Sarah Castell

The ippr

The Institute for Public Policy Research (ippr) is the UK's leading progressive think tank and was established in 1988. Its role is to bridge the political divide between the social democratic and liberal traditions, the intellectual divide between academia and the policy-making establishment and the cultural divide between government and civil society. It is first and foremost a research institute, aiming to provide innovative and credible policy solutions. Its work, the questions its research poses and the methods it uses are driven by the belief that the journey to a good society is one that places social justice, democratic participation and economic and environmental sustainability at its core.

D1460186

The Commission on Social Justice was established in 1992 at the instigation of the late John Smith and its report gave practical expression to his commitment to progressive change. ippr hopes that this publication continues to honour John Smith's legacy.

Rt Hon. John Smith QC, MP
1938–94

Social Justice

Building a Fairer Britain

Edited by **Nick Pearce** and **Will Paxton**

POLITICO'S

First published in Great Britain 2005 by
Politico's Publishing, an imprint of
Methuen Publishing Limited
215 Vauxhall Bridge Road
London SW1V 1EJ

10 9 8 7 6 5 4 3 2 1

ippr
30–32 Southampton Street
London WC2E 7RA
www.ippr.org

A CIP catalogue record for this book is available from the British Library.

ISBN 1 84275 133 6

Printed and bound in Great Britain by Bookmarque Ltd

Contents

Acknowledgements

Social Justice: Building a Fairer Britain could not have been written without assistance from many individuals and organisations. ippr would particularly like to thank Chris Ingram for his generous support. Without his willingness to invest in original and independent thinking the research work leading to this book could not have been undertaken. We would also like to thank Calouste Gulbenkian for its financial support. However, the analysis and recommendations in this report are entirely those of the various authors and do not necessarily represent those of the publication's supporters.

We would also like to thank the numerous external experts who have commented on drafts of the different chapters and on the interim report which was published in 2004. Thanks are particularly due for their generous time to Jo Wolff, Adam Swift, Stuart White, Alissa Goodman, Donald Hirsch, Tom Clark, Gosta Esping-Andersen, Lane Kenworthy, Bob Rowthorne, Colin Crouch, Fritz Scharpf, Anthony Giddens, Jane Miller, Fran Bennett, Ruth Lister, Bobby Duffy, Colin Hay, Tom Sefton, Nick Elison, Iain McLean, Dan Corry, Gerry Stoker, Geoff Whitty, Stephen Aldridge, John Van-Reenan, Nick Holgate, Pam Sammons, Leon Feinstein, John Hills, Tony Atkinson, Katherine Rake and Anne Phillips.

We would like to thank all those who have contributed to the publication or have been engaged in discussions on its ideas within the ippr. Thanks are due to Liane Lodhe, who provided early research support and to Matt Jackson, Richard Darlington and Rachel O'Brien who have helped in promoting the research. Particular thanks are due to Mike Dixon for his research on the project, without which this book would not have been completed.

Introduction

Nick Pearce and Will Paxton

This book arose out of a research project conducted at the Institute for Public Policy Research (ippr) to mark the tenth anniversary of the report of the Commission on Social Justice.

The Commission was established in the wake of the 1992 general election by the late John Smith MP, then leader of a Labour Party shell-shocked by its fourth successive defeat at the polls. The Commission's task was to conduct an independent inquiry, based at the ippr, into economic and social reform in the United Kingdom. Its terms of reference were broad, covering the theory and practice of social justice, particularly as these related to economic prosperity and reform of the welfare state. But its real ambition was to revitalise progressive thinking on social justice, equipping the broad currents of social democratic and liberal politics in Britain with a new vision of the future and a set of credible policy tools for achieving it.

The Commission's final report, *Social Justice: Strategies for National Renewal,* was a landmark document. It contained a compelling account of social injustice in Britain, a clear diagnosis of the forces shaping social, economic and political change, and a comprehensive vision of how social justice and economic prosperity could be achieved in the 21st century. It placed the core ideal of social justice centre-stage in public policy debate, helping to shift the climate of ideas on key issues such as the relationship between economic dynamism and social protection and the balance between rights and responsibilities. Many of its recommendations have since been implemented by the Labour government, perhaps the most important mark of its influence.

This book of essays was commissioned to re-examine the issue of social justice a decade on from the Commission's final report. It is not a systematic revaluation of all the policy analysis contained in that report. Nor does it lay out a comprehensive policy strategy for national renewal.

Instead it reflects on what has changed in Britain and the wider world since the early 1990s and asks how our understanding of social justice must adapt to keep pace with those changes. It combines discussion of first principles with detailed policy analysis in specific areas and draws together contributions from some of Britain's leading political theorists, social scientists and policy analysts to pose fundamental questions about how we can make further progress towards a fairer society.

The Commission on Social Justice was principally concerned with the core building blocks of domestic public policy: education, employment, social security and community renewal. This book returns to those areas to examine how much has been achieved over the last decade and to pinpoint where significant challenges remain. It pays particular attention to the question of the constitutional and democratic context in which social justice objectives should be pursued, rather than the separate but related question of how to reform public services to deliver equitable outcomes – these are the subject of other research projects being conducted at the ippr.

Midway into the first decade of a century, it is no longer possible to think about social justice without tackling challenges that reach beyond national boundaries: sustainability, migration and the fight against global poverty. This book therefore widens the scope of the original Commission to look across these fields. It also examines important new debates in political theory about the fundamental objectives of public policy: should we be aiming for a society in which people are happier or more equal, or should we aim for some other mix of goals?

Our primary purpose in publishing this collection of essays is to contribute to the renewal of progressive politics in Britain. We have set out to refresh contemporary thinking about social justice, grounding our vision of a fairer society in clear principles and robust empirical research evidence. Each chapter contains important new insights into the theory or practice of social justice. And running throughout the text is a fundamental question: what might it take to entrench progressive change – to embed social justice more firmly in the institutions, practices and habits of mind of the British people?

The theory and practice of social justice

What then are the core values that constitute social justice? In Chapter 1, David Miller outlines four principles of social justice:

- *equal citizenship*, understood as an equal set of basic rights, including the means to exercise these rights effectively;
- *the social minimum* of resources that allow all citizens to meet essential needs and to live a secure and dignified life in today's society;
- *equality of opportunity*, so that life chances depend only on motivation and aptitude, and not on factors such as class, gender or ethnicity; and
- *fair distribution*, such that resources that do not form part of equal citizenship or the social minimum may be distributed unequally, but that distribution must reflect relevant factors such as personal desert and personal choice.

These principles correspond fairly closely to those originally proposed by the Commission on Social Justice. They have the merit of capturing the complexity of how we often think about social justice, in contrast to theories which score the distribution of rights, opportunities and resources against single metrics, such as the maximisation of liberty or individual welfare. They are therefore likely to command a decent measure of public support, since popular attitudes to social justice are themselves complex and grounded in interlocking notions of equality, reciprocity, desert and reward.

Miller's four principles also embrace a wider understanding of wellbeing than traditional measures of fairness, such as the distribution of income and wealth. They enable us to frame such issues as the quality of the local environment, access to key public services and democratic participation through the lens of social justice. Consequently, they require us to think more broadly about how to achieve key objectives. Miller insists that social justice involves more than just action by the state. To move towards a fairer society involves changes in beliefs and practices at the grass roots as well: neighbours working together to clean up an estate, schools encouraging all children to aim high, employers taking care to avoid inadvertent discrimination, and so on. In some part, therefore, each of us has a responsibility.

The metric we should use for assessing social justice is explored at further length by Tania Burchardt in Chapter 11. She casts a critical eye over important recent debates on whether happiness should be the key goal of public policy.[1] She argues that the pursuit of happiness is not the same as the pursuit of social justice. We could all be happier but still not

---

1 See in particular, Layard, R (2005) *Happiness: Lessons from a New Science*, London: Allen Lane.

live in a society that deserved to be called fair and just. The selection of happiness as an object of value, she argues, suffers a number of problems. In its narrowest interpretations, it fails to distinguish between temporary states of mind and deeper personal fulfilment. Even when we think in broad terms about happiness – for example, as life satisfaction – the concept is problematic. In particular, it cannot explain the justness or otherwise of circumstances that condition expectations and attitudes.

Nonetheless, analyses of happiness are useful correctives to an exclusive focus on income poverty as the measure of inequality in social policy and they help us uncover important relationships between the concept of equality and how we actually think and feel about ourselves and others in our community. Consideration of happiness alongside other values, Burchardt argues, reminds us of the importance of 'subjective dynamics' – hope, expectation and disappointment – and of the need to promote individual and collective autonomy.

In Chapter 2, Mike Dixon and Will Paxton apply David Miller's four principles to a broad range of socio-economic indicators in Britain, charting a 2005 'state of the nation'. They show how in many respects Britain has become fairer in the decade or so since the Commission on Social Justice reported. The economy has experienced steady growth since 1993, employment rates have increased and registered unemployment continues to fall. Child and pensioner poverty have been reduced. The nation is healthier, living longer and experiencing far less crime than a decade ago.

Despite these improvements, however, Dixon and Paxton's analysis demonstrates how far Britain is from being a just society. Levels of child poverty continue to surpass those of many of our European partners and inequalities in income, wealth and wellbeing remain stubbornly high. Parental social class and ethnic background still heavily influence life chances, whilst democratic participation has fallen and political influence is polarising according to class and wealth. On almost every relevant measure, Britain must achieve substantial progress before it can claim that it meets the test of social justice.

Anglo-social justice?

In many respects, however, Britain is well placed to rise to this challenge. As Chapter 3 argues, the British welfare state is evolving towards what can be described as an 'Anglo-social' model in which high employment in flexible, service-based labour markets is combined with strong public services, an active welfare regime that prioritises entry into work and a redistributive tax and benefit system. This model seeks to combine the economic dynamism of the USA with the social equity of Scandinavian social democracies – moving away from the high levels of inequality, poverty and low social mobility of the former without sacrificing its economic strength.

It is argued that this emerging Anglo-social model is less exposed to the macro-economic instability and high unemployment levels characteristic of some continental European states and relatively well equipped to meet the cost pressures faced by all advanced societies that arise from demographic change and rising expectations of public services. It has also demonstrated significant capacity to diagnose and respond to new policy challenges, as Geoff Mulgan outlines in Chapter 4. But it suffers from the high levels of inequality typical of liberal welfare states with deregulated labour markets. In the absence of strong trade unions and a large public sector workforce, inequalities that arise from market distributions are high and greater strain is correspondingly placed on the tax and benefit system. This will continue to be the case for the foreseeable future, as Lisa Harker argues in her assessment of the changing welfare state in Chapter 12.

To tackle these inequalities and to realise fully the potential of the Anglo-social model for achieving social justice requires particular regard to gender inequalities. A major strength of the Commission on Social Justice's report was its attention to the inequality experienced by women in the workplace and in the domestic division of labour, a focus that fed through into a number of the policies introduced after 1997 – SureStart, the expansion of childcare, improved maternity pay and rights to parental leave. These reforms have begun to address the care deficit faced by women when balancing the pressures of working life with their caring responsibilities for children and/or elderly relatives, at the same time as they continue to shoulder a disproportionate share of the burden of domestic work. But childcare coverage remains incomplete and provision can be inflexible. Prices are relatively high and quality thresholds are far lower than in Scandinavia.

In the absence of public provision of childcare and a framework of parental employment rights, female participation in the workforce tends to be lower or disproportionately concentrated in lower-wage sectors. In countries such as the USA, women rely on informal childcare from friends and relatives or low cost private care services. They take up flexible lower wage jobs in order to combine caring responsibilities with work. The result is that social class inequalities in child development and gender inequalities at work are reinforced. Conversely, countries that rely on family support to provide many care functions tend to have lower levels of female employment, which places upward cost pressures on the welfare state and reproduces traditional inequalities between the sexes.

Increasing public investment in care provision should therefore be a social justice priority, as we outline below. But within that overall strategic priority, there remain tough questions to resolve about the balance between universal and targeted support and the relative priority given to child development and equality at work for women in different forms of childcare provision. These issues are analysed in detail in Chapter 13 by Jodie Reed and Peter Robinson, who build on the substantial evidence base now available on the effectiveness of childcare and early years education to pick up the challenge of how to maintain the momentum for equal life chances in the school system.

There have been substantial increases in education expenditure and attainment in qualifications since the Commission on Social Justice placed investment in learning at the core of its strategy for national renewal. Yet in recent years education outcomes appear to have reached a plateau. The rates of increase in primary school test results, GCSE scores and post-school staying on rates have slowed or stopped altogether. And while school achievement in disadvantaged areas has seen improvements, education outcomes remain more highly polarised by social class in the United Kingdom than in most other advanced economies.

Reed and Robinson's chapter addresses these issues against the background of an important contemporary academic debate as to whether education still matters for life chances as profoundly as the Commission on Social Justice believed it did. Some sociologists now argue that the link between formal educational achievement and positions in the social class hierarchy has weakened, while others contend that education remains a powerful determinant of life chances.[2] Reed and Robinson concur with the latter view but point out that in relation to schools policy, the evidence for how to promote social equity in education is less certain than for the early years. International data demonstrates that achievement is more equitable where school intakes are socially mixed

2 For full references, see p300.

but this still leaves open big questions as to how best to organise school admissions and allocate resources in support of social justice objectives. The development of school federations and collegiate provision, they argue, could offer a way forward between the Scylla of enforced allocations and Charybdis of choice-based markets.

Welfare-to-work policy was another major strand of the Commission on Social Justice's report, reflecting the circumstances of substantial unemployment in the early 1990s when Britain was emerging from a long process of deindustrialisation and a severe economic recession. Employment rates have risen substantially in the last decade but large numbers of people remain economically inactive and significant regional and local area differences exist in the distribution of jobs and prosperity. These differences are analysed in depth by Stephen Gibbons, Anne Green, Paul Gregg and Steve Machin in Chapter 14. They argue that at a regional or city level it is the least educated that suffer the largest and most persistent differences in employment. The solutions to these employment differentials, they argue, lie less in trying to increase the number of low skill jobs in deprived regions through industry subsidies and relocation grants, but more in seeking the high value-added economic activity usually associated with well-educated labour. Where there are skilled workers, there will be more jobs generated for those with lower skills. They conclude that an employment rate of 80 per cent is needed to draw the unskilled into work in every region, an objective that has now become official government policy.

Local area or community level disparities also exist in employment rates, education and crime. These neighbourhood disparities have social consequences for their residents, which are usually called 'neighbourhood effects'. Gibbons *et al* assess the evidence for these neighbourhood effects and conclude that they are large for crime, modest for child education and non-existent for adult employment except in geographically isolated areas. They draw a number of conclusions for policy, arguing that addressing these neighbourhood effects through increased funding for schools, crime reduction and wider neighbourhood renewal will help create a virtuous circle as these are factors that make neighbourhoods attractive.

New challenges for social justice

In contrast to education and employment policy, a number of areas of contemporary political debate were conspicuously absent from the

Commission on Social Justice's report. Migration is perhaps the most obvious. The highly charged, sometimes visceral, debate about migration that dominated the 2005 general election would have seemed inconceivable in the early 1990s, when policy discussions were focused on race equality and citizenship rights, not the pros and cons of immigration, cultural otherness or social cohesion.

The issue of migration challenges many conceptions of social justice by throwing into sharp relief the extent to which they assume a closed community, usually the nation state. Distributive notions of social justice, for example, ask how rights, opportunities or goods should be distributed between citizens of a community. But migration unsettles the concept of community, forcing us to define the rights and obligations of an often rapidly changing population of non-citizens: asylum seekers, temporary economic migrants and their dependants, illegal immigrants, and so on. After a decade or more of high net migration, policymakers in all advanced economies are grappling with these issues. But they are doing so without many of the conceptual tools necessary for the task, in conditions of significant public mistrust and concern.

In Chapter 7, Dhananjayan Sriskandarajah seeks to address the dilemmas facing policymakers and outline the components of a socially just approach to immigration. He advances five key areas of migration policy in which the pursuit of social justice can be furthered to the benefit of migrants, the communities they settle in and their societies of origin:

- a fair admission system based on current and future labour market needs for those whose arrival can be regulated;
- a clear set of entitlements for migrants to promote integration and pre-empt public fears about 'abuse' of the welfare state;
- early integration policies that prioritise socio-economic empowerment and support cultural diversity;
- action to mitigate the negative impacts of immigration to the UK on countries of origin; and
- a programme for regularising undocumented workers who may be vulnerable to exploitation.

Migration is one policy area which demonstrates that debates on social justice cannot be confined to the domestic issues with which the Commission on Social Justice was largely concerned. Today, our thinking about social justice is unavoidably international in scope. As David Mepham argues in Chapter 6, global interconnectedness means that the United Kingdom and other advanced economies have an instrumental self-interest in the prosperity of those beyond their borders, since the problems of disease, starvation and war sweep rapidly across national boundaries. But he also argues forcibly that the principles of social justice obtain globally. In contrast to theorists like David Miller, he argues that our moral obligations to other peoples extend beyond the protection of human rights and the provision of the basic means of existence, even though the implications of such obligations are themselves radical. Rather, he makes the case for principles of social justice to cover humanity as a whole, much as universalist theorists of cosmopolitan democracy have done. He outlines what a commitment to global social justice should mean for aid, trade, international development and foreign policies.

Our shared moral responsibilities also extend to the protection of the environment, another major area of policy concern that received only limited attention in the Commission on Social Justice's report. Although the environmental movement has successfully pushed green issues up the political agenda since the 1960s, it has been far less concerned with thinking about how environmental goals interact with social justice objectives.

In Chapter 8, Julie Foley, Tony Grayling and Mike Dixon address the conceptual task of bringing together environmental and social justice concerns. The core argument of their chapter is that environmental sustainability is compatible with fairness and equality; indeed in many instances it is a necessary condition of the achievement of wider progressive objectives. They outline a set of principles which should govern the importance attached to environmental objectives within a framework of social justice, which they apply to the overriding environmental challenge of the age – preventing climate change – before considering how the principles can be used to develop socially just policy in two domestic areas: energy use and transport policy.

Popular and progressive?

Having addressed this broad range of conceptual challenges for thinking about social justice, we turn in the final section of the book to the very practical questions of how to secure further progress towards

Britain. In particular, is there sufficient public support for the principles of social justice outlined in this book?

As Geoff Mulgan and Peter Taylor-Gooby demonstrate in Chapters 4 and 5 respectively, the British people do not respond to abstract concepts such as redistribution. Their views on taxation, public spending and the welfare state are expressed in the language of everyday social interaction and couched in terms of desert and contribution. Reciprocity is central to their notions of fairness and they single out certain groups, particularly children and pensioners, as deserving support.

These complex and sometimes contradictory views impose constraints on progressive political parties. Labour has been careful to go with the grain of public opinion, prioritising reductions in child and pensioner poverty and investment in valued public services like the NHS. It has not made explicit its support for a more equal society nor argued the moral case for progressive taxation.

In many respects, this strategy has been successful. It has allowed Labour to invest heavily in public services and fundamentally to shift the terms of political debate towards public goods without losing popular support. No mainstream political party now argues openly for reducing expenditure on core services like education or health in favour of tax cuts. At the same time income inequality has started to decline in recent years and impressive reductions in poverty among children and pensioners have been achieved.

After a third successive Labour general election victory, the question is whether this support for investment in public services and targeted poverty reduction can be generalised into a broader and deeper commitment to a fairer society. Can a truly 'progressive consensus' be achieved and if so, how?

Public opinion surveys give us some grounds for optimism. As Peter Taylor-Gooby argues, most people are concerned at inequalities and poverty and would like to see them reduced. They also think that the better off should pay more in tax and oppose regressive taxation of the worse off. They value key public services highly and want them improved. Importantly, they want women to have good opportunities in paid work and not to be solely responsible for childcare.

To translate these views into deeper support for progressive goals, against a background of distrust towards politicians, scepticism about the efficacy of government interventions and hostile countervailing elements of public and media opinion, is no simple task. It requres clear identification of priorities and a strategy for entrenching policy reforms.

As a starting point for debate, the final chapter of this book offers three priorities for building a fairer Britain: comprehensive early years education and childcare, investment in skills and lifelong learning, and reform of pension and personal care entitlements for the elderly. We offer a prospectus for raising the funds necessary for specified investments, chief amongst them the extension of early years education and care.

These three priorities reflect the empirical evidence marshalled in this book and elsewhere for the most efficacious means of promoting social justice objectives. Universal systems of high quality, intensive early years education and childcare decrease substantially the impact of family background on children's life chances and thereby promote equality of opportunity and fairness in social outcomes. As the Scandinavian experience demonstrates, universal childcare also enables women to participate on more equal terms in the workforce, strengthening efforts to achieve gender equality while promoting the long-term affordability of the welfare state.

Investment in skills and lifelong learning were at the heart of the recommendations of the Commission on Social Justice and now form a core part of the armoury of all centre-left governments. In the final chapter, the focus is on areas in which policy still needs development such as the 14–19 curriculum and qualifications structure and training entitlements for adults. Improved education and training, particularly for those at the lower ends of the labour market, can help stem income inequalities and promote upwards earnings mobility. But investments in these areas must be considered in conjunction with measures to reduce economic inactivity and exclusion from the labour market. As Peter Robinson documents in Chapter 15, there may be trade-offs, at least in the short term, between the objectives of furthering skills development and career progression, on the one hand, and reducing economic inactivity on the other.

We also advocate reforms to pension policy and the funding of personal care for the elderly. The proposals are based on previous research published by the ippr[3] and centre on increases to the basic state pension and new entitlements to free personal care, paid for on a self-financing basis over a generation by raising the retirement age and redirecting other

---

3 Brooks R, Regan S, and Robinson P (2002) *A New Contract for Retirement*, London: ippr

elements of public expenditure. The reforms aim to ensure the abolition of poverty in retirement, while contributing to gender equality for those with caring responsibilities.

These are major investments in social justice and accordingly come with a price tag. The funding requirements for each policy area are shown for both the short and long term, alongside estimates of the resources required for continued progress towards the government's existing target for abolishing child poverty.   Given Labour's general election manifesto commitment not to raise the basic and top rates of tax, the options presented for the 2005 Parliament focus on increases in National Insurance. In the longer term, the authors argue that a funda-mental overhaul of the tax system should be considered: integrating the tax and National Insurance systems, cutting tax for the lowest paid and increasing taxes for the very top earners.

These taxation proposals are progressive. They combine a redistribu-tion of the burden of taxation with an increased contribution from all, in recognition of the collective responsibility for funding the public services that help deliver social justice. They extend the proportion of Gross Domestic Product taken by public expenditure over the long term to around 45 per cent – still far short of levels in the Scandinavian countries but enough to make substantial progress towards a more just society. Public spending on these key priorities represents an investment in the future, not a drain on the country's resources. As the Commission on Social Justice argued over a decade ago, fairness and economic dynamism can go hand in hand.

Entrenching progressive change

Can progressive reforms carry popular conviction and leave a lasting legacy? The most successful progressive governments are those that set the terms by which future generations live, as did the Edwardian Liberal governments, Franklin D Roosevelt's New Deal administrations and the 1945 Labour government. These governments harnessed the economic and social forces of their times to progressive goals, leading public opinion behind a clear national purpose. What are the lessons we can learn from these administrations?

First, reform must be embedded in institutions and practices, as well as public discourse. The NHS is popular because it is perceived to embody values of fairness and reciprocity. As a public service funded through general taxation and available to all regardless of ability to pay, the NHS gives institutional life to widely and deeply held values.

Embedding entitlements to childcare and early years education in a high-quality, publicly regulated and comprehensive service should form the centrepiece of progressive institution-building in the early 21st century, just as the NHS did in the immediate post-war period. A comprehensive system of early years education and childcare services, supplied by a diverse range of providers but regulated as a public service with universal entitlements, would give institutional form to the principles of equal life chances for children and equality of opportunity for women, both of which attract significant public support.

Second, reform should embrace democratic pluralism and constitutional guarantees of the dispersion of power. Despite a major programme of democratic and constitutional reform since 1997, the British state remains highly centralised and dominated by the executive, particularly in England. This violates a core principle of social justice – that of equality of citizenship, which depends, as David Miller argues, on effective equality in the exercise of democratic decision-making. Historically many on the socialist left have argued that equality in outcomes, particularly in key public services, requires national definitions of entitlements and standards and hence the centralised exercise of power. But as Will Paxton and Andrew Gamble argue in Chapter 10, the twin goals of equality and decentralisation of democracy are neither mutually exclusive at the level of principle nor necessarily so in practice. They argue that a new constitutional settlement is required, one that enshrines the powers and funding of devolved administrations and local government. From a different perspective, Raymond Plant makes the argument in Chapter 9 for the compatibility of social democracy with the constitutional protection of positive social and economic rights.

In the context of declining respect for politicians, centralisation of power in the executive can also undermine public trust in democracy. Labour has been at its most vulnerable when its decisions have lacked transparency and openness. Conversely, many of its most successful reforms have involved devolving power or removing operational responsibility for policy implementation to external agencies, such as the Bank of England. Further constitutional reform may therefore help to renew trust in politics and the efficacy of public action. The list of candidates for reform is extensive: democratisation of the House of Lords; a new voting system for the House of Commons; constitutional protection of the powers of Parliament and the judiciary; and a new framework for local democracy.

Finally, progressive political visions stand the greatest chance of success when they give voice to a shared sense of national purpose. The 1945 Labour government carried forward the promise of social solidarity forged during the war years and successfully articulated national aspirations for a fairer society. When national identity coalesces around progressive values and ambitions in this way, the momentum for change can be powerful. Conversely, progressive parties suffer when they become divorced from patriotic sentiment or allow others to channel public fears and uncertainty into reactionary expressions of national identity.

National identity remains an important feature of advanced economies, despite the centrifugal pressures exerted by cultural globalisation and the growth of supra-national political institutions. In recent years, however, a number of academics and commentators have argued that the potential to forge a progressive national politics of social justice is undermined by the increased diversity characteristic of contemporary societies. Increased diversity, it is argued, makes it difficult to sustain the collective identities, trust and solidarity which underpin strong welfare states.[4]

There is evidence, particularly from the USA, to support this argument. But it is not overwhelming and, as Dhananjayan Sriskandarajah argues in Chapter 7, research in other countries, such as Canada, is more positive. Although anti-immigration sentiment has risen in many advanced economies, it does not hold that diversity necessarily conflicts with social solidarity. Political agency, particularly the presence of progressive political parties in national governments, can weaken the strength and popular appeal of anti-immigrant arguments and help sustain coalitions of support for the welfare state. Measures that foster economic and political integration of migrants also minimise distrust and community conflict.

Surveys of public attitudes in Britain show that the population increasingly holds an open and civic view of national identity, stressing its political and linguistic components, such as respect for the law and political institutions, and the ability to speak English. Exclusivist, ethnic-based accounts of national identity are on the decline.[5] The British

---

4   For a survey and response to these arguments, see Pearce N (2004), 'Diversity vs Solidarity: A new progressive dilemma?' *Renewal* Vol 12, No.3

5   See Tilley J, Exley S, and Heath A (2004), 'Dimensions of British Identity' in *British Social Attitudes: the 21st Report,* London: National Centre for Social Research

people appear to have recovered from the disorientation of a post-Empire world and the pessimistic view of irreversible national decline popular in the 1970s and 1980s. Over the last decade, they have become increasingly proud of the country's economic achievements, its fair treatment of different groups in society and its political influence in the world. These are strong foundations upon which to build a progressive sense of national identity – one which can support a wider political programme for achieving greater social justice.

Conclusion

We are at a critical juncture in British politics. The UK is no longer the 'tired, resentful, divided and failing country' that the Commission on Social Justice reported on in the early 1990s. It has become a fairer, more economically prosperous and democratic country, confident in its abilities and more certain of its place in the world. But it remains fundamentally divided by social class, with levels of poverty and inequality that still rank among the highest in Europe. Its democratic revolution is incomplete and it is only now waking up to the challenge of sustainable development. It is not a just society.

Achieving social justice is a generational project. It will take sustained investment and political will to close the gap between the values of social justice outlined in this book and the realities of contemporary Britain. But the country is set on the right course – income inequality is falling, there are fewer children and pensioners living in poverty, spending on public services is increasing and Britain is facing up to its environmental and moral responsibilities to the rest of the world.

The question is whether this progress can be cemented in an unprecedented third term of Labour government or whether the steady progress of recent years remains skin deep, vulnerable to challenge under a different government. The task now is to identify the key priorities for social justice and embed change in the institutions, attitudes and politics of British public life, so that a decisive and irreversible shift is made towards a better Britain. We hope this book contributes in some part to that goal.

Section 1

Understanding Social Justice in the Modern World

What is Social Justice?[1]

David Miller

The idea of social justice has been the driving force behind centre-left politics in Western societies for over a century. It is the idea that above all distinguishes social-democratic parties and movements from their neo-liberal and Marxist rivals. To pursue social justice is to believe that society can be reshaped – its major social and political institutions changed – so that each person gets a fair share of the benefits, and carries a fair share of the responsibilities, of living together in a community. Neo-liberals reject this idea because they believe it is destructive of a free market economy; Marxists reject it because they think that politics is always the slave of economics rather than its master, so social distribution cannot be changed without an economic revolution. In the light of 20th century experience, neither criticism holds up well. In every Western society, significant changes occurred in how wealth and income were distributed across society: in educational and job opportunities, in access to housing and health care, in provision for old age, in the rights of women, ethnic minorities and the disabled – the list could be extended indefinitely. These changes were politically driven, introduced by governments committed to social justice, and once introduced, largely left in place by governments of the right nominally opposed to them. It would not be an exaggeration to call the 20th century the century of social justice.

So why, at the beginning of the 21st century, is there still a social justice agenda for centre-left governments to pursue? One reason is that there is no single objective that defines social justice, but instead a series of objectives, corresponding to the different concrete goods and bads

1 I should like to thank Tania Burchardt, Will Paxton, Nick Pearce, Ben Rogers, Stuart White and Jo Wolff for their comments on an earlier draft of this chapter, and Zofia Stemplowska for invaluable research assistance.

whose distribution we care about. Getting educational opportunities fairly distributed does not, unfortunately, mean that access to housing or healthcare will also be fair. These are separate problems requiring different policies to tackle them. This also means that the philosophical quest for a single 'currency of justice' – some way of measuring each person's overall quota of social goods and bads – is doomed to fail. We cannot amalgamate educational opportunity and healthcare in such a way that we could regard someone who lives in an area with poor schools as being compensated by the existence of an above-average local hospital. We want each separate good to be fairly distributed across society. Moreover, what counts as a fair distribution will depend on the particular good in question.

Another reason why the social justice project is unlikely ever to be complete is that new issues are brought on to the agenda by technical and social change. Think, for example, of the growing significance of environmental questions. Are these also questions of social justice? Yes, because people benefit to different degrees when environmental goods like protected areas of natural beauty are created, and on the other hand suffer differentially when pollution or toxic waste is allowed to contaminate the places where they live. So alongside general policies that aim to preserve the environment for future generations, we need more specific policies to ensure that environmental goods and harms are fairly distributed among members of the present generation.

Or think of the implications for social justice of a society that is becoming increasingly multi-ethnic and multicultural. How should we understand equality of opportunity in such a society? Should our idea of social justice expand to take in justice towards groups as well as towards individuals, so when we find that members of a particular ethnic or religious group are faring badly in getting jobs or higher education places, we should adopt policies to combat that inequality?

So we need to rethink what social justice means for us at the beginning of the 21st century. What needs rethinking are not the fundamental principles themselves, because these still remain fully relevant, but how to put them into practice in the new circumstances that we face. Political philosophers continue to develop new ways of understanding social justice, and I shall refer to some of these as I proceed, but I want to start by laying out four basic principles which correspond fairly closely to those set out in the Commission on Social Justice's Report published in 1994 (CSJ, 1994). I have formulated them in a way that I hope is more precise, and that may help to answer some of the criticisms that have been made of the original phrasing. Then I ask what it would mean to apply these principles in a society like Britain today.

Four principles of social justice

Social justice tells us how different types of goods and bads should be distributed across a society. Because the goods are diverse, the principles of distribution should be diverse too. For instance, it would be folly to propose that income should be allocated by the same criteria as healthcare. But the core idea of social justice is contained in the following four principles:

- *Equal citizenship:* Every citizen is entitled to an equal set of civil, political and social rights, including the means to exercise these rights effectively.
- *The social minimum:* All citizens must have access to resources that adequately meet their essential needs, and allow them to live a secure and dignified life in today's society.
- *Equality of opportunity:* A person's life-chances, and especially their access to jobs and educational opportunities, should depend only on their own motivation and aptitudes, and not on irrelevant features such as gender, class or ethnicity.
- *Fair distribution:* Resources that do not form part of equal citizenship or the social minimum may be distributed unequally, but the distribution must reflect relevant factors such as personal desert and personal choice.

These principles would, I think, be widely accepted, and at first glance they might seem to be quite undemanding in relation to current policy. But in fact the reverse is true, as will shortly become apparent: a society that genuinely fulfilled these four principles would look quite different from the one we have today.

Equal citizenship

The idea of equal civil and political rights has long been recognised in democratic societies, but we still have far to go in ensuring that everyone can enjoy and exercise these rights to an equal degree. One of the most elementary civil rights is the right to personal security – the right to go about one's daily life without being robbed, assaulted, threatened or abused. This is not a right that is currently equally enjoyed by everyone. For instance, it is a striking fact that when people are asked about the problems that they experience in their neighbourhood – whether this means racial harassment, vandalism, or fear of crime generally – in every case those living in economically deprived areas reported a significantly higher level of concern than those in more affluent neighbourhoods. Twice as many Asians and black people as whites say that they are very afraid of becoming victims of violent crime. So while overall levels of crime have decreased in the last decades, as Mike Dixon and Will Paxton demonstrate in Chapter 2, inequalities between social groups in both their experience and perception of crime have, at least until very recently, tended to increase. Men and women also enjoy unequal levels of personal security; women are more likely to experience inter-personal violence than men, and very much more likely to be victims of sexual assault, including rape (Walby and Allen, 2004). All of this violates the principle of equal citizenship.

This example highlights an aspect of social justice that is often over-looked. We tend to think about it in top-down terms, as something that results from policies pursued by governments. This is partly true, and in the present case, an important objective of policing policy ought to be to ensure that the right to personal security is equally enjoyed by all. But social justice also depends on how ordinary citizens behave, and in this case what it requires is a widespread culture of equal respect, so that women can live free of verbal and physical harassment, members of racial or religious minorities are not subject to abuse or attack, and so forth. Laws can play a part here, but they cannot be a substitute for people voluntarily accepting and acting on the principle of respecting the equal rights of their fellow-citizens. Understanding what social justice means in everyday life should be a central element in the citizenship education that we now have as part of the school curriculum.

Another aspect of equal citizenship is the right to influence government, something that goes beyond the right to vote in elections, important though that is. At present the distribution of political influence is heavily skewed in favour of those who have resources of other kinds – wealth, communicative skills, industrial muscle – and although it is unrealistic to think that we could ever achieve perfect equality in this area, there are ways in which we can try to redress the balance. There have, for example, been a number of experiments with citizens' juries and deliberative opinion polls whose aim is to find ways in which people outside of professional political circles can be brought together to debate policy issues and to get beyond the sometimes rather superficial opinions expressed in opinion polls and focus groups. With a few exceptions, these experiments have not so far been formally linked to policy-making, but there is no reason why every major new policy initiative should not in due course be subject to scrutiny in a citizens' forum as well as by Parliament. Another idea along similar lines that has recently been aired is for a national 'Deliberation Day' to occur before elections (Ackerman and Fishkin, 2004). These proposals are often put forward under the rubric of enhancing democracy, but they also belong on the social justice agenda, as a way of moving towards greater equality in the exercise of political rights.

The principle of equal citizenship does not by itself tell us where the boundaries of citizenship should lie – who should be included and who should be left out. This is particularly relevant when we are considering immigration, one of the toughest challenges to social justice today. Justice does not require us to admit to citizenship everyone who wants to come in. But what it does require is that immigration decisions should be made consistently and fairly, using relevant criteria of selection, and that everyone who is admitted on a long-term basis – excluding students, seasonal workers and so forth – should be encouraged to become a fully-fledged citizen in due course.[2] What is unacceptable, in other words, is the existence of an underclass of residents who are either illegal immigrants or who have been granted denizen status without full civil and political rights, as has happened to guest workers in Germany and elsewhere. Holding this line is likely to prove difficult, given that many economically needy applicants would prefer to hold such a status rather than not be admitted at all. But this is what social justice means here and the principle of equal citizenship cannot be compromised.

The social minimum

This is sometimes treated as a part of equal citizenship, but the social minimum is not a principle of equality. Rather it is what political

---

2 It has sometimes been argued that there is a human right to migrate, so justice does require a policy of open borders. I don't accept such an argument – see my essay 'Immigration: The Case for Limits' in Wellman and Cohen (2004). Refugees, however, are a special case not to be confused with migrants generally; their human rights may oblige us to admit them.

philosophers call a principle of sufficiency – it tells us what the minimum share of resources is that everyone must have, but it says nothing directly about how resources above the minimum should be distributed. This is very clear when the resource in question is income. The social minimum includes the idea that there is a living income that everyone must have to cover food, clothing and other necessities, whether in the form of a minimum wage, a pension or an unemployment benefit. But social justice does not prohibit others from earning more than this although the fourth principle, fair distribution, is intended to apply to benefits over and above the social minimum.

The social minimum is often discussed as though it applied only to income. Conventional definitions of poverty, for example, refer to people receiving less than 50 per cent or 60 per cent of median income, and although this is obviously one important component, it is not the only one. The relevant question is a broader one: what must people have, given our circumstances, in order to be able to live a decent life? This brings in other dimensions of the social minimum, such as access to adequate healthcare. The problem here, a fairly intractable one, is to define a standard of adequacy, in light of the fact that medical advances mean that there will always be more potential forms of treatment for ill health available than resources to provide them. We need a way of establishing what all citizens are legitimately entitled to. General principles of social justice cannot by themselves tell us what adequate healthcare includes, they tell us only that once the minimum is set, everyone should have access to healthcare of that standard, and that when resources run short, they should be allocated according to need, not ability to pay. This is one area in which deliberation among citizens may provide a fruitful way forward: healthcare forums should invite people to indicate their priorities for different forms of medical treatment, and to say which treatments they regard as being essential and which discretionary (a line that we should expect to shift over time). Alternatively, following a proposal by Ronald Dworkin, we might gather relevant evidence by asking people what medical insurance cover they would buy, at what cost, assuming they did not know how likely they were to require any particular form of treatment (Dworkin, 2000).

Another, less familiar, dimension of the social minimum is the quality of the physical environment in which a person lives. Everyone should enjoy an environment of an adequate standard, which includes on the one hand not being exposed to excessive noise, excessive pollution, or the risk of serious harm, whether from collapsing buildings or the release of toxic chemicals, and on the other, enjoying amenities like clean streets, access to parks and playgrounds, and safe access to shops and leisure facilities. As in the case of healthcare, we need to find a way of setting the environmental minimum. Some would argue here that we should be aiming not for a minimum, but for equality – for an environment that is equally good for all. But I do not think that this is a requirement of social justice, even if it were feasible. Not all environmental goods are basic goods, and it is reasonable to expect people to use part of their income to buy additional goods, depending on their tastes, whether this means living in exceptionally quiet or secluded places, places of great physical beauty, or places with special amenities (living next to the golf course, for instance). This is only unjust if you think that all income inequality is unjust, which I shall argue later on is not the case. So our concern should not be with all differences in environmental value, but with people whose environmental quality falls below the threshold of adequacy.

There are other components of the social minimum, sufficient opportunities for mobility through the transport system for instance, but rather than attempt to be exhaustive I want to make two general points about this principle of social justice. The first is that the content of the social minimum is determined by what at any time is regarded as providing a decent standard of living, and this of course changes over time. We might therefore describe the social minimum as relative, but not in a damaging sense – at any moment there will be very considerable agreement about where the threshold should be set. For example, there are studies which ask people about items that they consider to be necessities that every household should be able to afford and there is a striking degree of consensus across income and age groups about which should be included (Gordon *et al*, 2000). So although the principle of guaranteeing everyone sufficient resources to meet essential needs and live decently might not seem very demanding, in fact it continues to provide a major challenge to governments even in the richest of societies.

The second, more controversial, issue is whether the social minimum should be combined with a principle that requires citizens to contribute to society in return, in line with the old slogan 'from each according to his abilities, to each according to his needs'. The contribution requirement has been defended on the grounds that it corresponds to a widely-accepted principle of reciprocity: citizens who benefit from resources created by their fellows should be willing to put something back into the pool, so long as they have the capacity and opportunity to do so. On the other side of the argument are those who claim that every citizen is entitled to a basic income regardless of whether he or she chooses to work or not, simply by virtue of membership. The corresponding practical issue is whether receipt of social security and other benefits should be conditional on the recipients' willingness to take available jobs, or to demonstrate social contribution in some other way.

In my view, the reciprocity requirement is sound in principle. The goods and services that are needed to guarantee the social minimum do not fall like manna from heaven, but are dependent on the productive work of others, by no means all of it intrinsically enjoyable, so somebody who chooses not to work but nonetheless receives basic income is taking unfair advantage of his fellows. The difficulties arise when we have to put the principle into practice, and say what level of contribution we expect people to make. Here we should be prepared to take a wider view than has happened up to now. In particular we should not equate contribution with paid employment, but should recognise the work involved in caring for young children and, increasingly important, for the elderly; people who do this work should qualify for income support from the state. And if we require others to take paid employment as a condition for receiving benefits, we must make sure that the terms are fair, which means, for instance, enforcing a minimum wage, giving adequate support to working parents through workplace nurseries and in other ways.

Equality of opportunity

Equality of opportunity has long been recognised as a basic principle of social justice, but what is often not understood is just how radical its implications are for the way that our society is currently organised. It is not simply a matter of allowing open competition for jobs and places in higher education. It is both wider and more demanding than this. The core idea is that a person's life chances – how successful they are in whatever career they decide to pursue – should only depend on their personal abilities and their motivation. This excludes a whole host of factors that currently influence life chances such as gender, ethnicity, and the social class of your parents. So it requires first of all effective anti-discrimination procedures when jobs and educational places are being allocated. This means not only choosing people on the basis of their ability to do a job or complete a course of study, but ensuring that people are not prevented or deterred from applying in the first place. Legislation aimed at ensuring this is now in place, but social justice still depends on the procedures used and choices made by thousands of independent admissions officers and selection committees who have constantly to guard against indirect forms of discrimination that favour particular candidates and exclude others.

To ensure equality of opportunity it is not enough that fair procedures are used at the point at which people are applying for jobs or educational places. It is also necessary that they should have had the same chance to acquire the relevant skills and abilities, despite differences in family background and so forth. One of the hard lessons we have had to take on board is just how much influence a child's experience in the first few years has on his or her chances later in life. A prominent American study, for instance, found that children raised in professional families had, by the age of three, vocabularies that were more than twice the size of those of children raised in families on welfare, and that the gap was continuing to widen.[3] This is an inequality that can only be partly remedied, short of getting rid of the nuclear family altogether, but it is important nonetheless to have pre-school programmes that by placing children in similar environments for part of the day can help to develop their linguistic and other capacities on more equal terms. The principle, in other words, does not just require that people's opportunities should be equalised at one point in their lives – at age eighteen, say – but that opportunities should as far as possible be equalised throughout, so that people can realise their full potential. For the same reason, since we cannot in practice achieve the same start for everyone – differences in family background will always matter – it is important to have multiple opportunity ladders, so that people who, for example, do not qualify for university at eighteen because they have missed out on educational opportunities beforehand, will have further chances to demonstrate ability and motivation.

Our understanding of equal opportunities should also be sensitive to cultural differences. We need to be clear here about the different ways in

---

3 Even more remarkably, in the same work by Hart and Risley (1995) three-year-old children from professional families used a wider vocabulary than parents receiving welfare. Moreover, among the children, vocabulary differences were strongly correlated with differences in measured IQ. Hart and Risley underline that the scale of outside intervention needed to compensate fully for these inequalities in the first three years of life would be massive, and presumably politically infeasible.

which culture can impact on opportunity, some raising issues of social justice and others not. If a person's cultural values are such that they prefer not to take on certain kinds of work, that does not amount to an inequality of opportunity – an opportunity is an option that someone can choose either to take or not to take in light of their values. To take extreme cases, it is not a failure of equal opportunity if there are no Anglicans working in synagogues or pacifists employed by the armed services. In contrast, if someone wants to take a job or some other opportunity, but is deterred by the associated costs – costs that are not part and parcel of the job itself – then this may violate the principle. Again, a simple example would be a job specified in such a way that its hours of work conflict with the religious requirements of a particular faith, even though the work pattern could easily be varied.

More difficult questions arise when changing a job specification does impose real costs on others, or when it seems that the person denied the opportunity is interpreting the demands of his or her culture in an unnecessarily rigid way. School authorities have argued, for instance, that teachers must be prepared to work a standard five-day week, even though this has proved a barrier to some Muslims for whom Friday afternoons are a time of prayer. The schools' case is that if teachers are going to be absent for part of the week then either classes will be disrupted, or other teachers will be overworked. If these arguments hold water, then it is fair to ask these applicants to choose between taking up opportunities that are otherwise open to them, and adhering to strict Islamic requirements. Parallel issues arise in the case of those who feel impelled to wear forms of clothing, such as the jilbab, that may conflict with the dress requirements of employers or schools. We need to establish on the one hand what purpose these dress codes serve for the latter, and on the other whether there are religiously sanctioned forms of dress that could be worn as an alternative.[4]

In a multicultural society equality of opportunity requires culturally sensitive educational and employment practices to ensure that opportu-

---

4 This example was prompted by the case of Shabina Begum, who was excluded from her school in Luton when she began to insist on wearing a jilbab. The school, almost 80 per cent of whose pupils are Muslims, had agreed a uniform policy after consultation with local mosques, which included the option of wearing a shalwar kameez (trousers and tunic). In March 2005, appeal court judges ruled that she had been excluded unlawfully according to the Human Rights Act. See BBC News Online, 2 March 2005.

nities are being made available to minority groups on reasonable terms. Not all barriers can be removed, but many can. Similar issues can arise in other cases – for instance over whether charging tuition fees for higher education denies effective opportunity to students from poorer families – but cultural differences pose particular problems for outsiders in establishing how central a religious practice or a dress requirement is to a way of life. There needs to be a dialogue between representatives of majority and minority communities in which the minority group are asked whether cultural practices that restrict their members' access to jobs and educational opportunities could be changed, while majority representatives are invited to scrutinise established norms – those governing school uniforms, or the pattern of the working week, for example – to see whether they are unnecessarily rigid.

So far I have been focusing on access to jobs and education as the centre-piece of equality of opportunity, but we should not overlook the very substantial inequalities that result from the inheritance of wealth. Since these also translate into unequal life-chances, and clearly bear no relation to the recipient's motivation and ability (other than the ability to remain on good terms with a wealthy parent!), they are incompatible with equal opportunities on any reasonable interpretation.

We may wonder why public opinion appears to care so little about the injustice of inherited wealth. This may in part be because of ignorance about the degree to which the pattern of inheritance is skewed, with large sums going only to a fairly small number of recipients. However, a recent study using deliberative workshops found that even when confronted with the facts, many people were reluctant to tax inheritance at all, and others opted for some variant on the present regime, perhaps with some progression built in, that would still leave large inequalities in net receipts (White and Paxton, 2005). Leaving aside general fatalism about the effectiveness of the tax system, it seems that the main factors driving this view were the idea that educational opportunities were the ones that really counted and the idea that the family rather than the individual was the proper unit of reward, so if someone deserves the wealth they have accumulated, their children in turn deserve to inherit it.

Most political philosophers who have tackled this problem would find the last idea very puzzling, and would argue that as far as social justice goes, we should be aiming for a system in which all inheritance above a certain low threshold should be taxed away and redistributed to those who do not inherit in the form of a capital grant – a greatly expanded version of the recently-introduced Child Trust Fund (Ackerman and Alstott, 1999). They might qualify this on efficiency grounds: the wish to bequeath is arguably at least a powerful motive behind economically desirable saving and investment. But this does not show that the beneficiaries are fairly entitled to receive their unequal inheritances. Might one argue that inheritance is analogous to a random windfall, like winning the lottery, and therefore not something that offends our sense of justice? I shall comment on justice and luck below, but clearly inheritance is strongly correlated with other advantages such as educational privileges, and therefore hardly a prize that each person has an equal chance of winning. It cannot be squared with equality of opportunity, but it will clearly take a considerable amount of argument – and perhaps experience of other ways in which the intergenerational transmission of wealth can be arranged – to persuade people of this truth.

I want to conclude my discussion of the equality of opportunity principle by pointing out what it does *not* entail. To begin with, it does not entail equality of outcome, or flat equality – everyone having similar jobs or the same income. This is perhaps obvious: the principle says that people's life chances, including their job opportunities, should depend on their motivation and their abilities, and these latter are not equally distributed across the population. What may be less obvious is that a society of equality of opportunity need not be one that completely removes any correlation between a person's demographic background – their class of origin or their ethnicity – and their life chances. In popular presentations of the idea it is sometimes suggested that for equal opportunities to exist, a dustman's son must have the same statistical chance of becoming Prime Minister as a surgeon's son. But this is misleading because it makes two potentially controversial assumptions. First, that the abilities that are relevant to career success have no inherited component, and second, that motivation, in the form of aspiration to pursue particular careers, for instance, is not affected by the culture of the family you are born into.

I shall not attempt to resolve the many controversies that surround the idea of inherited ability. It is clear, on the one hand, that there is no single gene that corresponds to 'ability' or 'talent' in the sense that correlates with economic success, and also that how successful a person with a given genetic profile will be depends a great deal on the environment in which he or she is placed. It is equally clear, on the other hand, that there is a significant correlation between the measured intelligence of parents and their children, and that this partially predicts future income and other advantages. On this basis alone, we should expect a just society to show a great deal of social mobility – much greater than our society does today – but still some overall correlation in occupational status and income across the generations. Equality of opportunity does not aim to defeat biology, but to ensure equal chances for those with similar ability and motivation.

Families not only transmit genes that may help to form relevant abilities, they also transmit values that shape children's aspirations in later life. For instance, they may encourage children to aim for particular careers, or inculcate religious beliefs that restrict their opportunity set, as our earlier discussion of culture suggested. How far is this consistent with equality of opportunity? If one family passes on educational values and another entrepreneurial ones, and as a result their offspring go into teaching and business respectively, there is nothing unfair about the fact that members of the second family end up earning more than the first. What is more disturbing is poverty of aspiration – children who are told that they can't expect to get anything better than an unskilled job, for instance. So we need to think carefully about the different ways in which families can affect the life chances of the next generation. Where opportunities are being restricted, either because abilities are not being given an adequate chance to develop at home or because aspirations are being kept low, then public policy, in particular educational policy, will have a large part to play in broadening them. But the transmission of ideas of what is valuable in life, whether of a whole culture or of a particular family, does not undermine social justice even where it results in some inequality.

This is important because there is a view of social justice that insists that the composition of every school, every college, every profession or career must exactly mirror the composition of the wider society, by gender, class, ethnicity, and so forth and that in turn lends support to forms of affirmative action that set quotas for appointing and admitting bodies to fulfil. Such a view is not only politically dangerous – it can lead to a backlash against all forms of affirmative action, including those whose aim is simply to ensure equal access and a fair chance to compete – but it also rests on a misunderstanding of equal opportunity. The principle is about giving equal chances to those with equivalent abilities and motivation; it leaves it open whether particular abilities and particular aspirations are evenly distributed between men and women, between ethnic groups, between social classes, and therefore what patterning, if any, a society of equal opportunities would display.

Fair distribution

This principle permits the unequal distribution of resources that are not part of the equal citizenship package, and not required to support the social minimum. Income is the most obvious example, but the principle also applies to many 'quality of life' goods such as job satisfaction, and the environmental benefits such as living in secluded places that may be purchased with income or traded off against it. It would be impossible for everyone to share these goods equally, and in any case this is not what justice requires – no one objects to someone getting paid more for working longer hours to pursue some dream that is expensive to fulfil, or someone who chooses more leisure time to cultivate his garden having to take a pay cut as a result. These are simple cases, but matters become more complicated when we ask, more generally, which inequalities are justified, and on what grounds?

Political philosophers often now answer this question by distinguishing between inequalities that arise from choice and those that arise from luck. The examples I just gave are unproblematic as far as justice is concerned, because the first person chooses to sacrifice leisure time for the sake of more income, while the second person makes the opposite choice. Contrast this with someone who cannot work because she is struck down with a disabling disease; her loss of income is the result of bad luck, and it is unfair for her to have to bear the consequences. So the proposed principle of fair distribution is that people should have equal resources unless they are personally responsible for having a greater or lesser share.

Attractive though it may appear at first glance, this principle faces some serious difficulties. The first of these is that attempting to eliminate the effects of all kinds of luck on people's fortunes would be an incredibly demanding undertaking. It is, after all, luck that we were born with the particular set of physical attributes and mental capacities that we have, so although it usually takes effort and discipline to turn these into economically valuable assets, it is still true that the resources different people can command for their services reflect the natural lottery that occurs as a person's genetic make-up is determined before birth. If we really wanted to eliminate the effects of luck of this kind, we would have to find a way of estimating the value of someone's natural talents, and then impose a redistributive tax that would nullify the advantages of the more talented and the disadvantages of the less talented. This would not only be practically unworkable, but would impose heavy costs on those who were born with (potentially lucrative) aptitudes that they had a great aversion to developing and using.

The luck of the natural lottery is not the only source of difficulty with the choice/luck principle of fairness. Even if we shift the line by allowing people to claim responsibility for their talents, it is still going to be difficult to decide how far they can genuinely claim to be responsible for the results of their actions. Suppose I decide to open a small café in the middle of town serving filled bagels and juices, and this turns out to be a big success. Can I claim all the credit, and the resulting profits, on the grounds that I spotted a market opening that no one else had noticed, and so it was my entrepreneurial flair that produced the result, or was it just luck that I happened to stumble across a product for which there was a latent demand, and there were no competitors around? We would never have the information that would enable us to settle the issue.

As a practical guide to policy social justice cannot aim at the wholesale elimination of luck. Instead, what we can do is protect people from the worst kinds of bad luck, and dampen down the cumulative effects of good luck. The policies guaranteeing the social minimum largely meet the first of these objectives. What about the second? Good luck that has no further consequences, like a lottery win, could be seen as neither fair nor unfair. What is more objectionable is when luck places people in positions of more or less permanent advantage. Much of the hostility justifiably directed at the chairmen of large corporations who receive big bonuses and share options regardless of their company's performance surely derives from the perception that it was, to a greater or lesser extent, chance that placed them where they are – once in the driving seat, they can ensure that the rewards of luck are multiplied. Luck also leads to excess in the case of film stars and sports personalities, where marginal differences in performance – being able to kick a football very slightly better than your nearest rivals – divide the superstars from the rest. Once superstar status is achieved, it routinely produces a huge stream of income, through sponsorship and the like, more or less regardless of what the star then does. Such inequalities are difficult to combat, but an important justification for taxing high levels of income and wealth progressively is that what is being taxed away is very largely the cumulative effects of luck rather than, say, of hard work.

The same point can be put more positively. Inequalities are fair when they result from some recognisable form of personal desert – someone has made a contribution that reflects their own particular talents and efforts, not merely the chance of being in the right place at the right time, and that contribution brings a proportionate reward. This allows in certain kinds of luck, including the luck of being born with talents you can exploit, but excludes others. If we apply this principle to the case of sporting superstars, then we can say that David Beckham deserves a high salary by virtue of the footballing skills that he displays, and that his many fans appreciate, but not the premium he can command just by virtue of his comparative ranking, as a sportsman and a celebrity.

How far should we be concerned about the extent of income inequality, over and above the question of luck and desert? Our principles of social justice don't set any direct limits to the size of income differentials, but very large inequalities will certainly make justice harder to achieve in the long run. They are likely to corrode equal citizenship, since money buys access to power; to exert upward pressure on the social minimum, as people compare their living standards to those of the wealthy elite; and to make equality of opportunity harder to achieve, since money buys educational and other advantages. They also weaken the sense of community that encourages people to support social justice in their daily lives. So although the main question we should be asking about economic inequalities is how far they are earned and how far unearned, we should also worry about their size. And perhaps these two concerns can be brought together, since a society where everyone was fairly rewarded for what they had contributed, and luck wasn't allowed to cumulate, would also be a society considerably more equal than ours.

Let me turn now to the other half of the luck/choice principle, that inequalities which reflect choice are always fair. This, too, has to be severely qualified. First of all, we may think that there are consequences that people should not have to bear, even if they result directly from personal choices. Indeed the idea of a social minimum to which everyone is entitled implies this. We think that smokers who develop cancers should be treated on the NHS, even if their decision to smoke was a fully informed choice. Taxing cigarettes is a legitimate way of ensuring that those who make this choice contribute more to the costs of treatment, but we should not pull the safety net away no matter how imprudent the choices people make.

A second qualification is that choices will produce just outcomes only if the circumstances in which they are made are also fair. If people are desperate they will choose to take jobs that involve them working under unhealthy or dangerous conditions, but such choices cannot justify the ills that then befall them. The same applies to the recent trend to allow citizens more choice in their use of public services. Introducing choice may have some desirable consequences, including giving the providers an incentive to improve the quality of their service, but it remains true that having a choice between several poor-quality schools or hospitals is not a fair choice if other people have a better range of alternatives.

Finally, it is important to be realistic about people's capacity to choose, particularly where choice involves making fairly complicated comparisons between long-term alternatives, for example between the merits of two rival pension policies. There is plenty of evidence that shows that people are generally not good at making choices of this kind – they are not rational maximisers of their future income, or of anything else, but are greatly influenced by the frame within which alternatives are presented to them. So there is a danger that if people's life chances come to depend heavily on the choices they make, this will work to the advantage of those who have a talent for choosing, or at least know where to turn for advice. Choice can sometimes justify unequal outcomes, but on condition that it is free and not forced, and based on an informed appraisal of the alternatives.

Conclusion

I have set out and defended four principles of social justice and it is natural to ask what priorities we should set if we have to choose between fulfilling each of them. From a philosophical perspective we may regard equal citizenship as the most fundamental principle insofar as the four principles together tell us what justice means in a society of free and equal citizens. Practically however, there are likely to be hard choices to make, since each of the principles makes demands on our resources. Money spent on community policing to protect equal rights to security is money that cannot be spent on increasing the state pension (part of the social minimum) or on pre-school education (necessary for equal opportunity). Faced with these choices, no one principle takes automatic priority. At the same time, we should look for policies that can take us forward on more than one dimension. Investment in education, deservedly popular at the moment, can help to safeguard the social minimum by reducing unemployment while at the same time increasing opportunities to move up the occupational ladder.

The principles I have outlined already enjoy widespread popular support (Miller, 1999). The challenge we face is to convince people of what needs to be done in practice to turn them into a reality. Although resources do matter, as I have just indicated, we should get away from the image of social justice as the state moving sums of money from one pocket to another. It is equally a matter of practice at the grass roots such as neighbours getting together to clean up an estate, schools encouraging all children to aim high and employers taking care to avoid inadvertent discrimination. Public policy needs to go hand in hand with an ethos of social justice that pervades society, and the state's role will often be to inform and support, rather than to intervene directly. We have travelled far over the last 50 or so years to combat injustice, but there is still much to do to create a society that treats all of its citizens with fairness and respect.

References

Ackerman B and Alstott A (1999) *The Stakeholder Society* New Haven: Yale University Press

Ackerman B and Fishkin J (2004) *Deliberation Day* New Haven: Yale University Press

BBC News Online (2005) *Schoolgirl wins Muslim gown case.* Available at
  http://news.bbc.co.uk/1/hi/england/beds/bucks/herts/4310545.stm

Commission on Social Justice (CSJ) (1994) *Social Justice: Strategies for National Renewal* London:
  Vintage Books

Dworkin R (2000) 'Justice and the High Cost of Health' in *Sovereign Virtue* Cambridge, MA.:
  Harvard University Press

Gordon D, Levitas R, Pantazis C, Patsios D, Payne S, Townsend P, Adelman L, Ashworth K,
  Middleton S, Bradshaw J and Williams J (2000) *Poverty and social exclusion in Britain* York: Joseph
  Rowntree Foundation

Hart B and Risley T (1995) *Meaningful Differences in the Everyday Experience of Young American
  Children* Baltimore: Paul H. Brookes

Miller D (1999) *Principles of Social Justice* Cambridge, MA.: Harvard University Press

Walby S and Allen J (2004) *Domestic violence, sexual assault and stalking: Findings from the British
  Crime Survey* Home Office Research Study 276, London: TSO

Wellman C and Cohen A (2004) *The Blackwell Companion to Applied Ethics* Oxford: Blackwell

White S and Paxton W (2005) *A Citizens' Stake: exploring the future of universal assets policies* Bristol:
  Policy Press

The State of the Nation: An Audit of Social Injustice in the UK

Mike Dixon and Will Paxton[1]

In this chapter we present key elements of social injustice in Britain today, using the framework outlined by David Miller in Chapter 1. We highlight key facts which bear on the four principles of social justice – equal citizenship, the social minimum, equality of opportunity and a fair distribution – with links, where relevant, made to subsequent chapters in this publication. While the distribution of material resources remains central, it is not the sole factor in determining social justice. The data in this chapter reflects a more complex view of social justice, covering wider indicators of wellbeing. Where possible we draw out the links between the different principles. Sometimes there may be trade-offs between policies' objectives – we may need to prioritise either reducing child poverty or promoting social mobility. But sometimes too, there will be win-wins.

Equal citizenship

Every citizen is entitled to an equal set of civil, political and social rights, including the means to exercise these rights effectively.

Many factors contribute towards equality of citizenship. At the most fundamental level this principle requires equality before the law, not least because experiencing civil justice problems can trigger other difficulties and foster social exclusion. Yet access to legal services is far from equal.

1 The authors would like to thank Tania Burchardt, Alissa Goodman and Donald Hirsch for comments on early drafts, Tony Atkinson for a useful presentation at an ippr seminar and colleagues at ippr, particularly Peter Robinson, Nick Pearce, Liane Lohde and Howard Reed, for invaluable input.

Some disadvantaged groups, such as unemployed people or those living in temporary housing, face significant hurdles in using such services despite being more likely to experience legal difficulties (Pleasance *et al*, 2004). Research shows that one in five people takes no action to solve an existing civil justice problem and around one million problems go unsolved each year because people don't understand their basic rights or know how to seek help (ibid). This is particularly true of the 1998 Human Rights Act, which appears to have had limited impact to date for those in the most deprived areas (Costigan *et al*, 2004).

If equal access to justice is central to equality of citizenship, so too are democratic participation and freedom from crime and anti-social behaviour. A vibrant political culture can be seen as a measure of a healthy society as well as being more likely to promote equality in other areas. Victimisation can seriously affect people's lives – making them unwilling to travel after dark, limiting their opportunities in the labour market and social lives, or reducing their sense of trust and involvement in the community.

Although we concentrate here on what could be seen as the foundations of equal citizenship, this does not mean that other factors should not be a concern, although some of these may be more difficult to measure and influence. For example, as Chapter 11 argues, the degree of respect and tolerance people show each other in their daily interactions is central but only indirectly affected by government action.

Personal safety

Most categories of crime are at their lowest level for 20 years. Official crime figures have fallen steadily since their peak in 1995 and in 2003/4 overall levels were down 39 per cent, burglary down 47 per cent and violent crime down 36 per cent on the 1995 figures (Home Office, 2004a). Britain appears to be a safer society than it has been for many years.

There are two caveats to this, however. First, apart from the 2003/4 figures, there has been a perception that low-level crimes and anti-social behaviour are actually increasing (ibid). Second, and more important from a social justice perspective, the pertinent issue is not just the aggregate level of crime, or the overall perceptions of crime, but on whom the burden falls most. Crime and the fear of crime are not evenly distributed across the population – some unfairly suffer more of the burden than others.

Concerns about anti-social behaviour are voiced particularly by the poor and those living in deprived areas (Home Office, 2003a). Similarly, many categories of crime, such as property crime, disproportionately affect those on low incomes and those who live in disadvantaged areas. Figure 2.1 shows that people living in disadvantaged areas in 2002/3 were much more likely to suffer from burglary, violent crime and have higher levels of worry about crime than those who live in more prosperous areas. The picture is even more unequal when looking at fear of crime; the correlation between income and fear of crime was stronger in 2002/3 than the correlation between income and victimisation (Home Office, 2003a).

Figure 2.1: People living in disadvantaged areas are more likely to suffer from crime and the fear of crime

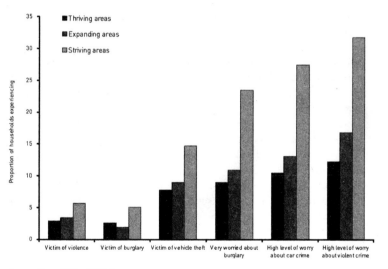

Source: Home Office (2003a)

Note: Figures for 2003/4 do not show fear of crime levels by area, so 2002/3 data has been used for ease of comparison. Area definitions used are ACORN area definitions produced by CACI Ltd. See http://www.homeoffice.gov.uk/rds/pdfs2/hosb703.pdf for further detail.

Trends in fear of crime and incidence of crime over time paint a slightly more positive picture. Though there is no established way of monitoring the distribution of crime over time, evidence suggests that the distribution of crime became more unequal through the 1980s (Tricket *et al,* 1995), but since 1997 it appears that this trend may have reversed.

Home Office data suggests the poor were less likely to suffer from violent crime and the fear of crime relative to the rich in 2003/4 than in 1997. In 2003/4, the poorest households were 1.02 times as likely to be victims of violent crime, compared to 1.29 times as likely in 1997, and they were 2.3 times as likely to be afraid of physical attack in 2002/3, compared to 2.6 times as likely in 1999 (Home Office, 1999; Home Office, 2003b).

There is a potential trade-off to be considered here between different elements of social justice. When should government prioritise increasing incomes (affecting the social minimum) over reducing crime or the fear of crime (affecting equal citizenship)? We know from 'willingness to pay' research that people are prepared to pay more in tax for a reduction in the level of crime in their local area, and that the amount they are prepared to pay increases with the seriousness of the crime.[2] This suggests not only that freedom from the fear of crime has a tangible value and that it significantly affects people's quality of life, but also that for some people, reducing crime may be preferable to an increase in their income. There may be times when people do not want increased financial support, but would like to see additional attempts to reduce crime.

Democratic participation

Equal citizenship also requires the right to be able to influence government. There has been a well-charted fall in formal, or traditional, forms of political participation. Nationally and locally, the trend in election turnout has been downward in the UK, as it has been in other developed countries. Likewise, 'satisfaction' with British democracy has fallen and fewer people believe they have a say in what government does (Seyd and Whiteley, 2002). But these overall figures mask a more worrying skew in the distribution of participation across the population.

At the general election in 2001, 68 per cent of the top two social classes are thought to have voted, compared to just 53 per cent of the bottom social class (MORI, 2001). Those on the highest incomes are also more likely to be aware of political issues and are twice as likely to have discussed politics in the last two years (Electoral Commission,

---

2 The mean amount people are willing to pay for a 50 per cent reduction in the risk of their being a victim of crime was found to be £106.31 for common assault, £154.29 for other wounding and £178.33 for serious wounding (Atkinson *et al*, 2003).

2004). Figure 2.2 shows how an existing class divide widened between 1991 and 1999. Interest in politics has fallen slightly across all social classes in recent decades, but for the lowest social classes it has decreased significantly – almost halving between 1981 and 1999.

Figure 2.2: Political interest by social class

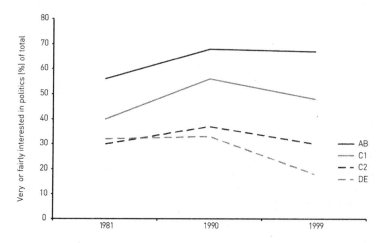

Source: World Values Survey quoted in Strategy Unit (2003).

Ethnic minorities are also less involved in political life. The Electoral Commission was told by 70 per cent that they had no interest in politics. They were also less likely to believe that they could change the way the UK is governed by getting involved in politics than the rest of the population (Electoral Commission, 2004). Worryingly, this is also the case for lower social classes. People's sense that they can influence decisions if they want to is lowest amongst the most deprived at local and at national levels (Home Office, 2003b; Home Office, 2004b).

Yet it is not just formal participation in democracy that should be of concern. Across a range of different activities which could still be defined as 'political', there is a correlation with class and income. Figure 2.3 shows engagement in 'collective', 'individual' and 'contact' forms of engagement. Collective activities include taking part in a strike, attending a political rally or being a member of a trade union; individual activities include signing a petition or shopping ethically; contact activities include making contact with your MP, councillor or the media.[3] It shows that those in the lowest social class, the poorest in society and the less educated were less likely to be politically active than those who are in a higher social class, better off or better educated in 2000, the last year for which data is available.

Figure 2.3: Engagement in political activity by social class and income

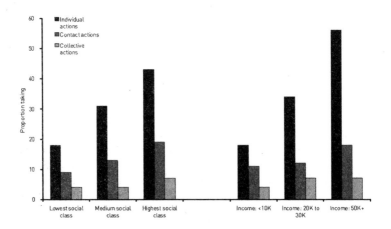

Source: Sheffield Citizens Audit (2001)

Importantly, the nature of political engagement appears to have fundamentally changed in the last 20 years. Although the picture is complex, with some people pointing to increased levels of 'protest' and direct action, such as that against fuel price increases or war in Iraq, the most noticeable shift has been away from collective forms of action. People increasingly express their political preferences through personal, market-related activity, such as contacting the media rather than politicians and boycotting products rather than signing petitions; they are paying for others to become engaged on their behalf.

If these trends continue, political power will be increasingly related to income and the ability to pay for change, further shifting the balance away from the poor and disadvantaged. It is noteworthy that

3 For a full explanation see Seyd and Whitely (2002) .

the class and income differentials in collective forms of political engagement are less severe. If 'individualised' political action continues to increase as it has done over the last two decades, and if turnout falls further still, there is a risk that the voices of the less well educated and the less well connected will become even less audible. The question we need to ask is whether the UK is witnessing a widening 'citizenship gap' between rich and poor. What are the impacts of this for achieving equal citizenship as well as wider social justice objectives?

The social minimum

All citizens must have access to resources that adequately meet their essential needs, and allow them to live a secure and dignified life in today's society.

Although income has traditionally been seen as being at the heart of the social minimum and carries the dual temptation for policymakers and government that it is relatively easy to both measure and affect, social justice requires a broader conception of disadvantage. Work by the Policy Studies Institute, Joseph Rowntree Foundation and others has drawn a distinction between poverty, which is based on income: and hardship, which is based on access to necessities – whether people can afford to heat their homes, whether they worry about money all the time and run out of it most weeks, and whether they can afford food, clothing and social participation (Hills, 2004). This hardship measure has the advantage of reflecting why we care about income; because poverty can reduce people's standards of living in unacceptable ways. Yet even this conception may not be broad enough. As Foley, Grayling and Dixon argue in Chapter 8, we need to think in terms of people's access to healthcare and transport, the environment they live in and other factors which allow them to live a secure and dignified life.

In this section we start by setting out what has happened to levels of income poverty for children and other groups. This is arguably the most accurate data available that shows how levels of wellbeing have changed over time. But we also concentrate on some of the wider aspects of a social minimum, including the possession of assets and access to a good local environment.

Income poverty

It is accepted by most people that income poverty should be measured in a relative way. Using the 60 per cent of median income after housing costs (AHC) measure to look at levels of poverty for all groups in society, we can see progress in the last decade. UK poverty levels increased dramatically during the 1980s: in 1981, 15 per cent of individuals lived in households in income poverty but by 1993/4 this had risen to 24 per cent. But by 2003/4 the overall proportion of people living in poverty had fallen to 21 per cent or twelve million people (DWP, 2005).

Looking at these aggregate figures reveals overall trends in poverty. However, the picture has been very different for different groups. Children have been the government's main priority, as shown by an explicit child poverty target. Although pensioner poverty has been a focus of the government's rhetoric, there has been no official target other than an aspiration to end pensioner poverty within a generation. For working-age adults with no children, however, there has been neither a target nor an aspiration. We consider these groups in turn.

Child poverty: mid-table respectability or Champion's League material?

In 1999, the Prime Minister stated that 'our historic aim [is] that ours is the first generation to end child poverty forever... It's a twenty year mission but I believe it can be done' (Blair, 1999a). Since then, significant progress has been made. In 1998, the UK was bottom of the European league, with the highest child poverty rate in the EU, but by 2001 the UK had risen to eleventh out of fifteen (Eurostat, 2002). Although significant progress has been made it now looks unlikely that the government will succeed in reducing child poverty by the first target it set – a quarter between 1999 and 2004/5 – on an AHC basis although it may meet the target on a before housing costs (BHC) basis (Brewer *et al*, 2005).

Yet, as Figure 2.4 shows, total child poverty remains high by international standards. Compared to the best-performing European countries the UK still has a shameful record. Of children in Britain, 21 per cent lived in households earning below 60 per cent of median income in 2003/4, compared to just 5 per cent in Denmark, 10 per cent in Sweden and 14 per cent in Germany in 2001 (Eurostat, 2002). The UK has also performed far better in the past. Only 10 per cent of children lived in poverty in 1968 and we are still a long way from achieving the 1979 level of 12 per cent (JRF, 1999; DWP, 2003a).

Figure 2.4: Child poverty levels: where does Britain stand?

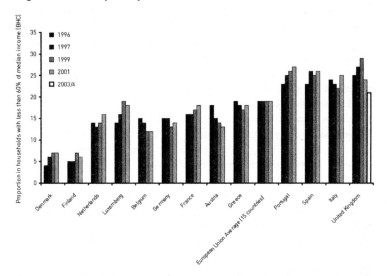

Source: Eurostat/European Community Household Panel. UK figures for 2003/4 are from HBAI 2003/4 and as such are not directly comparable.

In 2003, the Government announced a new measure of child poverty (DWP, 2003b). This will be used to assess progress on the goals of halving and then abolishing child poverty (HMT, 2004). A measure of relative income using the 60 per cent of median income will remain (though assessed on a BHC basis instead of AHC) but will complemented by two further measures:[4]

- One of absolute income which will measure the number of children living in households with a contemporary equivalised (taking account of household composition) income of less than 60 per cent of median income in 1998/9 on a BHC basis
- One which combines a less stringent relative income measure (70 per cent of median income) and levels of material deprivation

---

4 For further details on the Government's new measure of child poverty see http://www.dwp.gov.uk/consultations/consult/2003/childpov/poverty.pdf

Progress will be made towards tackling child poverty only when improvements are observed against all three of these tiers. There is much merit in moving away from a simple income based measure, but this also raises questions. In the short term, it raises a somewhat technocratic, but nonetheless important, issue about whether the shift from a BHC to an AHC measure is right. In the longer term, and more significantly in the context of 'the social minimum', it requires policy makers to think about the goods and services beyond household income that should be part of debates on poverty. The Sure Start pilots are an example of how effective this approach can be (NESS, 2004).

Pensioner poverty: another target needed?

The child poverty target has made a significant difference to the lives of millions of children. Yet no official target has been set for pensioner poverty, despite the Chancellor stating in 2002 that 'our aim is to end pensioner poverty in our country' and the Government putting significant resources into tackling pensioner poverty (Brown, 2002). As a result, will there be less attention and resources devoted to tackling pensioner poverty in the future? It is a national badge of shame that we fail to ensure adequate incomes in retirement and that many pensioners cannot afford to heat their homes – 20,000 more die in the winter months than in the summer each year (ONS, 2002a). To focus attention, consideration should be given to establishing an explicit target to abolish pensioner poverty.

If such a target were set, how should we measure progress? Government, as noted above, has decided to move from an AHC to a BHC measure for child poverty. This has been controversial because it makes it more likely to meet its targets. But it makes less sense for pensioner poverty because while on an AHC measure pensioner poverty has fallen from 27 per cent in 1994/5 to 20 per cent in 2003/4, on a BHC measure over the same period there has been little change. In 2003/4 20 per cent of pensioners were in poverty, just 1 per cent lower than in 1994/5. But it might be justifiable to measure pensioner poverty differently from child poverty. More pensioners now own their own home, which reduces their cash income but not their living standards compared to someone who does not own their home but does receive £50 a week in housing benefit.

Were we to accept that an AHC measure for pensioner poverty is more appropriate, then an increase the basic state pension to a level just above such a poverty line would effectively abolish pensioner poverty, as it would avoid the problem of low take-up of means-tested retirement benefits.[5] Despite some success in recent take-up campaigns, it remains the case that approximately 1.25 million pensioner households are not claiming the pension credit (DWP, 2004b).

Working-age adults: no target and no aspiration?

If pensioners have benefited less from efforts to reduce poverty than children, other groups have fared worse. This is particularly true for working-age adults without children. In 1994/5, of individuals in households with less than 60 per cent of median income AHC, only 15 per cent were single without children. By 2003/4 this same group made up 30 per cent of households in poverty (DWP, 2005). This might not be of concern if poverty among those of working age without children was falling, while child and pensioner poverty fell faster. However, this does not appear to be the case. Between 1994/5 and 2003/4 the absolute number of working-age adults without children in poverty has risen from 3.3 million to 3.6 million (DWP, 2005). One contributing factor here may be that benefit rates have not kept pace with average income.

Yet it is debatable what sort of attention needs to be attached to such 'unfavoured' groups. We would expect children and pensioners to be a priority and the existence of tax credits and the national minimum wage, which seek to sharpen work incentives and reduce in-work poverty, benefit working-age childless adults.

Hard-to-reach groups

Focusing on children, pensioners and working-age adults may miss important trends within these groups. Although overall levels of poverty have been reduced, there have been concerns that government policy has only benefited the 'low-hanging fruit' – those just below the poverty line, rather than harder-to-reach groups such as the homeless, pupils excluded from school, different ethnic minorities and asylum seekers. The picture with these groups has been mixed and the Government's own Social Exclusion Unit has argued that future policy must be more attentive to the needs of specific groups, particularly the poorest of the poor, the lowest educational attainers and the low-skilled (SEU, 2004).

---

5 Will Paxton, Nick Pearce and Howard Reed put forward this argument in detail in Chapter 16.

Furthermore, little has been done to reduce persistent poverty – defined as living at least three years out of the last four in poverty[6] – which is stubbornly high in Britain compared to the rest of Europe. Between 1998 and 2001, 10 per cent of UK citizens lived in persistent poverty, compared to an EU average of 9 per cent, 5 per cent in the Netherlands and 6 per cent in Germany and Norway (Eurostat, 2002). Below, though, we also focus on the disabled.

Hard to reach groups: the disabled

The importance of developing policy for disabled people is heightened by the increased incidence of disability in recent years. The best figures available, using the Local Area Labour Force Survey, indicate that between 1999/2000 and 2003/4, the number of disabled people of working age rose from 5,687,000 to 6,023,000 (ONS, 2005). Social justice demands greater policy attention is paid to disabled people as they face considerable barriers and disadvantage in a number of areas.

In 2001, 24 per cent of disabled people of working age had no qualifications, compared to 16 per cent of non-disabled people, which contributes to the difficulties people with disabilities face in finding employment; in 2002, they were five times more likely than non-disabled people to be out of work and claiming benefits (ONS, 2003a; DRC, 2003). In spring 2003, disabled people had an employment rate of only 49 per cent, compared with an employment rate of 81 per cent of those who were not disabled (ONS, 2004a). This employment rate gap has narrowed in recent years, yet there are still more than one million disabled people who say they want to work (Regan and Stanley, 2003).

Largely as a result of lower employment rates and poorer educational outcomes, the risk of being in poverty (measured as 60 per cent of median income) is higher for people with a disability. This is even before accounting for the additional costs which may be associated with their disability. Zaidi and Burchardt found that, using data from 1996/7, while official measures put 35.1 per cent of households with

---

6 Persistent poverty figures are on an AHC basis, due to data limitations in the British Household Panel Survey. Defining persistent poverty is problematic as measures which look over long time periods can miss individuals that experience real and lasting poverty whereas shorter measures can overstate the extent of such poverty. The 'three out of four years' measure is widely regarded as a good compromise, although it has widely recognised limitations. See Jenkins and Rigg (2001) for more information.

disabled people in poverty, when account is taken of additional costs of disability this figure became 60.8 per cent (Zaidi and Burchardt, 2002). In 2002/3, 35 per cent of households in poverty, on a BHC basis, contained at least one disabled adult, while only 21 per cent of households from across the population included a disabled adult. Importantly, there are links here to child poverty; only 17 per cent of children live in households with at least one disabled adults but 26 per cent of children in poverty (BHC) live in such households (DWP, 2004a).

The wider social minimum: beyond income

As noted above, the new three-tier definition to be used to measure progress towards tackling child poverty includes an index of material deprivation. The exact measure to be used is unconfirmed, though one similar to that in Ireland is likely (Nolan and Whelan, 2003). Were measures of deprivation correlated in a straightforward way with income, then policy would not need to change significantly. Government could continue to use tax credits and increasing employment rates to tackle poverty. However, the relationship is not clear. The Poverty and Social Exclusion Survey illustrates that households below certain income thresholds are not always the most deprived in terms of a range of non-monetary indicators (Bradshaw and Finch, 2002).

Already, the Treasury has started to integrate policy debates which are not primarily concerned with income with those about child poverty. The 2004 Child Poverty Review stressed the importance of financial inclusion and of improving the quality of housing (HMT, 2004). Consideration of what the wider social minimum, or some list of basic opportunity goods, should be will be an important element of future policy debates.

Continuing the transition from a debate about poverty (even with measure of material deprivation and accounting for benefit rates) to one about the social minimum will require further consideration in several areas.

The first is to think about the importance of expenditure as well as income. It can be expensive to be poor. In 2002/3, those who could not afford to take the risk of having a metered water bill faced payments up to £116 higher (NCC, 2004). For those without bank accounts it can be difficult to access cheap loans, which contributes to the difficulty poor people may have in 'smoothing' their consumption because they do not have assets. Work by Goodman and Oldfield has argued that, partly because of this smoothing effect, looking at expenditure rather than income reveals more about the longer-run, or lifetime, differences in living standards between people than looking at income (Goodman and Oldfield, 2004).

Second, the role of asset-exclusion needs to become more central. As well as enabling people to smooth consumption, asset ownership has other positive effects which are important in achieving a social minimum (Bynner and Paxton, 2001; Banks *et al*, 2002).

The third is in terms of access to public services. The better off still often receive better state-funded services, despite significant improvement since 1997 in focusing resources in a progressive direction. Research shows that higher education spending was regressive in 2002 and there are concerns that better off parents can 'work the system' in many cases (Sefton, 2004; Reid, 2003). There is also evidence that the NHS has remained inequitable in some key areas of healthcare provision; for many types of preventative healthcare services, such as health checks for cardiovascular disease and MMR vaccinations, the deprived have been less likely to access care, as well as being less likely to have inpatient treatment, and research suggests that children from low-income households may use fewer health services in relation to their needs than other children (Dixon *et al*, 2003; Sefton, 2004).

These three issues should become more important foci for policy over the next decade. Yet there are other central elements to the social minimum which may prove less easy to fit within a traditional framework, such as people's local quality of life.

Local quality of life

The state of the local environment makes a difference to health levels, as well as overall enjoyment of living in an area. Enjoying and experiencing the environment an integral part of living in Britain and, as such, all citizens should experience a minimum level of environmental quality. Policy makers' objectives should not just be overall reductions in pollution and improvements in the quality of local environments. We should be concerned with how different environmental 'bads' affect different groups and areas.

There is a mixed picture of environmental quality. Some indices have improved. Air quality was dramatically better in 2003 than in 1990, but between 1991/2 and 2001/2, the amount of household waste not recycled or composted increased (DEFRA, 2003). Unfortunately though, there is little evidence available in the UK on the relationship between environmental quality and social deprivation. That which exists

shows that deprived communities do suffer the worse effects of environmental degradation but the scope of such studies is limited. Recent
research showed that industrial sites were disproportionately located in
deprived areas (Walker *et al*, 2003).

Figure 2.5: Experience of problems at a neighbourhood level

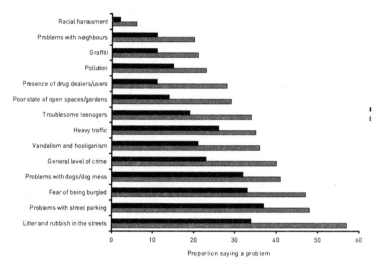

Source: English House Condition Survey, ODPM, 2001

Using a broader measure of the quality of the local environment, one
that includes crime and 'crime issues', it is evident in the latest data that
satisfaction with local areas is low across Britain and, as Figure 2.5 shows,
in 2001, it was those living in more deprived areas who were more likely
to report a problem across a range of different issues.

While it might be unsurprising that those in deprived areas reported
more problems, this should be a cause for concern. In 2000, 34 per cent of
people felt local facilities were poor or very poor, and over a third said they
had a high level of local problems, with those living in the most deprived
wards being more than twice as likely to report dissatisfaction. Forty-five per
cent of those in the most deprived 10 per cent of wards reported poor local
facilities, compared to 23 per cent of those in the least deprived ten per cent
of wards (ONS, 2002b). Poor local facilities can contribute towards other

problems, and promoting social justice and tackling disadvantage need to take notice of these environmental factors.

Equality of opportunity

A person's life chances, and especially their access to jobs and educational opportunities, should depend only on their own motivation and aptitudes, and not on irrelevant features such as gender, class or ethnicity.

Social mobility is a measure of equality of opportunity that describes the extent to which people move between groups during their lifetime, moves which bring advantages and disadvantages in terms of employment, income, education, crime, housing and quality of life. Levels of social mobility are influenced by a number of factors – education, social class, poverty, access to services, attitudes and aspirations, discrimination and the transparency and openness of societal institutions – not all of which are easy or desirable for government to influence.

Progressive policy makers should not necessarily want to fashion a purely meritocratic society; equality of opportunity may trade off against other objectives outlined by David Miller in Chapter 1. For example, promoting some kinds of mobility may mean less attention is paid to reducing income poverty and, perhaps more fundamentally, higher levels of social mobility may reduce social solidarity. It is worth noting that in the US perceptions of higher mobility mean that the public are more likely to think that people in poverty are there because they are 'lazy and lack willpower' and that benefit rates are too generous (Hills, 2004). In any case, a goal of completely equal life chances would be realistically unattainable. There will always be some correlation between people's origins and their destinations for perfectly acceptable reasons.

Yet progressives should undoubtedly be committed to greater equality of opportunity and social mobility than currently exists.[7] Social justice demands a society in which the social class, ethnicity or talents of your parents makes less difference to the kind of life you are able to lead or the opportunities open to you than is currently the case. People should be able to make greatest use of their talents and ability, not least because this implies

---

7 Some recent debate has focused on 'life chances'. Social mobility tends to be seen as one element of a wider 'life chances framework', one that also includes poverty and social exclusion. This could provide useful policy insights but in this section we focus on social mobility in its different forms, and not a broader conception of life chances.

a higher standard of living for everyone through greater economic efficiency. So how well is the UK fairing in terms of social mobility? It is important to be clear about what we mean here, as there are several complementary measures of mobility. Intragenerational mobility concerns the chances people have compared to others in their generation, whereas intergenerational mobility concerns the chances that people born into different social groups have of making it into other social groups between generations. Both of these can be usefully looked at in terms of income or social class and can be either relative – the relative chances people have compared to others in their group – or absolute – the actual number or proportion of people who are upwardly or downwardly mobile.

Limited chances for adults

Although there is a great deal of intragenerational income and earnings mobility in Britain (both upward and downward), much of this is short range, reflecting substantial inequality of opportunity. The most up to date analyses show that 65 per cent of those in the bottom income quintile in 1991 were in the bottom two quintiles in 2002 and just 8.7 per cent of those who were low paid in 1991 were in the top half of the income distribution in 1997 (DWP, 2004a; McKnight, 2000). The prospects for those with low skills and low educational attainment are much worse than those with better qualifications. Table 2.1 shows where people who were in the poorest fifth of the income distribution in 1991 were in the income distribution in 2002. While 79 per cent of those with no qualifications were in the bottom two quintiles after eleven years, just 45 per cent of those with qualifications above A-level were in the same position.

Table 2.1: Position in the income distribution in 2002 for the lowest income quintile in 1991 by educational level in 2002

Educational Level in 2002	Bottom Quintile	Second Quintile	Third Quintile	Fourth Quintile	Fifth Quintile
No qualifications	44	35	13	6	3
A-level or below	35	24	18	18	6
Above A-level	21	24	23	11	20

Source: Figures provided by DWP, based on BHPS 1991-2002. working-age adults only.

Looking at people's income 'trajectories' over the period 1991 to 2000 confirms this picture of a relatively static society. Around half of people had relatively flat incomes, around an eighth had steadily rising incomes and an eighth steadily falling incomes (Sefton and Rigg, 2004). The prospects of many of those on low wages in Britain are poor as those who are low paid can expect little improvement, even in the relatively long term.

Worryingly, there appears to have been a decline in earnings mobility between the late 1970s and late 1990s, particularly for prime age men (although there has been some improvement for women, reflecting their increased participation in the labour market).[8] This has been partly driven by declining mobility at the very top, as it has become more likely that those in the highest quartile of the earnings distribution remain there year on year, and considerable persistence of low pay at the bottom, with between 40 and 50 per cent of those who remained in employment over six year periods remaining in the lowest quarter of the earnings distribution (McKnight, 2000).

The need to consider the issue of wage progression is underlined when we look at increased levels of in-work poverty. In 2003/4, 28 per cent of households living in poverty (AHC) had one or more members in full-time work and 31 per cent of those in persistent poverty over the period 1998 to 2001 had one or employed members (DWP, 2005). Although tax credits and other welfare-to-work measures have helped reduce poverty, it is not enough to simply move people temporarily out; policy makers also need to seek to keep people out and ensure that they have the opportunity to make a sustained move away from poverty (see Chapter 16). The most recent research on the dynamics of poverty suggests that those who have been in income poverty longer are less likely to escape it, and that if people do escape, they are vulnerable to slipping back within a short period of time. The longer people can stay out, the more likely they are to maintain their improved situation (Jenkins and Rigg, 2001; Sefton, 2004).

Limited chances for children
Yet it is not just intragenerational mobility that we should be concerned with. Politicians of both the left and right claim to believe in greater equality of opportunity and there is widespread support for the notion

---

8   Unfortunately, little research evidence exists looking at trends after 1997.

that all children should start life with equal life chances. While inequality of opportunity later in the life cycle can be justified on the basis of differences in the choices individuals have made and the amount of effort they have expended in their lives, few would agree this should be the case for newborn children. Yet rarely is the radicalism of this commitment spelled out and carried through into practical policies.

In his 1999 conference speech the Prime Minister argued that:

> *We owe it to every child to unleash their potential. They are of equal worth. They deserve an equal chance… There is no more powerful symbol of our politics than the experience of being on a maternity ward. Seeing two babies side by side. Delivered by the same doctors and midwives. Yet two totally different lives ahead of them* (Blair, 1999b).

What are the respective chances of these babies today? We will have to wait to see what impact the changes Labour has made in the last eight years will have on the life chances of today's children. But there are two areas where we can look for evidence to underpin policy choices. First, we can assess the most up-to-date data on intergenerational social mobility in recent decades; and, second, we can examine the shorter-term impact of policy changes on drivers of social mobility, particularly educational attainment.

Measures of absolute intergenerational social mobility appear relatively positive, especially when seen in terms of social class, as this is partly driven by changes in the structure of society. Looking at a group of men born between 1950 and 1959 reveals that 42 per cent have been upwardly mobile (in that they are in a higher social class than their father at a similar age), while just 13 per cent have moved down (Payne and Roberts, 2002). This is partly because growth in professional and managerial jobs has been stronger than growth in manual jobs, resulting in more 'room at the top', enabling significant upwards mobility without substantial downwards mobility for children from higher class backgrounds. Yet we might be concerned that this pattern is in decline. Although absolute mobility increased very gradually between 1972 and 1992, it declined slightly in the period up to 1997 (ibid).

However, looking at absolute social mobility might not capture our concerns about equality of opportunity. Relative social mobility, the chance a disadvantaged child has compared to a relatively advantaged one, might paint a better picture.[9] Research that compares two different cohorts – groups of people all born at around the same time in 1958 and in 1970 – suggests that parental background makes more of a difference than it has done in the past. The first group of people who grew up in the 1960s and 1970s experienced higher relative income mobility than those who were brought up in the 1970s and 1980s. Such mobility became both less likely and also less far reaching for those in the later cohort. The experience of this group is shown by Figure 2.6, which reveals the make-up of income groups at age 30 for men in the 1970 cohort by parental income. (Women in this cohort experienced slightly more mobility than men, although less than the previous cohort.)

Figure 2.6: Relative intergenerational income mobility for men born in 1970, make-up of income quartiles by parental income

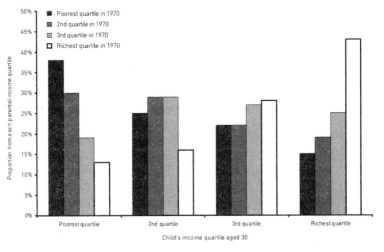

Source: Blanden *et al* (2004)

The chart shows that 34 per cent of those whose parents were in the bottom income quartile remained in this quartile and that 43 per cent of those whose parents were in the top quartile remained there themselves.

---

9   Income measures are arguably more useful than class measures in this context as they largely ignore changes in the class structure of society.

A further striking feature is that there has been less mobility out of the top quartile than out of any other group; once you make it into the top quartile, you are relatively unlikely to fall. Disconcertingly, compared to the 1958 cohort, income mobility appears to have declined significantly: the proportion of people remaining in the bottom quartile and top quartile were 30 per cent and 34 per cent respectively for this earlier cohort.

One important factor that we know more about, in relation to this 1970 cohort, is the early years of children's lives. Figure 2.7 shows that babies in this cohort with similar test scores at the age of 22 months developed cognitive skills at different rates depending on their social class. Only six months after birth, class differences in childhood cognitive development could be clearly seen and by the age of six the child with a low-cognitive ability from the rich family had already overtaken the poor but clever child.

Figure 2.7: Average rank in test scores by social class of parents and early position in tests

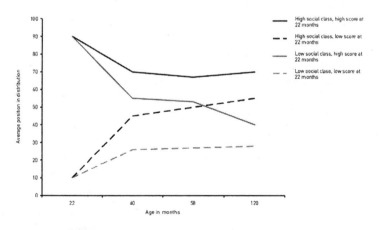

Source: Fenstein L (2003)

There are links here to children's health in their early years. The most recent data shows that the infant mortality rate in low-income areas is around 70 per cent higher than in the most affluent areas. Between 1998 and 2000, the rates amongst those in the lowest social class were double those in the highest (professional) social class – eight deaths per 1,000 births for the former and four for the latter. In 2002, birth weights continued to be linked to parental social class and accidental death amongst children was five times higher for children from the lowest social class than for those from a professional family (HMT, 2002).

This all paints a bleak picture. But declining social mobility is not inevitable. The UK's experience has not been shared by our international partners. Intragenerational mobility appears to have continued to rise in recent decades in France, Sweden and the Netherlands, largely, it is argued, due to a breakdown of the influence of social class on educational achievement in these countries (Solon, 1999). We also need to remember that contemporary and future policy changes intended to promote greater social mobility will have their most significant impact in a few decades time. Hence the importance of identifying the drivers of social mobility and assessing government success in positively influencing these.

Factors behind stubbornly high levels of immobility, including the importance of the early years, are discussed by Reed and Robinson in more detail in Chapter 13. Here we restrict ourselves to a discussion of trends in educational attainment.

'Education, Education, Education'

Sociologists have argued for many years that education has a profound impact on intergenerational social mobility. Political scientists have charted the links between educational attainment and later life chances, and have found correlations with higher levels of income and improved labour market performance (Machin and Gregg, 2003). However, a debate has recently started about whether education continues to be as important, or whether other factors, particularly the possession of 'soft skills' (such as the ability to communicate effectively), physical and psychological characteristics or even dress sense have become more important (Goldthorpe, 2003). In this section we assume that while formal educational achievement is not the only determinant of children's life chances, it should still be considered an important one and one which public policy can influence.

The UK has a mixed record on improving educational attainment. The aggregate figures are good: recent decades have seen sharp rises in educational achievement at all ages and increases in participation post-

sixteen. Yet the UK's longstanding leg.
achievement continues, with outstanding perf...
spectrum and consistent underachievement at th...
examine different stages in the education system and as...
recent policy developments.

Primary education

Primary school results are improving – in 2004, 74 per cent achieved Level Four or above in the mathematics test, four percentage points higher than in 1999, 78 per cent of pupils achieved Level Four or above in the English test, an increase of three percentage points on 2003 after remaining unchanged since 2000, and 86 per cent of eleven year olds achieved Level Four or above in the Key Stage Two science test, a decrease of one percentage point since 2003 but nine percentage points higher than in 1999 (DfES, 2005a). But significant inequalities remain. On average, those pupils receiving free school meals do consistently worse and make less progress in all subjects at all stages than those not receiving free school meals (DfES, 2005b). This difference is made all the more important because the UK education system continues to experience high levels of segregation (Gorard, 2003).

Secondary education

Educational attainment at secondary schools is largely determined by children's earlier development. But this does not mean that we should think secondary schools do not add value for children from lower income backgrounds. At the very least we should not want to see class or income gaps in educational attainment widen as children get older.

Again, looking at the aggregate data, there are signs that in recent years progress has been made; the numbers of pupils leaving school with no qualifications is falling and improvements in achievement at GCSE level have been fastest in schools facing challenging circumstances (DfES, 2004b). But the class gap remains: 74 per cent of children from the highest social classes achieved five or more GCSEs at grades A* to C in 2002, more than twice the proportion of children in the lowest social classes, and 86 per cent were participating in education post sixteen, 26 per cent more than the lowest social classes (DfES, 2004a). The implications of this for policy are developed in Chapter 13.

Inequalities in achievement are not only found when looking at class and income. Other factors, including ethnicity, also matter. Many ethnic

.nnorities still do less well at school than white pupils – particularly black, Bangladeshi and Pakistani pupils – and while the overall picture is complex, some trends can be drawn out. Of particular concern is that the disparity in achievement between ethnic groups increases significantly over the course of schooling. There is more inequality in attainment between ethnic groups after the completion of compulsory education than there is at entry to school (Bhattacharyya *et al*, 2003). Yet there are some encouraging signs. Indian and Chinese pupils are more likely to achieve the expected level compared with other ethnic groups at all key stages, and black and Asian young people are more likely to stay on in full-time education at age sixteen than white young people; 82 per cent of black and 85 per cent of Asian young people stay on in full-time education at age sixteen, compared to 69 per cent of white young people (ibid).

Higher and further education
There has been a dramatic expansion in the numbers entering higher education in the last fifteen years. The Government is committed to ensuring that half of all people under 30 participate in higher education by 2010, but the expansion thus far has disproportionately benefited those from more privileged backgrounds. Although participation rates for those from the manual social classes (classes C2, D and E) rose from 11 per cent in 1991/2 to 19 per cent in 2001/2, participation is still well below that of non-manual social classes, which rose from 35 per cent to 50 per cent over the same period (ONS, 2004b). While the chances of people from low-income backgrounds accessing university have increased, the relative prospects *vis-à-vis* those from wealthier backgrounds have not (Machin and Gregg, 2003).

However, it is not just access to higher education that should be of concern. Figure 2.8 shows what eighteen year olds were doing in 2002 by social class – whether they were in higher education, further education, working or doing something else.

A clear pattern is evident, with those from higher social classes being more likely to be in higher education and less likely to be in either full or part-time employment. Those from a routine or lower supervisory background are also more likely not to be in employment, education or training (the so-called NEET category). This group faces poorer prospects for the rest of their lives, which cannot be reconciled with a commitment to equality of opportunity. It should be of particular concern that the number of people who are NEET has remained relatively unchanged since 1997 (SEU, 2004).

Figure 2.8: Participation in education, training and employment, 18 year olds in England and Wales, 2002, by social class

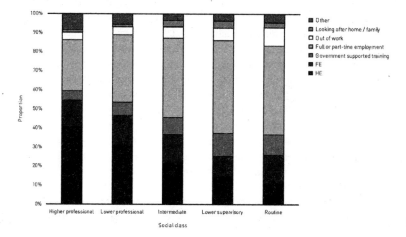

Source: ONS (2004c)

Fair distribution

Resources that do not form part of equal citizenship or the social minimum may be distributed unequally, but the distribution must reflect relevant factors such as personal desert and personal choice

In this section we move beyond poverty and a primary focus on the worst off, and examine the principle of fair distribution. This principle is concerned with the distribution of income but also with that of less tangible factors that affect people's quality of life, such as job satisfaction or the quality of the local environment. Here we focus primarily on the overall distribution of income and wealth, partly because this data provides a better picture of what has happened over the past decades. British society has become considerably richer as the UK economy has grown consistently since 1994; the challenge is to ensure that more citizens can share in the benefits of this growing prosperity.

As Taylor-Gooby argues in Chapter 5, people think financial inequality is currently too great in Britain. Responding to this concern also makes other elements of social justice easier to achieve. Poverty, measured in a relative way, is linked closely to levels of inequality. Although it has been possible, somewhat paradoxically, to reduce relative poverty without reducing overall income inequality since 1997, whether this pattern can be repeated in the future is unclear. The importance of overall income inequality is likely to increase. Likewise, there are links to subjective wellbeing; wide disparities of wealth and income can lead to more people being dissatisfied with the quality of their lives (Di Tella *et al*, 2002). Finally, an unfair distribution of prosperity could lead to unequal life chances and lower levels of social mobility (Erikson and Goldthorpe, 1992).

This section first outlines trends in income and wealth inequality and then goes on to examine fair distribution as it relates to territorial justice – different outcomes in different parts of the country.

Turning the tanker: a levelling-off of income inequality but no reduction?
Levels of income inequality increased dramatically during the 1980s. But from the early 1990s we have witnessed a clear break in trends with no increase in overall income inequality. Figure 2.9 demonstrates this well. It shows the Gini coefficient[10] for original income distribution and disposable income distribution.

'Original income distribution' is all market income, the majority of which comes from the labour market in the form of wages, but which also includes income gained from assets – for example rent on a property or dividends on shares.[11] (This is potentially significant given the increase in wealth inequality, which is charted later in the section.) Disposable income is income after tax and benefits. The gap between the two lines shows how hard the tax and benefit system is working: a wider gap means that the welfare state is reducing inequality more.

---

10 The Gini coefficient is a number between 0 and 1, where 0 means perfect equality and 1 means perfect inequality (that is, one person has everything and no one else has anything). See Goodman *et al* (1997) for further details and a discussion of the merits of alternative measures.

11 Strictly speaking what we have labelled 'original income' should be called 'pre-tax/benefit income' as there are certain components of income – for example, maintenance payments to partners and ex-partners – which are not market payments but are not taxes and benefits either.

Figure 2.9: Income inequality pre and post government intervention 1979–2003/4

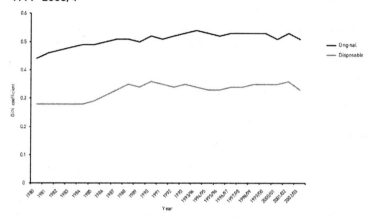

Source: ONS (2004c)

From the early 1990s there has been a clear break in trends in inequality of original income. In the decade up to 1992/3, original income inequality increased but since then it has stayed relatively level, rising by a few percentage points between 1994 and 2000/1 and then falling gradually since then. If we use ONS data, it was slightly lower in 2002/3 than it was in 1992/3, though the most recent Institute for Fiscal Studies data from 2003/4 suggests that the net effect of seven years of Labour government has been to leave inequality effectively unchanged (Brewer *et al*, 2005).

This picture is not only demonstrated by the Gini coefficient; it is also observed using other measures of income inequality. For example, the share of overall disposable income held by different parts of the population has hardly changed since the early 1990s. In 2003/4 the bottom 10 per cent of the population received 1.7 per cent of total income after housing costs, in contrast to 2.7 per cent of overall disposable income received by the top decile. This compares with 1.7 per cent and 27.7 per cent in 1994/5 (DWP, 2005).

Disposable income distribution: government working as hard as it could?
It is through the tax and benefit system that government can have the most direct impact on final income distribution. The gap between the

two lines in Figure 2.9 indicates how hard the tax and benefit system has worked to reduce original income inequality. Importantly, from around the time the Labour Government was elected the impact the welfare state appears to have had on inequality has changed relatively little. In 2002/3 the change in the Gini from original to disposable income was eighteen points, compared with nineteen points in 1996/7.

Much of this can be explained by the state of the economy. In a recession the welfare state 'kicks in' and works harder (Clark and Leicester, 2004). Hence when the economy recovered from the mid-1980s, tax and benefit policy had less of an impact on income inequality (with the help of Conservative tax changes). But the picture with the robust economic performance since the mid-1990s seems to be different. It is more puzzling because original income inequality has remained relatively steady and in theory the tax and benefit changes should have been progressive: the effect of major fiscal reforms between July 1997 and June 2001 should have increased incomes for the poorest 10 per cent by 13 per cent with virtually no increase for the wealthiest 10 per cent of the population (Clark *et al*, 2001). Yet the effect of tax and benefit policies seems to have reduced. There are two possible explanations for this. One is low take-up of means-tested benefits. The econometric models used by experts to estimate the effect of tax and benefit changes often assume 100 per cent take-up of means-tested benefits, which does not happen. The second is that the existence of 'unfavoured groups', identified in the previous section, has meant that the welfare state is working less hard overall.

The 10–89–1 society?
Figure 2.10 leads to similar conclusions. It shows the real increases in income for each percentile in the income distribution over a similar time period, between 1996/7 and 2001/2. The graph shows a broadly progressive impact. But at both ends of the income spectrum are issues of concern. Individuals with the lowest incomes – those in the bottom ten percentiles – experienced a smaller growth in income than the average. This could be due to measurement error, but it might also be due to the two factors highlighted above: poor take-up and unfavoured groups falling behind.

Figure 2.10: Mean annual income growth between 1996/7 and 2003/4 for each percentile of the income distribution.

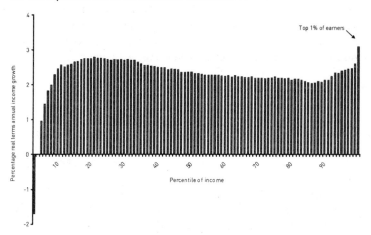

Source: Brewer *et al* (2005): 19
Note: Incomes measured before housing costs.

Worryingly, this chart also shows that income growth for the top 1 per cent of earners – such as a childless couple earning above £82,000 after tax in 2003/4 – continued to rise sharply after 1997 (Brewer *et al*, 2005). Commentators have previously talked of a 30–30–40 society, or a 20–60–20 society, but it seems we should be thinking about a 10–89–1 society (Hutton, 1996; Blair, 2003). Other research has shown that after a long period of decline following the Second World War, the proportion of income earned by the very richest in Britain started to rise in the early 1980s, and has continued to rise since – even from the early 1990s when increases in overall income inequality were arrested. The top 1 per cent of the population increased its share of overall income from approximately 6.5 per cent in 1980 to approximately 13 per cent in 1999. The top 0.1 per cent more than doubled its share over a similar period. Between 1980 and 1995 its share increased from 1.5 per cent to over 4 per cent. A similar pattern since the Second World War can be seen in the US, but not in other European countries where the share of income earned by the very richest has continued to decrease (Atkinson, 2003; Atkinson and Salverden, 2003).

One contributing factor might be differing tax regimes. Only Denmark, Greece and Portugal raised more revenue from regressive taxes on consumption (OECD, 2003).[12] The impact of this is that the UK has a largely regressive tax system, despite strong public support for a progressive tax system (see Chapter 5). Figure 2.11 shows the proportions of income paid in tax across the income distribution.

Figure 2.11: Tax as share of gross income, by decile, 2001–2, UK (%)

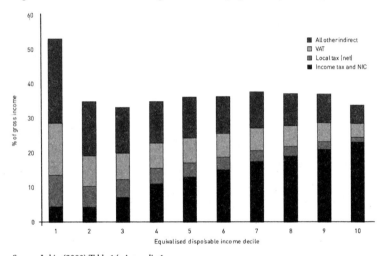

Source: Lakin (2003) Table 14, Appendix 1
Note: WTFC treated as part of gross income, not a deduction from income tax. Local taxes, fuel duties and VED are those levied directly on households. Those levied on businesses are part of other indirect taxes.

Gender inequality

Gender inequality remains a stubborn issue. Though women's situation in the workplace is improving and, as Figure 2.12 shows, the full-time pay gap in 2003 was at its lowest ever level,[13] there are two causes of concern. First, the gap is still large: women earned 85.7 per cent of what men earned in 2003, compared to 82.6 per cent in 1998. Second, for

12 For Denmark this is partly explained by higher rates of tax for certain luxuries.
13 The pay gap here is measured as full-time female median earnings as a percentage of full-time male median earnings (excluding overtime).

part-time work (the bottom line on the chart) the gap has not narrowed in recent years and remains far higher than for full-time work. This is significant as, consistent with previous trends, almost half the increase in women's employment since 1994 has been in part-time work.

Figure 2.12: The gender pay gap

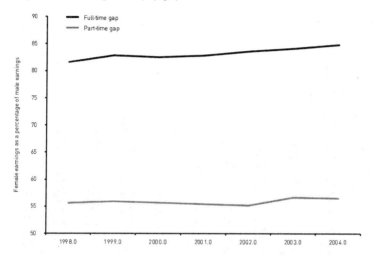

Source: ONS (2004d) Annual Survey of Hours and Earnings
Note: The full-time pay gap compares median full-time female hourly earnings (excluding overtime) with median full-time male hourly earnings (excluding overtime). The part-time pay gap compares median part-time female hourly earnings (excluding overtime) with median part-time male hourly earnings (excluding overtime).

The pay gap is much higher for older women than for younger women. For those aged 21 to 24 it was less than 4 per cent in 2003, compared to 24 per cent for those aged 40 to 49 (WEU, 2003). This is partly because there is a larger educational difference between genders in older generations and partly because many younger women have not yet taken time out of their careers to have children. It remains to be seen whether women's improved educational attainment will feed through into significant reductions in the pay gap, although it is likely that without further policy efforts targeted at helping women, progress will continue to be relatively slow.

Research has shown that 15 per cent of the gap is caused by interruptions to women's employment as a result of childcare responsibilities, 26 per cent by lack of full-time experience in the workplace, and 29 per cent by discrimination and other factors associated with being female (WEU, 2003). This suggests policy aimed at reducing the gender pay gap needs to focus on broader concerns than just tackling discrimination, although this is still clearly important (see Chapter 16). Providing more flexible working arrangements that enable women to continue to work if they choose to and ensuring that childcare arrangements do not penalise women for having children could go a long way.

Women also continue to be more likely to live in poverty: 20 per cent of women lived in poverty in 2003/4, compared to 18 per cent of men (DWP, 2005). Furthermore, despite increased participation in the labour market, women have continued to do much more unpaid labour than men. In 2000/1, women living in a couple and working full time spent nearly four and a half hours on childcare and other activities with their children on a weekday on average, compared to just over three and a half hours for men on the same tasks (ONS, 2002c). The persistent gender pay gap is in part because of this unequal division of labour. Women still lose most ground in the labour market after childbirth (DTI, 2003).

While women continue to experience worse labour market outcomes than men, monetary factors will continue to encourage women rather than men to take up new caring roles as families have less income to lose if women give up work. Of course, women should have the right to choose how to bring up their families and they should not be forced to work if they choose to care instead, but the situation as it stands places undue pressure on women to take up care responsibilities when they may not wish to, reducing their opportunities and freedom.

Wealth inequality

We should not just be concerned with income. Who owns the nation's wealth also matters. There is a well-established argument that concentrations of wealth may have a corrosive effect on the health of a democracy and in addition to this recent policy developments, such as the Child Trust Fund (CTF), have moved questions about wealth up the agenda.

Wealth inequality is high and rising. The Gini coefficient for wealth distribution in 2002 was 0.7, which compares with 0.36 for disposable income in 2002/3. Figure 2.13 shows how wealth inequality and concentrations of wealth have changed between 1980 and 2002. The wealth held by the most prosperous 1 and 10 per cent is shown on the left-hand axis, and inequality measured by the Gini coefficient is shown on the right-hand axis. The chart shows that in 2002, 23 per cent of personal wealth was held by the top 1 per cent of the population, an increase from 18 per cent in 1990. Over the same period the increase in the share of wealth held by the top 10 per cent of the population has increased from 47 per cent to 56 per cent (Inland Revenue, 2004).

Interestingly, the break in trends in this chart occurs at approximately the same time as that for original income distribution, but in exactly the reverse direction. Wealth inequality stayed level throughout the 1980s (when income inequality was increasing dramatically) but then it increased rapidly from the early 1990s onwards. It is unclear why this has occurred, although one explanation is that many people who increased their incomes in the 1980s have invested in various forms of wealth – there has simply been a time lag before this has fed through into the wealth data. In one sense, while income inequality has levelled off, we are still feeling the effects of the 1990s polarisation through today's rising wealth inequalities.

Figure 2.13: Wealth held by the very richest individuals and inequality

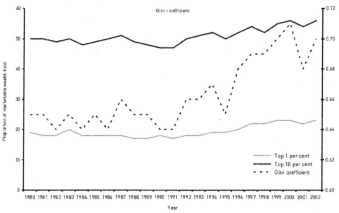

Source: Inland Revenue (2004) Table 13.5

There is another concern. If increased income inequality in the 1980s fuelled growing wealth inequality in the 1990s, is there a danger that wealth inequality will now contribute to growing income inequality? Market income other than wages and salaries, which is mostly investment income, contributes more to the income of the wealthiest decile than to the remainder of the population. In 2002/3 the top 10 per cent of the working-age population received over 4 per cent of their income from investments compared with under 1 per cent for those in the lowest 10 per cent of the income distribution (Lakin, 2003). If wealth inequality goes unchecked, will it reduce the ability of governments to tackle wide disparities in income?

An important issue here is inheritance. Although only one in 40 people inherits in each year, those in higher social classes are more likely both to receive an inheritance and to inherit a greater amount. Between 1996 and 2000, just over 4 per cent of those in the top two social classes inherited, with a mean inheritance of about £18,000, compared to 2 per cent of the bottom social class inheriting an average of £10,000 (Future Foundation, 2002). More fine grained data from 1995/6 suggests that inheritance may be even more polarised than this, with the top social class inheriting an average of £100,600, compared to £12,400 for the bottom social class (Rowlingson and McKay, 2004). Although this data is relatively old, it is unlikely that patterns have changed dramatically since then. As Miller points out in Chapter 1, opinion is sharply divided over the legitimacy of inheritance tax. Yet even if it could be permitted under the principle of fair distribution, it seems likely that it stands at odds with a commitment to equality of opportunity.

Geographical inequalities

Prosperity is also distributed unfairly spatially. It is unacceptable that people's life chances should be restricted simply because they happen to be born in one place rather than another. Yet considerable concentrations of disadvantage and differential outcomes remain. The policy implications of some of the data presented here are discussed in further detail in Chapter 14.

Regional inequalities

Regional differences in rates of poverty are striking. In 2003/4, 28 per cent of people in London were in poverty, compared to only 16 per cent in the South East (DWP, 2005). Worklessness was nearly twice as high in the North East as in the South East and unemployment was 3.3 per cent in the East, compared to 6.9 per cent in London in 2003 (ONS,

2004a). Many of these differences are accounted for by levels of disability, which have a strong regional slant. To give an idea of the scale of the challenge, to bring employment levels in London up to the UK national rate, more than 200,000 people would need to start working. This is more than double that required in any other region. Given its low starting point, substantial increases would also be required in the North East despite its relatively small size.

Furthermore, regional inequalities seem to have widened over the last two decades. Figure 2.14 looks at Gross Value Added (GVA), a measure of output used by economists. It shows that between 1990 and 2002, the gap between regions has widened. On the chart the UK mean is 100 for each year; the gradual movement away from the mean indicates widening differences between regions (with London, the East of England and the South East above the line and doing better, and other regions below the line and doing worse). Between 2000 and 2002, there appears to have been some narrowing of inequalities with a move back towards the UK average in some parts of the country. This could be a temporary effect reflecting the recent modest downturn in the London economy following a shake-out in financial services after falls in the stock market. We should not lose sight of the fact that inequalities remain greater than they were before 1994/5.

Figure 2.14: Changes in regional prosperity (GVA)

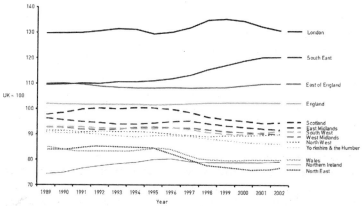

Source: ONS (2004e)

Area inequalities
Such regional inequalities are noteworthy. Looking at regional disparities gives us an indication of the overall condition of the regional economy which is an important driver of employment outcomes at a more local level. But focusing merely on the bigger picture can mask inequalities within regions. Pockets of great deprivation exist alongside relatively affluent neighbourhoods. Analysis of inequalities at a local level tends to focus on the situation of the 10 per cent of most deprived electoral wards as identified by the Index of Multiple Deprivation (IMD) in 2000 or the Index of Local Deprivation (ILD) in 1991 and 1998. The IMD is constructed from measures of a number of factors: income, employment, health, education and skills, crime and the quality of the local environment. These factors are combined to assess how deprived local areas are.[14] Figure 2.15 uses this data to compares the distribution of deprivation in 2000 and 2004 and illustrates how concentrated this is within small areas.

There is also some evidence that, on important measures, the inequalities between local areas have increased. The most deprived areas have not been catching up with wealthier areas. Evans *et al* (2002), for example, found that between 1995 and 2000 there was a fall in the number of benefit claimants in all areas, but that the percentage fall was higher in less deprived areas.

The challenges ahead

This overview of the state of the nation raises significant policy and political challenges. In many respects Britain has become fairer in the last ten years. The economy has experienced steady growth since 1993, employment rates have increased and registered unemployment continues to fall. The Government's commitment to reducing child poverty has thus far been successful, with tax credits and support for getting a job forming the central planks of policy. Life is improving in many ways for the very worst off. The nation is healthier, living longer and experiencing far less crime than a decade ago.

Yet despite these improvements, Britain is far from being a progressive or just society. Levels of child poverty continue to surpass those of many

---

14 The IMD, and its forerunner the ILD, have been subject to regular revisions over the years. The weighting given to the different components of the index has changed. While it is possible to track changes in areas over time, it is important to be aware of its limitations.

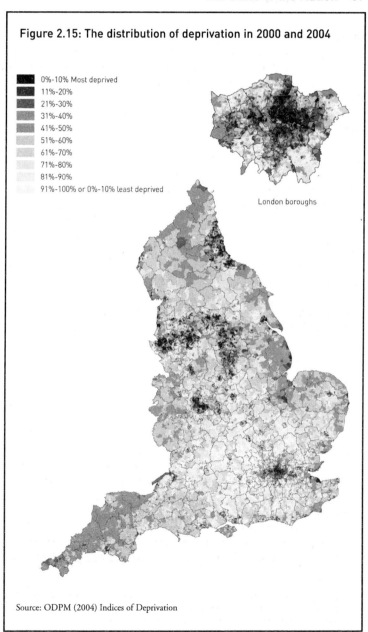

Figure 2.15: The distribution of deprivation in 2000 and 2004

0%-10% Most deprived
11%-20%
21%-30%
31%-40%
41%-50%
51%-60%
61%-70%
71%-80%
81%-90%
91%-100% or 0%-10% least deprived

London boroughs

Source: ODPM (2004) Indices of Deprivation

of our more successful European partners, and inequalities in income, wealth and wellbeing remain stubbornly high. Parental social class and ethnic background still heavily influence life chances, while democratic participation is falling and political influence is polarising according to class and wealth. Despite significant extra resources for the public services and the reduction of poverty over recent years, major progress is still need to transform Britain into a truly prosperous, fair and decent society.

References

Atkinson T (2003) *Income Tax and Top Incomes over the Twentieth Century* (Unpublished). Available at http://www.nuff.ox.ac.uk/users/atkinson/TAXATION.htm

Atkinson A and Salverda W (2003) *Top Incomes in the Netherlands and the United Kingdom over the Twentieth Century* (Unpublished). Available at http://www.nuff.ox.ac.uk/users/atkinson/NLandUK12.pdf

Banks J, Smith Z and Wakefield M (2002) *The distribution of financial wealth in the UK: evidence from the 2000 BHPS data* London: IFS. Available at http://www.ifs.org.uk/ workingpapers/wp0221.pdf

Bhattacharyya G, Ison L and Blair M (2003) *Minority Ethnic Attainment and Participation in Education and Training: the evidence* TSO. Available at http://www.basic-skills observatory.co.uk/uploads/doc_uploads/751.pdf

Blair T (1999a) 'Beveridge revisited: a welfare state for the 21st century' reproduced in Walker R (ed) *Ending Child Poverty* Bristol: Policy Press

Blair T (1999b) Speech to Labour Party conference, 28 September 1999. Available at http://news.bbc.co.uk/1/hi/uk_politics/460009.stm

Blair T (2003) Opening Speech to the Progressive Governance Conference. Available at http://www.policy-network.net/php/article.php?sid=5&aid=171

Blanden J, Goodman A, Gregg P and Machin S (2004) 'Changes in Intergenerational Mobility' in M Corak (ed) *Generational Income Mobility* Cambridge: Cambridge University Press

Bradshaw J and Finch N (2002) 'A comparison of child benefit packages in 22 countries' *Department for Work and Pensions (DWP) Research Report 174* London: TSO

Brewer M (2005) 'Child Poverty: Maintaining Momentum' in *Social Mobility and Life Chances* London: Institute for Public Policy Research (ippr)

Brewer M, Goodman A, Shaw J and Shephard A (2005) *Poverty and Inequality in Britain: 2005* London: Institute for Fiscal Studies (IFS)

Brown G (2002) Speech to the Labour Party Conference in Blackpool. Available at: http://politics.guardian.co.uk/labour2002/story/0,12294,801869,00.html

Bynner J and Paxton W (2001) *The Asset Effect* London: ippr

Clark T, Myck M and Smith Z (2001) *Fiscal Reforms Affecting Households, 1997–2001* London: Institute for Fiscal Studies (IFS). Available at http://www.ifs.org.uk/election/ebn5.pdf

Clark T and Leicester A (2004) 'Inequality and two decades of British tax and benefit reform' *Fiscal Studies 25 (2)* London: Institute for Fiscal Studies (IFS)

Costigan R, Sheehan J, Thomas P A (2004) *The Human Rights Act 1998: An Impact Study in South Wales* Cardiff University: Cardiff Law School

Department for Environment, Food and Rural Affairs (DEFRA) (2003) *The environment in your pocket* London: TSO

Department for Education and Skills (DfES) (2004a) *National Curriculum Assesment and GCSE/GNVQ Attainment by Pupil Characteristics, in England (2002 final) and 2003 (provisional) SFR04* London: TSO

Department for Education and Skills (DfES) (2004b) *GCSE/GNVQ Examination Results for Young People in England 2002/2003 (provisional)* London: TSO. Available at http://www.dfes.gov.uk/rsgateway/DB/SFR/s000419/tab001.shtml

Department for Education and Skills (DfES) (2005a) *Trends in Education and Skills* London: TSO. Available at http://www.dfes.gov.uk/trends/index.cfm?fuseaction= home.showChart&cid=5& iid=30&chid=117

Department for Education and Skills (DfES) (2005b) *National Curriculum Assessment, GCSE and Equivalent Attainment and Post-16 Attainment by Pupil Characteristics in England 2004* London: TSO. Available at http://www.dfes.gov.uk/rsgateway/DB/SFR/s000564/SFR08-2005v2.pdf

Di Tella R, MacCulloch R and Layard R (2002) *Income, happiness and inequality as measures of welfare* London: LSE Mimeo

Department of Trade and Industry (DTI) (2003) *Individual incomes of men and women 1996/7 to 2002/3 a summary* London: TSO

Department of Work and Pensions (DWP) (2003a) *Opportunity for All 2003* London: TSO. Available at http://www.dwp.gov.uk/ofa/reports/2003

Department of Work and Pensions (DWP) (2003b) *Measuring Child Poverty* London: TSO. Available at http://www.dwp.gov.uk/consultations/consult/2003/childpov/final.pdf

Department of Work and Pensions (DWP) (2004a) *Households Below Average Income: An analysis of the income distribution from 1994/5 to 2002/3* London: TSO

Department of Work and Pensions (DWP) (2004b) *The New Pension Credit: A review of the campaign to May 2004* Available at http://www.dwp.gov.uk/publications/dwp/2004/pension_credit/ rev_campaign_may04.pdf

Department of Work and Pensions (DWP) (2004c) *Households Below Average Income: An analysis of the income distribution from 1994/5 to 2003/4* London: TSO

Disability Rights Commission (DRC) (2003) *Disability Briefing: February 2003* London: DRC

Electoral Commission (2004) *Audit of political engagement* London: The Electoral Commission. Available at http://www.electoralcommission.org.uk/about-us/auditofengagement.cfm

Erikson and Goldthorpe (1992) *The Constant Flux – A study of class mobility in industrial societies* Oxford: Clarendon Press

Eurostat (2002) *Free data* Brussels: European Communities. Available at http://www.eustatistics. gov.uk/products.asp

Evans M, Noble M, Wright G, Smith G, Lloyd M and Dibben C (2002) *Growing together or growing apart? Geographic patterns of change of Income Support and income-based Jobseeker's Allowance claimants in England between (1995-2000)* London: Joseph Rowntree Foundation (JRF)

Future Foundation (2002) *The giving age: inheritance in the context of an ageing population* London: The International Longevity Centre UK

Goldthorpe J (2003) 'The myth of education based meritocracy: why the theory isn't working' *New Economy* 10.4, London: ippr

Goodman A and Oldfield Z (2004) *Permanent differences? Income and expenditure inequality in the 1990s and 2000s* London: Institute for Fiscal Studies (IFS). Available at http://www.ifs.org.uk/ inequality/permanent_differences.pdf

Goodman A, Johnson P and Webb S (1997) *Inequality in the UK* Oxford: OUP

Gorard S (2003) *School Choice Policies and Social Integration: The Experience of England and Wales* (Unpublished). Available at http://www.ippr.org/research/files/team23/ project159/Microsoft%20Office%20Word%20-%20Gorard%20paper.doc.pdf

Hills J (2004) *Inequality and the State* Oxford: Oxford University Press

HM Treasury (HMT) (2002) *Tackling Health Inequalities, 2002 Cross cutting review* London: TSO
Available at http://www.hm-treasury.gov.uk/media/EEDDE/Exec %20sum
Tackling%20Health.pdf#page=16

HM Treasury (HMT) (2004) *Child Poverty Review* London: TSO. Available at http://www.hm-treasury.gov.uk/media//22FFA/childpoverty_fwd-1.pdf

Home Office (1999) *The 1998 British Crime Survey* London: TSO

Home Office (2003a) *Crime in England and Wales 2002/3* London: TSO. Available at
http://www.homeoffice.gov.uk/rds/pdfs2/hosb703.pdf

Home Office (2003b) *2001 Home Office Citizenships Survey: people, families and communities* London:
The Stationery Office

Home Office (2004a) *Crime in England and Wales 2003/04* London: TSO. Available at
http://www.homeoffice.gov.uk/rds/bcs1.html

Home Office (2004b) Home *Office Research Study 289: 2003 Home Office Citizenship Survey: People,
Families and Communities* London: TSO

Hutton W (1996) *The State We're In: Why Britain is in crisis and how to overcome it* London: Vintage

Inland Revenue (2004) *Distribution of Personal Wealth* London: TSO. Available at http://www.inland-drevenue.gov.uk/stats/

Jenkins S and Rigg J (2001) *Department for Work and Pensions Research Report 157: The Dynamics of
Poverty in Britain* Colchester: University of Essex, Institute for Social and Economic Research.
Available at http://www.dwp.gov.uk/asd/asd5/rrep157.asp

JRF (1999) *Child Poverty and its Consequences* London: Joseph Rowntree Foundation (JRF). Available
at http://www.jrf.org.uk/knowledge/findings/socialpolicy/389.asp

Lakin C (2003) 'The effects of taxes and benefits on household income 2001/2' *Economic Trends* May
2003, London: TSO. Available at http://www.nationalstatistics.gov.uk/articles/economic_trends
/ET607Lakin.pdf

Machin S and Gregg P (2003) 'A lesson for education: university expansion and falling income
mobility' *New Economy* 10 (4), London: ippr

McKnight A (2000) 'Trends in Earnings Inequality and Earnings Mobility, 1977-1997: the impact of
Mobility on Long-Term Inequality' *DTI Employment Relations Research Series No 8,* London: TSO

MORI (2001) *How Britain Voted in 2001* London: MORI. Available at:
http://www.MORI.com/polls/2001/election.shtml

National Evaluation of Sure Start (NESS) (2004) *The Impact of Sure Start local programmes on child
development and family functioning: a report on preliminary findings* London: Institute for the Study
of Children, Families and Social Issues, Birkbeck University of London. Available at:
www.ness.bbk.ac.uk/documents/activities/impact/397.pdf

National Consumer Council (NCC) (2004) *Life Lines: affordable utilities* London: NCC. Available at
http://nccdev.keymedia.info/access/ppm6utilities.pdf

Nolan B and Whelan C (2003) *Multi-dimensional measures of well-being.* Available at http://www.nuff.
ox.ac.uk/projects/ChangeQual/papers/public/themes/2/theme_2_331_Multi_measur.doc

Office of the Deputy Prime Minister (ODPM) (2001) *English House Condition Survey* London: TSO

Office of National Statistics (ONS) (2001) *Labour Force Survey* London: TSO

Office of National Statistics (ONS) (2002a) *Mortality Data* London: TSO

Office of National Statistics (ONS) (2002b) *People's perceptions of their neighbourhood and community
involvement: Results from the social capital module of the General Household Survey 2000* London:
The Stationery Office

Office of National Statistics (ONS) (2002c) *UK 2000 Time Use Survey* London: TSO

Office of National Statistics (ONS) (2003a) *Annual Local Area Labour Force Survey* London: TSO

Office of National Statistics (ONS) (2003b) *New Earnings Survey* London: TSO

Office of National Statistics (ONS) (2004a) *Labour Force Survey* London: TSO

Office of National Statistics (ONS) (2004b) *Social Trends 34* London: TSO

Office of National Statistics (ONS) (2004c) *Gini Coefficient* London: TSO

Office of National Statistics (ONS) (2004d) *Annual Survey of Hours and Earnings (ASHE)* London: TSO

Office of National Statistics (ONS) (2004e) *Regional Gross Value Added* (GVA) London: TSO

Office of National Statistics (ONS) (2005) *Local Area Labour Force Survey* London: TSO. Available at www.nomisweb.co.uk

Organisation for Economic Co-operation and Development (OECD) (2003) *OECD Tax Database* Paris: OECD

Payne G and Roberts J (2002), 'Opening and closing the gates: recent developments in male social mobility in Britain' *Sociological Research Online* 6. Available at http://www.socresonline.org.uk/6/3/contents.html

Pleasance P, Buck A, Balmer N J, O'Grady A and Genn H (2004) *Causes of Action: Civil Law and Social Justice* London: Legal Services Research Centre

Reid P (2003) *Equity, Choice, Capacity and Culture* Speech 7 November 2003. Available at: http://www.dh.gov.uk/NewsHome/Speeches/SpeechesList/SpeechesArticle/ fs/en?CONTENT_ID=4066541&chk=1lueKl

Regan S and Stanley K (2003) *The Missing Million* London: ippr

Rowlingson K and McKay S (2004) *Attitudes to inheritance: A literature review and secondary analysis of data* London: Joseph Rowntree Foundation (JRF)

Sefton T (2004) A *Fair Share of Welfare: Public Spending on Children in England* London: LSE. Available at http://sticerd.lse.ac.uk/dps/case/CR/CASEreport25.pdf

Sefton T and Rigg J (2004) *Income dynamics and the life cycle* London: LSE. Available at http://sticerd.lse.ac.uk/dps/case/cp/CASEpaper81.pdf

Seyd P and Whiteley P (2002) 'Is Britain Still A Civic Culture?' *Paper presented at the American Political Science Association Annual Conference, Boston, US, August 2002*. Available at http://www.shef.ac.uk/politics/citizenaudit/apsa2002.doc

Sheffield Citizen's Audit (2001) Available at www.shef.ac.uk/politics/citizenaudit

Social Exclusion Unit (SEU) (2004) *Breaking the Cycle: Taking stock of progress and priorities for the future* London: TSO

Solon G (1999) 'Intergenerational mobility in the labour market' in Ashenfelter O and Card D (eds) (1999) *Handbook of Labour Economics 3a* The Netherlands: Elsevier Science BV

Strategy Unit (2003) *Strategic Audit: Discussion Document* London: TSO

Tricket A, Ellingworth T, Hope T and Pease K (1995) 'Crime Victimsation in the Eighties: Changes in area and regional inequality' *British Journal of Criminology* 35: 3, Oxford: Oxford University Press

Walker G, Fairburn J, Smith G and Mitchell G (2003) *Environmental Quality and Social Deprivation R&D technical report, Environment Agency* London: TSO

Women and Equality Unit (WEU) (2003) *The Gender Pay Gap in Great Britain* London: TSO. Available at http://www.womenandequalityunit.gov.uk/research/factsheets/ equal_pay_nov_2003.doc

Zaidi A and Burchardt T (2002) 'Comparing income when needs differ: equivalisation for the extra costs of disability in the UK' *CASEpaper 64* London: London School of Economics (LSE)

Social Justice in a Changing World: The Emerging Anglo-Social Model

Mike Dixon and Nick Pearce[1]

There are significant challenges ahead if Britain is to become more socially just. As Paxton and Dixon show in Chapter 2, although changes in the priorities of government can have measurable lasting effects on the life chances of citizens and the fairness and prosperity of society, policy does not operate in a vacuum or against a static background. There are constantly shifting pressures resulting from social, demographic, economic and technological changes in the modern world and governments must take these into account when framing policy.

These changes impact on different welfare states around the world in very different ways. It is therefore important to understand the nature of the British welfare state and how and why it differs from those of other countries. In some senses it is an idiosyncratic hybrid, with elements that resemble parts of both the US and Scandinavian models. Importantly, it has the potential to become more progressive over the next decade, incorporating and developing the best features of each of these models into what could be thought of as a distinctive 'Anglo-Social' welfare state.

This chapter looks at the most important trends and drivers which will affect this emerging Anglo-social model over the next ten years, with the aim of identifying some of the important pressures, challenges ahead and options for government to respond. We begin by outlining the impact of globalisation and regionalisation, before focusing on the trends and drivers within nation states which will create new pressures and shape priorities. Finally, we place these in a British context, identifying

1 Thanks to Gosta Esping-Andersen, Lane Kenworthy, Anthony Giddens, Colin Hay, Howard Reed, Will Paxton and Fritz Scharpf for comments.

the Anglo-social model's unique features, the main challenges it faces and the opportunity it provides for achieving social justice.

The myths and realities of globalisation

Ten years ago, when the Commission on Social Justice reported, many analysts thought the most important challenge welfare states faced was global economic integration. It was widely believed that economic globalisation would make generous welfare states increasingly unsustainable and that governments would have to cut back on social services and other forms of welfare (Cerny, 1994; Strange, 1996; Scharpf, 2000a). In part, these concerns derived from the recognition that advanced welfare states had come under increasingly difficult cost and revenue pressures since the late 1970s, during a period of considerable structural changes in international markets (Scharpf, 2000a). From the perspective of the early 1990s, the most important of these appeared to be rising competition from newly industrialised countries in markets which had traditionally generated manufacturing employment in advanced industrial societies; and the global integration of financial markets, stimulated by the lifting of capital controls, advances in information and communication technology and the growth of 'footloose' multinational firms.

While these developments have undoubtedly had some effect on both developed and developing nations, a growing body of research shows that the Commission's relative scepticism about the importance of globalisation was largely correct (CSJ, 1994; Swank, 2002; Pierson, 2001a; Genschel, 1999; Rowthorn and Ramaswamy, 1997; Rowthorn and Coutts, 2004). In fact, many commentators now doubt whether globalisation as traditionally understood has actually taken place; while it is clear that the volume of cross border transactions has increased significantly since the 1960s, most economies (and particularly those in Europe) have become more integrated with their regional neighbours rather than their global ones (Hay, 2004a; Hirst and Thompson, 1999). Intra-regional trade accounts for a growing share of global economic activity suggest that for Britain, competition, integration and trade with European neighbours are more important phenomena.

The impact of these processes of economic globalisation and regionalisation has been less extensive than was initially feared; they do not seriously threaten the capacity of nation states to work towards aims of social justice, although they do create some challenges that require careful policy responses.

A shift to high-skill employment in advanced industrial economies?

Advanced industrial economies have high wages compared to newly industrialising ones and there can be significant differences even within regions – Western Europe currently has much higher wages than Eastern Europe. This has led some globalisation theorists to argue that advanced welfare states face insurmountable pressure to specialise in high skill employment. Their argument is that in sectors which depend on traded goods and services, such as low-skilled manufacturing and (increasingly) some services, lower production costs, low transport costs and technological improvements in distribution mean that these sectors cannot compete internationally (Rhodes, 2000a, 2000b). In the absence of government intervention, low-skill industries will therefore be faced with irreversible decline in advanced welfare states as cheaper production in other countries shifts consumer demand and investment capital away from domestically produced goods.

The theorists therefore argue that advanced economies must dramatically shift employment to high skill production, where they are relatively competitive. However, growth in these areas would result in worsening relative prospects for low-skilled workers compared to high-skilled workers (Gottschalk and Joyce, 1995; Streek, 1999). The consequence would be that income inequality will rise significantly as those without skills are left behind in a polarising labour market, which would be of particular concern in the UK context because income inequality is already at historically high levels.

In such circumstances advanced nations have been offered four options in the globalisation literature. The first is to put up trade barriers to protect domestic industries. This is increasingly unfeasible in the modern economy where international political pressure is largely against protectionism. Although selective tariffs have been deployed by governments and international bodies seeking to protect particular industries for domestic political reasons, these can now be challenged through the auspices of the World Trade Organisation and other mechanisms (however, this does not prevent trade-distorting subsidies, such as the EU Common Agricultural Policy).

The second is to deregulate labour markets and accept extremely low wages and the resulting poverty and inequality. This option often features in neo-liberal responses and is unacceptable on social justice grounds. The third is to retrain the labour force to compete in high-skill sectors, requiring high levels of public spending on education and training, which has been central to repertoire of most centre-left analyses. The fourth is to protect labour through high public sector employment and wage subsidies, again placing significant pressure on state spending and revenues.

If the low skill competition argument was supported by the evidence, this list of options would be an unenviable but inescapable one. Most progressive governments would seek to compete on the basis of high-skill, high-value added goods and services, and this indeed is the rhetoric of many public policy announcements in countries such as the UK.

However, although other factors, which we outline below, may pressure governments into following some of these policy prescriptions, greater economic integration does not entail a relentlessly competitive struggle that advanced economies are doomed to lose unless they make significant adjustments. It is very difficult to import or outsource goods and services in many sectors, such as nursing and hospitality. Although there has been a decline in the GDP and employment shares of the manufacturing sector in all advanced economies and a corresponding increase in the shares of the service sector, international trade between developed and developing countries has only been responsible for a small proportion of this shift. Between 1992 and 2002, the manufacturing share of employment in OECD countries shrunk by 4 per cent, of which just 1.2 percentage points were the result of cheaper imports (Rowthorn and Coutts, 2004). As we show below, a much more significant driver has been the changing demand and productivity trends within advanced economies, rather than the forces of external competition, and it is these trends that welfare states must respond to in this area, rather than concerns arising from globalisation (Iverson and Cusack, 2000; Scharpf, 2000a; McQuaid, 2002; Hills, 2004).

This is particularly so for the UK. The speed of manufacturing decline in Britain has been much faster than anywhere else. Although the most important driver has been changing demand and productivity trends, the decline of British manufacturing was also partly as a result of a loss of privileged access to Commonwealth markets, the impact of the recession in the early 1980s and monetary policy in the early and mid 1980s which halted the long-term fall of sterling and priced British exports out of international markets. At the same time, the UK built on its existing strengths and developed internationally competitive services, particularly in the financial and business sectors and, to a lesser extent, education and the media (Rowthorn and Coutts, 2004).

Britain therefore faces less pressure from the growing 'Europeanisation' that may affect other welfare states in Europe as the EU becomes more economically integrated. The increased competition from new Eastern members whose workforces have comparable skill levels to those in Western Europe will have a greater impact on other welfare states which have higher manufacturing employment and less flexible labour markets, although it is likely that wages will rise more rapidly in the new EU countries than in older members, resulting in less competitive pressure over time.

A tax 'race to the bottom'?

A related argument in the globalisation debate is that increasing international competition and economic integration will promote a 'tax race to the bottom' due to 'cut throat tax competition' (Scharpf, 1997; Maystadt, 1994). Increased international mobility of capital means that economies have to compete with each other to attract investment by reducing rates of corporation tax to make business more profitable (Sinn, 1990; Sinn, 1993; European Commission, 1996; OECD, 1998). This places pressure on government finances to reduce expenditure, increase budget deficits, somehow increase growth rates, expand the tax base through higher levels of employment or shift the burden of taxation away from mobile bases (such as capital) towards less mobile bases. In Europe, where there are still significant language barriers between countries which restrict economic migration to some extent, this would mean increasing taxes on labour and consumption as well as encouraging organised labour to be less demanding in claims related to social provision and public sector pay.

If this argument holds force, the implications for social justice would be profound. Many consumption taxes are regressive so a redistribution of the tax burden towards these could result in a more unequal distribution of income. Pressures on wage restraint would be fiercest in low wage, low productivity sectors as these generate the least profit in advanced economies, while wages could rise without such damaging effects to competitiveness in higher skill occupations. Falling government revenue would mean governments faced tough choices over social spending decisions and significant budgetary pressure to cut back where possible.

Again, however, although this argument has a plausible gloss, it is not supported by the evidence. High degrees of global and regional market integration have not translated into systematically lower corporation tax rates and despite increased economic interdependence, neither capital income tax revenues, total tax revenues, nor public expenditures in advanced economies have shown an average downwards trend (Quinn, 1997; Swank, 1998; Garrettt, 1998a; Scharpf, 2000a; Ganghoff, 2000; Hay, 2004). In the UK, the proportion of total tax revenue raised from corporation tax rose from 6 per cent in 1978/9 to 8 per cent in 2003/4 (Inland Revenue, 2004). There is no evidence that tax burdens have shifted substantially towards immobile bases of labour. Furthermore, there is no evidence that employment in sectors which are open to competition is affected by the tax burden (Scharpf, 2000b).

This might seem puzzling, particularly given the influence that the 'race to the bottom' argument has had over policy makers and politicians in the last two decades, which might have placed pressure towards lower corporate taxation whether supported by the evidence or not (Hay, 2004). Part of the explanation is that cost is not the first consideration for the majority of investors. The educational skill level of the workforce is the most important factor in determining the attractiveness of a labour market regime to mobile investors after access and proximity (Swank, 2002; Traxler and Woitech, 2000). Other factors such as the ease of setting up a business and the simplicity of tax filing and collection play an important part. Business can also benefit from high social spending in other indirect ways, such as a healthy workforce, good transport infrastructure and low crime levels (Garrett, 2000). This is supported by the fact that the vast majority of Foreign Direct Investment (FDI) flow – a reflection of the investment decisions taken by internationally mobile capital – is between developed nations with relatively high labour costs, rather than from these to developing states with relatively low labour costs, which partly explains why regionalisation has been a more dominant trend than globalisation (Brewer and Young, 1998; Callaghan, 2001; UN, 2004).

A further consideration is that there are other significant demands on governments that have prevented them from reducing corporation taxes. These include substantial cost pressures in maintaining the standard of public services and making good on existing commitments (Glennerster, 1999; Hills, 2004). If corporation tax was consistently reduced, governments would need to find other ways of raising revenue but high levels of unemployment in many OECD countries place limits on how far the tax base can be shifted towards labour and consumption (Genschel, 1999).

The changing focus of government?

Economic regionalisation and globalisation have not caused a generalised shift to high-skill service employment in advanced economies, nor have they catalysed a 'tax race to the bottom'. Governments are still able to raise revenue through corporation tax and much industry remains internationally competitive. The ability of advanced nation states to achieve social justice has not been compromised by greater economic integration; government policy remains at least as influential and crucial as it has ever been.

This does not mean that globalisation is irrelevant as far as achieving social justice is concerned. As Mepham argues in Chapter 6, the implications for developing nations are far reaching; very few countries have industrialised in the last 50 years without participating in the global economy, yet economic integration brings considerable challenges.

There are important implications for advanced economies too. Although the UK is in a stronger position than many other European welfare states because of its low manufacturing employment and downwards flexibility in the labour market, the growth of outsourcing may create pressures in some areas. Much of the industrial employment in the North of England was replaced by contact centre work during the late 1990s and early 2000s and more than 450,000 people there work in call centres, help desks or related or ancillary occupations. These workers tend to be low-skilled and their jobs are particularly vulnerable to offshoring. While the number of contact centres placed offshore so far is small, the potential is very large, which could exacerbate the existing regional inequalities outlined in the previous chapter (Rowthorn, 2004; DTI, 2004). However, excessive concern is not warranted at the current time. There is no evidence of adverse employment effects from offshoring as the small number job losses so far have been more than compensated for by gains elsewhere.

Perhaps more fundamentally, globalisation may also place limits on the policy options open to government. Operational responsibility for monetary policy has been passed to central banks in large parts of the developed world, as governments have sought to ensure low inflation and macro-economic stability. The power to increase demand in the economy through monetary policy has therefore weakened, particularly if governments are concerned about keeping exchange rates stable (Hirst and Thompson 1999; Gilpin, 2000). This restriction is counterbalanced to some extent by the fact that access to global finance enables governments to borrow more freely to finance expansionary policies or the welfare state. This makes them less sensitive to being reliant on domestic lenders who may demand higher interest rates if they feel government has borrowed too extensively, although for EU countries there is a 3 per cent deficit ceiling and currency traders tend to punish countries which borrow too heavily.

Despite these restraints on monetary policy, fiscal policy can still play an important role in maintaining aggregate demand during periods of low economic growth, and significant policy options remain for the active promotion of employment and general economic performance through supply side measures, such as enhancing the productivity of human and physical capital (Boix, 1998; Garrett, 2000; Rodrick, 2000). In many senses, greater regional and global economic integration has meant that governments have never been so powerful or so crucial to the management of their national economies as the importance of the state has increased in respect to promoting international competitiveness through support for a higher skilled labour force, for research and development, for technology policy and other assistance to domestic firms (Garrett, 2000). Far from signalling the end of the British welfare state, this suggests that regionalisation and globalisation may in fact have helped to entrench it. Yet globalisation is only one of many drivers affecting welfare states and, as we argue below, it is far from being the most important.

Trends and drivers within nation states

There are three main domestic areas in which significant changes will occur over the next decade: the structure of the labour market, household composition and the cost pressures on states resulting from the increasing expectations of citizens and demographic shifts. We can say with relative certainty how the drivers and trends underlying these will continue to act over the next decade and these create real opportunity for governments to harness future trends to create a more socially just society, affecting policy far more than just at the margins. The following section looks at each of these policy areas in terms of the challenges it brings for achieving social justice.

The evolving labour market
The labour market is evolving in developed nations in ways that are unrelated to globalisation. Technological change and shifts in patterns of

demand by consumers have had a profound impact and will continue to do so. Nearly all OECD nations have experienced both a shift towards a service economy and greater female participation in the labour force in the last three decades; these trends are projected to continue. Other key drivers have included substantial technological advance, which has had a marked effect on the quality of work available to different groups. Yet despite these similarities, the extent and effects of these changes have varied considerably between different welfare states.

The continued growth of the service sector and the relative decline of manufacturing

The share of manufacturing employment has been declining and the share of employment in the service sectors has been increasing in all countries in the OECD since the early 1980s, although the scale of this shift has varied markedly between countries (Rowthorn and Coutts, 2004). It is not clear that the implications of this have been thought through by the centre-left.

This shift is a result of many factors, but there are several prominent ones. Rising GDP has led to a greater demand for services because as their income rises people tend to spend more on them (Hills, 2004). Somewhat paradoxically, technological advances which have led to greater productivity increases in manufacturing than services have also led to higher levels of employment in services. This is because if the relative demand for services and goods remains the same and the services cannot be imported, as is the case for care services, then as firms become more efficient at manufacturing they need less people to produce the demanded amount of goods and more people need to be employed in services to meet demand (Rowthorn, 2004).

Similar patterns have been seen across advanced industrial nations but the UK and US have seen particularly dramatic shifts in recent years (McQuaid, 2002; Rowthorn and Coutts, 2004). There has been a sustained process of deindustrialisation in the British economy for many years. In 1982, 33.6 per cent of total employment was in the manufacturing, construction and utilities sectors and 65.4 per cent was in the service sector; by 1992 the figures were 27.1 per cent and 72.8 per cent respectively; and by 2002 they were 21.7 per cent and 78.3. This trend is expected to continue over the next decade at least: by 2012 service sector employment is projected to be 81.8 per cent of all employment, with manufacturing, construction and utilities having shrunk to just

18.2 per cent (IER, 2004). As noted above, an important implication of this is that fewer and fewer jobs in the UK are dependent on competitive advantage and open to international competition, making the impact of greater economic integration within the EU less problematic.

A shift towards a service economy is not necessarily undesirable. Britain had the second largest surplus in its service current account transactions in Europe in 2003, at 24.1 billion Euros, nearly half that of the much larger US economy, reflecting the international competitiveness of British services (Eurostat, 2004). However, it does create significant challenges from a social justice perspective. As Iverson argues, skills do not transfer easily from many jobs within manufacturing to jobs in the service economy (Iverson, 2001). Even relatively highly skilled manufacturing workers may find it difficult to find acceptable employment in the service sectors (although there are many who find the transition relatively easy, as they were doing service-type jobs within a manufacturing firm).

Part of the problem here is that many workers may be unable to find jobs that have comparable remuneration to their previous work and are unwilling to work for what they perceive as very low wages, preferring to remain inactive. If they do become employed it is often in lower skilled jobs, which often leads to declining skill levels as people lose the skills they have and are less likely to retrain (Hay, 2004b). In the UK, this may account for the considerable rise in inactivity rates in areas in which manufacturing decline has been most marked, as well as having some impact on the numbers receiving incapacity benefit (see Chapter 15). These effects have significant regional and gender bias with the greatest impact concentrated in the North of England on working class men and go some way to explaining the marked regional inequality that exists in Britain today, as well as the much greater proportion of public sector employment in the North than was the case a decade ago (see Chapter 14) (Gregg, 2000; Rhodes, 2000a, 2000b; Rowthorn, 2003).

A second concern is that many families may be priced out of some services, particularly childcare and care for the elderly. This is because services which require a high degree of labour, such as nursing or teaching, tend to see slower productivity growth than other sectors which are more suited to take advantage of technological change to boost productivity (Baumol, 1967). This means that they become more expensive over time compared to other goods and are therefore less affordable for people at the bottom of the income distribution, who are often those who would benefit most from affordable childcare.

A third concern for social justice arising from greater service sector employment is in relation to people's life chances and equality of opportunity. It may be that it is harder to progress from low-skill jobs to better jobs in the service sector than it is in the manufacturing sector as service employers face greater disincentives to invest in training for their low-skilled staff. Many low wage jobs in the service sector require relatively little experience and are seasonal, resulting in relatively high degrees of turnover as staff are easy to replace (CIPD, 2004). Although the evidence is limited, this may mean that progression through the labour market is harder in some parts of the service sector than in comparable jobs in manufacturing as there are fewer ladders of opportunity.

The polarisation of work and worklessness
The second major concern for social justice arising from the evolving labour market is the 'polarisation of work'. There are two elements to this and it is important to distinguish between them. The first concerns the quality of jobs that people have and the second concerns the amount of work that people have. Both are important and both have been particularly dominant features of the British and American labour markets compared to Scandinavian and continental ones (Wright and Dwyer, 2003).

The quality of employment has become increasingly polarised in advanced industrial economies, as the proportion of both 'lovely' and 'lousy' jobs has increased over recent decades at the expense of 'average' jobs. This has been very evident in the UK, as the share of jobs at the bottom of the job 'quality' distribution increased by 17 per cent and the share of jobs at the top increased by nearly 80 per cent over the period 1979 to 1999 (Goos and Manning, 2004).

This polarisation of work is not fully explained by the shift from a manufacturing economy to a service economy, as there has been significant job polarisation within sectors. Although this shift has had some effects, a much more important driver has been technological change. Goos and Manning argue that technology has become adept at replacing human labour in routine tasks but not in non-routine tasks (ibid). This means that technology has replaced human labour in some areas that require precision and so were never unskilled, such as craft manual jobs and book-keeping, but has not been able to replace human labour in jobs that require either hand-eye coordination or creative or managerial thinking. These types of jobs tend to be concentrated at the bottom and the top of the labour market; jobs like shelf stacking and managerial roles jobs have therefore experienced stronger relative growth compared to jobs like book-keeping and craft manual jobs.

In Britain, this polarisation may increase over the next few years as growth in high end occupations is projected to be faster than that of less well paid professions. The share of total employment taken up by managers and senior officials is expected to increase from 14.9 per cent in 2002 to 16.2 per cent by 2012, while the share of skilled trades occupations is expected to decrease from 10.2 per cent in 2002 to 9.1 per cent over the same time period (IER, 2004). Over the coming decade it is also likely that further technological change will continue to replace human labour in a wider range of jobs and that the polarisation of the labour market will continue.

This matters from a social justice perspective as it places pressure towards increased inequality in income; those jobs at the top have seen wages rise faster than those in the middle and the bottom, partly due to increased relative demand (see previous chapter). Much of the growth in income inequality in the US has been a result of stagnant wages at the bottom of the income distribution (Kenworthy, 2004a). Another implication and challenge is that it may make progression through the labour market more difficult, as there are less intermediate jobs that provide a stepping stone, compared to the more gradual career progression biographies associated with (particularly) skilled manufacturing employment. We might also be concerned about the effects on social cohesion as there is a more marked gap between professions, leading to a clearer divide between the well off and the badly off.

The second aspect of the polarisation of work relates to the amount of work in households. During the 1980s, levels of worklessness rose dramatically and during the 1990s worklessness became increasingly concentrated in certain groups and areas as the pattern of employment became increasingly unevenly distributed across households (Gregg, 2000). Despite a prolonged period of sustained economic growth in the late 1990s, levels of worklessness have not decreased substantially (see Chapter 15). This is partly due to changes in household structures: more people are living on their own than ever before and single person households are at greater risk of being workless than other households, just by virtue of the fact that if one person is unemployed this counts as all members being unemployed, but it still presents a significant challenge (DWP, 2004).

One particularly worrying trend here concerns disability. Disabled people have low employment rates relative to other groups, despite well over a million disabled people who are out of work saying that they want to work, and the proportion of people who consider themselves disabled has increased substantially over recent decades (ONS, 2004a; Stanley and Regan, 2003). There are estimated to be as many as 6.9 million people of working age with a disability (DRC, 2004). Most notable has been the significant rise in the number of people who report mental health impairments. This is especially worrying because people with mental health impairments have the lowest employment rates of all impairment groups, at about 20 per cent (although this may partly be to do with people no longer perceiving themselves as physically disabled when they move into employment).

There have also been significant increases in the number of women claiming benefits on the grounds of disability and health problems, reflecting the increased labour participation of women in the labour market. However, no plausible explanations have been offered for the increase in younger men claiming disability-related benefits or for the rise in mental health impairments.

Female participation in the labour force

The third major structural shift in the labour market is the increased participation of women in part-time and full-time employment. The last decades have seen a slow but steady expansion in the female labour force in nearly all OECD countries, a trend that is set to continue. Yet the levels of female participation differ dramatically between countries, with 71.5 per cent of women of working age in employment in Sweden in 2003 compared to 42.7 per cent in Italy (Eurostat, 2004). National policy differences matter a great deal here. Countries with high levels of social protection, good state childcare provision and flexible working allowances tend to have the highest participation rates, while those with low social protection where a significant responsibility for care is taken up by women have much lower rates on average.

In the UK, female labour force employment is relatively high with 65.3 per cent of women of working age in employment in 2003, up from 60.8 per cent in 1992 (Eurostat, 2004). This equates to 46.7 per cent of total employment in 1992 to 47 per cent in 2002 and is projected to increase to 48 per cent in 2012, significantly driven by growth in the service sector. Women are much more likely to be in flexible employment than males as 20.9 per cent of women work part time, compared to just 6.5 per cent of men. They are also much more likely to work in the service sector, as female labour makes up 70.5 per cent of total employment in the public services sector and is high in other service sectors (IER, 2004).

High female participation in the labour force can be an important step in increasing social justice. It may help to reduce income inequality as women are able to improve their incomes above that provided by the state. Since one-earner (and obviously zero-earner) households are disproportionately at the low end of the income distribution, adding a second earner (almost always a woman) usually reduces income inequality because it boosts household incomes more at the bottom than at the top. This has been particularly pronounced in the Netherlands over the past two decades (Kenworthy, 2004b). It may also raise government revenue by increasing the income tax base and stimulating consumption through higher production and spending.

Yet it may also place new demands on the state. Women's increased employment means that they are less able to provide unpaid care, particularly for children and elderly relatives, and there may be greater political and moral demands on the state to take up this responsibility (Esping-Andersen, 1999a; Pierson, 2001a). International comparisons are revealing here. Both the US and Sweden have relatively high levels of female participation in the labour force but very different levels of state provision of childcare and flexible working arrangements. In the US, this means that many children attend unregistered day-care and that a larger proportion of women work in low wage jobs which offer greater flexibility. In Sweden, where childcare is provided by the state to a much greater extent, women tend to participate in the labour market on a more equal footing, although there is a greater proportion of women in public sector jobs in Sweden than the US as public sector jobs in Sweden tend to be more flexible than private sector ones (Esping-Andersen, 2002).

There are difficult choices to be made here and there may be trade-offs that policy needs to be sensitive to. These new demands have led some commentators to predicted that support for caring, in response to the pressures placed by increasing female employment, may constitute one of the few growth areas for contemporary welfare states (Bonoli, 2005).

As highlighted in the previous chapter, significant challenges concerning female employment still exist. Perhaps most obviously, the gender pay gap is still substantial and does not appear to be closing with any urgency. Yet there are other concerns. The kind of work that women do tends to be flexible and part time and opportunities for progression in these jobs may be more limited than in full-time work. We need to find a way of creating an employment sector that provides decent progression opportunities for women.

A changing demography

Policy must be sensitive to these shifts in the structure of the labour market in working towards a more just society. Yet it also needs to respond to a changing demographic picture as family structures continue to alter and populations continue to age in developed economies.

The way people live together is changing. In Britain, people are spending more time on their own, either before forming relationships or after a relationship has broken down. The average size of households in the UK, which fell from 2.64 in 1982 to 2.46 in 1992 and 2.33 in 2002, is projected to fall further to 2.19 by 2016, partly due to the increasing numbers of single person households (ODPM, 2004a). There were 5.8 million single person households in England in 1996, compared to 6.3 million in 2002 and a projected 7.9 million in 2016, with substantial rises in single parent households also projected (ODPM, 2004b).

This presents a challenge for social justice because single person households (and particularly single parent households) are much more likely to be poor than households with two or more adults of working age (DWP, 2004). This is partly because families are more able to pool resources between them and thereby spread the risks of unemployment or low pay. They are also more able to provide care for children and elderly relatives,[2] meaning that trends towards smaller households may place the dual pressures of greater poverty and increased demand for state provision of care services on the state (Esping-Andersen, 1999a; Esping-Andersen, 2002).

Ageing populations also present significant challenges for many welfare states for two important reasons. The first of these is the potential 'generational clash'. The political priorities of older and younger generations tend to be very different, with the former more concerned with healthcare and pension provision, and the latter more concerned with education and childcare. In Britain in 2000, 15.6 per cent of the population was over 65, compared to 13.2 per cent in 1971. By 2050, this will

---

2 These risks may be exacerbated by any increased geographical mobility of the population. More research is needed to look at the precise implications of geographical mobility on the requirement for care.

have risen to 24.4 per cent and, perhaps more significantly, the proportion of people over 80 will have risen from 4 per cent in 2000 to 9.1 per cent. This will mean that it is increasingly difficult to balance political and justicial priorities.

The second challenge ageing populations present is due to existing pension commitments, particularly those that are funded by pay-as-you-go systems. Importantly, Britain does not face as serious a demographic challenge as most other states in Europe, partly as a result of a younger population and high fertility rates and partly as a result of less generous state pensions commitments. Even so, the healthcare and benefit costs of an ageing population could be substantial in the UK as income shortfalls for pensioners resulting from relatively low state pensions may result in high levels of means-tested benefits payments under the current system (SCEA, 2003).

A further source of pressure relates to the changing ethnic composition of the UK. Migration levels are relatively high and have increased over the last decade. In 1993, the UK experienced a small net outflow of migrants. Net inflows were recorded in each year from 1994 onwards. These increased in the late 1990s to 172,000 in 2001, but fell slightly to 153,000 in 2002 (ONS, 2004b). While this is a relatively small number in terms of the overall population, and certainly nowhere near high enough to counterbalance an ageing population, it does create some tensions that need to reconciled – although these are often rather more political than economic. One such tension is whether diversity undermines support for the welfare state, which international evidence suggests not to be the case; another concerns competition for low-skilled jobs (see Chapter 7).

A more important driver in terms of ethnicity concerns ageing. Population growth has been rapid for some groups, the result of higher fertility rates and lower mortality due to a younger population, which has resulted in the ethnic proportion in Britain growing by 53 per cent between 1991 and 2001. However, many ethnic groups now have large cohorts approaching retirement. By 2009, the number of elderly people from ethnic groups will have increased substantially, raising concerns about ethnic minority pensioner poverty. In 2002/3, ethnic minority pensioners were far more likely to be poor and there are genuine concerns that many of those approaching retirement have not had time to build up significant capital for private pension provision (DWP, 2004).

Cost pressures on welfare states

The cost of an ageing population is one source of financial pressure on the welfare state that will increase over the coming decade. Yet there are good reasons to think that this is indicative of a wider trend and that governments will come under increasing budgetary pressures in many policy areas.

As discussed above, part of the reason that there has been no 'tax race to the bottom' is that welfare states face substantial cost and revenue pressures that have not allowed them to reduce taxation or spending. These are partly due to the constantly increasing expectations of electorates who expect to see year-on-year improvement in public service delivery, while providing cutting edge services becomes ever more expensive. In healthcare, for example, privatised drug-orientated medical research has rapidly escalated the cost of public provision. One driver behind these changing expectations is increasing affluence; as people get richer they tend to spend more of their income on healthcare and education and consequently are more demanding of the services supplied by the state (Hills, 2004). Another factor is the comparisons people naturally make with the private sector, which is providing increasingly tailored, professional and personal services, particularly as political rhetoric shifts in the direction of citizen-consumers.

Existing commitments are also an important source of pressure. Some of this is the result of strategic choices, such as the British Government's commitment to eradicating child poverty and increase expenditure on the NHS from 5.5 per cent of GDP in 1996/7 to 7.9 per cent in 2007/8, but demographic changes are also important (HMT, 2004).

These fiscal pressures are not new but the responses available to governments have become more limited. A very stylised picture would be that in the post war period until the OPEC crises in the mid 1970s, strong growth meant that the state could rely on steadily increasing revenues to fund public service expansion. In the 1980s, there was a realisation that this expansion had placed too much pressure on state spending and there was 'a retreat to the core' as the state cut spending in areas where it could afford to, such as support for industry and earnings related pensions, and (arguably) in areas in which it could not, such as housing, pensions, benefits and social services (Glennerster, 1999). In the late 1980s and 1990s, there was a focus on doing things more efficiently, through public private partnerships, targets, audits, civil service restructuring and reducing 'waste'.

This legacy makes for a particularly tough set of choices facing governments in 2005 (Robinson, 2004). It is doubtful whether there is the practical possibility of much greater efficiency gains being made or services cut and it is questionable whether doing so would be a wise long-term strategy in achieving greater social justice.

Different states, different responses?

All advanced welfare states must respond to these changes over the coming decade. Yet the way that states need to react depends greatly on their welfare model, providing strong support for the claim that state action and structure make a real and lasting difference to levels of inequality and prosperity. It is therefore helpful to consider the way these challenges impact on different types of welfare state as this puts the choices facing Britain into perspective.

Following Esping-Andersen (1990) we can look at these trends as they affect three different welfare state models under which advanced economies can be broadly grouped, in terms of how reliant citizens are on the market for their welfare, how equal the distribution of income is and the nature of state-economy relations.[3] While the analysis below is a necessarily incomplete sketch, it nevertheless provides a useful point of comparison.

Social democratic models

Social democratic states, such as Sweden and Denmark, are broadly characterised by universalism, egalitarianism, comprehensive social citizenship and high levels of taxation and social spending. Although these states are performing well, the dominant pressures they face, arising from the trends outlined above, are high rates of taxation and high non-wage

---

3   Esping-Anderson's classification scheme has come under criticism. There are clear limitations to dividing welfare regimes into such broad categories, as there are important differences between countries within categories, although doing so is still useful and revealing. Australia and New Zealand are sometimes cited as distinctive models (Castles and Mitchell, 1992). Alternatively, a fourth model might be that of the dynamic market economies of East Asia such as Hong Kong, Taiwan and Korea. These states have relatively equal distributions of income, low tax levels and high degrees of employment stability. Low levels of female employment mean that a substantial proportion of care is provided by private individuals. The main pressures facing these states will result from future growth in female employment and rapidly ageing populations increasing the demand for state provision of care, placing significant cost and revenue pressures on state spending.

labour costs threatening the domestic labour supply, and insufficient revenue to fund social programmes (Scharpf, 2000b). To free resources for further investment in human capital, further cuts may be necessary in social transfers; these may undermine the corporatist institutions and consensual policy making on which the system partly rests (Esping-Andersen, 2002).

Corporatist models

These states, such as Germany and France, are characterised by a social insurance system of taxation fused with corporatist and social catholic subsidiarity traditions (Esping-Andersen, 1990). Public service employment is limited and labour market regulations and high fixed costs (including payroll taxes) impede private sector employment growth. The dominant problems posed by the drivers outlined above are lagging employment and financial instability (Scharpf, 2000a; Pierson, 2001a).

Liberal models

Liberal welfare states favour individualism and markets with the welfare state cast as a relatively minimal and residual player. Several countries are commonly categorised as liberal welfare states, including the US, Britain, Australia, New Zealand and (in some respects) Switzerland. These states are relatively economically viable as the problems of lost budgetary restraint and unemployment have been largely avoided through policies which encourage the growth of a large low-wage service sector, but they face mounting pressures related to poverty and inequality as well as large gaps in the support for human capital development and an array of associated social problems (Scharpf, 2000b).

A new Anglo-social welfare model?

Although the UK has often been categorised as a typical liberal welfare model, there have always been important differences that distinguish the British welfare state.

Britain's welfare state is in some respects a hybrid of the liberal and social democratic models outlined above, combining selective and universal features. This means it faces a distinct set of challenges in the light of the trends and drivers outlined above and a considered policy response needs be sensitive to this. While Britain is currently closer to a liberal model than a social democratic one, the next decade presents a genuine opportunity to develop its best features and move towards what could be thought of as a new 'Anglo-social' welfare model, incorporating and reconciling economic performance and flexibility with equality and social justice (see Chapter 16).

Britain's political economy is essentially liberal. There are relatively few constraints on the market in determining the initial distribution of income, so any reductions in inequality are largely a result of the tax and benefit system (see previous chapter). Although Britain does have significant public sector employment which places some constraint on market determination of wages, this stands in contrast to social democratic states where union strength and the centralisation of wage bargaining mean that the market does not produce such marked inequalities and corporatist states where a heavily regulated labour market has a similar effect (Wallerstein, 1999; Rueda and Pontusson, 2000). Although the Labour Government has introduced the minimum wage and is committed to raising it, it has resisted restoring the link between pensions and earnings or much of the employment protection lost by workers under the previous Conservative Government (Gamble, 2004).

The labour market in the UK is also similar to that in liberal welfare states, particularly the US, in the extent to which it is highly deregulated and flexible. This has resulted in relatively low levels of temporary employment as employers do not face disincentives in hiring staff on a permanent basis, as is the case in the highly regulated labour markets of countries such as Spain and Italy (Robinson, 1999). Employment is higher than in corporatist democracies which face significant challenges related to employment, although it is at a similar level to the social democratic welfare states such as Sweden and Denmark. Yet there are marked differences in the way these levels have been achieved. Britain has an extensive low-wage, low-skill private (service) sector and low levels of unionisation which contribute to the much greater income inequality generated by the labour market in the UK, whereas wages in the low-skill service sector tend to be kept high in social democracies as these jobs are often unionised and in the public sector. Although this makes Britain less vulnerable to pressures resulting from Europeanisation, it leaves it much more open to pressures of rising inequality resulting from further polarisation in the labour market and relatively high levels of migration. To achieve the Anglo-social welfare state, greater emphasis needs to be placed on measures that harness the labour market to produce greater equality through higher wage mobility, increased workforce skill levels, and more widespread care provision (see Chapter 16).

The extensive service sector in Britain has a very high level of female participation, meaning that overall female labour market participation is much higher than it is in corporatist welfare states. However, it is still lower than in the social democratic states and the kind of work women do is also different. The gender pay gap is much higher in the UK than it is in Sweden or Denmark, partly due to the greater level of overall income inequality. This also related to both the much greater provision of childcare and more flexible working arrangements (particularly in the public sector) in social democracies, although recent moves in Britain towards expanding the universal provision of childcare have gone some way in redressing the balance.

As well as these primarily liberal features, the British welfare state shares some characteristics of social democratic models, particularly those that concern the use of active labour market policy, public service provision and some forms of benefits. Healthcare is free at the point of use and there have been substantial redistributive measures in favour of reducing child and pensioner poverty. Recent reforms have consolidated some universal programmes and introduced a new one in the form of the Child Trust Fund (Kelly *et al*, 2003). Further reforming the pension system, as recommended in Chapter 16 would bring Britain closer to an Anglo-social model through more extensive universal provision.

British public services are largely financed through income taxation and to some extent through consumption (indirect) taxation. Contrary to much popular opinion, (see Chapter 5) the British tax system is not very progressive: the bottom 10 per cent of the income distribution pay a higher proportion of their income in tax than the top 10 per cent (Hills, 2004). This stands in marked contrast to corporatist democracies which rely to a greater extent on social insurance contributions as a source of revenue and have significantly higher levels of public spending, although this is partly due to higher unemployment levels and greater cost pressures due to more rapidly ageing populations and more generous pensions commitments (Esping-Andersen, 2002). While Scandinavian countries do not have a particularly progressive tax system, they achieve much more redistribution through transfers and public spending (Kenworthy, 2004c). Although tax levels will probably remain relatively low in the UK, there is scope for movement towards an expansion of some public services, particularly in relation to childcare (see Chapter 16).

The regressive tax system in the UK means that the onus of redressing injustice and reducing inequality is largely placed on the benefits system

(Hills, 2004). Although there are (relatively low) universal income guarantees, social spending is focused on those most in need by extensive means-testing, with an emphasis on labour market activation policies in tackling poverty. Many benefits, such as the Working Families Tax Credit, are means-tested to past median income, giving incentives to the unemployed to find work while maintaining popular support (Hills, 2004). Unemployment benefits also have a limited degree of conditionality, and initiatives such as the New Deal for Skills aim to help people to find work by improving their skill sets.

Like Sweden, and to a greater extent than the US, the British welfare state recognises that the government has an important role to play in helping people into work through training and placement and in making work pay through a higher minimum wage and an employment-conditional tax credit that provides more help to those with no children, despite them being a relatively unfavoured group. This focus has had significant success in helping people into paid work (see Chapter 15). Yet there is little opportunity for progression in the UK labour market and productivity is low compared to other European nations, suggesting a skills shortage (DfES, 2004). The British welfare state has undoubtedly been successful in many areas, such as generating employment and prosperity while avoiding the very worst excesses of inequality seen in the liberal US economy through a commitment to elements of progressive universalism, significant challenges remain in achieving social justice. We suggest that these might be overcome by further movement towards the Anglo-social model of the welfare state.

The challenge ahead

The hybrid nature of this emerging Anglo-social model means that the evolving labour market, changes in household structures and demographic shifts will impact in distinctive ways in Britain and require nuanced policy responses that differ substantially from that suitable for liberal or social democratic states. In many ways Britain is well positioned to work towards goals of social justice. High levels of both male and female employment, low employment taxes, a flexible labour market, a strong and flexible service economy, a relatively youthful demographic structure and large recent increases in spending on public services provide a firm foundation. Yet the trends and drivers outlined in this chapter and the inequalities highlighted by Dixon and Paxton in

Chapter 2 will require careful, considered responses. The most important challenges are:

- Pressures towards income and wealth inequality arising from the evolving labour market
- Women's increased participation in the labour force and the implications of the pursuit of gender equality for the provision of care
- Stalled or declining social mobility
- Marked local and regional inequality
- Rising cost pressures on the public sector
- The management of relatively high levels of migration and migrant participation in the labour market.

References

Baumol W J (1967) 'Macroeconomics of Unbalanced Growth: The Anatomy of Urban Crisis' *American Economic Review* 57, Nashvill: American Economic Association.

Boix C (1998) *Political Parties, Growth and Inequality: Conservative and Social Democratic Party Strategies in the World Economy* New York: Cambridge University Press

Bonoli G (2005) 'The politics of new social risks and policies' in Armingeon K and Bonoli G (eds) *The Politics of Post-Industrial Welfare States* London: Routledge

Brewer T L and Young S (1998) *The Multilateral Investment System and Multinational Enterprises* Oxford: Oxford University Press.

Callaghan J (2001) 'Globalisation and Social Democracy: What difference does it make?' *Paper for the 51st Political Studies Association Conference* Manchester: 10-12 April 2001

Castles F and Mitchell D (1992) 'Identifying Welfare State Regimes: The Links Between Politics, Instruments and Outcomes' *Governance: An International Journal of Policy and Administration* 5 (1), Oxford: Blackwells

Cerny (1994) 'The dynamics of financial globalization: technology, market structure, and policy response' *Policy Sciences* 27, New York: Springer

Chartered Institute of Professional Development (CIPD) (2004) *Recruitment, retention and turnover 2004: a survey of the UK and Ireland* London: CIPD. Available at: www.cipd.co.uk/surveys

Commission on Social Justice (1994) *Rethinking Social Justice: Strategies for National Renewal* London: Vintage and ippr

Department for Education and Skills (DfES) (2004) *5 Year Strategy for Children and Learners* London: The Stationery Office

Department of Trade and Industry (DTI) (2004) *The UK Contact Centre Industry: A Study* London: The Stationery Office

Department of Work and Pensions (DWP) (2004) *Households Below Average Income* (series) London: The Stationery Office

Disability Rights Commission (DRC) (2004) *Disability Briefing: January 2004* London: DRC

Esping-Andersen G (1990) *The Three Worlds of Welfare Capitalism* Princeton: Princeton University Press

Esping-Andersen G (1999a) *Social Foundations of Post-Industrial Economies* Oxford: Oxford University Press

Esping-Andersen G (2002) *Why we need a new welfare state* Oxford: OUP

European Commission (1996) *Taxation in the European Union* Brussels: European Commission

Eurostat (2005) *Free data* Brussels: European Communities. Available at http://www.eustatistics.
gov.uk/products.asp

Gamble A (2004) 'New Directions in the British Welfare State' *Paper prepared for the 2004 Annual
Meeting of the American Political Science Association* September 2-5 2004.

Ganghoff S (2000) 'Adjusting National Tax Policy to Economic Internationalization' in Scharp F and
Schmidt V (eds.) (2000) *Welfare and work in the open economy* Oxford: Oxford University Press

Garrett G (1998a) *Partisan Politics in the Global Economy* Cambridge: Cambridge University Press

Garrett G (1998b) 'Global Markets and national politics: collision course or virtuous circle?'
International Organisation 52, Cambridge: Cambridge University Press

Garrett L (2000) 'The Causes of Globalisation' *Comparative Political Studies*, 33 (6/7): 941–91

Genschel P (1999) *Tax competition and the welfare state* Köln: Max-Planck-institut fur
Gesellschaftsforschung

Gilpin (2000) 'The Nation State in the Global Economy' in Held D and McGrew A (2000) (eds) *The
Global Transformations Reader* Cambridge: Polity Press

Glennerster H (1999) 'Which Welfare States are most likely to survive?' in *International Journal of
Social Welfare* 8, Oxford: Blackwells

Goos M and Manning A (2004) *Lovely and Lousy Jobs: The rising polarisation of work in Britain*
London: Centre for Economic Perfomance (CEP)

Gottschalk P and Joyce M (1995) 'The Impact of Technological Change, Deindustrialisation and
Internationalization of Trade and Earnings Inequality: An International Perspective' in McFate K,
Lawson R, Wilson W J (eds) (1995) *Poverty, Inequality and the Future of Social Policy* New York:
Russell Sage

Gregg (2000) *Measuring the polarisation of work across households* London: Centre for Economic
Performance (CEP)

Hay C (2004) 'Common Trajectories, variable paces, divergent outcomes? Models of European capitalism under conditions of complex economic interdependence' *Review of International Political
Economy* 11 (2), London: Routledge

Hills J (2004) *Inequality and the State* Oxford: Oxford University Press

Hirst P and Thompson G (1999) *Globalisation in Question* Cambridge: Polity Press

HMT (2004) *The 2004 Spending Review* London: TSO

Inland Revenue (2004) *Table 1.2.* Available at
http://www.inlandrevenue.gov.uk/stats/tax_receipts/table1-2.pdf

Institute for Employment Research (IER) (2004) *Working Futures: National Report 2003-4* University
of Warwick: IER

Iverson T and Cusack R (2000) 'The causes of welfare state expansion: deindustrialisation or globalization?' *World Politics* 52, Baltimore: Johns Hopkins University Press

Iverson T (2001) 'The dynamics of welfare state expansion' in Pierson P (ed) (2001) *The New Politics
of the Welfare State* Oxford: Oxford University Press

Kelly G, Gamble A and Paxton W (2003) 'Stakeholding and Individual Ownership Accounts' in
Dowding K, De Wispelaere and White S (eds) *The Ethics of Stakeholding* London: Palgrave
Macmillan

Kenworthy L (2004a) 'Rising Inequality not a surge at the top' *Challenge* 47 (5),

Kenworthy L (2004b) *Jobs with Equality* book in progress: 22 November 2004. Available at
http://www.u.arizona.edu/~lkenwor/jobswithequality.pdf

Kenworthy L (2004c) Calculations based on Luxemburg Income Study data see

Maystadt P (1994) 'EMU: The Tax Challenges Ahead' *EC Tax Review 2*, Kingston-upon-Thames:
Kluwer

McQuaid R (2002) *Employability and Employment Change – some lessons for the future* Professorial
Lecture, Napier University, Edinburgh

ODPM (2004a) *Household Estimates and Projections: Great Britain, 1961-2021* London: TSO

86 Social Justice

ODPM (2004b) *Household Estimates and Projections: by composition and region, 1991–2021* London: TSO

OECD (1998) *Harmful Tax Competition. An Emerging Global Issue* Paris: OECD

ONS (2004) *Labour Force Survey* London: TSO

ONS (2004b) *International Migration* London: TSO. Available at
http://www.statistics.gov.uk/cci/nugget.asp?id=766

Pierson P (2001) 'Post-Industrial pressures on the Mature Welfare States' in Pierson P (ed) *The New Politics of the Welfare State* Oxford: OUP

Quinn D (1997) 'The correlates of change in international financial regulation' *American Political Science Review* 91, Cambridge: Cambridge University Press

Rhodes M (2000a) 'Restructuring the British Welfare State: Between Domestic Constraints and Global Imperatives' in Scharpf F and Schmidt V (eds.) (2000) *Welfare and work in the open economy* Oxford: OUP

Rhodes M (2000b) 'Challenges to Welfare: External Constraints' in Pierson C and Castles F G (eds.) (2000) *The Welfare State Reader* Cambridge: Polity

Robinson P (1999) 'Explaining the relationship between flexible employment and labour market regulation' in Felstead A and Jewson N (eds.) *Global trends in flexible labour* London: MacMillan

Robinson P (2004) *Tough Choices: the 2004 spending review* London: ippr

Rodrick D (2000) 'Has Globalisation Gone Too Far?' in Held D and McGrew A (2000) *The Global transformations reader* Cambridge: Polity

Rowthorn R (2004) *The impact on advanced economies of North-South trade in manufacturing and services* Paper presented at the First International Forum for Development, New York City, 18 October 2004

Rowthorn R and Ramaswamy R (1997) *Deindustrialisation: causes and implications* IMF Working Paper, WP/97/42 Washington: IMF

Rowthorn R and Coutts K (2004) *Commentary: De-industrialisation and the Balance of Payments in Advanced Economies* Paper presented at an international conference on 'De-industrialisation and Industrial Re-structuring' on 5 December 2004 at the Renaissance Seoul Hotel, Seoul, Korea

Rueda D and Pontusson J (2000) 'Wage Inequality and Varieties of Capitalism' *World Politics* 52:, Baltimore: Johns Hopkins University Press

Scharpf F (1997) 'Introduction: the problem-solving capacity of multi-level governance' *Journal of European Public Policy* 4,, London: Routledge

Scharpf F (2000a) 'The Viability of advanced welfare states in the international economy: vulnerabilities and options' in *European Review* Vol. 8 No 3, London: Routledge

Scharpf F (2000b) 'Globalization and the political economy of capitalist democracies' in Held D and McGrew A (2000) *The Global transformations reader* Cambridge: Polity

Select Committee on Economic Affairs (SCEA) (2003) *Aspects of the Economics of an Ageing Population* London: TSO

Sinn S (1990) 'Tax harmonization and tax competition in Europe' *European Economic Review* 34, , London: Elsevier

Sinn S (1993) 'The taming of leviathan: competition among governments' *Constitutional Political Economy* 3, Southampton: University of Southampton

Stanley K and Regan S (2003) *The Missing Million: supporting disabled people into work* London: ippr

Strange S (1996) *The Retreat of the State: The Diffusion of Power in the World Economy* New York: Cambridge University Press

Streek W (1999) *Comparative Solidarity: Rethinking the "European Social Model"* MPIfG Working Paper 99/8. Köln: Max Planck Institute for the Study of Societies

Swank D (1998) 'Funding the welfare state: globalization and the taxation of business in advanced market economies' *Political Studies* 46, Oxford: Blackwells

Swank D (2002) *Diminished democracy? Global Capital, Political Institutions and Policy Change in Developed Welfare States* Cambridge: Cambridge University Press

Traxler F and Woitech B (2000) 'Transnational Investment and Labour Market Regimes: A Case of "Regime Shopping"?' *European Journal of Industrial Relations* 6:2, London: Sage

United Nations (2004) *World Investment Report 2004* New York and Geneva: United Nations

Wallerstein M (1999) 'Wage-Setting Institutions and Pay Inequality in Advanced Industrial Societies' *American Journal of Political Science* 43, Bloomington: Midwest Political Science Association

Wright E and Dwyer R (2003) 'The patterns of job expansions in the USA: a comparison of the 1960s and 1990s' *Socio-Economic Review* 1:3, Oxford: Oxford University Press

Going With and Against the Grain: Social Policy in Practice Since 1997

Geoff Mulgan

This chapter is concerned with how, over the last decade, British social policy has coped with what Immanuel Kant called 'the crooked timbre of humanity' – the messy problems, aspirations and attitudes of the people who pay for social programmes and are affected by them.

A decade can be a very long time in social policy. Seen in retrospect, 1994, the year of the Commission on Social Justice, now looks like the tail end of the Thatcherite era, on the cusp of a profound change in perceptions of social issues. The previous decade had brought a marked widening of inequalities with few parallels either in British history or in other countries. Poverty had fallen off the Government's public policy agenda, apart from occasional attacks on single mothers and the work-shy. The term 'social exclusion' wasn't used on any side in politics. Within the elite it was widely believed that with tough law and order policies in place, Britain, like other societies, could get by with much higher levels of poverty and exclusion than had been acceptable in the past. Mass unemployment did not have to mean electoral annihilation so long as the majority of voters were experiencing rising living standards. In any case, trickle down from a booming economy would solve most problems. Path dependency meant that the UK had little choice but to make the most of a polarised labour market in which a highly paid professional elite enjoyed the greatest benefits of globalisation while a low paid and poorly educated bottom tier learnt to work more flexibly in the new service economy.

There was by no means a consensus. Researchers, think tanks, activists and others were convinced for moral and practical reasons that the position was unsustainable. Interestingly, in retrospect, the civil service during this period was also doing some serious work on exclusion – albeit kept at arms length from ministers. However, most of the important decisions taken by government were refracted through a prism in which greater inequality, and the prospect of rising inequality, was taken as given.

Ten years later the position is unrecognisable. This Government has committed itself to three ambitious goals: abolishing child poverty within 20 years; moving towards full employment; and narrowing the gap between the poorest areas and the rest. None of these will be easy to achieve, but the Government can point to some progress towards each of them. In addition, a slew of more precise targets has been set, on everything from crime levels in poor areas to mortality. A major expansion of redistribution has been implemented, largely through the tax credits programme, without any political backlash. A sign of the change in mood is that the Conservative opposition is keen to proclaim its commitment to reducing poverty, and anxious to replace its image as mean and amoral.

There are still powerful pressures driving greater inequality, at both the very top and the very bottom of the income range. Yet, to the surprise of many commentators, most of British society has become both wealthier and more equal, partly as a result of government actions and partly as a result of complex shifts in patterns of supply and demand for different kinds of labour. Some of the worst aspects of exclusion and poverty – from long-term unemployment to rough sleeping (down to further than the Government's target reduction of two thirds) – have been successfully treated, although not by any stretch of the imagination cured. As Chapter 3 points out, relative poverty has marginally improved. The number of individuals in households with incomes below 60 per cent of the median fell from 13.9m, or 25 per cent in 1996/7, to 12.4m, or 22 per cent, six years later (DWP, 2004). The number of children in relative poverty fell by a quarter during the same period (even if by European standards the numbers remain high). And although the Gini coefficient remains high this reflects some of the oddities at either end of the income scale (including a highly globalised elite in London at one end of the spectrum and the freezing of benefits for non-parents at the other end), and misses out on broader trends towards equalisation across most of the income range.[1]

In matters of policy it is always a sign of success when attention shifts to new problems. Few now would dare propose, even in private, that an

---

1 The Gini coefficient is a number between 0 and 1, where 0 means perfect equality and 1 means perfect inequality (where one person has everything and no one else has anything). See Goodman *et al* (1997) for further details and a discussion of the merits of alternative measures.

underclass can be policed into submission. Indeed, barring some of the less analytically interested broadsheets and high octane commentators, few serious observers now believe that there is such a thing as a permanent underclass anyway and Burchardt *et al* (2001) present a convincing argument as to why the UK does not have an underclass.

Partial success has also contributed to an air of optimism about the capacity of policy to resolve problems that is probably unmatched since the 1960s. No one today would repeat Francois Mitterand's infamous comment in the late 1980s that in relation to unemployment everything had been tried, and nothing worked. Instead, the UK, like many other countries, has experienced consistent success in applying, testing and improving labour market policies that have helped to bring unemployment down to levels not seen since the mid-1970s.

The positive aspects of this story deserve to be celebrated. They were not predicted, and were by no means inevitable. However, in what follows I want to focus less on the successes than on three sets of changes that have taken place since 1994, all of which pose difficult challenges for government over the next few years. These are:

- changes in the nature of the problems;
- changes in the nature of the politics;
- changes in the nature of policy tools.

In particular I want to suggest that in the next phases of social policy less will be achieved by thinking and acting around the broad aggregates than has been the case in the past. Instead, more finely grained analysis and policy will be essential to deal with the problems of a more differentiated society and to cope with the crooked timber of the post-industrial landscape.

The changing problems

Some features of poverty and exclusion change depressingly little over time. Many of the places that were amongst the poorest 100 years ago are poor today. There have been some striking changes, like the rapid decline of seaside towns that has left once-booming Blackpool as a symbol of deprivation. But generally the places that are now most at risk of deprivation are the same as the places that were 20 years ago: the big industrial centres and former mining areas. Within cities many of the same areas have remained poor over very long periods. In London, for example, the same streets show up as in Booth's famous surveys a century ago. There are also continuities of family; the UK remains a relatively immobile society, and the best predictor of poverty continues to be family background (see Chapter 2 for an overview).

However, relative success in sustaining overall economic growth and bringing down joblessness, in redistribution through tax credits, and in improving performance in public services, has, like the tide going out, left other things more visible than a decade ago.

A first example is low pay and immobility. A booming jobs market underpinned by the minimum wage has still left many in dead-end jobs, with few opportunities for progression. The combination of an often ramshackle training system, low levels of literacy and numeracy, and government unwillingness to introduce the more directive policies on training followed in other countries (like France or Singapore) have arguably left millions with blunted opportunities. During the 1980s and 1990s, most commentators assumed that Britain was becoming a more open society. Instead, the best available data suggests that social mobility is at best stagnant, at worst declining (Aldridge, 2004), a position that is mirrored in the supposedly open US. The prosperity of an affluent service class engaged in high value activities in the big cities appears if anything to have further entrenched the immobility of people in low pay and low-skilled service jobs.

A second example is inactivity. Although UK employment rates remain high, since 1997 there has been little progress in bringing down either the proportion of households that are workless or the numbers of the inactive (see Chapter 15). This reflects a combination of political nervousness and the genuinely intractable nature of the problems. Many more lone parents are now in work than in the mid-1990s, and many have benefited from enhanced training, advice and childcare. But there remains a very large group, of several hundred thousand, who claim that they would like to work but don't. Some of the reasons have to do with the practicalities of the labour market: inflexible employers, poor transport and lack of childcare. But supply is also part of the story. The UK has opted not to copy some of the north European countries that impose stringent requirements on lone parents to seek work once their children reach three or four, and despite sometimes fierce rhetoric for the benefit of the right-wing press, little has been done to tighten up conditionality beyond loosely policed requirements to show up for an interview with a personal adviser.

The position on disability is even more striking. There are some clear worsening trends on disability in many countries, particularly involving mental illness, stress and addictions. However, again despite sometimes firm rhetoric, relatively little has been done either to deal with the practical barriers in the way of disabled people working (although legal obligations on public buildings and transport operators have started to bite) or to tighten up the conditions attached to incapacity benefit and other supports for people with disabilities. Early in the Government's life, when some tougher measures were proposed, the strength of the reaction from the disability lobby (including wheelchairs chained to the gates of Downing Street) took many ministers aback. As a result it has been hard to open up a sober discussion of policy options for the many hundreds of thousands with minor disabilities, many of whom would like to work (ONS, 2002; Stanley and Regan, 2003).

The existing system has many perverse consequences. It incentivises people to be classified as disabled, and it is slow to act, allowing many to drift from a temporary disability into a permanent state of worklessness; recent Strategy Unit report on disability provides a good overview of recent evidence (Strategy Unit, 2004). In South Wales and the North-East I have met second generation incapacity benefit claimants who have gone directly onto incapacity benefit as soon as they were eligible – a disturbing new phenomenon that has yet to be analysed by researchers. The general point is that Government has not made anything like as much headway on economic activity as it might have done. The success in offering a different kind of deal to the young unemployed, with both enhanced rights and enhanced responsibilities, has not been replicated with other groups, despite the fact that so many of the criticisms originally made of the New Deal (which was caricatured by some on the liberal left as coercive workfare, indistinguishable from the policies of the right) have turned out to be flawed.

A third example is public health. Improved service standards in the NHS, and success in bringing down cancer and heart disease death rates, have shifted the focus of attention more onto other aspects of health, in particular the behavioural contributions to public health, heightening awareness of the widening class divide in smoking, drinking and diet, and the weakness of the classic social democratic toolkit of policy responses.

A fourth example is the changing position of Britain's ethnic minorities. Back in the 1970s it made sense to talk about ethnic minorities as a whole, and to focus policies on the divide between the majority and these minorities. Today such approaches look anachronistic. Some minorities have quickly overtaken the white majority in schools and earnings, including Chinese, Indians and Africans. Some 75 per cent of each Indian age cohort now goes to university, nearly double the average. Others, meanwhile, are falling behind in terms of unemployment, earnings and school performance, including many in the Pakistani, Bangladeshi, and Afro-Caribbean communities (Bhattacharyya *et al*, 2003). All minorities are still losing out on jobs and wages relative to their qualifications, but despite this evidence of continuing discrimination a much more complicated pattern is taking shape (Strategy Unit, 2003a). Much of the explanation for this pattern can be found in the class backgrounds of migrants to the UK, and the cultural and social capital they bring with them. But there are also other forces at work. Gender makes the picture even more complicated, for example, with Afro-Caribbean girls doing far better than boys.

As a result the policy challenge has become far more fine grained, and bound up with highly controversial questions of family structure and culture. Crude measures to increase ethnic minority employment, of the kinds used in many public sector organisations in the 1980s and 1990s, are likely to benefit the already relatively privileged, rather than reaching into the real sources of deprivation.

A fifth example is migration. Over the last decade, migration – both legal and illegal – has grown rapidly, prompted by the combination of instability and war in east Africa and Eastern Europe, the attractions of a dynamic economy, and the accessibility of an English language culture with a relatively unregulated labour market. For politicians, the problems of asylum have been most prominent – and certainly contributed to the downfall of more than one centre-left government in Europe. Asylum has brought back to the surface all of Europe's fears about out of control migration, fed perhaps (according to some of the ethnographic research) by subliminal fears of strangers willing to work hard. For policy makers, the acute challenge has been both to restore confidence in the overall system of migration and asylum and to better integrate migrants once they are here (something which the UK has been notably poor at in the past, the result of a combination of neglect and nervousness at imposing the sorts of language requirements that are common in other European countries).

A sixth example is the availability of new data and research on social capital and community which were largely absent from the Commission on Social Justice perspective. British social policy has traditionally tended to be somewhat statist and centralist, perhaps reflecting the dominance of the common rooms of Oxbridge and the corridors of Whitehall. It is possible to read whole bookshelves of policy and analysis without any sense of real people, their voices and relationships. That has changed little. However, there is now much more data available on social capital and networks, and their roles in the labour market and growth – soft realities which often explain much which is lost in the more traditional aggregated datasets of social policy makers.

A seventh example is geographical polarisation. Despite the continuities, some features of the geography of exclusion have changed markedly. In the 1980s wide inequalities opened up between regions and cities as a result of the differential effects of economic shocks. Since then, however, the pattern has changed. There are still some signs of widening gaps between regions, but there are now much greater inequalities within regions and cities than between them, and pressures in housing markets, reinforced by variations in school performance and crime patterns, have further concentrated poverty and claimants in fewer areas (see Chapter 14 and the early work of the Social Exclusion Unit on the National Strategy for Neighbourhood Renewal). A new hierarchy of urban spaces is taking shape that has greatly benefited some parts of some UK cities, but has locked others into a subordinate position (Hall, 2003).

These examples show how the problems faced by policy-makers have changed over the last decade. They reveal a more complex picture than ten years ago that is partly the result of success, partly the result of larger global trends, and in which many of the problems have become more varied and more tied up with issues of behaviour and culture rather than just economics.

Changing politics

If the problems have changed, how have the political arguments adapted? The big concern of progressive politicians in the early 1990s was that society had changed shape from something akin to a pyramid to something more like a rugby ball. Whereas once their task was to redistribute from an affluent minority at the top to a poor majority at the bottom, the position had now changed. The large majority in the middle needed new arguments to persuade them to support those below them, while also being more likely to aspire to reach the top themselves.

For the Labour Party in particular, as a class-based party, the challenge was essentially the same as the one that had been argued about obsessively ever since the 1950s: how to forge an alliance between the mainstream working class, whose traditional roots in manufacturing and mining were in inevitable decline, a new and growing body of skilled and semi-skilled workers in services, and a growing middle-class of white collar workers and professionals.

The conclusions reached in the late 1980s and early 1990s involved reshaping the political rhetoric and policy mix through a series of different frames. One was to talk much more about child poverty rather than poverty *per se*. Taxpayers, and particularly swing voters, were much more willing to see their money redistributed to help needy children than to help their parents, who might be indolent and stupid rather than just unlucky, even though the difference was far more presentational than real (Sefton, 2004). This move was in part justified analytically by the mounting weight of evidence on the effects of early years experiences – from diet and parenting to cognitive development in schools – on subsequent achievements (Stipek and Ryan, 1997; Feinstein, 2003; Carneiro and Heckman, 2002).

Another prism for reframing the debate about poverty was to talk more about the externalities of poverty: the many ways in which its indirect impact on drug abuse, crime and antisocial behaviour affected the more affluent, particularly in a dense, primarily urban society like the UK. The argument became a mirror of Conservative 'trickle down' rhetoric; instead poverty would trickle up through society, whether in the form of heroin dealers targeting the teenage children of the rich, or burglars stealing BMWs.

A third way of shifting the argument was to direct attention to the economic benefits that would flow from a society with fuller employment, simultaneously cutting spending on unemployment benefits, reducing the waste of talent and energy, and raising the sustainable growth rate.

The other crucial issue of the new politics was the position of the very top. At times, Labour toyed with more direct assaults on the 'fat cats' and the very rich. However, Labour has been influenced by the very powerful trends in the UK and many other advanced industrial societies towards oligarchy, increasing concentrations of power and wealth at the very top, amongst groups who are able to shape public agendas and exercise very disproportionate influence over political parties and media elites.

While politicians largely sidestepped the question of the inequality at the top, the new generation of leaders who took over the Labour Party in the 1990s proved very effective at making the case for a different approach to poverty and inequality. They drew on a somewhat different analysis to the largely Rawlsian arguments that underpinned the Commission on Social Justice. Political theorists have tended to deduce principles of justice either from notions of natural law or from theoretical thought experiments like John Rawls' 'veil of ignorance'. The alternative has been to examine how words and concepts are used in daily life (in philosophical terms this could be characterised as the approach of the later rather than the younger Wittgenstein). Such approaches reveal the complexity of public views about fairness and justice that give rather greater weight to merit, desert and hard work than the deductive theories of philosophers. The British public certainly tended to be less tolerant of failure and self-inflicted problems than the theorists. Many had internalised some of the more lurid claims made by the tabloid media about welfare 'scroungers', and much of Labour's electoral base accepted the argument that somehow those hard-working families who were playing by the rules were not getting a fair deal.

Ten years on, Labour's repositioning still looks broadly right. It is supported by the theoretical work of Michael Walzer, David Miller, Jon Elster and others who have analysed the complexity of notions of justice that are not easily aggregated into a single idea of social justice, whether from a purely philosophical perspective or a political one (Miller, 1999; Walzer, 1983; Elster, 1992). Public perceptions distinguish between the different dimensions of fairness and justice that are often in tension with each other: just distributions, opportunities and procedures very rarely point in the same direction. The same is true of justice based on rights or needs; justice based on scalar distribution (the more you put in the more you get out) or justice based on contract (you get what you agree to); just responsibilities or just distributions of power.

The work of Elster has also pointed out that our conceptions of justice, which are essentially moral conceptions, are highly context specific. Taking only one aspect of justice as an example, we view very differently issues such as just access to exemption from conscription, just access to abortion, just access to bus travel and just access to the media to correct a mistake. By aggregating different dimensions of justice into a single definition we lose more insights than we gain, and once policies reach the world of real politics and argument, all of these complex moral dimensions soon reappear.

These different approaches to justice do not constitute a single alternative to traditional deductive notions of social justice. But they do show why theoretical attempts to pin down a single consistent view and apply it in practice always unravel, and why towards the end of his life Rawls concluded that any viable conception of justice needed to be 'political not metaphysical', by which he meant that people might more easily agree on the applications of justice than on the fundamental principles from which they derived.

Miller's recasting of the four principles of social justice in Chapter 1 is a brave attempt at synthesising principles that would be 'widely accepted'. Yet even his own discussion shows that this is not quite true. So, for example, the idea that everyone should have precisely equal rights regardless of their past contributions is far from self-evident (and recent UK policy towards migrants from the accession countries in the EU has moved away from this principle precisely because it was seen as unfair by so many of the public). Likewise, as his own discussion shows, any strict interpretation of the third principle of equality of opportunity has to mean severely limiting inheritance, and thus fighting deeply held views about the nature of family and kinship.

It is precisely for these reasons that politicians now face a difficult job in building on the progress made in reducing poverty and exclusion over the last decade. For despite the success in reframing political arguments better to fit the reality of public understandings of justice, and despite some success in adjusting public attitudes (always a responsibility for progressive politicians), many of the most pressing issues come up against contradictory or resistant public attitudes.

Just as the analysis of problems has had to become more fine grained, so is the politics no longer usefully understood through broad aggregations and broad brush concepts of redistribution and justice.

Asylum is a good example. For some of the public, asylum became a social justice issue in the early part of this decade, in the sense that people who were not seen by them as legitimate members of the community were seen to be getting preferential access to housing and healthcare. For others, asylum was a social justice issue in precisely the opposite sense; here were people in need to whom we owed a responsibility of care.

The continuing interaction of race and class is another example. Some of the most problematic lines of social exclusion are now those that demarcate parts of some Muslim communities from the rest. The dynamics of housing allocations and school choice have encouraged some communities to congregate together, particularly in the North West. Since these communities start off with high levels of unemployment these shifts can further increase their economic isolation. They also exacerbate conflicts over resources with predominantly white communities (such as regeneration funding or money for upgrading housing). The forthcoming book on *Race, Community and Conflict* (Dench *et al*, 2005) which updates the Institute of Community Studies' classic analyses of the East End working class in the 1950s, will be a rare empirical dissection of the many tensions between a migrant community and the white working class, and will show that many of these tensions are essentially about conflicting views of fairness rather than being ascribable to racism and prejudice.

In the very different environment of the US, a large part of the explanation for low welfare spending is that it is associated by the white majority with spending on blacks. It is seen as a race issue rather than a social justice issue (Alesina *et al*, 2001). The UK is a long way from reaching a similar point, but it is not hard to imagine louder arguments against spending on regeneration and employment programmes that seek to present these as subsidies for a hostile, or at least 'other', Muslim community.

A third example is the continuing debate around conditionality in welfare. In relation to single young men and women without children it is now widely accepted that rights should be balanced with responsibilities. But in relation to disabled people of working age and single mothers, public perceptions of fairness and justice are highly complex, and rather distant from the assumptions of many policy makers. Ask any representative sample of the public to discuss questions like 'How much should a young man or woman be held responsible for choosing to have a child early in life when they lack the means to finance a family?' or 'Should the welfare system incentivise or penalise unemployed people for having children?' and it becomes clear just how large the gap is.

A fourth set of examples are those involving public health and paternalism. Middle-class attitudes have shifted fairly fast towards supporting a much more activist stance by government on diet, obesity, and smoking. The lobby for local bans on smoking in public spaces is now gaining ground, emboldened not only by the US experience but also by recent moves in Ireland and Norway. Activists point to the widening class gulf around smoking and other behavioural 'bads' to advocate a much more paternalistic approach, seeing this as decisive for social justice. But for many people, particularly those whose behaviour might be influenced, this is simply not legitimate territory for the state to enter and impinges on very basic moral freedoms.

So in all of these areas we need subtler and more differentiated arguments that make sense not only in theoretical terms or in relation to the available evidence, but also in relation to public values; how the public sees the world and how they understand justice.

Changing experience of policy tools and efficacy

The changing nature of the problems and the political arguments is matched by changing understandings of how government can act. In the early 1990s, Labour was very timid in its thinking about policy tools and Whitehall machineries. The level of debate had not progressed much beyond Gerald Kaufman's advice on how to handle civil servants, a sort of 'Yes Minister' in reverse. Labour in the past had tended to oscillate between a rather naïve assumption that the civil service machine is a Rolls Royce machine just waiting to be told where to go, and a paranoid assumption that its main objective was to frustrate Labour's radical intentions.

The Commission on Social Justice reflected its time in that it tended towards the first view, largely assuming that the existing structures were fit for implementing whatever policy package was proposed.

Yet in power, and particularly in social policy, Labour has been highly innovative, and has learned to use more finely tuned policy tools. There have been at least ten distinctive new approaches.

First, much of government has now moved beyond the traditional linear approach to policy which took ideas from manifestos through green papers and white papers to legislation. Instead it is widely recognised that policy and delivery are much better understood as continuous processes of implementation, assessment and improvement in which legislation every few years symbolises change rather than being at the heart of it. The Health Collaboratives are a good symbol of this new approach, as is the continuing evolution of the New Deal, with constant testing of new approaches and the more radical experiments with Employment Zones.

Second, in many areas of social policy, government has gone beyond the old model dominated by a small cadre of specialist policy makers (a model that was actually intensified by the new public management and Next Steps agencies ideas of the late 1980s) towards a much more open system in which large numbers of outsiders are employed within government (half the staff of the Strategy Unit, Social Exclusion Unit and others). There is thus far more involvement of academics, NGOs and business in the process of both policy design and delivery.

Third, much tighter performance management has been introduced into many areas of policy, addressing not only literacy and numeracy in schools, but also cancer and heart disease, burglary and street crime and welfare. The UK has now probably gone further in terms of transparency and active management than anywhere else in the world. There have been many criticisms of targets; they can create perverse incentives, and have often been ill-designed, criticisms set out in the Strategy Unit papers *Better Policy Design* and *Delivery and Devolved Decision-Making Review* (Strategy Unit, 2001; Strategy Unit, 2004). However, the need to use some transparent metrics to judge success and hold agencies to account is now widely accepted. Moreover, poor people, who have traditionally had to make do with poor services, have been the main beneficiaries of tighter performance management (as the relative performance of schools, hospitals and police forces in poorer areas has risen faster than the average), and are likely to continue to be the main beneficiaries as government makes more use of floor standards and guaranteed minimums.

Fourth, policy has become more evidence based, or, to be more precise, more informed by evidence, with extensive use of pilots, pathfinders and trailblazers, and systematic evidence reviews. Sure Start, for example, was very overtly based on social science research, as was the literacy strategy. Pilots have sometimes been misused, for example by ministers proclaiming success too early, and often political pressures have made it impossible to await their full results. These lessons are summarised in the Strategy Unit study on pilots, *Trying it Out* (Strategy Unit, 2003b). But the long run shift towards policy more informed by evidence looks unstoppable and should be helped by the fact that devolution creates more opportunities to test policies out. The complexities of evidence based policy making were recently set out in my essay *Government and Knowledge* (Mulgan, 2005).

Fifth, both policy design and implementation have become more holistic, notably in programmes aimed at rough sleepers, youth justice, early years and regeneration. Sure Start is one example. Others include

Connexions, the New Deal for Communities (both recently strongly backed by the National Audit Office even though many traditional vested interests in Whitehall and elsewhere remain hostile), support for children at risk, and the embryonic National Offender Management Service, which has the potential to revolutionise criminal justice policy. In some ways joined-up policy and delivery remain in their infancy. Certainly the traditional hierarchies remain very strong. But much more progress has been made than was expected a decade ago.

Sixth, a host of new roles have been created, many of them standing between the traditional professionals and the public, that have made the day-to-day experience of policy much more supportive. These include personal advisers in Jobcentre Plus and Connexions, learning mentors, teaching assistants and community support officers in policing. These are all aspects of a broader move to make government more personal in its nature; treating people as rounded individuals rather than simply as categories.

Seventh, a remarkable new architecture of tax credits has been built up which has not only transformed the living standards of millions of people but also, after some serious teething troubles, offered a wholly new way of thinking about welfare. These credits are important, in part because of the generosity of the funding that flows through them and in part because they have relinked welfare to the workplace. Their main problems are now essentially design problems; how to manage the right incentives at different levels, how to avoid perverse side-effects (such as pension credits reducing incentives to save), and how to cope with the continuing problems of stigma.

Eighth, in many areas of delivery there has been a strong emphasis on contestability and diversity, breaking open public sector monopolies and allowing private and non-profit organisations to compete. This has long been the case in social care and it is now commonplace in welfare, employment services, drug treatment and prisons (and it has long been commonplace in many other European countries with strong social democratic traditions). For those designing policies, new issues have become critical in a more mixed economy: how to design contracts to avoid cream-skimming, how to grow markets so that there is genuine choice of providers (rather than, as in IT, a handful of global firms which can all too often fleece government), and how to avoid flawed contracting models that leave government with all the risk and lead to excessive spending (as happened with many of the first waves of the PFI).

Ninth, there has been a strong emphasis on prevention: preventing diseases and behaviours that cause health inequality, taking earlier action to prevent children falling into patterns of risk, and raising spending on crime prevention, all disproving the cynical conventional wisdom that politicians will never spend in ways that will deliver results only in ten or twenty years time.

Tenth, there has been more long-termism: higher investment in prevention, five-year strategies in the main public service areas, and a recognition that most things worth doing take time. This has undoubtedly been helped by relative economic and political stability. But it also reflects the seriousness of purpose of many ministers. As *The Times* reported on the Government's Strategic Audit in 2003, 'governments usually overestimate how much can be achieved in the short-term and underestimate how much can be achieved in the long-term' (Strategy Unit, 2003a; Riddell, 2003). Many mistakes have been made as ministers tried to take short cuts to win credit, or tried to dismantle the changes their predecessors had put in place. But by and large most of the social programmes have been reasonably long term in ethos and implementation.

Each of these innovative approaches is admirable and more likely to succeed than the traditional models of policy and delivery. But none of them is unproblematic. Ministerial understanding of, and interest in, the practicalities of delivery remain very uneven. The fact that so few Labour ministers had ever run anything before entering Parliament remains a problem and continues to encourage a spin culture which values announcements and the appearance of activity rather than real achievements (and makes British government very different from counterparts in Europe that are largely populated with ministers who have run towns, cities and regions). This lack of practical delivery experience is also found amongst much of the senior civil service.

Some of the new tools also create political problems of their own. In some cases the problems are ideological, like whether to use a better performing private company in place of a mediocre public organisation. In other cases they are the problems of a more open system, like how to handle evidence which shows that a policy isn't working.

Looking ahead, many intellectual challenges still stand in the way of genuinely mature social policy analysis and implementation. They include some quite technical tasks, such as the design of better techniques for assessing and managing public programmes, whether through the rubric of public value (Strategy Unit, 2002), or through the more sophisticated means for assessing spending on human capital and social programmes (we still have far better tools for appraising investment in bridges and airports than in childcare or vocational training). Others include the need for better understanding of organisational and delivery issues in social policy; the need for smarter understanding of the crucial trade-offs between simplicity and complexity (too often, policy makers devise marvellously detailed programmes that take little or no account of how they will be delivered); and the need for more rigour on the precise roles played by ethos and motivation in public service delivery.

There are also some critical areas where knowledge remains inadequate: the dynamics of business investment in poor areas and how it can best be changed the effects of different policies on ownership, knowledge of what really works; in accelerating progression in the labour market and at work, and empirically grounded ideas about what to do with the low wage, dead-end jobs that continue to be needed in any developed society.

What next? In the future, as in the recent past, the central issue for British social policy will be how to better align the three dimensions of successful change I described earlier: clarity about the critical tasks, smart politics grounded in well-grounded ethical arguments, and effective tools. For the reasons cited above, the job of achieving this sort of alignment may become harder as the problems become more complex, and as society becomes more diverse, even though the critical tasks – eliminating child poverty, achieving full employment and narrowing the gap between rich and poor areas – are likely to remain valid.

For the centre-left there will also be a continuing intellectual and practical challenge. We currently lack a synthetic framework for thinking about how all of the different aspects of social policy fit together. A single grand theory is unlikely to be viable for all sorts of reasons. But there is much to be gained from having some common frames, a common language and common ways of thinking about how different policies impact on the same individuals, families and communities.

I've already suggested why social justice may not be quite adequate as a unifying framework. Another contender which may have more reach is the life chances framework, which in different forms has been around for several decades (and which has recently been developed further by the Strategy Unit). It may provide the necessary bridge between thinking about equality of outcomes and equal opportunities, as well as rescuing back from the right the insight that politics and policy are fundamentally moral activities, and that they are most likely to succeed when they both resonate with, and help to shape, the moral metaphors through which the public see the world.

The limitation of the life chances framework, however, which it shares with social justice arguments, is the lack of a convincing link to broader questions of economic development, a coherent account of what kinds of labour market, education system and workplace organisation will be viable in the capitalism of the 21st century.

None of these intellectual or political tasks will be easy. Moving away from the broad brush aggregates of much traditional social policy inevitably makes both the analyses and the prescriptions more complex. The moral basis for social policy will never be finally settled, nor pinned down in simple precepts. Instead it has to be constantly reframed and argued about anew. But the conditions are propitious. Remarkable progress has been made in healing the scars of the Thatcher years. Since progressive politics depends on confidence in the efficacy of government, we should not forget to celebrate just how much has been achieved, while also tooling up for the challenges ahead.

References

Aldridge S (2004) *Life chances and Social Mobility: an overview of the evidence* London: TSO

Alesina A, Glaeser E and Sacerdote B (2001) 'Why Doesn't the US Have a European-Style Welfare System?' *NBER Working Paper Number W8524* Cambridge MA: National Bureau of Economic Research (NBER)

Bhattacharyya G, Ison L and Blair M (2003) *Minority Ethnic Attainment and Participation in Education and Training: the evidence* London: TSO

Burchardt T, Le Grand J and Piachaud D (2001) 'Degrees of Exclusion: Developing a Dynamic, Multidimensional Measure' in *Understanding Social Exclusion* Oxford: Oxford University Press

Carneiro P, and Heckman J (2002) 'Human Capital Policy' *NBER Working Paper Number W9495* Cambridge MA: National Bureau of Economic Research (NBER)

Dench G, Young M and Gavron K (2005) *Race, Community and Conflict* London: Institute for Community Studies

Department for Work and Pensions (2004) *Households Below Average Income* London: TSO

Elster J (1992) *Local Justice* New York: Russell Sage Foundation and Cambridge University Press

Feinstein L (2003) 'Inequality in the early cognitive development of British Children in the 1970 cohort' *Economica* 70, Oxford: Blackwell

Goodman A, Johnson P and Webb S (1997) *Inequality in the UK* Oxford: Oxford University Press

Hall P (2003) *Growing the European Urban System* London: Institute of Community Studies

Miller D (1999) *Principles of Social Justice* London: Harvard University Press

Mulgan G (2005) 'Government and Knowledge' *Evidence and Policy* 1 (2), Bristol: Policy Press

Office of National Statistics (ONS) (Spring 2002, Autumn 2002) *Labour Force Survey* London: TSO

Riddell P, Article in *The Times*, 12 November 2003

Sefton T (2004) 'What we want from the welfare state' in Park A, Curtice J, Thomson K, Jarvis L and Bromley C (eds) *British Social Attitudes, the 20th report, continuity and change over two decades* London: Sage Publications

Stanley K and Regan S (2003) *The missing million: supporting disabled people into work* London: ippr

Stipek D J and Ryan R H (1997) 'Economically disadvantaged preschoolers: Ready to learn but further to go' *Developmental Psychology* 33, Washington: American Psychological Association

Strategy Unit (2001) *Better Policy Design and Delivery* London: TSO

Strategy Unit (2002) *Creating Public Value* London: TSO

Strategy Unit (2003a) *Ethnic Minorities and the Labour Market: Final report* London: TSO

Strategy Unit (2003b) *Trying it out* London: TSO

Strategy Unit (2004) *Improving the life chances of disabled people: interim report* London: TSO

Walzer M (1983) *Spheres of Justice* New York: Basic Books

Attitudes to Social Justice

Peter Taylor-Gooby[1]

In Chapter 1, Miller identified four principles of social justice:

- Equal citizenship – every citizen is entitled to an equal set of civil, political and social rights, including the means to exercise these rights effectively.
- The social minimum – all citizens must have access to resources that adequately meet their essential needs, and allow them to live a secure and dignified life in today's society.
- Equality of opportunity – a person's life chances, and especially their access to jobs and educational opportunities, should depend only on their own motivation and aptitudes, and not on irrelevant features such as gender, class or ethnicity.
- Fair distribution – resources that do not form part of equal citizenship or the social minimum may be distributed unequally, but the distribution must reflect relevant factors such as personal desert and personal choice.

But understanding what the goals of the centre-left should be is only half the battle. It is also vital to understand public attitudes, how policy can work with the grain of these views, and where they may need to be challenged.

This chapter outlines what we know about the public's views on some elements of Miller's four principles. We focus on the social minimum (which is understood primarily in terms of attitudes to income poverty), fair distribution and on the emerging policy debate about childcare as it

1 The author and ippr would like to thank Tom Sefton, whose presentation at an ippr seminar contributes to this chapter, MORI for providing analysis of the European Social Survey and NATCEN for contributing original analyses of the BSA regarding attitudes towards childcare and work-life balance.

relates to a concern for equality of opportunity, particularly in relation to gender equality. Fair distribution is a key issue given the increase in income inequalities, particularly at the top end in recent years. To what extent do people find these inequalities acceptable?

The analysis is based mainly on the annual British Social Attitudes (BSA) survey, the leading survey of public attitudes in the UK. We reinforced this data with some findings from recent qualitative work carried out by Alan Hedges and Peter Dwyer, which uses focus groups to explore ideas about tax, the role of government in welfare and the circumstances under which different groups merit help. We also draw on the European Social Survey (ESS), which allows us to compare public opinion in the UK to that across Europe.[2]

This chapter shows that most people support the principles of social justice, but have reservations when it comes to paying more tax, particularly if it is intended primarily to help the poor. Views are complex, and support for greater fairness, a social minimum and more equal opportunities appears to be much stronger in relation to some groups than others. The extent of need is relevant – those with children are more likely to be supported – but, at the same time, groups which are seen to be contributing to society in some way, rather than just being passive recipients of welfare, are also likely to be favoured. In other words, there are indications in the data that, while most people support the four principles outlined above, in practice they may add a fifth, a principle of reciprocity or entitlement through social contribution.

Income inequality and a fair distribution

A clear majority of the British public see income inequalities as too large and believe they should be reduced. A considerable and increasing majority of those interviewed in the BSA survey (now about 80 per cent) say that 'the gap between those with high and low incomes is too wide' (Sefton, 2003; Hills, 2004; Bromley, 2003). Looking more specifically at market or wage inequality (as opposed to income inequality which takes

---

2 The British Social Attitudes survey is the leading survey of public attitudes in the UK. It has run on an annual basis since 1983 (see Park *et al* (2001) Appendix I). The European Social Survey provides high quality data on social attitudes across EU member states and some associated countries. The 2001 and 2002 rounds of the survey are now available (see www.europeansocialsurvey.org for details and access to the data).

account of tax and benefits) most people also believe these to be too great, especially at the top end. When people's perceptions of the general pattern of inequalities between occupations are compared with their views on what inequalities should be (see Table 5.1), it is clear that people would prefer the groups that they see as low paid to receive more and the higher paid to receive less. Looking at the ratio of bottom to top in Table 5.1, we see that people, starting from what they perceive wage levels to be, would like to compress the earnings distribution by over half; from 1:14 to 1:6. Most people greatly underestimate the spread of incomes. The actual earnings ratio is 1:55, four times the 1:14 of popular perception. In short, people appear to want differentials reduced by increasing income at the bottom and reducing it at the top.

Table 5.1: Perceptions of annual earnings before tax, 1999

	Perceptions (£K)	What they should earn (£K)	Actual earnings (£K)
Shop assistant	9	12	10.3
Unskilled factory worker	10	12	13.1
Skilled factory worker	15	18	18
GP	35	40	50.8
Appeal court judge	80	50	139.9
Chair of large corporation	125	75	555
Ratio, bottom to top	1:14	1:6	1:55
Base 819			

Source: adapted from Hills (2004) table 2.9

How strongly do people feel about this? Levels of income inequality are not at the forefront of people's minds when they are asked about the most important issues facing the country. The public continue to put public services, particularly the NHS and the education system, at the top of their list although one issue that is related to inequality and was a major issue a decade ago is unemployment. MORI data shows that in October 1994, when the Commission on Social Justice reported, 62 per cent of people thought that unemployment was an 'important issue facing Britain today'. By August 2004 this figure had fallen to just 7 per cent (MORI, 2004). Hedges' qualitative research for the BSA survey also suggests that, while people do care about income inequality, it is their views on, and often their dissatisfaction with, public services that comes uppermost in their minds.

The argument that the UK public do care about income and wage inequality, but without great conviction, is reflected in the international data from the European Social Survey. Some care needs to be taken with the relevant survey question – it asks whether people agree with the statement: 'Government should reduce differences in income'. This may mix people's views on the justice or otherwise of income differentials, with opinion on whether government has a role to play in reducing them. That said, some interesting patterns do emerge from the data. In the chart countries are arranged into 'welfare-state regimes': one conservative, one southern European and one social democratic, with the UK as a liberal outlier.[3] Both the percentage of people who 'agree strongly' and 'agree' with the statement, are shown.[4]

Figure 5.1: 'Government should reduce differences in income levels'

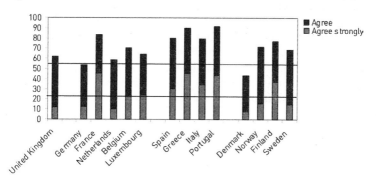

3 For a fuller discussion, see Esping-Andersen (1990) and Ferrera (1996) who deal with Southern Europe as a separate category of welfare state. Data are also available for Eastern Europe, but differences in recent national experience especially in relation to the role of government make direct comparisons with the UK difficult.

4 In this paper we make straightforward comparisons between different countries. Such cross-national comparisons, though, should be approached with caution, since cultural factors may influence response. While answers may be influenced by national dispositions (for example, social democratic countries have more egalitarian views), they can also be influenced by different characteristics – people in one country may be less prone to telling researchers they have strong views on issues than they are in another.

Though there are differences between countries within each of the welfare state regimes, there is generally higher support for government redistributive action in southern Europe than in social democratic and conservative countries. This pattern is likely, at least in part, to be affected by differences in existing levels of inequality. The views expressed in response to this question are influenced by two factors: support for redistributive intervention and perceptions of how severe the inequality gap is. The social democratic countries are most equal followed by the established European core conservative countries – Germany, France and Benelux. Mediterranean countries are more unequal and the level of inequality in the UK is slightly higher than for this group (Luxembourg Income Study, 2004; Blekesaune and Quadagno, 2003)

Support for government redistribution is slightly lower in Britain than elsewhere, but the most striking feature is weaker level of conviction. In the UK 62 per cent of respondents 'strongly agree' or 'agree' with the statement, against an average for all countries shown of 76 per cent. However, the UK, along with Germany, the Netherlands, and somewhat surprisingly, Denmark and Sweden, has under 15 per cent 'definitely agreeing' that government should reduce differences in income inequality. All other countries have significantly more 'definitely agreeing'. Taking into account the fact that inequality in the UK is greater than elsewhere, this indicates that people in this country do care about income inequalities, but do not necessarily feel strongly, and may be less inclined to think it is the government's job to reduce them.

Poverty and the social minimum

Public attitudes to poverty are similar to those regarding income inequality. People do think that it is an issue, but not one they feel strongly about.[5] In 2003 a majority of those interviewed believed 'there is quite a lot of real poverty in Britain today'. However, as Table 5.2 shows, the proportion holding this view has declined since the early

---

5   It is worth considering what the public understand when they talk about 'poverty'. Though officially rates of poverty are measured by counting the number of people or households that fall short of a particular level of income, in the last decade academic and policy debate has emphasised wider measures of deprivation and exclusion (NPI/Rowntree, 2002). The close relation between views on inequality and poverty and the equivalent concern about both areas strengthens the case for poverty measures that reflect social inequalities more broadly, rather than simply assessing the number falling below a particular income threshold.

1990s. Likewise, the proportion of people who think that poverty is growing has fallen, from 68 per cent in the early 1990s to 35 per cent by 2003. MORI includes a standard question on 'the important issues facing Britain' in its monthly omnibus survey. In 1997–8 the percentage who identified poverty and inequality as a priority was located in the band between 7 and 10 per cent. By 2004, the range had fallen to between 3 and 6 per cent (MORI, 2004). In some ways the public attitudes accurately match officially measured trends. As Chapter 2 demonstrates, the Government has been successful in reducing poverty since 1997, most notably among children, a group seen as deserving across a wide range of opinions. The attitude data implies that it may be difficult to ensure continuing public support for policies to achieve further reductions in the level of child poverty, either because people have become less concerned, or because they believe that the problem is already addressed.

Table 5.2: Perceptions of poverty in Britain, 1986–2003

	1986	1989	1994	2000	2003
Quite a lot	55	63	71	62	54
Very little real poverty	41	34	28	35	41

Turning to international comparisons, we rely on an ESS question asking people what they think of the question: 'To be a good citizen, how important is it to support those who are worse off?' Though this does not necessarily translate into views on poverty, the findings are again interesting. In Figure 5.2, we again seek to show overall differences in attitudes, but at the same time to assess the salience with which people hold views. People were asked to rank on a scale of one to ten how strongly they agreed with the statement, with a score of one representing the strongest approval. The chart shows the respective percentages for people answering one to three, and percentages for those answering either four or five.

The cumulative percentage of people who answered one to five in the UK is not significantly different from other countries. The average for the countries shown is 74.7 and the percentage in the UK is 77.8. Only two countries have higher levels of support. But taking the more stringent measure of agreement, we see a different picture. The UK figure for people answering between one and three is 48 per cent, considerably lower than the European mean of 55.5.

Figure 5.2: 'To be a good citizen, how important is it to support those who are worse off?'

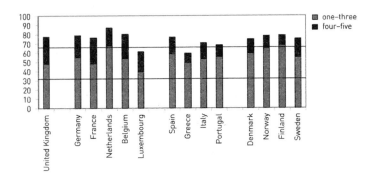

People think that income inequalities in the UK are too great, that the distribution should be narrowed, and that there is a significant amount of poverty, although perhaps rather less than in the past. However, at present they do not hold these views strongly. In addition, there is some evidence that people feel less strongly about these issues than they did seven years ago.

The Government's responsibility

Notwithstanding the weakness of people's views in this area, the fact remains that majorities, when asked, do support core elements of social justice. Figure 5.1 has already touched on people's views on the role of government. Figure 5.3 shows BSA data on a similar question. Given the level of government caution about raising the question of redistribution in public debate, support is surprisingly high. In 2003, 42 per cent agreed that 'the government should redistribute income to the less well off' and that only 26 per cent disagreed.[6] The remainder, a signifi-

---

6   Redistribution is complex. It may involve redistributing income horizontally, over the lifecycle, from working age to pensioners or to children, or it may involve vertical redistribution from rich to poor (with no temporal aspect). Hedges (forthcoming), suggests that people tend to think in terms of the latter.

cant proportion, were undecided. The percentage of people agreeing that government has a role to play in redistribution has increased only slowly since 1999. Indeed, support is still lower than in the late 1980s and early 1990s when around 50 per cent of people agreed. In other words, while opinions have not hardened against redistribution under Labour, neither have they been turned around to support a greater measure of equality.

Figure 5.3: 'Government should redistribute incomes from better off to less well off . . .'

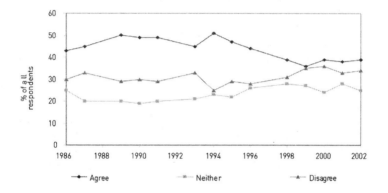

The gap between the 80 per cent of the population who think that income differences are too large and the 42 per cent who would support government action is striking. As we shall see below, support for higher taxes to improve welfare is also relatively low. There remains an important disjunction between support for the highly valued mass services like the NHS, and the lower level of support for services directed at specific minorities such as unemployed people, lone parents and the poor. A number of factors may contribute to this pattern of views.

Misconceptions about levels of spending
Most people are able to judge the rough relative cost of most areas of state provision reasonably accurately, and to rank services correctly in order of the cost to the exchequer (Taylor-Gooby and Hastie, 2002). However, when the questions turn to the detail of specific components of social security and, in particular, benefits directed at the poorest

groups, widespread misconceptions emerge. In 2001, more than two-thirds of those interviewed saw the cost of benefits for the unemployed as the largest or the second largest item in the social security budget, whereas in fact they account for about 6 per cent.

Distinctions between different groups

'The poor' are not universally regarded as a needy group. Attitudes are affected strongly by the level of need a person experiences. If people are asked whose wages they think government should supplement, support is much stronger for helping those with children than it is for either single adults or couples without children. In 2003, 66 and 59 per cent respectively thought that government should top up the wages of lone parents and couples with children. Only 26 per cent thought the same policies should be applied to couples with no children.

Existing government policy could be seen as going with the grain of public opinion. Benefit increases have been significantly more generous for the groups that stand high in public favour and that are judged deserving. The central theme in provision remains 'work for those who can, security for those who can't' as the DSS analysis of the Changing Welfare State succinctly puts it (DSS, 2000). This implies 'selective universalism and patchwork redistribution' (Hills and Lelkes, 1998). One recent change is that, since April 2003, support for low wage earners has been extended to adults without children through the working tax credit. This is one instance where policy is potentially pushing ahead of public opinion.

People worry about the effects of benefits on behaviour

The moralistic concerns about the impact of welfare benefits on work incentives have grown stronger since 1997. Figure 5.4 shows that from 1983 to 1996, between 40 and 55 per cent of people thought that benefits for the unemployed were too low and caused hardship and between 35 and 28 per cent thought the contrary – that they were too high and discouraged work. After 1997, there is no clear trend, but it does appear that rather more people have taken the view that benefits are too generous and discourage work. This is supported by answers to other questions. In 2003, 39 per cent of people also felt that 'many people who get social security don't really deserve any help', an increase from 26 per cent in 1994. The next section explores views on this central issue more thoroughly.

Figure 5.4: 'Benefits for the unemployed are too high or too low', 1983–2003

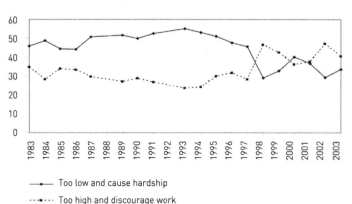

—•— Too low and cause hardship

···•··· Too high and discourage work

Welfare conditionality and reciprocity

The welfare state, in the minds of most people, is not simply an engine of redistribution from better to worse off and of universal public provision. Similarly, most people do not think of social justice simply in terms of redistribution. Instead views are more complex. containing only elements of traditional centre-left egalitarian concerns, and might be better summed up in terms of a strong sense of fairness shaped by a valuing of reciprocity or mutuality (Hedges, 2003; Mau, 2004; Dwyer, 2002). Such a view suggests that policies which reinforce reciprocity might provide a source of social cohesion and offer a way of building social capital in a virtuous dynamic (Putnam, 2000).

The data suggests people believe the welfare state should not be simply a funnel to direct resources downwards, but should also be a system of reciprocity, which provides good opportunities and support for those who participate, but does not waste resources on those who fail to do so. People should share a basic set of rights and responsibilities, which can mean recipients of welfare should abide by certain rules (Hedges, 2003; Dwyer, 2004). To gain public support, policies on welfare spending need to be linked to the way people behave, and in particular the extent to which they actively pursue paid work or other socially valued activities.

Table 5.3 looks beyond the able-bodied and childless to other groups. Substantial numbers, though not majorities, believe sick people or carers should not have benefits cut, regardless of whether they report to job centres, and very few people think they should suffer major benefit cuts. However, views with regards to single parents, whom (as we saw earlier) most people see as meriting supplements if they earn poverty wages, are more authoritarian. 79 per cent think their benefits should be affected in some way if they do not visit a job centre when asked.

Table 5.3: Benefit sanctions for those failing to visit the job centre, when asked, to talk about ways of finding work (2003, %)

Benefits for people failing to attend job centre interviews should be...

% who say	...not affected	...reduced a little	...reduced a lot	...stopped
Lone parent	17	38	14	27
Sick or disabled person	41	32	9	13
Carer on benefits	48	28	7	13

At present, Government policy seems to match opinion closely. Sanctions are currently being implemented for lone parents and for some (very small) groups of the sick and disabled, but are not anticipated for carers. Divisions arise in the public mind in relation to lone parents and the age which children should attain before mothers are expected to seek paid work. Table 5.4 shows the public's views on the 'duty' of different women to look for work. In all situations there was some reluctance to prescribe what the mother should do, but the most telling comparison is that between the single mother with a child under school age and the single mother with a child over school age. A significantly greater number of people (but not a majority) believe that a single parent in the latter situation has a responsibility to work. At present this is out of step with Government policy, and indeed the situation in most other European countries, where there are stronger requirements to attend work-focused interviews and to take work (Stanley and Lohde, 2004). The pattern of attitudes displays a division between an obligation to pursue paid work and freedom of choice on this issue for lone mothers with children of school age.

Table 5.4: What are the responsibilities of mothers in different circumstances?

	Duty to work	Duty to stay at home	Do as she chooses	Base
Single mother, child under school age	14.3	23.1	51.7	2900
Single mother, child at school age	45.3	4.0	43.7	2900
Married mother, child under school age	6.4	30.6	56.0	2900

Chapter 12 of this publication will examine this question in some more detail, including a discussion of the future of the contributory principle and National Insurance. The link between welfare payments and some form of valued social participation or reciprocity appears to act as a source of legitimacy for welfare spending. The next section considers the potential of a progressive tax system for tackling unfair income disparities.

Progressive taxation to reduce inequality?

The issue of tax and tax increases is addressed below. Willingness to pay and potentially to accept increases in taxes is essential to maintaining good public services, but the structure of the taxation system is also important, since it can be used to promote greater equality.

An important aspect of inequality, as highlighted in Chapter 2, is the growing gap between those at the top and the mass of the population. Even if we accept that it is difficult to gain widespread support for policies which will tax the better off to pay for benefits for those at the bottom, it may still be possible to enlist popular enthusiasm for progressive taxation, which may at least help contain trends towards greater market inequality. This could be done by directing tax cuts towards the poor, taking proportionately more from the better off, or by combining the two policies. There are difficulties with all these strategies.

The current structure of taxation does not fit neatly with current opinions. At present, the combined impact of all taxes, including direct taxation (on income) and indirect taxation (on spending), is roughly proportional across the greater part of the income distribution (see Chapter 2). Almost all income groups pay between 32 and 37 per cent of income in tax. Perversely, it is only in the very bottom tenth of the population that people pay a significantly greater percentage of their income in tax – 53 per cent (Hills, 2004). Table 5.5 shows that most people believe this to be unfair. In 2001, 11 per cent thought that those on higher incomes should pay a 'much larger' share of their incomes in tax, and over half thought they should pay a 'larger' amount. This suggests that, within limits and contrary to the current situation, people do agree in principle that the taxation system should be progressive.

Table 5.5: Share of income that should be paid in tax by those with high incomes, compared to those with low incomes, 1987–2001

	1987	1992	1999	2001
Much larger	9	20	21	11
Larger	55	58	55	55
Same	21	18	20	29
Smaller/much smaller	1	1	–	1
Base	1212	1066	804	2821

Interestingly though, the proportion endorsing a more steeply progressive tax system has fallen sharply since 1999. This is possibly in response to the perception that the tax policies of Labour in office have taken more from high earners, though we can't be clear. The period for which we have data does not include the 2002 announcement and 2003 implementation of an increase in National Insurance. Since this did not provoke an expression of concern in the media, it is unlikely to have produced a substantial shift in opinion. This may mean that support has fallen further, but an overall majority for a more progressive taxation is likely to continue. However, popular support for such a system does not make any policy change straightforward, for a number of reasons.

First, people have a poor intuitive understanding of the current distributive impact of taxation. They are surprised when they find out that under the current system different income groups pay broadly the same proportion of their income in tax. 8 per cent of those interviewed in the 2001 survey thought that those on higher incomes pay a much larger share of income in tax than low-income people, and 56 per cent thought they pay a larger share, roughly in line with what people thought they should pay as reported in Table 5.5.

Second, it is also unclear what people mean by 'those on higher incomes'. The threshold of 'high income' seems to be set in many people's minds at a level where the potential impact on inequalities is limited. The Fabian Society's Commission on Taxation in 2000 asked what people thought of the tax rates on those earning below £15,000, between £15,000 and £30,000, between £30,000 and £70,000, and above £70,000 a year (Fabian Society, 2000). When confronted with these figures only 29 per cent said the top band were taxed at too low a rate and only 11 per cent thought the £30,000 to £70,000 band were taxed too lightly. The largest proportion of the sample (40 and 46 per cent respectively) thought tax levels for these groups were about right. Recent qualitative work also found that it was difficult to get widespread support for tax increases on any group earning below £100,000 a year – tax as an engine of fairness was seen as only appropriate to the real 'fat cats' (Hedges, forthcoming).

Third, as in other areas, support for tax changes presented in general terms tends to become diluted the more precisely and concretely the issues are expressed. Many of those with above average incomes do not actually count themselves as falling into the group who should pay more. While 55 per cent of those interviewed thought high income people should pay more, when asked to assign themselves to high, middle or low income categories, only 4 per cent chose the former as against 53 per cent middle-income and 42 per cent low income. The vast majority of those who endorse progressive taxes think that someone else will actually pay them. This suggests that making the tax system more progressive, though not impossible, would be extremely difficult. Raising more revenue could be more challenging still.

Paying for social justice?

Altering the tax system, to make it more progressive without necessarily increasing overall tax revenue raised, is one way of reducing inequality. However, to pursue wider social justice objectives, extra resources may be required, for example to invest in education or, as is argued in the final chapter of this book, expanded childcare.

The vast majority of people do endorse tax-financed provision in most policy areas. Looking across different areas of the welfare state, there is still a widely held view that government intervention is necessary to solve a range of social problems, though people think this applies to a greater extent in some areas than others. Securing good public services for all is still regarded as a central task of government. In 2003, 87 per cent of those interviewed thought that government should be responsible for paying the cost of health care when someone is ill, when offered a choice between government, an employer or the person themselves and their family (Park *et al*, 2003). Only in pensions has there been any significant fall in levels for support for tax financed provision (Taylor-Gooby, 2004).

The main division lies not between those who favour lower overall tax and those endorsing the present situation. Rather, it is between those who favour the status quo and those who want spending and, by implication taxation, to be increased. Table 5.6 shows that the balance has shifted somewhat over time, with support for increased state provision rising up to 1991 and thereafter falling back. The fall in support has been quite significant between 1999 and 2003, possibly corresponding to the perception that Labour has already implemented increases.

Table 5.6: Attitudes to taxation and spending, 1983–2001

Government should:	1983	1987	1991	1995	1999	2003
Increase taxes and spend more on health, educational and social benefits	32	50	65	61	58	51
Keep tax and spending the same	54	42	29	31	35	38
Reduce tax and spending	9	3	3	5	4	6
Base	1761	2847	2918	1234	3143	3276

Reflecting the discussion above about what people see as priorities for government action, willingness to pay more tax still appears to be linked to specific services. There are clear differences in the services that are highly supported and in the amounts that people are willing to pay for them. The NHS, education and state pensions are consistently the highest priorities for extra resources. Figure 5.5 below shows that far fewer people would be willing to pay higher taxes for 'welfare benefits' directed specifically at the poor, such as income support and housing benefit. Indeed, throughout much of Labour's first term there was a fall in the percentage of people who would support such spending. This percentage has recovered since 2001, but to a level no higher than that of the mid-1990s. Such attitudes tend to track the economic cycle, as higher unemployment increases the legitimacy of welfare spending.

Figure 5.5: Views on public spending and taxation

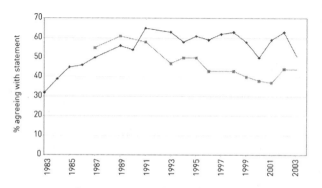

—●— increase taxes and spend more on health, education and social benefits
—■— spend more money on welfare benefits for the poor even if it means higher taxes

Endorsement of higher taxation, even in the case of highly popular services like the NHS, education and pensions, is more limited than an initial reading of the data might indicate, and currently appears to be falling. Above, we highlighted the extent to which people misunderstand the current system and how views of what 'higher income' means shape whether they themselves would actually wish to pay more in tax. In addition, and perhaps more fundamentally, levels of mistrust in government present a considerable barrier.

A striking finding from qualitative research is the high level of dissatisfaction with and mistrust of the state. Trust in government and politicians has remained consistently low during the past two decades. For example, no more than 23 per cent of those interviewed during the period 1983 to 2003 trust politicians and government to 'tell the truth' – only slightly above the figure for journalists and substantially below that for any other of the sixteen categories of people in public life reviewed (Hedges, forthcoming; Norris, 1998). At the same time, trust in government 'to put the needs of the nation above those of party' has roughly halved, from 39 to 20 per cent during the same period. The impression of an increasingly critical public is reinforced by evidence on dissatisfaction with specific services.

The latest BSA data shows that, even in the case of the most widely supported and highly valued service, the NHS, dissatisfaction is high and, until recently, rising. Dissatisfaction with this service reached a peak of 49 per cent in 1996. After 1997 the new government initially enjoyed a 'honeymoon' in public opinion and dissatisfaction fell to 33 per cent by 1999. Since then it has risen, and by 2002 was at 41 per cent but then fell to 37 per cent in 2003, indicating that increased spending may be feeding through into service improvements which are acknowledged in public perceptions (Taylor-Gooby and Hastie, 2002; Sefton, 2003). Other services follow a similar pattern.

The impression that public trust has to be earned is reinforced by data on service spending. Table 5.7 shows that in 2002 few people trusted government to spend taxpayers' money wisely 'a great deal'.

Table 5.7: Do you trust government [and the specified services] to spend taxpayers'/service consumers' money wisely in the interests of service users (2002, %)?

	A great deal	Quite a bit	Number of responses
Government	9	26	2663
Local council	9	32	2698
Police	10	46	2600
State pension	11	39	2572
Private pension	12	44	2550
NHS hospital	12	47	2688
Private hospital	16	49	2466
State school	16	54	2611
Fee-paying school	22	57	2384

The last six rows of the Table 5.7 deal with 'matched pairs' – areas where there are both state and private services which are to some extent alternatives, directed at similar needs. In general, the private alternative receives slightly higher support. The pattern of responses is consonant with the general direction of recent work in sociology. This argues that, as people become generally better informed about the shortcomings of experts and officials, and more self-confident in their judgements, they are less inclined to trust them (Giddens, 1994; Beck *et al,* 2003). Low trust may also reflect what could be labelled a sense of 'welfare fatalism'. People want better public services and support in principle the notion of greater equality of opportunity, reduced inequality and a strong social minimum, but are sceptical of the ability of government to make progress on these ideals (White, 2003). They also have a relatively low opinion of politicians and are much more inclined to call the services offered by government into question.

Childcare: an emerging priority?

One area of public spending on which a link to any net increase in tax has not been tested is childcare. This is an issue intricately tied up with a desire to improve women's life chances and achieve a higher degree of gender equality. Enhancing opportunities for women has been a strong theme of recent public debate. Social and economic change in this area has been profound in recent decades. The big increase in overall levels of women's involvement in paid work occurred during the three decades from the 1950s to the 1980s and since then participation has increased only slightly (from 71 per cent in 1990 to 72 per cent by 2001). However, the rates of participation in paid work for mothers with a child under five have changed more rapidly. The employment rate for mothers with children under five has increased from 48 per cent in 1990 to 57 per cent by 2001 (Dench *et al,* 2002 quoted in Crompton *et al,* 2003).

Public attitudes have shifted too. The proportion believing that a woman's primary role is to stay at home and provide domestic support for a male bread-winner has halved during the past fifteen years from about a third to a sixth. Substantial majorities now believe that mothers can establish warm relationships with their children as well as working, and that family life is not undermined when women are in full-time paid work. This decline of traditionalism is slightly tempered by the widely-held view that women should interrupt careers or work part time when children are under school age (Crompton *et al,* 2003). Many people accept that women should seek work, but tend to see domestic duties and particularly care of young children as primarily the responsibility of mothers, rather than fathers. Public attitudes assume a high degree of gender equality in the public sphere of paid work, but not in the private sphere of the home, with sombre implications for the 'double burden' on some women.

As Table 5.8 shows, it is only when children are under school age that significant numbers of people think their mothers should stay at home. Asking just mothers this question produces very similar results. 70 per cent of mothers think that women should return to work after their youngest child starts school; 57 per cent think they should work full time again when their children leave home.

Table 5.8: Should women work in different circumstances? (2003)

Should women work outside the home full-time, part-time or not at all in these circumstances?

	Full -time	Part -time	Stay home	Can't choose	Base
...after marrying and before you had children	78.2	7.7	1.3	10.6	1960
...when a child was under school age	3.4	34.1	48.1	11.7	1960
...after the youngest child started school	15.7	65.6	5.4	11.7	1960
...after the children left home	62.1	9.2	1.3	15.1	1960

Despite higher demand among women themselves to work, gender inequalities remain persistent. Furthermore, issues such as stress at work, particularly for middle-class women, are increasing in prevalence (Compton *et al*, 2003). Demand for more equal female participation in the labour market, and for a better work-life balance, raises questions about the availability, or otherwise, of high quality childcare. It also raises the issue of whether people think that government should contribute to the cost of provision, assuming that women are still expected to carry the lion's share of domestic responsibilities. Table 5.9 shows that in 2002 there were high levels of support for government help with the costs of childcare. This view holds for all groups of mothers shown, though it is weaker in the case of married mothers where the child is under school age. It is only with regards to single mothers with children of school age that we can track attitudes over time. Contrary to the trends in many other areas, there has been a growth in the percentage of people who think the government should help meet the costs. In 1994 only 52 per cent agreed with the statement. This rose to 57 per cent by 1995 and reached 62 per cent in 1998, since when it has been roughly constant.

It is striking that the earlier question (Table 5.3), which asked about sanctions for lone mothers as benefit recipients who do not attend work-focused interviews, produced a punitive response. Focus on single parents as mothers and providers (Table 5.9) generates more positive support. The greater public backing when a role in which a parent provides care for children, rather than one in which she is presented as a passive beneficiary, is emphasised, and adds to the evidence that welfare redistribution is more strongly endorsed when it is seen to go to those making a reciprocal contribution.

Table 5.9: When should government provide money to help with the costs of childcare? (2002)

Government should provide money to help with childcare for...

	Single mother, child under school age	Single mother, child at school age	Married mother, child under school age
Agree	73.2	60.7	49.8
Neither agree nor disagree	11.4	17.1	18.9
Disagree	10.8	16.2	24.8
Base	1614	1614	1614

Current policies are not successful in enabling people to achieve satisfactory work-life balance, and the impact is not confined to women. At the same time, endorsement for provision that enables women to participate in employment while also sustaining childcare is strong. The approach has the advantage that it combines the promotion of equal opportunities with meeting the needs of children, two themes both strongly supported in public opinion. This may well be an area in which tax increases would be tolerated, provided that they were linked to ensuring the availability of reliable and affordable daycare. It is noteworthy that improving the quality of life for children has been one of the strongest themes in progressive discussion of welfare policy across Europe (Esping-Andersen *et al*, 2002: ch 2).

Conclusion: three challenges

Survey evidence shows that the core social justice ideals of a social minimum, equal opportunities and the fair distribution of rewards in society, are shared by the majority of UK citizens, at least at the level of principle, although attaining the social minimum is often valued more than equality. Most people are concerned at inequalities and poverty and would like to see them reduced, think that the better off should pay more in tax and oppose regressive taxation of the worse off. They value the key public services highly and want them improved, and want women to have good opportunities in paid work and not to be solely responsible for childcare.

However, widely-held patterns of belief impose limitations on the relevance of these attitudes to practical support for the centre-left's political programme. Most people still believe that public services offer low standards and represent poor value for money. While they support progressive taxation in principle, they set the threshold at which higher taxes should bite comfortably above their own income, typically at over £100,000 a year. There are long-standing moralistic concerns about the impact of welfare benefits on the poor. Those with children are more deserving of help, but pursuit of paid work is also valued. While equal opportunities are supported in principle, many still believe that the mother should be the main carer for young children. So government faces three key challenges.

Changing views: challenging fatalism

One key challenge for government is to consider where it can lead and shape public opinion. Subservience to prevailing attitudes can be unduly limiting and dangerous. Unduly limiting because it is a government responsibility to promote progressive reform, and this bears particularly heavily on the centre-left. Dangerous because by accommodating public opinion government may actually strengthen attitudes which prevent it from reaching its policy goals. There is some evidence that policy can lead opinion, for example by presenting unemployed people as active, by stressing training and the pursuit of paid work or by emphasising the social contribution made by single parents and carers. The dilemma between following and leading opinion has been particularly acute since 1997. In much of the data presented there are clear trends in attitudes with a break after 1997 reflecting expectations of or assumptions about the impact of the policies of the new government.

Some of these attitude shifts may not sustain progressive policy-making. For example, a decreasing number of people think that levels of child poverty remain high. This could reflect public recognition that there have been some reductions in poverty, but may undermine attempts to reduce poverty further. The increase in the number of people who consider unemployment benefits too generous may be seen as positive and a shift in public attitudes towards welfare more in tune with the government's emphasis on rights and responsibilities. However, this may make it more difficult to press for greater fairness in the distribution of rewards in society. The proportion of people who think government should redistribute incomes from the better off to the worse off has fallen substantially since 1994, and this presents a challenge to government policy.

A further issue concerns the extent of public misinformation. The evidence on trust in politicians and government indicates that the public is always likely to view any evidence from this source as tainted. However, the same material shows that more independent experts (scientists, academics, the judiciary, civil servants) enjoy much higher (and in fact rising) levels of public confidence. A continued emphasis on the independence of agencies and the transparency of the procedures by which data is gathered on issues like tax-incidence, and the costs of services for different groups, together with reiteration of some of the widely misunderstood points made in this chapter, would, over time, improve the quality of public debate.

Continuing to building reciprocity into the welfare system
Redistribution from rich to poor is supported by people, but people's views on welfare are complex. Majorities want the welfare system to support a society where the needs of groups such as children are especially valued. Able-bodied adults are expected to contribute, typically through paid work or through the care of young children or other

dependents, and are to be supported in doing so. Government policies are expected to ensure that rewards and opportunities in employment are fair and the availability of childcare is clearly important here. Benefits are valued to the extent that they are seen to fit within this framework, not because they simply redistribute resources indiscriminately to those with low incomes.

Support appears to be much stronger in relation to some groups than others. The extent of need is relevant and those with children are more likely to be thought deserving. At the same time, groups which are seen to be contributing to society in some way, rather than taking a passive role as recipients of welfare, are also likely to be favoured. Where there is no sense of reciprocity, public support is more limited. In other words, there are indications in the data that, while most people support the four principles outlined at the beginning of the chapter, in practice they may add a fifth, a principle of reciprocity or entitlement through social contribution.

The pattern of attitudes is complex, so policy which is to be acceptable to the mass public must also reflect this complexity. It must include elements of progressivism, to contain the trends to ever greater inequalities. However, specific benefits must be directed to favoured need groups, pre-eminently children and their mothers. The importance of work, or perhaps a wider sense of 'participation', in most people's minds must be respected, which implies a wide range of supportive measures to help people into work, top-ups for low earners, schemes to address work-life balance issues and a degree of sanctioning for able-bodied people who fail to take jobs when these are available. Rewards for paid work and promotion opportunities must also be fair, so that the gender gap in pay is seriously engaged.

Tax and trust

The Government is faced with a dilemma on taxation. On the one hand improvements in services which the public desire cannot be delivered without higher taxes. More progressive taxation is necessary to address the inequalities which are also a cause for public concern, and will contribute to a centre-left programme. On the other hand, while more people endorse higher taxes in principle (provided they are spent on valued services), they are much less willing to pay them or to accept a more progressive system of taxation in practice.

The material discussed in this paper indicates that the case for higher taxation cannot be made through an appeal to social justice as redistribution from better off to worse off. People are much more likely to accept higher taxes if they are convinced that these will pay for improvements in highly valued services, and if they believe that the emerging welfare system respects the principles of reciprocity and entitlement which are widely held. From this perspective those on the receiving end of state welfare can be seen as reconnected with society through the contribution they make in terms of care or pursuit of work. Practical policies for implementing social justice depend on a remoralising of provision for the poor in line with the principles embodied in popular conceptions of social justice at the overall societal level. The work of writers as diverse as Fukuyama (1995), Galbraith (1992), Putnam (2000), Sennett (1998), Dayton-Johnson (2001), Le Grand (2003), Goodhart (2004) and Alesina and Glaeser (2004) points to a decline in the moral bases for social cohesion as a central problem in an increasingly diverse and individualised society. Examination of the way people think about social justice in everyday life offers a possibility for developing policies which engage with these issues and allow the centre-left to develop a feasible programme that advances fairness.

References

Alesina A and Glaeser E (2004) *Fighting Poverty in the US and Europe* Oxford: Oxford University Press

Beck U, Bonss W and Lau C (2003) 'The theory of reflexive modernity' in *Theory, Culture and Society* 20 (2)

Blekesaune M and Quadagno J (2003) 'Public attitudes towards welfare state policies: a comparative analysis of 24 nations' in *European Sociological Review* 19 (5), Oxford: Oxford University Press

Bromley C (2003) 'Has Britain become immune to inequality?' in Park A, Curtice J, Thomson K, Bromley C and Phillips M (eds) *British Social Attitudes, The 20th Report* London: Sage Publications

Crompton R, Brockmann M and Wiggins R (2003) 'A woman's place…Employment and family life for men and women' in Park A, Curtice J, Thomson K, Bromley C and Phillips M (eds) *British Social Attitudes, The 20th Report* London: Sage Publications

Dayton-Johnson J (2001) *Social Cohesion and Economic Prosperity* Toronto: James Lorimer

Dench S, Ashton J, Evans C, Meeager N, Williams M, Willison R (2002) *Key Indicators of Womens' Position in Britain* London: TSO

Department of Social Security (DSS) (2000) *The Changing Welfare State: Social Security Spending,* London: TSO

Dwyer P (2002) 'Making sense of social citizenship' *Critical Social Policy* 22 (3), London: Sage

Dwyer P (2004) *Understanding Social Citizenship* London: Policy Press

Esping-Andersen G (1990) *The Three Worlds of Welfare Capitalism* Cambridge: Princeton University Press

Esping-Andersen G, Gallie D, Hemerijck A and Myles J (2002) *Why We Need a New Welfare State* Oxford: Oxford University Press

Fabian Society (2000) *Commission on Taxation and Citizenship* London: Fabian Society

Ferrera, M (1996) 'The southern model of welfare in Europe' *Journal of European Social Policy* 6 (1), London: Sage

130   Social Justice

Fukuyama F (1995) *Trust* London: Penguin Books

Galbraith J (1992) *The Culture of Contentment* London: Sinclair-Stevenson

Giddens A (1994) *Beyond Left and Right* Cambridge: Polity Press

Goodhart D (2004) 'Is Britain too diverse?' *Prospect* February 2004,

Hedges A (2003) *Perceptions of Redistribution* London: CASE and NatCen

Hedges A (forthcoming) *Perceptions of Redistribution* London: CASE and NatCen

Hills J and Lelkes O (1998) 'Social Security, Selective Universalism and Patchwork Redistribution' in Jowell R, Curtice J, Park A, Brook L, Thomson K and Bryson C (eds) (1998) *British Social Attitudes, 15th Report* Aldershot: Ashgate Publishing

Hills J (2004) *Inequality and the State* Oxford: Oxford University Press

Le Grand J (2003) *Motivation, Agency and Public Policy* Oxford: Oxford University Press.

Luxembourg Income Study (2004) *Key Figures*, Available at www.lisproject.org

Mau S (2004) 'Welfare Regimes and the Norms of Reciprocal Exchange' *Current Sociology* 52, London: Sage

MORI (2004) *MORI Political Monitor: long-term trends, the most important issues facing Britain today* Available at www.MORI.com/polls/trends/issues.shtml#1994

Norris P (ed) (1998) *Critical Citizens: Global Support For Democratic Governance* Oxford: Oxford University Press

NPI/Rowntree (2002) *Responsibility for All: A National Social Inclusion Strategy* London: NPI. Available at www.poverty.org.uk/reports/rfa.htm

Park A, Curtice J, Thomson K, Jarvis L and Bromley C (eds) (2001) *British Social Attitudes, the 18th report* London: Sage Publications

Park A, Curtice J, Thomson K, Jarvis L and Bromley C (eds) (2003) *British Social Attitudes, the 20th report* London: Sage Publications

Putnam R (2000) *Bowling Alone* New York: Simon and Schuster

Sefton T (2003) 'What we want from the welfare state' in Park A, Curtice J, Thomson K, Bromley C and Phillips M (eds) *British Social Attitudes, The 20th Report* London: Sage Publications

Sennett R (1998) *The Corrosion of Character* New York: W W Norton

Stanley K and Lohde L (2004) *Sanctions and Sweeteners* London: ippr

Taylor-Gooby P (2004) 'New Social Risks in Post-Industrial Society' *International Social Security Review* (57) 3, Oxford: Blackwells

Taylor-Gooby P and Hastie C (2002) 'Support for state spending' in Park A, Curtice J, Thomson K, Bromley C and Phillips M (eds) *British Social Attitudes, the 19th report* London: Sage Publications

White S (2003) *The Civic Minimum* Oxford: Oxford University Press

Section 2

Themes and Issues

Social Justice in a Shrinking World

David Mepham

The report of the Commission on Social Justice in 1994 focused its analysis and policy prescriptions almost entirely on the United Kingdom (CSJ, 1994). It dealt briefly with the impact of international economic developments on the capacity of the UK Government to pursue strategies for social justice at home. But its terms of reference did not include issues of justice beyond the UK's shores.

Today an exclusively national interpretation of social justice is neither morally defensible nor politically or intellectually tenable. It is not morally defensible because the extent of poverty and human suffering across the world demands a comprehensive moral response. There is now a growing body of political philosophy that addresses 'global justice' and that considers the responsibilities of citizens and governments in developed countries towards poorer parts of the world or towards people in other countries whose human rights are abused. It is not politically or intellectually tenable because global interdependence and interconnectedness are reducing the distinction between domestic and international policy and increasing the number of issues that require a genuinely global response.

This chapter will seek to illustrate how citizens in developed countries like the UK are affected more extensively than ever before by events and processes taking place elsewhere. The traditional narrow interpretation and pursuit of the national interest are therefore increasingly obsolete. 'Our' interests – 'our' prosperity and security for example – are now dependent on achieving greater prosperity and security for others and on greater international cooperation to manage global problems.

The chapter will briefly assess the record of the UK Government on some of these issues since 1997; the significant progress that has been made but also those issues on which the Government's performance has been more modest or disappointing. Finally, the chapter will outline what a progressive agenda for global social justice should look like.

Justice beyond borders

The Peace of Westphalia, which ended the Thirty Years War in 1648, is conventionally taken to mark the beginning of the modern international system.[1] This system was based on sovereign states, each with exclusive authority within its own geographic boundaries. While the Westphalia model was a political construct rather than a precise description of the evolving international order, the impact of this model over the last three and a half centuries has been profound. It continues to influence thinking on international politics to this day.

The Westphalia model has two particularly significant features relevant to the focus of this chapter. First, the principle of state sovereignty has been linked generally to a presumption of 'non-interference' by states in the internal affairs of other states.[2] Rules and institutions could be developed to regulate international relations, but these rules applied to states and not to individuals, and to the external not the internal behaviour of those states. Second, it suggests a sharp distinction between domestic policy (where states are sovereign) and international policy (where there is no single source of sovereign authority).

Throughout the 20th century, especially since 1945, the principles of state sovereignty and non-interference have faced a serious challenge, not least with the development of international human rights and humanitarian law. Before the Second World War, only states had rights in international law. With the Universal Declaration of Human Rights of 1948, the rights of individuals received international legal recognition for the first time. Over the subsequent five decades, there has been a massive expansion of international human rights treaties, setting out the civil, cultural, economic, political and social

1 It would be more accurate perhaps to describe it as the beginning of the modern European state system given the very different political structures existing in other parts of the world. However, as a consequence of European colonialism, subsequent decolonisation and other developments, a system of sovereign states has now become a worldwide phenomenon.

2 In practice, the non-intervention norm of the Westphalia system has been very frequently overridden over the last three and a half centuries, not least through massive intervention by colonial powers. However, following the ending of European colonialism, many of the newly independent states of Africa and Asia have strongly endorsed the norm of non-intervention.

rights to which all human beings are entitled, regardless of race, creed, gender or age. In societies across the world, individuals and groups have adopted the language of rights to assert their claim to fair treatment, decent living conditions and greater justice. As Ignatieff says: 'Human rights has gone global not because it serves the interests of the powerful but primarily because it has advanced the interests of the powerless.' (Ignatieff, 2001). The international human rights framework therefore provides a strong intellectual basis for a concept of global justice (see propositions one and two below).

But there remains a clear tension or ambiguity between these universal human rights and state sovereignty, a tension that is reflected within the UN Charter itself. While Articles 2.1 and 2.7 define state sovereignty in terms of inviolability and non-interference, various other parts of the Charter call on states to uphold human rights.

For most of the last century, the alleged distinction between domestic and international policy has been reflected in the division between political theory and the new academic discipline of international relations (Brown, 2002). Issues of justice and moral obligation were viewed as central to the former but of questionable value or feasibility in respect of the latter. While this division has been seriously questioned over recent decades, considerations of justice at the global level clearly raise very specific and highly complex issues:

> The distinguishing feature of international political theory is that it deals with the implications of a world in which there are multiple political units, each claiming to be, in some sense, autonomous. A political arrangement of the world's surface based on sovereignty rests on processes of inclusion and exclusion which may well cut across considerations of rights and justice. (Brown, 2002).

While most political philosophers would now argue that we have moral obligations towards people living elsewhere in the world, few assert that these obligations are the same as those we owe to members of our 'own' society. A particularly clear example of this is the work of the late John Rawls. His most famous book *A Theory of Justice* makes no mention what-soever of wealth inequalities between different societies (Rawls, 1971). Rawls' method – 'the veil of ignorance' – is to seek justice by asking what principles people would choose in a so-called 'original position', where they had no idea of the place they would occupy in that society, for example whether they would be rich or poor. He suggests that under these conditions people would choose an equal distribution of basic liberties and would accept economic inequalities where these worked to the benefit of the least advantaged in society. Applied internationally, if people were ignorant of which society they belonged to, this approach would have enormously radical implications. However, Rawls chooses to relate his theory to a single developed society and to the principles of distributive justice within it.

Issues of transnational justice are addressed, albeit selectively, in Rawls' later work *The Law of Peoples*. In this book, Rawls argues that:

> *Well-ordered peoples have a duty to assist burdened societies, that is, those societies that lack the political and cultural traditions, the human capital and know-how, and, often, the material and techno-logical resources needed to be well-ordered.* (Rawls, 1999)

But he is less than specific about the extent of those duties. He places emphasis on the need for societies to develop a suitable culture, seen as essential for effective development in the long term. But he has very little to say about the plight of those hundreds of millions of people worldwide living in absolute poverty today. And he rejects any notion of global distributive justice. He argues that: 'No people organised by its government is prepared to count, as a first principle, the benefits for another people as outweighing the hardships imposed on itself.' (Rawls, 1999) For Rawls, obligations towards 'insiders' take clear priority over obligations to 'outsiders'.

Philosophers like Michael Walzer and David Miller agree with Rawls that there is an important distinction between insiders and outsiders and that it is not necessarily unjust to give greater attention to the interests and needs of one's co-nationals (Walzer, 1983; Miller, 2000). Walzer's and Miller's view is based on the advantages that are seen to result from stable and liberal political communities. They do not dispute – and it is not prejudicial to their argument – that state borders are essentially arbitrary products of war and conquest. However, like Rawls, they assert that distributive justice can only really occur where there is a well-developed sense of community and that this is missing at the global level.

Miller has additional objections to theories of global distributive justice. He argues that there is a complex relationship between national self-determination and global justice, and that there are strong grounds for valuing the former very highly, especially when these institutions of self-determination incorporate deliberative democracy, protection for civil and political rights and a guaranteed right to emigrate (Miller, 2000).

But Miller does believe that there are moral obligations to promote justice beyond national borders. He suggests three. First, the obligation 'to respect the basic human rights of people everywhere'. Second, he argues that wealthier individuals and societies should 'refrain from exploiting those who are vulnerable to their actions'. Third, he asserts that all political communities should 'have the opportunity to determine their own future and practise justice among their members' (Miller, 2000).

Miller's three principles have potentially far-reaching implications for resource distribution and for our understanding of moral obligation, and they set clear limits to national self-determination. As he puts it, if the only way to have an extensive national health service in our own country is 'by exploiting the members of another political community – for instance, through exploitative trading relationships... then it is wrong to do so' (Miller, 2000). Miller's arguments provide a clear foundation for moral obligations beyond national borders, including respect for human rights, the requirement to end exploitative practices and support for accountable government (see propositions two, three and four below).

The views of Rawls, Miller and Walzer – and the distinction they draw between insiders and outsiders – has been challenged in different ways by the philosophers Brian Barry, Charles Beitz and Thomas Pogge. Barry questions the fictional social contract at the heart of Rawls' *A Theory of Justice*, a model which necessarily takes no account of those whose interests are not represented at the 'original position', including foreigners and future generations. Beitz and Pogge dispute the thesis of the self-contained society, arguing that global interdependence has invalidated this premise and that the world should be treated as though it were a single society. They call for the core principles set out in *A Theory of Justice* to be applied globally. Beitz and Pogge also point out the essential arbitrariness of the existing global distribution of resources. This latter argument has considerable force. However, the claim that the globe can be considered as a single society – comparable to existing national societies and with similar feelings of obligation and allegiance – is harder to sustain (Barry, 1973; Beitz, 1979; Beitz, 2000; Pogge, 2002).

The controversial philosopher Peter Singer also rejects the insider/outsider distinction and puts forward a radical utilitarian theory of global justice. His key principle is that: 'If it is in our power to prevent something bad from happening, without thereby sacrificing anything of comparable moral importance, we ought morally to do it.' (Singer, 1972) This argument has two further components; that distance is unimportant (the suffering of a child in Bangladesh counts for as much as the suffering of a child in England, for example), and that this moral obligation applies to individuals as well as to their governments.

It should be noted that Singer does not argue for the achievement of global equality, but rather for action to end avoidable human suffering worldwide. While an attempt to implement Singer's principle of global justice would involve substantial resource transfers from the world's rich to the world's poor, these resource transfers would not, according to more recent versions of his principle, be unlimited (they would end at the point where adequate provision had been made to prevent human suffering).

There are three specific criticisms that can be made of Singer's approach. First, he says very little about how development occurs in poor countries. Over the years, large amounts of development aid have been allocated to poor countries, but its impact on poverty reduction has been limited. Reducing poverty is clearly more complicated than writing a large cheque. Second, if the goal is to end human suffering, a utilitarian will be indifferent as to how this goal is achieved. Questions of process, autonomy and sustainability are largely absent from Singer's argument. Third, the alleged irrelevance of distance can be challenged. People tend to have a stronger sense of moral duty towards those nearest and dearest to them than they do towards distant strangers.

This is not to argue that we don't have very extensive moral responsibilities towards humanity as a whole – Singer is right about that – but it does suggest that a single utilitarian calculus may be an inadequate guide in helping to judge the appropriate balance between these conflicting responsibilities (Brown, 2002).

Another perspective on issues of global justice is provided by 'cosmopolitan' theorists like David Held, Allen Buchanan and Mathias Koenig-Archibugi. They argue that globalisation is transforming the world at a rapid pace and that effective political power can no longer be automatically assumed to rest with national governments:

> We no longer live, if we ever did, in a world of discrete national communities. Instead, we live in a world of 'overlapping communities of fate' where the trajectories of countries are deeply enmeshed with each other. (Held 2004: x)

Held *et al* reject the notion that our moral obligations should be limited by geographical boundaries. Their approach is squarely in the tradition of moral universalism and egalitarian individualism, as set out in the Universal Declaration of Human Rights (1948). They call for what they term 'cosmopolitan democracy', a programme to reform and democratise the existing structures of global governance and to build new global democratic institutions better able to tackle global issues, such as HIV/AIDS, climate change and migration (Held, 2003; Held, 2004; Buchanan, 2000; Koenig-Archibugi, 2004).

The most common criticism of this approach concerns its feasibility: whether the conditions really exist for the emergence of global democracy. In the short term, the answer to this is clearly no. But this easy dismissal ignores two critical points. First, the cosmopolitans are not proposing an end to the nation-state; rather they envisage global demo-cratic institutions working together with nation-states in a new multi-layered framework of global governance (Held, 2004). Second, the cosmopolitans are engaged in a long-term, gradualist project. This will take a long time, but there is a strong case now for trying to build greater accountability at the global level.

What the work of Held *et al* does provide is a sharp critique of the existing global distribution of wealth and a powerful foundation for global distributive justice. If many of 'our' actions impact on others beyond our shores, including on the distribution of income within and between countries, it is hard to argue that issues of distributive justice should be confined within national borders.

This can be illustrated well by reference to the environment. Current patterns of production and consumption are imposing huge strains on the global environment and it is the world's developed countries that are making the biggest contribution to these global environmental problems. If all of the world's six billion people were to consume at the level of the world's richest people, the consequences would be ecologi-cally disastrous. On what moral basis, therefore, do the world's richest people defend a lifestyle for themselves that would be impossible to extend to others and which imposes huge costs on people elsewhere? A moral response to this question surely implies a shift to more sustain-able patterns of production and consumption globally and a commit-ment to a fairer distribution of global wealth (see propositions five and six below).

Global social justice – six propositions

As the discussion above illustrates, there is a huge amount of thinking and analysis on issues of global justice. Drawing on the best of this work, it is possible to identify some core propositions relevant to the consideration of justice beyond the borders of states. These propositions are particularly focused on defining the moral responsibilities of the world's rich towards the world's poor and the responsibilities of those who live in relatively free societies towards those living under authoritarian regimes or whose human rights are abused.

1. There are universal human rights – a set of basic entitlements that should be available to all human beings everywhere.
2. There is a moral obligation on the world's governments to help all of the world's people secure their basic human rights, drawing on the international human rights framework.
3. There is a moral obligation on the world's richer countries and people to end or curb those policies – unfair trade rules or excessive greenhouse gas emissions – that exploit, systematically disadvantage, or worsen the living conditions and life chances of poor people.
4. There is a moral obligation on the world's richer countries and people to help poor people in poor countries to secure accountable and effective political institutions.
5. The existing allocation of global resources is morally unjust and unsustainable; a more equal distribution of the world's wealth should be promoted as a moral necessity.
6. There is a moral obligation to pursue a form of economic development in the present that does not compromise the ability of others to meet their needs, including future generations.

These propositions will be drawn on throughout the remainder of this chapter, both in the assessment of Labour's record and in thinking through a progressive agenda for global social justice.

Global interdependence

Alongside these moral concerns, there are a host of prudential reasons why global poverty, human misery, state failure, conflict and the violation of human rights in other countries should matter to 'us' – that is, to people living in wealthy societies like the UK. Growing global interdependence and interconnectedness are shrinking the world and increasing the extent to which we affect, and are affected by, events and processes in poor countries.

A clear example of this is the link between poverty, state failure and terrorism. 11 September 2001 demonstrated in the most dramatic fashion possible that no country, however prosperous, powerful or apparently invulnerable, can remain isolated from the impact of insecurity and state failure elsewhere. Afghanistan – a quintessential 'failed state' – provided a convenient base and training ground for Al-Qaeda. In many other poor countries, terrorist groups have taken advantage of porous borders and weak regulatory and law enforcement systems to move men, weapons and finance around the globe (Rice, 2003).

Of course, it is true that the particular individuals involved in organising these attacks were not themselves poor. But political extremists are adept at playing on poverty and grievance, particularly amongst the young. Al-Qaeda appears to have been very successful, for example, in drawing support from disaffected young people in the Middle East and in Asia (Burke, 2003). Too often this underlying political context for terrorism and extremism is overlooked:

> *If there is one fact above all that western informed opinion has to take into account it is what can be called 'global rancour': the enormous, and ever expanding, divide between the developed west, and the large areas of crisis and anger that surround it – in the Middle East, Latin America, Africa and Asia.* (Halliday, 2004)

The huge culpability of successive western governments in creating the conditions for some of today's terrorist violence is also often conveniently forgotten. The US has a particular responsibility for financing and supporting Islamic movements during the Cold War period and in helping to create Al-Qaeda (Halliday, 2002). This was a deeply immoral and foolish policy, and its consequences are likely to be with us for many years to come.

There are important links, too, between poverty and civil war. Civil wars reflect not just a problem for development, but a failure of development. As the World Bank has shown, the risk of civil war is fifteen times higher in low-income countries than in wealthier countries (World Bank, 2003). These conflicts have devastating human and developmental consequences for people living in these countries and in surrounding states. But they have impacts on developed countries too. Developed countries will often be expected to provide substantial humanitarian assistance or even to intervene militarily in response to the crises brought on by violent conflict. There is an important connection, too, between poverty, conflict and large scale migration flows.

Civil wars create territory outside the control of any recognised government, facilitating illicit arms trafficking, the trade in hard drugs and international crime. An estimated 95 per cent of the global production of these drugs occurs in countries with civil wars and the major supply routes run through conflict territories, including 70 to 90 per cent of the heroin found in European markets (World Bank, 2003).

And there are critical linkages between human displacement and the spread of disease. Global efforts to eradicate malaria have been considerably hampered by civil war. The same is true for HIV/AIDS. Those uprooted by war are at greater risk of contracting the disease, and the social dislocation brought on by war is an important means by which the disease is spread (World Bank, 2003). Our global interdependence is also particularly acute in respect of the natural environment.

These examples of our global interdependence provide an additional and very powerful reason for strengthening efforts to combat poverty, state failure and conflict in the poorest parts of the world.

The 'ethical dimension' to UK foreign policy

The UK Labour Government, first elected in 1997, asserted that moral concerns would form an important part of its approach to global politics. In May 1997, the then foreign secretary, Robin Cook, set out a new mission statement for the Foreign Office and the Government. Amongst other objectives, the mission statement asserted that the UK would 'work through international forums and bilateral relationships to spread the values of human rights, civil liberties and democracy' (Cook, 1997a). In introducing the statement, Robin Cook famously said that UK foreign policy would have 'an ethical dimension' and that the Labour Government would 'put human rights at the heart of foreign policy' (Cook, 1997b). Later that year, the Government published a White Paper on International Development that asserted that the UK had a 'moral duty' to reach out to the world's poor and needy and to try to create 'a more just world' (DfID, 1997).

Though subsequently much derided and misrepresented, these commitments to global ethics were important. Even if the term 'ethical dimension' is no longer used, over eight years the Government has retained a stated commitment to global social justice and international human rights. This rhetorical commitment has been matched by some significant shifts in policy.

Since 1997, the Government has hugely strengthened the UK's efforts to combat poverty in the world's poorest countries. The Government has increased the aid budget significantly: up from the 0.26 per cent of GNP it inherited in 1997 to 0.47 per cent by 2007/8. And it has set a date for reaching the UN 0.7 per cent aid/GNP target. As importantly, it has worked on improving aid quality, by untying aid and using it to help countries undertake social, economic and governance reform. The Government has played a leading role internationally in pushing for debt relief and has taken some steps to help make the global trading system fairer for poorer countries.

On civil and political rights the Government has been a strong supporter of tougher action to combat torture and the use of the death penalty internationally. It has allocated substantial resources for justice and penal reform in poorer countries and backed initiatives to support freedom of association and expression, including a free press and media.

The UK has been a strong advocate of the International Criminal Court (ICC), which came into force in July 2002. It has contributed significantly to the work of the United Nations, including its peace-keeping and development activities, and supported a stronger role for the European Union and the Commonwealth on development, human rights and global justice issues.

More controversially, over the last eight years UK troops have been fairly regularly deployed overseas on ostensibly 'humanitarian' missions. In the cases of Sierra Leone and Kosovo, human rights concerns were a dominant motive for UK intervention and this brought some improvements in the human rights situations there. In Afghanistan the intervention was not motivated by human rights concerns. While the overthrow of the Taliban has brought significant dividends to some Afghans, the human rights situation in much of the rest of the country remains very poor.

For its policies on many of these issues, the Government deserves credit. Its actions in these areas are consistent with the moral propositions set out in this chapter. There are other areas, however, where UK international policy has fallen short of the moral claims made in 1997, including policy towards Iraq, the detention of terrorist suspects in Guantanamo Bay, arms exports, and the promotion of human rights towards particular countries.

For human rights advocates, the arguments for and against military action in Iraq were always complex and finely balanced. Saddam Hussein's human rights record was appalling and his removal and capture are very welcome developments, as are the recent elections in Iraq. But the UK Government's support for military action against Iraq in the absence of a second UN resolution seriously undermined its claim to be a supporter of international law and the UN. To invest unprecedented diplomatic energy and political capital in the attempt to secure a second UN resolution and then to dismiss its necessity when support for that resolution could not be secured was not a tenable position. The case for war has been further undermined by the failure to uncover any weapons of mass destruction in Iraq following the removal of Saddam Hussein's regime (the declared justification for war), by the shocking lack of planning for the post-Saddam period and by the pervasiveness of violence and terrorism in Iraq under the US and UK occupation.

UK support for war in Iraq was driven less by a concern for human rights, international law or the authority of the UN, and much more by a calculation that it would be dangerous for the world if the US were to take action unilaterally. The UK Government's decision to align itself very closely with the foreign policy of the Bush administration has had wider implications for its human rights policy. For example, the UK has muted its criticism of US policy in Guantanamo Bay, where large numbers of detainees have been held in clear violation of international humanitarian law.

Despite some strengthening of its arms export controls, the UK Government's overall record on arms exports is also disappointing. Since 1997, the UK Government has licensed arms and military equipment to a large number of countries guilty of violating human rights (Mepham and Eavis, 2002).

In addition, the UK Government has been inconsistent in its policy towards rights-violating governments. Where there are no major trade or other interests at stake, the UK has been prepared to be quite tough on human rights issues, for example with Zimbabwe over recent years. While responding to rights abuses in more powerful states is obviously much more complex – with other issues coming into play – the Government has not given adequate priority to human rights in its relations with countries like Russia, Saudi Arabia or China. On these and other issues, UK policy has been out of step with the kind of moral propositions set out in this chapter.

A progressive agenda for global social justice

Drawing on the discussion of moral principles, the prudential arguments and our brief assessment of Labour's record, it is now possible to identify some essential building blocks of a progressive agenda for global social justice.

The world is already committed to a series of ambitious targets for poverty reduction and development: the Millennium Development Goals (MDGs), agreed by 189 countries at the UN Millennium Assembly in 2000.[3] The achievement of these goals should remain central to an agenda for global social justice.

Progress towards the MDGs has been very mixed. Thanks to rapid economic development in China and India, the dollar a day poverty target is likely to be achieved globally by 2015 – a quite remarkable demonstration of what is possible in development. But this success is not matched elsewhere. For many countries in Africa, Asia and Latin America, the last decade has been a lost decade, with 54 countries poorer today than they were ten years ago (UNDP, 2003). On current trends, none of the MDGs will be met in Africa. Indeed, at existing rates of progress they will not be achieved in Africa within the next 100 years.

How can these deeply disturbing trends be turned around? How can poorer countries be helped to promote more inclusive and sustainable development? Many of the steps that are necessary depend on actions taken by the governments of poor countries and people themselves. As the New Partnership for Africa's Development (NEPAD) acknowledges, more effective development progress in Africa requires Africans to take more responsibility for their own development strategies and reform

---

3   The MDGs include halving the proportion of the world's population living on less than one dollar a day between 1990 and 2015, and, over the same period, halving the proportion of people that regularly go hungry. They also include commitments to get all children into primary school, a reduction by two-thirds in the under-five mortality rate, a three-quarters reduction in the maternal mortality rate, a halt to the spread of HIV/AIDS and a halving of the proportion of the world's people without access to safe drinking water – all to be achieved by 2015.

their governance systems to encourage increased economic activity, investment, trade and growth (Amoako, 2004).

A similar point can be made about the Middle East. The influential UN Arab Development Reports have identified 'deeply rooted shortcomings in institutional structures', lack of access to education, and weak observance of human rights, especially for women, as central causes of poverty, inequality and unemployment in the region (UNDP, 2002).

It is hard to overstate the importance of national leadership and popular participation to effective development. For many years, development was seen as an essentially technical problem requiring technical solutions and it was dominated by a very narrow conception of economics. But the reality is that development is about the transformation of societies. To effect that transformation successfully, culture and politics matter as much as macro-economic stability.

Similarly, development has suffered – and to some extent still suffers – from heavy-handed intervention and the attempt to impose a one-size-fits-all economic model on a very diverse group of countries. The success stories in development – the countries of East Asia for example – have pursued their own development models, which differ in significant respects from today's economic orthodoxy (Chang, 2002). Progressives should support greater discretion for countries to determine their own pathways out of poverty and greater room to manoeuvre, so that different communities can fashion their own visions of the just society (Edwards, 1999).

This doesn't mean, of course, indulging policies that are patently destructive. To be successful, all governments need reasonably effective institutions and competent public administration in order to enforce the rule of law and take action against corruption. Governments also need to put in place economic policies that generate higher and more inclusive levels of economic growth and that attract and retain savings for investment. They need to invest in their people: in health, education, water and sanitation. They must also expand poor people's access to land, credit and skills and assist small farmers with productivity and diversification. And they need to strengthen the rights, freedoms and opportunities of poor people (Sen, 1999).

Action in all these areas can bring real benefits. But progress could be greater still within a more supportive global environment. Poorer countries operate in a global economic and political context largely shaped to suit the interests of the world's richer countries.

There are five areas in particular where far-reaching changes in developed countries' policies are required: trade and investment; development aid; good governance, human rights and democracy; state failure and intervention; and global governance.

Trade and investment

The Doha Trade meeting in 2001 called for the new multilateral trade round to be a 'development round'. However, for almost two and a half years negotiations on implementing this round were deadlocked. In August 2004 a breakthrough of sorts occurred at a World Trade Organisation (WTO) meeting in Geneva. It is critical to seize this opportunity.

While international trade has the potential to bring huge benefits to the poor, the existing global rules of trade and the policies of developed countries are rigged against them. The average OECD tariff on manufactured goods from developing countries is more than four times that on manufactured goods from other OECD countries (Oxfam, 2002). There are also huge double standards in relation to agriculture. Three-quarters of the world's people living on less than one dollar a day (that is 900 million people) are small farmers. But massive agricultural subsidies in the EU and the US and the dumping of agricultural surpluses on poorer countries are forcing many of them out of business.

Poor countries also suffer the effects of tariff escalation, with countries like Ghana facing much higher tariffs on processed chocolate than on unprocessed cocoa beans when they try to export into developed country markets. And many poor countries remain heavily dependent on the primary commodities market. The price of these commodities has fallen dramatically over recent decades: prices are also enormously volatile, which can lead to severe economic shocks. Another very controversial trade agreement is TRIPS – the Agreement on Trade Related Aspects of Intellectual Property. TRIPS has the effect of pushing up the price of technology and other essential products, including drugs, for many poor countries.

A progressive agenda for trade should include deep cuts in agricultural subsidies and controls on tariff escalation. It should involve strengthening poor countries' capacity to export, for example through investments in transport infrastructure. Increased attention should be given to the problem of economic volatility in countries heavily dependent on primary exports, as well as reforms to TRIPS to ensure poor people get access to essential drugs and technology. Additional support should be provided to African countries to diversify out of dependence on primary commodities and developed countries need to re-examine their policies on trade and services, given the advantages that could accrue to poor countries from greater labour mobility, migration and remittances.

The role of transnational companies and inward investment in poor countries also raises important issues. Managed well, investment flows can bring real development benefits. Managed badly, they can distort local development, fuel conflict and contribute to human rights abuses. This is particularly the case in poor countries heavily dependent on natural resources, a dependence that can significantly increase countries' vulnerability to violent conflict (World Bank, 2003).

So far, the main way in which the governments of developed countries and companies have sought to address these concerns has been through strategies for corporate social responsibility (CSR). But the impact of CSR has been limited (Mepham and Cooper, 2004). Some existing international initiatives – such as the OECD *Guidelines on Multinational Enterprises*, the *Extractive Industries Transparency Initiative* and the UN *Norms on the Responsibilities of Business* – have a role to play in promoting high standards, but again they lack adequate enforcement mechanisms.

A progressive agenda should involve helping poor countries to create a more attractive environment for inward investment, at the same time as strengthening the capacity of governments to regulate the private sector in the public interest. The provisions of the OECD *Guidelines* should be used to take action against errant companies. The UN Convention against Corruption should also be strongly supported, and prosecutions brought against those who engage in corrupt practices abroad. More generally, progressives should assert that a global economy needs global regulation. Having secured reputations for prudent economic management, progressive governments should be much more self-confident about making the case for a changed relationship with the international business sector, one in which corporate rights are matched by a stronger set of global corporate responsibilities (Mepham and Cooper, 2004).

Development aid
The World Bank and the UN have estimated that it will cost an extra $50 billion a year, every year for the next ten years, if the MDGs are to

be achieved. Gordon Brown has been a particularly strong advocate of the case for increased aid, and has put forward a proposal for an International Finance Facility (IFF) to help leverage additional resources for development from the international capital markets (Brown, 2004). But despite recent increases in aid by some donors, substantially more global aid is still required, not least to meet the huge additional costs of tackling the HIV/AIDS pandemic.

HIV/AIDS poses an unparalleled threat to development. Around 58 million people worldwide have been infected and 20 million people have died. In sub-Saharan Africa it is the leading cause of death and is inflicting massive costs across the continent. Life expectancy in some African countries has fallen by 20 years. In many African countries around 60 per cent of fifteen year olds are unlikely to live to old age as a consequence of the disease (UNAIDS, 2004). By 2010, life expectancy in some African countries could be lower than at the start of the twentieth century (Gordon, 2001).

Massive additional investment is required to tackle this epidemic, not just in anti-retroviral drugs but also in prevention, care and treatment services, support for healthcare systems and the development of a vaccine. Increased investments are also needed if the poorest countries are to meet the goals on access to education, clean water and safe sanitation (Mepham, 2003).

A progressive approach to aid should include a clear commitment by all developed countries to increase levels of development aid to the UN 0.7 per cent GNP/aid target. Additional aid for development could be generated through a much more generous approach to debt relief through the Heavily Indebted Poor Countries Initiative (HIPC). While HIPC has brought benefits, for many poor countries debt burdens remain unacceptably high.

Progressives should also seriously consider other potential sources of finance for global development, including the Tobin tax, an arms tax, a new issue of IMF special drawing rights or an airline fuel tax (Brown, 2004; Soros, 2002). Over time, the allocation of a certain proportion of national income to meet global development goals might become mandatory, something to be set out in a binding international agreement, rather than the current system of discretionary aid spending.

At the same time, aid needs to be provided in radically new ways. Too often in the past, aid has served to strengthen local elites but has done little to improve the lives of ordinary people. In other circumstances, aid has weakened not strengthened national systems of governance and left governments more accountable to external actors than to their own people (de Waal, 2004). Instead, aid should be seen as an investment to help countries build capacity and run their political and economic systems more effectively and with greater accountability to local people. Wherever possible, aid should be allocated directly in support of poor countries' own development strategies.

Developed countries need to do far more to improve the quality of their aid and the way it is delivered, so that it does not impose heavy transaction costs on recipient governments. An international agreement on aid untying should also be sought, to increase the cost-effectiveness of aid and to help poorer countries to strengthen local procurement systems.

Good governance, human rights and democracy

Reducing poverty and promoting development require an effective state and good governance. If that development is to be genuinely inclusive and sustainable, it also requires countries to respect human rights and to introduce more accountable and democratic government (see propositions two and four).

Developed country support for good governance can often be done in partnership with poor country governments, helping them to strengthen systems of public administration, the rule of law or action against corruption.

Human rights – particularly civil and political rights – are a more sensitive matter. Many governments resent pressure and criticism from outsiders. Getting countries to better protect human rights therefore needs to be handled with considerable diplomacy and with a good understanding of where or when encouragement or pressure is most likely to be effective.

At the same time, there should be no question that the way in which a government treats its citizens is a legitimate matter for international interest and concern. One of our core propositions of global social justice is the moral obligation to help all of the world's people secure their basic human rights (see proposition two).

Of course, there is also a clear responsibility on developed countries to ensure that their own human rights performance is in line with their international legal obligations and that they are not contributing to human rights abuses in other countries, for example through arms sales or support to rights-abusing governments (see proposition three) (Mepham and Lorge, 2005).

The issue of democracy raises very sensitive issues, including its relationship with freedom and human rights. Today, 119 countries, comprising 62 per cent of all countries in the world, have a government created by elections in which every citizen could vote (Zakaria, 2003). However, far from being a cause for celebration, some see in this development as cause for concern.

Across the globe, democratically elected regimes, often ones that have been re-elected or reaffirmed through referenda, are routinely ignoring constitutional limits on their power and depriving their citizens of basic rights. This disturbing phenomenon has been called 'illiberal democracy' (Zakaria, 2003).

Similar doubts have been raised about the transition to democracy in post-conflict societies, with some arguing that the early introduction of multi-party elections in poor, ethnically divided societies may trigger or intensify violent conflict.

These concerns are real and significant. But we should be careful about the conclusions that are drawn from them. Democratic freedoms have intrinsic as well as instrumental value. For all its imperfections, democracy remains the best system yet devised for organising complex societies and millions of people around the world have suffered and still suffer from the absence of accountable and legitimate government. But our understanding of democracy, the policies adopted in support of it, and the time required to embed effective democratic institutions, do need to be much more sophisticated (Ottaway and Carothers, 2005).

Democracy is more than majority rule. It depends critically on a credible opposition whose role is respected, properly funded parliaments, the rule of law, constitutional checks and balances, security sector reform, a free press and media and an effective and non-corrupt system of public administration. And it requires a vibrant civil society: a space in which voluntary groups such as free trade unions and NGOs can organise and deliberate, promote social change, and hold governments to account at all levels (Edwards, 2004).

A progressive agenda should include support for effective states, good governance and human rights, especially the rights of women and minority communities. Tackling some of the worst human rights violations – for example, slave and bonded labour, 'honour' killings and female genital mutilation – should also be priorities for action. Progressives should be unapologetic in their support for democracy, but they should stress that it requires more than the holding of elections;

support for the development of democracy needs to be properly sequenced, particularly in post-conflict societies, but also in societies without a strong democratic culture or tradition.

State failure and intervention

State failure comes in many different forms. At one end of the spectrum are countries like Liberia or the Democratic Republic of Congo, where state institutions have disintegrated and the writ of the central government barely extends beyond the capital. At the other end are states plagued by poor governance or pervasive corruption. Many countries in between suffer from weak and fragile state institutions. What all these states share, albeit to varying degrees, is an inability to secure real progress in the reduction of poverty. As noted above, effective states are an essential precondition for effective development and for greater progress towards the MDGs.

The causes of state failure are extremely diverse. Every state has its own complex history. Many of the governments in these countries have pursued highly damaging economic strategies that have weakened the capacity of the state and its ability to deliver services to its people (Rotberg, 2003). At the same time, there are numerous people within these countries who benefit from state crisis and failure: corrupt rulers and warlords, unscrupulous businesses, and traders in arms, drugs and illicit commodities.

Too much of the debate about state failure treats it as an internal phenomenon in need of an external remedy. But developed countries are often complicit in state failure – through colonialism and support for proxy governments during the Cold War, but in the present too. In many weak and failing states today, civil conflicts are fuelled by arms and monetary transfers that originate in the developed world. The proceeds of national plunder by corrupt leaders are generally stored in western bank accounts or laundered through international financial institutions. And state institutions can be undermined by unfair international trade rules or by donor conditionality. A progressive approach to state failure should involve developed countries 'putting their own house in order' on these issues (see proposition three) (Mepham and Lorge, 2005).

The most controversial issue in relation to state failure or dysfunction concerns intervention: how bad does a situation have to be to warrant intervention? This question brings to the fore the tension between state sovereignty and universal humanitarian principles.

> *If humanitarian intervention is, indeed, an unacceptable assault on sovereignty, how should we respond to a Rwanda, to a Srebrenica and to other gross and systematic violations of human rights that offend every precept of our common humanity? (Annan, 2000)*

The best attempt to address this issue in recent years is *The Responsibility to Protect*, the report of the International Commission on Intervention and State Sovereignty (ICISS, 2001). The Commission suggests that all the relevant decision-making criteria can be summarised under the following six headings: right authority, just cause, right intention, last resort, proportional means and reasonable prospects (ibid).

This issue of intervention and these specific criteria are discussed in detail in a separate ippr report (Mepham and Cooper, 2004). Here it is worth highlighting four issues that require further thought and analysis. First, opportunity cost. The Iraq war has already cost the US around $126 billion, almost twice the annual global spending on aid (Institute for Policy Studies, 2004). Could this money be better spent – with greater overall humanitarian benefit – supporting long-term prevention, specific development or human rights initiatives in various countries around the world? Second, where interventions are necessary to prevent massive human rights violations, can we ensure that decent motives are not tarnished by inappropriate means? For example, it is hard to reconcile 'humanitarian intervention' with the use of cluster munitions or the sight of US soldiers torturing Iraqi prisoners. Third, how do we mobilise the necessary political will to act from key governments and institutions when faced with massive human rights violations? Too often in these situations the political will to act is lacking, including in the case of Darfur (Podesta, 2004). Fourth, do we have the necessary understanding and capacity – military and non-military – to intervene effectively and to help build peace over the longer term? And if that understanding and capacity is lacking, how do we develop it? (UN, 2004).

Global governance

A more socially just global order depends upon a more equitable system of global governance, one in which poor countries have a bigger and more effective voice. Global governance should not be confused with global government. There is not yet a global society in the way that there are national societies, and nation states remain the core focus of citizen identification.

But an uncoordinated system of structures, institutions and norms – a system of global governance – has grown up over the last half century. Some parts of this system rest on universal, supranational values, notably the UN Declaration of Human Rights, the Geneva Convention and, most recently, the International Criminal Court. Other parts of the system are more firmly rooted in the existing distribution of state power, or, more accurately, that which existed at the end of the Second World War.

Today's dominant institutions of global governance – the UN, World Bank, International Monetary Fund (IMF), World Trade Organisation (WTO) and the G8 – are effectively controlled by a very small number of countries. In the case of the UN, five countries exercise disproportionate power as veto-wielding permanent members of the UN Security Council. Less well known – but equally iniquitous – is the power structure within the World Bank and the IMF, where voting power is a reflection of financial contributions and a constitutional structure biased towards the interests of the US. While the WTO is nominally more democratic – based on the principle of one nation one vote – in practice the US and the EU exercise disproportionate influence over the agenda.

However, even this description doesn't adequately capture the realities of global power. At the top of the pyramid sits the US, the world's strongest military and economic power by a very long way. As the policies of the Bush administration on Iraq and Kyoto demonstrate, the existing rules and structures of global governance will often not constrain the US when it refuses to play by these rules. Does this mean then that the attempt to create a better system of global governance is fanciful and naive?

There are three reasons for thinking it is not. First, US power is not unlimited and the US will not always act unilaterally (Nye, 2002). As the Bush administration discovered in Iraq, not even the world's strongest nation can secure its objectives through independent action. The belated US effort to involve the UN and other nations in Iraq confirms this. Second, the proliferation of global rules, norms and structures has had a real impact. We should not belittle what global governance has already achieved, especially on issues like human rights. Third, the extent of global interdependence will only grow in the years to come and with it the need for global institutions and structures that can address global problems (UN, 2004). The international financial system, for example, is crying out for a more effective system of global regulation, to minimise the risks of currency crises and the damage they inflict on the global economy, particularly the world's poor (Jacobs *et al*, 2003). These global institutions and structures will often derive their legitimacy from national systems of political accountability, but they will be necessarily global in their focus and their reach.

While change will not come easily, and while reforms cannot ignore realities of power, progressives should continue to make the case for a more equitable and effective system of global governance and a stronger role for poor countries within it.

Conclusion

Fairer rules on trade and investment; increased and better used development aid; support for good governance, human rights and democracy; a willingness to tackle state failure; and the reform of global governance – these would all help poorer countries to make greater progress towards the Millennium Development Goals and the realisation of human rights.

Not only would these actions be morally right (consistent with our six propositions); they would also be in our common interest. In a shrinking world, there can be no secure future for any of us without greater global social justice.

References

Amoako KY (2004) 'The Capable State' *New Economy* September 2004 London: ippr

Annan K (2000) Speech to the UN Millennium Assembly

Barry B (1973) *The Liberal Theory of Justice* Oxford: Clarendon Press

Beitz C (2000) *Political theory and international relations* Princeton: Princeton University Press

Brown C (2002) *Sovereignty, rights and justice – international political theory today* Cambridge: Polity Press

Brown G (2004) 'The challenges of 2005' *New Economy* September 2004 London: ippr

Buchanan A (2000) 'Rawls' Law of Peoples: Rules for a Vanished Westphalian World' *Ethics* 110,

Burke J (2003) *Al-Qaeda – Casting a shadow of terror* London: I B Tauris

Chang H J (2002) *Kicking Away the Ladder: Development Policy in Historical Perspective* London: Anthem Press

Commission on Social Justice (1994) *Social Justice: strategies for national renewal* London: ippr

Cook R (1997a) *Mission Statement* 12 May 1997 London: TSO. Available at www.fco.gov.uk

Cook R (1997b) *Speech at the launch of the FCO Mission Statement* 12 May 1997 available at www.fco.gov.uk

De Waal A (2004) 'Rethinking Aid' *New Economy* September 2004 London: ippr

Department for International Development (DfID) (1997) *Eliminating World Poverty* London: TSO

Edwards M (1999) *Future Positive – International Co-operation in the 21st Century* London: Earthscan

Edwards M (2004) *Civil Society* Cambridge: Polity Press

Gordon D (2001) *Plague upon plague: AIDS and violent conflict in Africa*, available at https://www.usip.org/events/pre2002/plague_cib.pdf

Halliday F (2002) *Two Hours that Shook the World: September 11, 2001: Causes and Consequences* London: Saqi Books

Halliday F (2004) *Terrorism in historical perspective* opendemocracy.net

Held D and Koenig-Archibugi S (2003) *Taming globalisation: frontiers of governance* Cambridge: Polity Press

Held D (2004) *Global Covenant: the Social Democratic Alternative to the Washington Consensus* Cambridge: Polity Press

International Commission on Intervention and State Sovereignty (ICISS) (2001) *The Responsibility to Protect* Ottawa: International Development Research Centre. Available at www.dfait-maeci.gc.ca/iciss-ciis

Ignatieff M (2001) 'Human Rights as Politics and Idolatry' in Gutman A (ed) *Human Rights as Politics and Idolatry* Princeton: Princeton University Press

Institute for Policy Studies and Foreign Policy in Focus (FPIF) (2004) *Paying the Price – the Mounting Costs of the Iraq War* Washington: FPIF. Available at http://www.ips-dc.org/iraq/costsofwar/

Intergovernmental Panel on Climate Change (IPCC) (2001) *Climate Change 2001: The Scientific Basis* Cambridge: Cambridge University Press

Jacobs M, Lent A, Watkins K (2003) *Progressive Globalisation: Towards an international social democracy* London: Fabian Society

Mepham D and Eavis P (2002) *The Missing Link in Labour's Foreign Policy: the case for tighter controls over arms exports* London: ippr and Saferworld

Mepham D (2003) *Clean Water, Safe Sanitation* London: ippr

Mepham D and Cooper J (2004) *Human rights and global responsibility: an international agenda for the UK* London: ippr

Mepham D and Lorge J (2005) *Putting our house in order: recasting G8 policy towards Africa* London: ippr

Miller D (2000) *Citizenship and national identity* Cambridge: Polity Press

Nye J (2002) *The Paradox of American Power* Oxford: Oxford University Press

Ottaway M and Carothers T (2005) *Uncharted Journey: Promoting Democracy in the Middle East* Washington DC: Carnegie Endowment for International Peace

Oxfam (2002) *Rigged Rules and Double Standards – trade, globalisation and the fight against poverty* Oxford: Oxfam

Podesta J (2004) *Dealing with Darfur: can the world act on its responsibility to protect?* Yale Harper Fowler Fellow Lecture, Yale Law School, 6 December 2004

Pogge T (2002) *World Poverty and Human Rights: Cosmopolitan Responsibilities and Reforms* Cambridge: Polity Press

Rawls J (1971) *A Theory of Justice* Oxford: Oxford University Press

Rawls J (1999) *The Law of Peoples* Boston: Harvard University Press

Rice S (2003) *The New National Security Strategy: Focus on Failed States* Washington DC: The Brookings Institution

Rotberg R (ed) (2003) *When States Fail: Causes and Consequences* Princeton: Princeton University Press

Sen A (1999) *Development as Freedom* Oxford: Oxford University Press

Singer P (1972) 'Famine, Affluence, and Morality' *Philosophy & Public Affairs* (1) 3, Oxford: Blackwells

Singer P (2002) *One World: the ethics of globalisation* Princeton: Yale University Press

Soros G (2002) *George Soros on Globalisation* New York: PublicAffairs

United Nations Development Programme and Arab Fund for Economic and Social Development (UNDP and AFESD) (2002) *Arab Human Development Report* Oxford: Oxford University Press

United Nations Development Programme (UNDP) *Human Development Report 2003* Oxford: Oxford University Press

UNAIDS 2004 *AIDS Epidemic update,* December 2004, available at https://www.unaids.org/wad2004/report.html

UN High Level Panel (2004), *A More Secure World: Our Shared Responsibility*, New York: United Nations

Walzer M (1983) *Spheres of Justice* London: Martin Robinson

World Bank (2003) *Breaking the conflict trap – Civil War and Development Policy* Washington DC: World Bank

Zakaria F (2003) *The Future of Freedom: Illiberal Democracy at Home and Abroad* New York: W.W. Norton & Company

Outsiders on the Inside:
Towards Socially Just Migration Policies

Dhananjayan Sriskandarajah[1]

Growing numbers of asylum claims in the UK (some 650,000 claims over the last decade), rising net immigration (an estimated 1.5 million new non-British immigrants since 1993), racial tensions that led to riots in several northern towns, and security issues since 11 September 2001 have combined to fuel public concern about the scale, nature and impact of immigration into the UK. These issues, and the political context in which they have been discussed, have proved tricky for the Labour Government and for the left more generally. Moving beyond the concerns of the report of the 1994 Commission on Social Justice, it seems timely and important to consider the implications migration holds for the pursuit of social justice in the UK and what the pursuit of social justice means for migration policy.

For the Government, asylum and migration policy has been a minefield. Increasingly complex migratory flows (in/out; temporary/permanent; voluntary/forced; visa-free/subject to visa control) are hard to understand, let alone manage effectively. Balancing competing interests has not been easy: for example, employers have shown an almost insatiable demand for migrant workers while more than 60 per cent of the population feels that there are too many immigrants in Britain (Page, 2004). Worse still, the migration issue of the day changes often and the list seems endless: asylum numbers, benefit tourism, security concerns, the treatment of asylum seekers, illegal working, problems in the visa processing system, European Union (EU) enlargement, unreliable statistics and so on. With each new issue, scare-mongering headline and exposé

---

1 The author is grateful for comments from David Goodhart, Sarah Kyambi, Will Paxton, Nick Pearce, Shamit Saggar, Saskia Sassen and Sarah Spencer.

about failings in the migration system, public confidence in the Government's ability to manage the system is further undermined. Worst of all, public fears have played into the hands of the far right and racists.

The left has found it difficult to articulate a cogent or confident position on migration, ethnic diversity and social cohesion. Instead there has been pessimism about the impact of immigration and increased ethnic diversity on the pursuit of equality. On immigration, there is unease about migrants pushing down wages, competing against the poorest sections of society, and increasing capital's share of national income relative to labour. According to journalist Polly Toynbee, this is 'the real reason why we should fear immigration' (Toynbee, 2004). On ethnic diversity there is a fear, most recently associated with David Goodhart, that mix of cultures can undermine the social solidarity required to support the welfare state (Goodhart, 2004; RSA/Prospect, 2003). Two further concerns also linger in the minds of those on the left: asylum policies that are seen as too tough and the neo-imperialist implications of higher levels of immigration exacerbating global inequalities through 'brain drain' from the developing world. Thus, with growing public concern about the effectiveness of migration policies, increasingly hostile politics of migration and race, and pessimism from the left about the principle of promoting migration, there is a pressing need to articulate a progressive agenda for managing migration and promoting social cohesion.

The institutional arrangements for the pursuit of equality, justice and governance in contemporary liberal democracies rely on boundaries that demarcate membership (citizenship), thereby creating insiders (citizens) and outsiders (non-citizens). Mobility between political communities throws up challenges to the liberal commitment to the moral equality of all persons and the democratic principle of collective rule. Yet, liberal theories of equality and justice are, at best, silent. At worst they are inconsistent on the question of the admission of outsiders (Jordan and Düvell, 2003; Cole, 2000). Immigration also brings the globalist challenge for the pursuit of social justice (see Chapter 6) closer to home, literally. When the 'outsider' moves in next door, questions of membership and distribution become far more pertinent than when he or she was a television image beamed from a faraway land.

As Miller outlines in Chapter 1, immigration raises a fundamental question for the pursuit of social justice: is there an equality commitment to the new citizen? Answering his question requires addressing other, equally difficult, questions: when and how does a migrant qualify for a social minimum? Should migration status be taken into account when assessing equality of opportunity? Does the notion of fairness/entitlement change according the nature or length of one's membership of a community? Should assessments of fair distribution include non-citizens who live, work and produce in a community?

Efforts to address these questions are plagued by the increasing complexity of migrant flows and experiences. Not all migrants require visas to enter, live or work in the UK. Those who do need visas have several routes of entry open to them including work visas, asylum, and family reunion, each with distinct rules around duration of stay permitted, recourse to public funds, and renewability. In addition there are those who enter illegally, over-stay, infringe the entitlements of their visa or switch between categories. Not all migrants settle permanently in the UK, even though many may be entitled to. Similarly, the links between migration and increasing ethnic diversity are not always straightforward – not all migrants belong to ethnic minority communities, and not all members of ethnic minority communities are migrants. Not surprisingly, this complexity has often meant that attempts to discuss migration and diversity in abstract get lost in the minutiae of migration management.

What's more, debate on migration and integration does not fit easily into the left-right divide. There has been a growing consensus amongst all mainstream parties in the UK on the economic need for immigration. Meanwhile business leaders and trade unions support greater freedom of movement and groups with completely different starting points, such as the far right and environmentalists concerned with optimal populations, share a common suspicion of higher immigration.

If progressives are to manage migration and its impacts effectively, then they must have something to say on five central, and thorny, issues:

- Admission – who can enter and the rules of their entry
- Entitlements – what rights and services migrants have access to
- Integration – how effectively they integrate into their host society
- Overseas impacts – what impact their movement has on their erstwhile home
- Undocumented migrants – how to handle those already here but living and working without permission

A substantial section of this chapter is devoted to how policies in these five areas can help deliver better social justice outcomes for migrants,

their host societies and sending countries, and at the same time help
outflank (or pre-empt) an assault from the far right.[2] However, before we
turn to these issues, it is worth surveying the empirical landscape to see
what impact migration has had and is likely to have on the UK.

Britain's changing face?

It is certainly true that immigration has been on the rise lately. In contrast
to periods of net emigration from the UK during the 1970s, the number
of immigrants has started to exceed the number of emigrants over the last
two decades (Figure 7.1). This is largely due to rising net annual inflows of
non-British citizens: net flows in 2003 were nearly four times those in
1993 and nearly eight times more than in 1983. By 2003, foreign nationals
(not including naturalised migrants) made up 4.8 per cent of the UK
population, up from 3.5 per cent in 1993 and representing an addition of
864,000 foreigners over a decade (OECD, 2003; Salt, 2003).

Figure 7.1 Net international migration by citizenship, 1975-2003

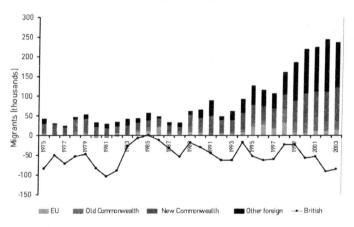

Source: International Passenger Survey and ONS. EU refers to nationals of fourteen member states in 2001.

---

2 This chapter does not discuss a universal right to migrate or the possibility of an 'open borders'
   policy. While it is vital that states do not place undue restrictions on the mobility of people, especially when they have relinquished so much of their control over capital flows, and are obliged to
   protect the fundamental right to seek refuge from persecution, it is assumed that states can and do
   exercise significant controls over the movement of people.

It is also true that, in recent years, immigrants have come from more diverse parts of the world. In net terms, migrants from the 'old' Commonwealth (countries such as Australia, Canada, New Zealand and South Africa) and the rest of the 'old' EU have not been contributing to the rise in immigrant numbers (Table 7.1). While there may be substantial circulation of people between the UK and these countries, net contributions have been most significant from the 'new' Commonwealth and further afield. These rises and changes in immigration have been reflected in changing patterns of applications for British citizenship. The number of people granted British citizenship has risen threefold in the decade to 2003 and, while Indian, Pakistani and Bangladeshi nationals have consistently featured at the top of the citizenship table, several other nationalities (Somalis, former Yugoslavs, Nigerian, Sri Lankan, Turkish and Zimbabwean) have increased their numbers dramatically (Home Office, various years).

Increasingly diverse immigration, combined with higher fertility amongst some sections of the non-white resident population, seems to have had a discernible impact on the ethnic make-up of the population. In the two decades to 2001, the proportion of ethnic minorities has risen from 4.6 per cent to 8.7 per cent, representing a doubling of actual numbers (see Table 7.1).

Table 7.1 Rising ethnic diversity, 1981–2001

Census	Ethnic group as % of total population					Number of minorities (millions)
	White	South Asian	Black	Chinese & other Asian	Other Groups	
1981	95.40	2.20	1.51	0.45	0.44	2.152
1991	93.68	3.10	1.91	0.70	0.60	3.028
2001	91.43	4.28	2.62	0.93	0.74	4.213

Source: Census data, categorised to correct for methodological differences between censuses particularly with regard to the 'mixed' group, (Rees and Butt, 2004). Figures are for England only; overall figures for the UK are slightly lower for minority proportions and numbers.

However, not all migrants are minorities – a third of all foreigners living in the UK in 2003 were from the then fourteen other members of the EU (Salt, 2003). Nor are all members of minorities migrants – more than three-quarters of black other, nearly 60 per cent of black Caribbean, and a third of Indian and Pakistani groups in 2002 were born in the UK (Lindley *et al*, 2004). Referring to UK-born ethnic minorities as immigrants is at best, misleading, and at worst, offensive. Further, despite recent increases in immigration and ethnic diversity in the UK, the proportion of foreigners (5 per cent compared to 6 per cent in France, 9 per cent in Germany and nearly 20 per cent in Switzerland) and ethnic minorities (8 per cent compared to 23 per cent in the US) remains smaller than many other Western countries.

Dealing with diversity

The disadvantaged position of ethnic minority groups has been and continues to be a matter of concern. A report on *Ethnic Minorities and the Labour Market* (Strategy Unit, 2003) found wide variations in the labour market achievements of different ethnic minority groups. Indians and Chinese often out-perform whites in schools, and in the labour market, other groups such as Pakistanis, Bangladeshis and Black Caribbeans experience, on average, significantly higher unemployment and lower earnings than whites.

While the disadvantage experienced by some groups is worrying, progressives should draw two important lessons. First, the differential performance amongst ethnic minority groups confirms that there are no insurmountable barriers to their successful economic integration. Second, it is this existence of an 'ethnic penalty' in economic perform-ance that may lead to relative underachievement amongst all ethnic minorities compared to the white group, rather than actual deprivation *per se*. As a recent report by the Government's Social Exclusion Unit observes, ethnic minority groups are more likely to have health inequal-ities, are more likely to be homeless, and enjoy fewer life chances, and like-for-like all ethnic groups are disadvantaged compared to white people in similar circumstances (SEU, 2004). Perhaps more worrying, the report notes that 'people from some ethnic minority groups, including asylum seekers and refugees' are one of three main broad groups of people (along with those who have physical/mental health problems and those who lack skills/qualifications) for whom policies consistently seem less effective. Reducing the scale of the ethnic penalty has to be a priority within wider efforts to reduce disadvantage of all underperforming groups.

A second set of issues, this time about the impact of ethnic diversity on trust, social cohesion and support for the welfare state (Goodhart, 2004; Pearce, 2004), have also been received attention in recent years. While the central thesis – that ethnic diversity correlates negatively with trust or social capital, and therefore reduces support for the welfare state – is appealing, those on left should be wary. Increased ethnic diversity does indeed add yet another layer of complexity to the rich diversity that already exists in the UK but it is not clear whether this necessarily poses a fundamental challenge to the moral bases of social solidarity at all, or a challenge sufficient to undermine the pursuit of redistribution.

Most importantly, while migration policies must recognise and address the real and perceived links between migration and ethnicity, good migration policies should also recognise that these linkages are not as straightforward as often assumed. While the danger of exclusionist nationalist ideologies is always present, there is evidence that a broad inclusive identity seems both possible and preferable. Significant majorities of most non-white ethnic groups living in Britain identify as British, either on its own or in conjunction with other identities (ONS, 2004; Thompson, 2005). We also know that people born outside Europe are likely to take up British citizenship; for example, more than 70 per cent of people born in the Indian subcontinent, Africa, Caribbean, and Central and South America who have lived in the UK for more than six years had applied for British citizenship, while only about a quarter of those born in Ireland, and about half of those born in the US, Canada and Australasia had done so (Home Office, 2004). The challenge will be to transform these sentiments and enthusiasm into active forms of civic engagement.

Getting the basics right

Admission

There is often a disjuncture between rhetoric and reality in the management of migration. On the one hand, most EU member states have spent the best part of the last decade in a competitive race to be the least attractive destination for asylum seekers and some types of economic migrants. On the other hand, the reality is that migrants to the UK continue to fill large-scale vacancies in the immediate term (Sriskandarajah *et al*, 2004), are likely to contribute to maintaining economic competitiveness in the medium term, and are almost certainly going to play a role in mitigating some of the long-term demographic problems posed by an ageing society.

This highlights why recent political consensus on 'limiting' and 'controlling' immigration is so problematic. A sensible and sustainable migration policy needs to acknowledge that some routes of entry cannot be limited (asylum, spouse migration), some should move flexibly according to economic conditions (employment-related migration), and some should actually be promoted (foreign students). A key question that emerges is 'what principles guide the admission of those routes of entry that the state can interfere in legitimately?'

Most importantly, the UK's admissions policy must be consistent, fair and based on relevant criteria of selection. For a start, admission policies must be race-blind. We cannot assume, or let immigration rules and officials assume, to be able to judge a person's ability to integrate or contribute to society based on their ethnic characteristics. While historical, cultural and economic links can explain some differences in admission requirements, the vast incongruence between the visa-free employment access enjoyed by nationals of some countries and the considerable requirements made of some nationals who want simply to holiday in the UK calls this principle into question. One way to address this would be to consolidate admission categories. The more parsimonious the system, the easier it should be to manage.

The Government's five-year plan announced in early 2005 goes some way in pursuing parsimony but also signals two worrying reversals in policy-making. First, the UK's relatively good record of allowing permanent settlement for non-EU nationals is under threat as the Government pursues more temporary flows for many categories of migrants. Not only does allowing permanent settlement allow for better integration of migrants (who can strike roots knowing that they are here permanently), it can also help meet some the demographic challenges mentioned above. The proposals to limit the leave to remain of those granted refugee status is doubly worrying. Rather than seeking to limit the settlement potential of migrants, the UK should establish a permanent settlement programme such as those in place in Canada, the US and Australia. A settlement visa would give participants full citizenship rights, promote early integration and pre-empt claims that temporary migrant schemes are being used as a 'back door' to permanent settlement.

There may be potential here for EU-wide cooperation to maximise the benefits of migration for the region. One option would be an EU version of the US Green Card (a 'Blue Card' perhaps) through which a certain number of migrants are permitted to migrate to the EU and choose where they wish to settle. This would reduce some of the current disparities between EU nationals and third country nationals, and also help realise the potential that freedom of movement within the EU has for economic efficiency and flexibility. It would also help attract highly-skilled migrants who may wish to move within the EU without waiting to qualify for full citizenship rights of one member state.

The second worrying trend involves proposals to restrict routes of entry for low-skill migrants from outside the EU. These moves are presumably based on the belief that nationals of the newest member states of the EU will fill some of the low-skill vacancies in the UK (an assumption that is unlikely to hold for long, because these economies will grow and age) and that low-skill immigration is less politically attractive than high-skill immigration.

On asylum, recent initiatives to limit the numbers of in-port or in-country asylum claims have resulted in a significant drop in the number of asylum claims in the UK and the rest of the EU. While this fall has given political leaders greater room for manoeuvre in defending the migration system, there are genuine concerns that the UK and other EU members are failing to provide protection for those who may genuinely need it. The most effective way of responding to this challenge would be to increase the scale of refugee resettlement programmes. Resettlement offers several advantages – it provides refuge to those without the means to travel legally or illegally to get somewhere to lodge a claim, and by limiting resettlement to those whose status has already been established it would be possible to circumvent the negative politics about 'undeserving' cases gaining the right to live in the UK. Resettlement also provides a positive reaffirmation of the UK's commitment to refugee protection.

Entitlements

Getting admission right is the first and critical step in managing migration: matching supply to demand, being fair, meeting international obligations and laying the foundation for integration. However, firming up access to a country is meaningless unless there is an effective set of rules governing membership of a society. This is where entitlements emerge as a critical and hotly debated issue, especially where the usual response to greater immigration has been to tighten the limits on entitlement to the welfare state (Geddes, 2003). First, there are structural challenges of calibrating entitlement levels for migrants, taking into account their needs, their contribution to society and any potential (yet unproven) impact that generous entitlements may have on drawing other migrants. Second, there are operational challenges in making sure those who have the right to services can access them (paying special attention to those who may be unfamiliar with often complex rules) and minimising fraud. Third, public opinion sees migrants as a drain on society underpinned perhaps by a perceived lack of reciprocity between the entitlements given to some groups of migrants (for example, asylum seekers and, arguably, foreign spouses) and their contribution to society. These factors have led to recent moves to restrict entitlements, based in part on perceptions of the free rider problems.

Discussions about reforming immigrants' entitlements in the UK have been part of wider discussions about saving costs and promoting self-sufficiency. While this is understandable when so many services are funded out of general taxation, policy makers must be aware of the potential dangers of trimming down immigrant entitlements. Migrants should not be used as an easy scapegoat for cutting costs. Similarly, while shifting the burden of supporting new migrants from state to sponsors (often family members in the case of reunion) can make sense in many circumstances, this should have firm limits: sponsors should never be expected to meet the costs of providing basic entitlements such as universal healthcare or education and migrant self-sufficiency cannot be the sole criteria for service provision or for qualification for citizenship.

Most importantly, the provision of entitlements to migrants needs to be premised on a commitment to equality rather than a desire to save costs. The UK cannot simply import labour – often to staff key public services – without accepting some of the burden of providing for those workers on broadly similar terms to those applicable to resident workers and at least while they reside in a host country.

Similarly, equal citizenship presupposes relatively equal access to public goods and justifies the redistribution of resources for the sake of promoting integration. This may actually mean extra allocations to vulnerable groups such as refugees or recently-arrived migrants. Indeed, if the UK is to be an 'opportunity society' then it cannot curb the opportunities for newcomers to better themselves (nor can their successes be resented). Finally, there is evidence that migrant access to the welfare state actually contributes to the positive attitudes of many immigrants towards their host society and may be critical in promoting social cohesion and inclusion (Thompson, 2005).

While it is easy to conceive of and justify special entitlements that prevent social exclusion for other vulnerable groups in society such as low paid workers or single-parents, doing so for migrants is a harder political pill to swallow. The responsibility falls on political leaders to make the arguments that all migrants have a clear set of basic entitlements and that many migrants are also entitled to the benefits distributed according to the same strict rules that govern the resident population.

A simplified system with a fair and graduated scale for entitlement to public services will ensure that migrants know what to expect, and that migrants' entitlements cannot be misrepresented easily by those who wish to stir resentment. Distributed along the following tiers, these entitlements would also aid the pursuit of social justice for migrants:

1. A basic 'safety net' of entitlements for all residents, regardless of status, based on universal moral obligations of humanity. This requirement to equal access to some basic rights arises clearly, in the case of adults, from judicial interpretations on the provision of shelter and food under Article Three of the European Convention on Human Rights and, in the case of children, from the 1989 Children Act. The UK's ratification of the International Convention on the Protection of the Rights of All Migrant Workers and Members of Their Families that came into force in July 2003 would also help clarify legal duties to migrants.
2. A set of instrumental entitlements that further the interests of the community at large, such as universal primary healthcare and measures to promote social cohesion such as accessible (though not necessarily compulsory) English, Welsh or Gaelic language provision.
3. A more expansive and clearly defined set of entitlements where individual need justifies extra provision, especially where someone risks

falling dangerously below the social minimum or where a lack of entitlements prevents them from exercising their full capabilities.

4. A full or almost-full set of civic entitlements and equal opportunity commitments to those who are entitled to stay permanently. Everyone who is admitted on a long-term basis – excluding students, seasonal workers and so forth – should be encouraged to become a fully-fledged citizen in due course. Even those who are here for a short period should be encouraged to engage with local community life – as a way of enhancing the community, their own experiences and also of ensuring social cohesion.

There is a potential that generous migrant entitlements, rather than attracting potential asylum seekers who often have little knowledge of or control over where they end up, will actually impact on the choices made by a highly mobile, highly skilled and well-informed pool of migrant labour. If the UK wants to keep up with countries like the US and Australia that are going out of their way to attract these workers, it must ensure that migrant workers are offered an attractive package of economic and civic entitlements.

Integration

Successful integration makes for successful communities, but unsuccessful integration can lead to social exclusion and racial tensions. Moreover, integration sits at the heart of the nexus between migration and ethnic diversity.

Integration begins early (not, for example, only when someone is granted British citizenship or refugee status) and, given that early experiences and formative social networks can shape later attitudes. Integration is also a two-way process, involving an ongoing, perhaps never-ending, iterative process of change involving both migrant and host society (summarised in Table 7.2 below). And, integration is multi-dimensional, involving socio-economic, social and civic aspects.

In keeping with a broad commitment to economic inclusion for all groups in society, the integration of migrants should prioritise socio-economic integration. The faster and more effectively immigrants integrate into the workforce, the more likely the perception that newcomers are making a positive contribution to society.

The challenge of integration also raises some difficult questions about multicultural policies (Phillips, 2004). In addition to the immigration pessimism and diversity pessimism outlined above, there has also been scepticism about whether multiculturalism can work in a society such as the UK. Here there is much to learn from societies such as Canada and Australia where multiculturalism seems not to have been inimical to the promotion of an inclusive society. Measures to promote integration (such as state-funded English-language classes for immigrants) in conjunction with measures to foster minority identities and cultures (such as state-subsidised bilingual education) can be effective tools for achieving social cohesion, not least because migrants themselves feel more attached to their host society.

Table 7.2. The challenges of integration

	Primary challenge for migrants	Primary challenge for host society
Socio-economic	Effective socio-economic integration that fits skills, experience and aspirations, and maximises life chances	Encouraging socio-economic integration of migrants without (being seen to be) unfairly favouring migrants over established residents.
Political/Cultural	Adjusting to the new political and cultural context of the host community	Balancing everyone's right (including, say, the 'English') to retain and promote autochthonous identities with the need to promote social solidarity.

There is also scope for integration strategies to prioritise local-level action. Local initiatives make sense not just because migrants and ethnic minorities are distributed unevenly across the UK but also because it is the local-level interaction that underpins social cohesion.

Overseas impacts

It is very easy when discussing migration to focus solely on the impacts of *im*migration. Yet, we know that *em*igration can also have significant impacts, especially on some countries in the developing world. Therefore, good migration policies need to go beyond local impacts and take account of these mutual, global impacts.

The most obvious of these mutual impacts involves the flows of highly skilled people from the developing world. Countries like the UK benefit immensely from the contributions of these workers. Two thirds of all work permits issued in recent years went to workers from countries with low or medium levels of human development, and one in three new doctors recruited to the NHS over the last decade qualified outside Europe, most in developing countries. This demand for migrant workers in rapidly ageing developed countries is likely to increase. But this brain drain, the sustained loss of the best and brightest from the developing world, has the potential to hamper economic growth and development in the sending countries. Where this occurs in critical sectors such as health and education in the poorest countries it can lead to what might be called 'brain strain' – the undermining of progress towards critical development objectives such as those listed in the Millennium Development Goals (MDGs).

The apparently obvious solution to these challenges – and one frequently espoused by 'compassionate racists' who want to 'help' the developing world – would be to place severe restrictions on the movement of highly skilled people from developing countries. But simply closing the door or clogging the drain could have deeply troubling implications for the human rights of the people involved, might not be effective, would limit the benefits that immigration can deliver for a country like the UK (especially in the key contribution that migrant workers make to the functioning of the welfare state) and may deny some countries access to the positive impacts to be gained from emigration (remittance and investment flows from diasporas can often fuel local development).

A progressive response to the challenges should start from the recognition that migration can have positive impacts for those who move, the societies they move to and the societies they leave behind. In the general terms, the most effective way would be to promote greater skill circulation, thereby securing the economic benefits greater mobility can deliver while avoiding permanent loss of skills from developing countries. This could even be done by something as straightforward as providing more funding to support skilled young UK residents who want to spend time working in developing countries.

Where particular brain strain hotspots are identified, it may be necessary to place some limits on large-scale recruitment of migrant workers. Here, the UK has made progress in devising codes of practice for overseas recruitment – particularly to the NHS – but these need to be widespread across sectors, involve coordination between all developed countries and be implemented better. More ambitiously, a multilateral framework could channel funds to these hotspots to encourage human capital formation and promote retention and return of highly skilled workers. All of this needs to be done in conjunction with efforts to promote development, democracy and human rights in the developing world, and correct global inequalities.

The key question however becomes one of finding the political will to identify and fund these sorts of initiatives – not an easy task given the primary political concern with immigration and an already stretched development budget. Naturally, a progressive commitment to global social justice requires rich countries to do something to ameliorate the impacts of their demand for skilled migrant workers. Private remittances from migrants themselves will go some way in doing this but if we are serious about commitments such as the MDGs then identifying and tackling the impacts of brain strain is a priority. There are also more instrumental reasons for tackling the developmental impacts of migration: the more incentives there are for potential migrants from poor countries to stay and for those who have already migrated to return, the more manageable immigration becomes for rich country policy-makers. In a mutually interdependent world, the push and pull factors generated by massive global inequality cannot be ignored.

Undocumented migrants

Tragic events such as the deaths of 58 people locked in the back of a lorry *en route* to the UK in 2000 and of 22 cockle pickers at Morecambe Bay in 2004 draw stark attention to the dark underbelly of the UK's migration policies. Anecdotal evidence (Pai, 2004) suggests that these deaths are just the tip of the iceberg. There seems to be a systemic problem of people being smuggled across borders, being bonded to pay back their traffickers, and living and working in atrocious conditions – something the Home Secretary has called a 'modern day slave trade'.[3] Indeed, it is thought that there are at least three million unauthorised foreigners in the EU, up from two million a decade ago (IOM, 2003).

---

3 http://www.homeoffice.gov.uk/n_story.asp?item_id=877; see also TUC report on 'Forced Labour and Migration to the UK' at http://www.tuc.org.uk/international/tuc-9317-f0.cfm

As borders become more secure and faking one's identity becomes more difficult, there is a risk that those already here illegally will stay and form an excluded underclass. A strategy of flushing these people out may be tempting, but criminalising undocumented migrants or stripping them of access to basic public services risks punishing the exploited rather than the exploiter. Not only will such measures lead to a damaging culture of suspicion but those already on the fringes of society may be driven further underground.

Instead, there needs to be better targeting of crooked employers. Despite wide-ranging powers to punish those employing undocumented workers, only 22 prosecutions and eight convictions were brought between 1998 and 2002 (Stevens, 2004). But getting tough is not enough and the Government must be congratulated for recognising this, at least in relation to workers from the new member states of the EU. Resisting calls to restrict access to the labour market for workers from the latest round of new EU member states was an admirable stance that recognised the need for migrant workers but also the need to provide incentives to those already here before 1 May 2004 to regularise their status.

The logical and pragmatic next step in this realistic, humane and effective approach would be to encourage the regularisation of other undocumented workers. Regularisation allows undocumented workers to move in an orderly manner from illegal to legal to permanent resident over a set time period (Papademetriou, 2002). Such schemes have been used with considerable success in several other EU members with more than two million migrants becoming regularised in the 1990s (OECD, 2003), including in Spain where the latest amnesty began in early 2005, and have been discussed in the US, most notably by President Bush, with regard to what to do about its estimated 9.3 million undocumented migrants (Passel *et al*, 2004).

The Government's imminent introduction of biometric identity cards may be the perfect opportunity for the UK to regularise those undocumented migrants who could prove that they have been resident and employed in the UK for a certain period and have not been engaged in criminal activities. They could be offered temporary, extendable leave to remain and after a designated period, if the person is still in stable employment (thus contributing to the economy) and demonstrates the requisite language skills, they might then be offered permanent residence.

Conclusion

The central argument running through this chapter has been that, while increased net immigration and greater diversity present challenges for the pursuit of social justice, these challenges are by no means new, significant or insurmountable. We should be careful not to exaggerate the role or impact of migration. Migration is neither the root cause nor the ultimate panacea for all of society's ills. While we must acknowledge the inherent difficulties of managing migration and promoting integration, we must also remember that migration can aid economic competitiveness (giving policy-makers more scope to achieve other policy ambitions), mitigate some of the demographic problems of an ageing society, and help the UK become more a more vibrant, diverse and cosmopolitan society.

When it comes to ethnic diversity, it is important to reiterate that, while there have been some changes in the UK's ethnic composition, the impact of these changes should not be exaggerated, especially when it comes to any real or perceived impact on the fundamentals of national identity. That said, the existence of an 'ethnic penalty' (or, in the case of recently-arrived minority immigrants, an 'ethnic penalty plus') needs to be addressed urgently, both for its own sake and for the sake of social cohesion. Importantly, the success of previous immigrants should not make us complacent about the integration prospects of recent immigrants. Nor should the problems of existing minority communities prejudice us against further migration, even from those communities that are seen to be doing badly.

This chapter has sought to outline five key areas of migration policy in which the pursuit of social justice can be furthered to the benefit of migrants themselves, the communities they live in and the societies they came from:

- a fair admission system based on current and future labour markets' needs for those whose arrival can be regulated;
- a clear set of entitlements for migrants to promote effective integration and pre-empt public fears about 'abuse';
- early and effective integration policies that prioritise socio-economic empowerment and support cultural diversity;
- a recognition of and action towards the negative impacts of immigration to the UK on countries of origin;
- efforts to regularise undocumented workers who may be exploited.

Three further challenges are also evident: we need to change the language with which we discuss migration, to deepen the linkages between migration policies and other areas of public policies, and to strengthen the evidence base on which migration policies are made.

First, contemporary public discourse on migration is deeply problematic. At worst, migration is cast as a 'problem' that needs to be solved or kept in check. At best, discussions often oscillate unhelpfully between instrumentalism and obligation: what can migrants do for society and what should society do for migrants? If the material strategies outlined earlier in the chapter are to stand any chance of success, they need to be bolstered by discursive strategies: less essentialising of ethnic difference (after all it is need and not difference that should underpin progressive policies); more representations of migrants as agents, capable of changing themselves and also of effecting change; more political leadership to shape and lead public opinion in these areas rather than be held hostage by the views of xenophobic or racist segments of society; and more voices of migrants and ethnic minorities in shaping public policy in this area.

Second, contemporary policy development on migration is made problematic by the temptation of many to see migration as somehow a uniquely difficult challenge. Of course migration involves complicated trade-offs such as those between employer need and greed, or between investing in the domestic labour force and importing ready-to-work migrants. Yet, it is also important to recognise that these are neither new nor isolated trade-offs. All public policy involves these sorts of trade-offs and governments succeed or fail according to how well they deal them. While migration adds a layer of complexity to these challenges, it does not create anything wholly unfamiliar to policy-makers.

Third, good migration policies also need a good evidence base. This is critical to efforts to identify and address the size and nature of the ethnic penalty. More reliable data will also be critical in restoring public confidence and take out some of the political heat from the migration debate. The Government should think seriously about an independent panel to monitor immigration flows and report to Parliament (Sriskandarajah, 2004). Most ambitiously, such a panel could mimic the functions of the Bank of England's Monetary Policy Committee (a Managed Migration Policy Committee perhaps) and identify the broad parameters for the appropriate scale of immigration into the UK.

The question of what happens when an outsider becomes an insider, especially when that outsider is ethnically different from the majority of insiders, is a vexed one for both liberal theorists and progressive policy-makers. While the former stand accused of ignoring outsiders, the latter are faced with an unenviable combination of a hostile political climate, a plethora of hard to manage policies and lingering doubts about first principles. Yet, as we rethink social justice, the challenge is to frame a set of fair, cogent and sustainable immigration and integration policies. Failure to do so could have disastrous effects: permanent social exclusion for some groups of migrants, strains on social cohesion, growing support for the far right, and increasing global inequality.

References

Cole P (2000) *Philosophies of Exclusion: liberal political theory and immigration* Edinburgh: Edinburgh University Press

Geddes A (2003) 'Migration and the Welfare State in Europe' in Spencer S (ed) *The Politics of Migration: Managing Opportunity, Conflict and Change* Oxford: The Political Quarterly

Goodhart D (2004) 'Too diverse?', *Prospect*, , see http://www.prospect magazine.co.uk/start.asp?P_Article=12394 See also responses to this piece by several commentators at http://www.prospect-magazine.co.uk/HtmlPages/replies.asp

Home Office (2004) *Persons Granted British Citizenship United Kingdom* London: Home Office 2003 figures: http://www.homeoffice.gov.uk/rds/pdfs04/hosb0704.pdf, 1993 figures: http://www.home-office.gov.uk/rds/pdfs2/hosb1294.pdf

International Organization for Migration (IOM) (2003) *World Migration 2000* Geneva: IOM

Jordan B and Düvell F (2003) *Migration: The boundaries of equality and justice* Cambridge: Polity Pres

Lindley J, Dale A and Dex S (2004) 'Ethnic differences in women's demographic, family characteristics and economic activity profiles, 1992 to 2002' *Labour Market Trends*, April, London: ONS http://www.statistics.gov.uk/articles/labour_market_trends/ethnic_differences.pdf

ONS (2004) *Focus on Ethnicity* London: ONS http://www.statistics.gov.uk/cci/nugget.asp?id=459

Organisation for Economic Cooperation and Development (OECD) (2003) *Trends in International Migration 2003* Paris: OECD http://www1.oecd.org/publications/e-book/8103061E.PDF

Page B (2004) *The Second Death Of Liberal England?* London: MORI http://www.mori.com/pubinfo/bp/the-second-death-of-liberal-england.shtml

Pai H-H (2004) 'Inside the grim world of the gangmasters' *The Guardian*, 27 March 2004 http://www.guardian.co.uk/uk_news/story/0,,1179164,00.html

Papademetriou D (2002) *Converging Realities of the US-Mexico Relationship* Washington, DC: Migration Policy Institute http://www.migrationinformation.org/USfocus/display.cfm?ID=35

Passel J S, Capps R and Fix M (2004) *Undocumented Immigrants: Facts And Figures* Washington, DC: Urban Institute http://www.urban.org/UploadedPDF/1000587_undoc_immigrants_facts.pdf

Pearce N (2004) 'Diversity versus Solidarity: A New Progressive Dilemma?' *Renewal*, Vol. 12 (3), London: Lawrence and Wishart http://www.renewal.org.uk/vol12no32004diversityversussolidarity.htm

Phillips T (2004) 'Multiculturalism's legacy is 'have a nice day' racism' *The Guardian*, 28 May 2004

Prime Minister's Strategy Unit (2003) *Ethnic Minorities and the Labour Market*,London: Prime Minister's Strategy Unity http://www.number-10.gov.uk/su/ethnic%20minorities/report/index.htm

Rees P and Butt F (2004) 'Ethnic change and diversity in England, 1981–2001', *Area*, vol. 36(2), Oxford: Blackwells

RSA/Prospect (2003) Diversity versus solidarity conference, London, 28 January 2003

Salt J (2003) *International Migration and the United Kingdom: Report of the United Kingdom SOPEMI Correspondent to the OECD 2003* London: Migration Research Unit http://www.geog.ucl.ac.uk /mru/docs/uk_sopemi_03.pdf

Social Exclusion Unit (2004) *Breaking the Cycle: Taking stock of progress and priorities for the future* London: Office of the Deputy Prime Minister

Stevens D (2004) 'The Nationality, Immigration and Asylum Act 2002:

Secure Borders, Safe Haven?' *Modern Law Review*, 67(4), Oxford: Blackwells

Sriskandarajah D (2004) Migration targets? *Prospect, October 2004*,

Sriskandarajah *et al.* (2004) *FactFile: Labour Migration to the UK* London: ippr http://www.ippr.org/research/files/team19/project158/FFLabMigFINAL.pdf

Thompson A (2005) *Asian 'Britishness':* London: ippr

Toynbee P (2004) 'The real reason why we should fear immigration', *The Guardian*, 11 February 2004

Sustainability and Social Justice

Julie Foley, Tony Grayling and Mike Dixon

The connection between environmental protection and distributive justice should underpin our modern day understanding of sustainable development. It has become more widely recognised that the poor tend to suffer disproportionately from environmental degradation and indeed that social inequalities are amongst the very causes of environmental harm. Yet while there is much common ground between the goals of sustainable development and social justice, there can potentially be difficult trade-offs; sometimes policies which would be most effective in protecting the environment are those which could have unacceptably regressive impacts.

These trade-offs are rarely explicitly spelt out and as a result those whose primary interest is in achieving social justice have traditionally devoted little attention to sustainable development. However, there is growing recognition that some environmental problems require immediate action to protect the rights and development choices of the most deprived communities. Climate change is already creating injustices around the world with the poorest and most vulnerable communities, in both developed and developing nations, most at risk from weather-related hazards such as drought and floods. Progressive governments need to seriously consider how social justice and environmental sustainability interrelate. Does social justice require sustainability? How should we manage any trade-offs between them? Are there policies which help achieve environmental objectives while at the same time being consistent with wider social justice objectives?

One reason for the lack of discussion of the way social justice and sustainable development fit together has been that proponents of each have tended to use very different rhetoric. Those talking about social justice in the economic sphere tend to favour arguments that promote GDP growth and the promotion of human welfare through economic means, placing little value on the environment. Some environmental groups, on the other hand, have traditionally placed more emphasis on the intrinsic value of the natural environment; they have focused on the protection of the countryside, wildlife habitats and endangered species. Many environmental campaign groups could arguably be seen as occupying unpopular anti-consumerist ground (Jacobs, 1997; Agyeman and Evans, 2004). The emergence of the 'pragmatic environmentalist', who has tried to use a more appealing language to express concerns about consumption and economic growth, has had some impact though. The objective has been to shift the argument away from what people will lose as a result of environmentally damaging policies, towards what they will gain (Foley, 2004a). But a full reconciliation between the two progressive objectives remains elusive.

While there have been some notable successes in recent years – the advancement of the environmental taxes and charges for enforcing the 'polluter pays' principle and the 2003 *Energy White Paper* which put climate change at the heart of energy policy are two examples – in many areas the Government's performance has been less than impressive. For example, it has not managed to reverse the trend towards faster, longer distance transport, mainly made by car, away from local modes like walking, cycling and taking the bus. Like administrations before it, this Government has struggled to handle accusations that any environmental policies are simply 'anti-motorist'. The fuel tax protests in 2000 resulted in lasting reductions to fuel duty in real terms. It is not clear that government policy is driven by clearly thought through principles or expressing a consistent message about the importance of environmental concerns.

The next decade is a crucial one for environmental policy. There is unprecedented scientific evidence about the detrimental effects of current levels of production and consumption on the state and abundance of future environmental resources, and hence unprecedented need for government. This makes the issue of how to reconcile environmental concerns with social justice a pressing one. This chapter suggests how this can be achieved.

Our core argument is that environmental sustainability is compatible with social justice; indeed, in many instances it is a necessary condition to achieve wider social justice objectives. We argue that this is the case for two main reasons, both of which stem from a concern for human welfare.

The first of these results from the obligation of the current generation to future generations. There must be some resources available in the long term which can be distributed fairly; without sustainability there could be no social justice in anything but our own generation (or very few generations hence). Social justice, over the long term, therefore requires us to preserve, renew or find substitutes for those natural resources which are critical for human life. Although there are difficult questions here about the nature and scale of intergenerational obligations, there can be little doubt that our responsibilities are at least significant. Action in some areas of environmental sustainability is therefore required as a precondition for the pursuit of social justice.

The second reason concerns human welfare in a shorter timeframe. As both Miller and Burchardt argue (in Chapter 1 and Chapter 11 respectively), material resources, which invariably means a focus on income and wealth, are not the only goods which should be distributed in a socially just way. Environmental goods too contribute directly to human welfare and their distribution and availability are a matter of social justice. In terms of the principle of social justice presented in Chapter 1 some environmental goods form part of the social minimum, while others are subject to the principle of fair distribution. So, for example, access to green spaces should be part of the minimum to which all citizens should be entitled.

These two arguments help us to weigh the importance of environmental sustainability against other priorities within a framework of social justice. But wherever possible progress towards meeting these two objectives must be conditional on a third objective: ensuring that policies designed to achieve primarily environmental objectives are not regressive in their impact. For example, how can we ensure that a system of road user charging does not disproportionately impact on the poor? This chapter draws these arguments together by presenting three principles:

1. The precondition principle – any natural resource which is a precondition for human life and wellbeing, must be protected for the foreseeable future unless it can be renewed or its contribution to human welfare provided by other means.
2. The distributive principle – environmental 'goods' and 'bads' should be distributed according to the principles of social justice. In some instances this requires a minimum standard for all citizens, while in others it requires fair distribution.

3. The just impact principle – policy responses designed to ensure the protection or renewal of natural resources must, in so far as is possible, have a progressive impact.

The final section of the chapter applies this framework to the overriding environmental challenge of the age – preventing climate change – and considers how these principles can be used to develop socially just policy in two domestic areas related to this: domestic energy use and transport policy.

Why should the centre-left care about the environment? The three principles

Concern for the environment can be motivated by many factors. We might think that the environment is only worth preserving or renewing to the extent that it contributes to human welfare, we might think that the natural environment has an intrinsic worth which places an obligation on us to preserve it, or we might be drawn to some combination of the two. As Dobson argues, the source of our concern for the environment makes a considerable difference to which elements of the natural world we think it is important to preserve and hence to the way we should think about policy design (Dobson, 1998). If we think that nature has an intrinsic value independent of whether it is useful for humans then we would face much stronger pressures to preserve some parts of it than if we think its value is instrumental, deriving from its contribution to human welfare.

For progressives, arguments about the intrinsic value of nature independent of its contribution to human welfare tend to hold little sway. Although other values may guide us to preserve nature for its own sake, human welfare is the central issue in relation to social justice. For progressive policy-makers, it is the interaction between people and the environment that offers greatest political appeal. This view was reflected in the Brundtland report for the 1987 World Commission on Environment and Development (WCED) which proposed that sustainable development should understood as 'development that meets the needs of present generations without compromising the ability of future generations to meet their own needs' (Bruntland, 1987). This is the most widely accepted definition and is explicitly anthropocentric, confirming the view that, as far as social justice is concerned, we should only care about the environment to the extent that it impacts upon human welfare.

It is worth noting that, in practice, this may mean a broader range of responsibilities than it might seem at first. Norton argues that there may be relatively little practical difference between the two positions – one seeing all nature as intrinsically valuable and the other only seeing it as being important when it contributes to human welfare because human welfare depends on closely integrated and finely balanced ecosystems (Norton, 1991). Preserving the parts of ecosystems which contribute to human welfare may mean preserving the whole system in many cases.

This leads us to consider which elements of the natural world social justice requires us to preserve or renew. Which environmental factors are important for human welfare and why? There are two separate arguments here which stem from three fundamental principles and we will discuss them in turn. The first of these is the precondition principle, which concerns those environmental goods which are critical for – in the sense of being necessary for – the production and reproduction of human life (Dobson, 1998). If the benefits of a natural resource cannot be provided by any other man-made or natural means, social justice requires us to renew and sustain it.

The precondition principle

A breathable atmosphere, drinkable water and fertile soil are necessary for human life and the precondition principle requires us to preserve them for current and future generations. Other cases are more difficult. Take biological species; we have to consider the role that these species play in preserving environmental ecosystems that are valuable, as well as the potential medicines and scientific advances that such species may enable. The difficulty arises because there is an element of scientific uncertainty – we cannot predict with any great accuracy how much damage will be caused by certain types of environmental degradation. Should we divert precious energy into protecting natural resources when we do not know if they are worth protecting in the long term?

The standard way of dealing with this difficulty is through invoking what has become known as the 'precautionary principle'. This has been endorsed internationally on many occasions, including at the Earth Summit meeting in Rio in 1992. The idea here is that 'where there are threats of serious or irreversible damage, lack of full scientific certainty shall not be used as a reason for postponing cost-effective measures to prevent environmental degredation' (Rio Declaration, 1992). It is important to realise that the precautionary principle is unclear on one crucial point: what exactly counts as 'damage'. One reading of the Rio Declaration is that the precautionary principle would be compatible with valuing nature for nature's sake. Yet from a social justice perspective, as we have argued above, this is not what is important about the environment. For this reason we present the precondition principle which, while being closely related to and incorporating the precautionary principle, is more explicit about which environmental goods it covers; those which can be expected to be important for future human welfare.

Implicit in the precondition principle (and the precautionary principle on which it draws) is the assumption that we have obligations to future generations and to those living in other countries.

Theories of social justice usually assume a 'population' across which goods and bads are distributed. Why should this population be restricted only to people alive at any one moment in time? While it seems undeniably right that present human wants should be placed below the needs of some future generations, it is unclear that this should extend indefinitely. We cannot reasonably have the same obligation to every future generation, however many there may be in the future, as this would require that we use an absolute minimum of natural resources consistent with our survival (Laslet and Fishkin, 1992). A more convincing argument is that our responsibility to future generations diminishes over time, so our responsibility to the next generation is very nearly the same as to our own but our responsibility to a generation many millennia away is almost negligible. These obligations should fade slowly enough to deal properly with long-term environmental issues such as the decay of radioactive waste (Dobson, 1998).

The question of our obligations to those living in other countries is also problematic, as Chapter 9 illustrates. There are two related issues here. The first is that many environmental problems require global solutions; there is no unilateral solution to the problem of climate change so any effort must be a united one. The second is that actions taken in one country can have dramatic repercussions in other countries and it is generally the poorest that suffer most as a result of the actions of the richest. In 2001, CO_2 emissions per capita in low-income countries were 23 times smaller than those in the US and ten times smaller than those in the UK; per capita energy use in sub-Saharan Africa was less than an eighth of that in the US and a quarter of that in the UK

(World Bank, 2004). Yet it is the developing world which suffers most from environmental degradation. Climate change is undermining food security in places such as sub-Saharan Africa and there is a growing consensus that a rapidly changing climate in Africa could be highly damaging to development (Juniper, 2004).

Despite differences amongst theorists in terms of how exactly to motivate and define our responsibility to both future generations and to other countries, three things are clear. First, that we do have obligations to future generations and to those living in other countries; second, that these obligations are substantial, at least in the foreseeable future; and third, that we are currently failing to meet these obligations in many areas and, as the Brundtland definition recognises, the claims of justice to resources and environmental goods by every individual in present and future generations will be denied if existing patterns of consumption and development are allowed to continue, particularly in developing countries (Miller, 1999; Juniper, 2004; Retallack, 2005).

The distributive principle

Natural resources that are necessary as a precondition for human life and wellbeing are not the only part of the environment we should be concerned about as a matter of social justice. Once these are accounted for, there are some environmental goods which should be distributed between different people and communities in a socially just fashion. Some environmental goods should form part of the social minimum and all citizens should have a basic level of the good, though above this there could be significant levels of inequality. Other environmental goods should be distributed across the population fairly. Once environmental protection which falls under the precondition principle or the distributive principle have been achieved, it is a matter of democratic decision making and individual choice over whether to invest extra resources in environmental preservation.

Understanding the social minimum as including environmental goods builds on a well-established train of thought. There has been a shift in thinking about measures of success that are not solely dependent on economic indications, putting wider quality of life concerns at the centre of development policies. While we do not wish to catalogue an exhaustive list of the environmental goods which should be part of the social minimum, it is certain that this would include clean air, clean water, access to green space and a right of access to the countryside. There are undoubtedly difficult trade-offs here but this should not be surprising. Where the social minimum is comprised of different elements, there will always be debate about the appropriate balance of resources in achieving different elements of this. Yet this does not mean that any decision is arbitrary; even when the trade-offs are complex there are still preferable options.

Environmental goods that do not form part of the social minimum should be distributed in accordance with the principle of fair distribution (see Chapter 1). They can be distributed unequally as long as the distribution reflects relevant factors such as personal desert and personal choice. For example, it is not unjust that those people who have chosen to live in cities with better employment opportunities and other advantages have worse access to the benefits of the countryside than those who choose to live there. However, as Chapter 2 shows, the distribution of environmental 'goods' such as clean air and access to open spaces, and 'bads' such as pollution, can be strikingly unequal. These are important for both intrinsic and instrumental reasons; access to a good local environment is an important part of a good quality of life and living in an area with unclean air and little space to exercise can often exacerbate respiratory diseases, like asthma, and other health problems such as obesity (Duxbury, 2004).

It is the poorest communities which are often most affected by environmental health issues and the lack of access to environmental goods. The gap in mortality rates between different social groups in the UK has increased almost two and a half times since the 1930s with a major factor being where people live (DoH, 2003). This may be partly linked to the fact that the most deprived wards have had highest pollutant concentrations. Those in the most deprived wards were exposed to 41 per cent higher concentrations of poisonous nitrous dioxide gas than those in averagely deprived wards in 2002. Industrial sites are disproportionately located in deprived areas, with five times as many sites in the wards containing the most deprived 10 per cent of the population and seven times as many emission sources, than in wards with the least deprived 10 per cent (Walker et al, 2003). There is also some evidence which shows that landfill sites are more likely to be near deprived areas and there is also a clear relationship between risk of flooding and deprivation in England, with eight times more people in the most deprived deciles living in a tidal floodplain than in the least deprived decile (Elliott et al, 2001; Walker et al, 2003).

Aligned with increasing awareness of the connections between environmental and social deprivation is the concept of 'liveability'; there is a growing recognition across government that communities which look down-at-heel and uncared for are more likely to attract environmental crime and low-level disorder which in turn can jeopardise economic success (ODPM, 2003). These kinds of liveability issues can also play a central role in determining how people relate to local civic and political institutions. Frustration breeds resentment and fuels a sense of hopelessness in the ability of those in power to effect change.

The two principles above, including the precautionary principle, provide guidance about the extent to which we should invest resources in protecting and improving the environment. Yet these are not enough. They say nothing about how this should be achieved or who should bear the brunt of any costs. The third principle addresses these issues.

The just impact principle

This principle is aimed at ensuring that the distribution of the costs and benefits of preventing environmental degradation is socially just, using the framework outlined in Chapter 1. Policies should not impinge on the social minimum, nor should they compromise equality of opportunity or equal citizenship. Where possible, environmental policies should promote these aims while ensuring that the distribution of costs and benefits is fair.

The just distribution principle draws on the established idea that the polluter should pay and that the person or organisation that is responsible for creating environmental degradation should be responsible for rectifying or compensating for any damage. Environmental economists have long argued for internalising environmental externalities, such as pollution, into the costs of goods and services and this government has explored the use of various charging and taxation measures as a means of putting a market value on environmental costs and encouraging greater resource efficiency. The impacts of these kinds of measures are, however, not neutral across society as the costs will tend to fall more heavily on some people than on others, and the environmental benefits will tend to advantage some more than others. Progressive policy makers are often cautious about environmental charges or taxes on social equity grounds in terms of their potential impacts on low-income individuals or households. For example, it may be that employment in low-skill manufacturing jobs would be affected much more seriously than employment in high-skill services by a tax on automobile production, while those that would see most benefit (in terms of reduced congestion) would be wealthier people who tend not to work in low-skill manufacturing jobs.

While the principle of just distribution is important, we recognise that there may be cases in which other principles take precedence over it. This is particularly the case with the precautionary principle. Where this requires action and no policy which would satisfy the just impact principle is available, social justice requires that we implement a policy which does not have a just impact. On the whole though, every effort should be made to design policy so that it fulfils all three principles outlined above.

Applying the principles: climate change

We now consider how these principles can be applied in practice, focusing on the overriding environmental challenge of the age – preventing dangerous climate change. This helps illustrate some of the synergies, difficulties and trade-offs that reconciling social justice and sustainable development can create.

A few sceptics continue to deny the link between greenhouse gas emissions and dangerous climate change, or downplay its significance. However, the overwhelming consensus of expert scientific opinion, led by the UN's Intergovernmental Panel on Climate Change (IPCC) is that the accumulation of carbon dioxide (CO_2) and other greenhouse gases in the atmosphere from human activities, mainly the combustion of fossil fuels, is causing global warming and dangerous climate change. Unless action is soon taken to drastically reduce emissions of greenhouse gases from human activities, while preserving and enhancing the capacity of natural sinks for carbon dioxide including soils, forests and oceans, we are likely to be heading for environmental disaster.

Some communities such as those in the Arctic and low-lying island nations like Tuvalu are already experiencing adverse impacts directly attributable to global warming (Lynas, 2004). Extreme weather events such as heat waves, droughts, storms and floods appear to be happening more often and with greater severity worldwide, consistent with the climatologists' predictions. The poorest countries are the most vulnerable but no country is immune from the impacts. For example, the heat wave across Europe in the summer of 2003, which killed 30,000 people, has been strongly linked to global warming (Stott *et al*, 2004).

No amount of climate change can be considered safe but there is increasing scientific evidence to suggest that beyond a certain level the adverse impacts increase markedly (Hare, 2003; Retallack, 2005). If average global temperature exceeds about 2°C above the pre-industrial level for a sustained period, then the evidence suggests that billions of people worldwide will face water shortages, especially in developing countries, crop losses will hit major food exporting countries and irreversible damage may be done to whole ecosystems on which people rely, such as coral reefs and the Amazon rainforest.

Beyond 2°C, the risk of abrupt or runaway climate change also increases, such as would be caused by the collapse of the Gulf Stream (ironically plunging Britain into a period colder than experienced during the 'Mini Ice Age' of the 17th and 18th centuries when people skated on the Thames), or the collapse of the West Antarctic Ice Sheet that would increase sea levels by several metres and inundate low-lying lands, including world cities like London and New York, or the transformation of the world's forests and soils into a net source rather a sink for carbon dioxide that would accelerate global warming, or the release of huge quantities of methane (a more powerful greenhouse gas than carbon dioxide) stored on the ocean bed as methane hydrates, which would do likewise.

On a precautionary basis, the precondition principle therefore suggests taking action to limit average global temperature rise to no more than 2°C above the pre-industrial level. A number of significant individuals and organisations have come to this conclusion including the UK Secretary of State for the Environment, Food and Rural Affairs, Margaret Beckett (2003); the chief executive of BP, Lord Browne; the EU's Environment Council; the German Advisory Council on Global Change (2003); the Association of Small Island States (AOSIS); the Government of the Philippines; the North-South Dialogue on Equity in the Greenhouse; Climate Action Network International (2003) and the International Climate Change Taskforce (ICCT, 2005; Retallack, 2005).

Average surface global temperature rose by about 0.6°C during the 20th century. Some further warming is inevitable due to the inertia of the global climate and energy systems. The most authoritative report to date, the third assessment report of the IPCC, suggests that average temperature could rise by another 1.4°C to 5.8°C between 1990 and 2100, depending on the global emissions trajectory and the actual relationship between greenhouse gas concentrations and temperature changes (IPCC, 2001). It is likely to be very difficult to avoid breaching the 2°C threshold but by making deep cuts in greenhouse gas emissions while preserving the natural sinks for CO_2, it may be possible to limit the peak temperature rise and bring the temperature back below the threshold in the long term – and hope that irreversible damage has not already been done.

Reducing global greenhouse gas emissions

Scientists are not yet able to specify the exact relationship between atmospheric concentrations of greenhouse gases and temperature changes. The precautionary clause of the precondition principle must once again apply. Analysis commissioned by ippr based on IPCC scenarios suggests that to have a high probability (about 80 per cent) of long-term stabilisation at or below the 2°C threshold requires stabilising the atmospheric concentration of greenhouse gases at no more than about 400 parts per million (ppm) CO_2 equivalent (Retallack, 2005). Including the non-CO_2 elements, total atmospheric greenhouse gas concentration has probably already exceeded this level and will rise well above it. But if the emissions are subsequently reduced below the rate at which they are absorbed by the biosphere, then the concentration can be reduced again. Meeting 400 ppm CO_2 equivalent by the end of this century is likely to require ensuring that global emissions of CO_2 peak by 2020 and are then reduced by more than half from the 1990 level by the middle of this century and continue to be reduced thereafter. Equally concerted efforts will need to be made to reduce emissions of other greenhouse gases. It can be done through the deployment of energy saving, renewable energy and other low-carbon technologies on a vast scale but the longer that action is delayed the harder it becomes.

If a precautionary approach applies to mitigating dangerous climate change, then the just distribution and just impact principles apply to the means by which it is done. Article 3.1 of the United Nations Framework Convention on Climate Change (UNFCCC), ratified by 189 countries representing 98 per cent of the world's population, requires that the parties protect the climate system 'on the basis of equity and in accordance with their common but differentiated responsibilities and respective capabilities' (United Nations, 1992). Per capita emissions are far higher in developed countries, which are also far richer than developing countries. In social justice terms, this means that cuts in emissions should be far steeper in developed countries, which should provide assistance to developing countries both for low-emission economic development and for adaptation to the climate change for which they are largely responsible. Developing countries should be allowed to grow their per capita emissions initially to enable economic development.

A reasonable way to apply the just impact principle internationally would be to converge on equal per capita emission entitlements between countries as global emissions contract. A pure 'contraction and convergence' framework as proposed by the Global Commons Institute would mean specifying the convergence date and level and the trajectory of emissions entitlements for each country from the outset, with a global emissions trading scheme as a balancing mechanism and a means of transferring resources from rich countries to poor countries (Meyer, 2000). The International Climate Change Taskforce (ICCT, 2005) has proposed a staged process towards eventual convergence, building on the UNFCCC and Kyoto Protocol. Countries would take on different levels of commitment according to their stage of development between least developed and fully industrialised, with commitments periodically negotiated consistent with the long-term objective and the latest scientific evidence and technological developments.

The Brazilian Government has proposed a different principle: historical responsibility with emission cuts proportionate to cumulative emissions since industrialisation (Evans, 2002). This would mean, for example, that the UK would be required to reduce emissions even more sharply while recently industrialised countries would have less stringent commitments. However, historical responsibility is probably a more appropriate principle of equity to apply to addressing the impacts of climate change, particularly on developing countries. In this respect, the International Climate Change Taskforce recommended the establishment of an international compensation fund, with contributions linked, in part at least, to historical responsibility for emissions (ICCT, 2005).

Reducing UK greenhouse gas emissions

If Britain is to take its fair share of responsibility for combating climate change, then ippr has proposed that it should not only meet its Kyoto commitments and voluntary target to cut CO_2 emissions by 20 per cent from the 1990 level by 2010 (DEFRA, 2004a). It should also commit to cutting CO_2 emissions by 40 per cent by 2020, towards the likely need to cut emissions by about 90 per cent by 2050 (Retallack, 2005). This is based on convergence on equal per capita emission entitlements between countries by 2050 and a global emissions trajectory consistent with meeting 400 ppm CO_2 equivalent by the end of the century. The Government's current long-term goal of a 60 per cent cut by 2050, as set out in the energy White Paper (DTI, 2003) and recommended by the Royal Commission on Environmental Pollution (RCEP, 2000) is based on the assumption that stabilising at 550 ppm CO_2 would be consistent with limiting temperature rise to 2°C. Our analysis suggests only a 10 to 20 per cent chance of keeping to this threshold at this concentration (Retallack, 2005), which is not consistent with the precautionary principle.

As it stands, Britain is meeting its Kyoto commitment but falling short of its domestic target, on course for only a 14 per cent reduction in CO_2 emissions by 2010. Targets for renewable electricity, combined heat and power, industrial and domestic energy saving and transport emissions are likely to be missed (Mitchell and Woodman, 2004). The UK climate change programme is currently under review (DEFRA, 2004b). New measures are required to get back on track. Below we consider how the principles of just sustainability can be applied to two difficult areas of UK climate change policy: household energy and transport policy.

Domestic energy consumption
Household energy demand is growing in the UK. Electricity use grew by 16.5 per cent between 1990 and 2000 and is projected to grow by 12 per cent between 2000 and 2010 (Cambridge Econometrics, 2004). This energy demand was responsible for 27 per cent of total UK carbon emissions in 2004 (DEFRA, 2004c). While the Government has been able to mitigate the effects of much of the growth in energy use by switching from coal to less carbon-intensive gas in energy production, there are limited possibilities for further substitution (Ekins and Dresner, 2004). It is clear that we need to find ways of reducing carbon emissions by reducing domestic energy consumption (as well as by reducing the carbon intensity of domestic energy sources). Although the Government has a target of reducing carbon emissions by 20 per cent from 1990 levels by 2010 and by 60 per cent by 2050, it looks increasingly unlikely that this will happen. In this case the challenge is to develop policies that are consistent with the just impact principle. This is not easy.

The *Energy White Paper* and the *Energy Green Paper*, issued by the European Commission in 2002, both place an emphasis on 'doing more with less' and 'decoupling' economic growth from energy use through greater energy efficiency, particularly in the domestic sector. Many other European countries, including Norway, Sweden, Germany and Italy have introduced carbon taxes on household energy aimed at incentivising households to reduce their energy consumption. In the Netherlands, this has been shown to be highly effective (Foley, 2004b). Yet these countries differ from the UK in an important way; they have relatively low levels of 'fuel poverty', understood as the proportion of households that need to spend more than 10 per cent of income on heating in order to obtain an adequate level of warmth. In 2001, there were an estimated three million UK households in fuel poverty, of which two million contained people aged 60 years or over, a child under sixteen years, a disabled person or someone suffering from a long-term illness (DTI, 2003).

A significant proportion of preventable illness and deaths in the UK are caused by people living in damp and cold housing, suggesting that fuel poverty is not just a priority for energy policy by public health policy. It is estimated that 23,500 more people died in winter 2003/4 (December to March) in the UK than would be expected from death rates occurring over the rest of the year (ONS, 2004). Over half of these deaths were from heart attacks and strokes and the rest were from respiratory diseases, influenza and hypothermia. Each winter a higher proportion of the UK population die as a direct result of unseasonal cold weather than in either Finland or Russia (Faculty of Public Health, 2003).

The aim of reducing household carbon emissions therefore needs to be achieved in a way that is sensitive to the extent of fuel poverty. In light of the poor energy efficiency of the much of the UK's housing stock there have been concerns that a domestic energy tax could unfairly impact on the fuel poor, violating the just impact principle. Research by Ekins and Dresner (2004) found it would be impossible to introduce an energy tax combined with a means-tested compensation package which did not exacerbate fuel poverty for the very worst off, as the variation in domestic energy use between households is too great. Recent proposals for a domestic energy tax have therefore included the idea of the government borrowing the money to finance a five-year crash programme to eliminate fuel poverty, then introducing the tax and using the proceeds to pay off the loan (Fabian Society, 2000). It is questionable, however, whether there would be enough sufficiently skilled people available to insulate enough homes within five years. In addition, the existing Warm Front scheme has already found that it is difficult to identify fuel poor households.

Introducing a domestic energy tax in the not too distant future is also unlikely given that energy prices are forecast to start rising. The DTI forecasts that there will be a steady rise in electricity and gas prices over the period to 2010 (DTI, 2004). If energy prices start to rise, it will be politically impossible to introduce a domestic energy tax. There is no doubt that the *Energy White Paper* measures are essential for reducing greenhouse gas emissions and increasing energy efficiency. But their contribution to increasing energy prices could potentially make it even more difficult to meet the Government's fuel poverty pledge

For political reasons (the likely increase in fuel prices) and for principles reasons (the difficulty with developing a policy consistent with the just impact principle), policy makers face a dilemma in relation to domestic energy use. A possible solution could be threefold. First, government should revise the eligibility criteria for Warm Front grants and provide energy efficiency options appropriate for hard to treat homes. This is the fairest way to achieve reductions consistent with the just impact principle. Second, it should increase renewable electricity use as laid out in the 2002 Renewables Obligation. The offshore wind industry has already proven to be a catalyst for economic regeneration and in Denmark 16,000 jobs are accounted for by wind turbine companies (DTI, 2003; Danish Wind Power Association, 2003). The huge wind resource in the UK represents manufacturing investment opportunities, although there are undoubtedly difficult trade-offs involved in balancing the views of individuals and communities which are against the visual intrusion of wind farms with national and international interests to advance renewable energy. Third, government should encourage innovation in future low carbon industries, like wave and hydrogen power.

Transport

Road transport's share of total UK CO_2 emissions could rise to 29 per cent by 2020 overtaking the domestic, industry and service sectors. Transport is likely to be the only sector with rising emissions in the period to 2020, largely due to increases from road transport. If the Government's policies in other sectors prove successful, the increase in CO_2 emissions from road transport will not be so great as to reverse the downward trend predicted for total UK emissions. After 2020, the continued increase in emissions from road transport could start to raise total UK CO_2 emissions again and begin to erode the carbon savings anticipated from greater energy efficiency and renewable electricity use (Foley and Ferguson, 2003).

There are a number of challenges in the area of transport policy. One is unrelated to the principles identified above; instead it concerns the need to reconcile freedom of choice with the common good. Left to their own devices, the transport choices of individuals and organisations do not add up to a common good and may ultimately be self-defeating. It is not that people are making more journeys or spending more time on the move. The number of journeys made and the time spent travelling has not changed significantly for at least 30 years (Metz, 2003). What has changed is that people are making longer journeys by faster means. The long-term trend is away from slow, local modes like walking, cycling and taking the bus, towards faster, longer distance transport, mainly by car (DfT, 2004a).

In relation to social justice though, there are two key challenges. The first, because of the precondition principle, is how to reduce emissions in a way consistent with the just impact principle. This links transport policy back to the overriding challenge of climate change. But there is a second issue; the need to ensure that transport policy develops in such a way that it provides a basic minimum level of access to geographical mobility for all. This relates to the distributive principle outlined above.

Regarding climate change, the question for policy makers is how to respond to this situation. How can the environmental costs of these changes in behaviour be minimised? How can public policy change people's behaviour? Some of the problems can be tackled by technology. Advancements in pollution abatement technologies and cleaner fuels have led to significant reductions in the exhaust emissions of air pollutants from new cars. To date, the carbon dioxide emissions from increases in road traffic have been largely offset by improvements in vehicle efficiency. But future fuel efficiency improvements are unlikely to keep pace with traffic growth. In the long term, hydrogen power, which is far cleaner, holds the potential to replace fossil fuels in transport (Foley, 2001; DfT, 2004b).

But this form of technological response will not be sufficient. Some problems are less amenable to technological interventions and, in any case, shorter-term measures are required. One option, which must be pursued, is to ensure that land use and spatial planning is used to promote compact urban developments that mix housing, shops, services and employment together, so that people can meet their needs closer to home (Urban Task Force, 1999). The Government's Sustainable Communities Plan edges in the right direction but the minimum densities it proposes are not high enough to make a real difference (ODPM, 2003). The concern, however, is that major new housing developments in the South East growth areas may generate additional traffic, worsening journey times as well as local air quality, adversely affecting public health.

Another way of influencing behaviour and reducing emissions is to extend road user charging. Above we rejected the option of user charges on domestic energy consumption. In transport, however, the success of the central London congestion charge, introduced in February 2003, has changed the terms of the debate and encouraged government to conduct a feasibility study into the extension of road user charging (DfT, 2004c). Confounding the critics, traffic levels in London are down by 16 per cent and congestion has been cut by 30 per cent (TfL, 2005). Although the scheme has been criticised for pricing the poor off the roads, it is in fact broadly progressive, fulfilling our just impact principle. It falls mainly on businesses and people on higher incomes. Most Londoners on low incomes do not own a car but get about by foot and public transport. In fact, more than eight out of ten people who travel into central London do so by public transport (TfL, 2003). Some of the surplus money raised has been used to put on extra bus services, which are flowing better due to less congestion.

In some ways London is a special case, but some general rules do apply. The richer the household, the more likely it is to own one or more cars and the more miles it is likely to travel by car. Road user charging is then broadly progressive, particularly if the money raised is earmarked for local transport improvements. The most significant problem is low-income households in rural areas who are poorly served by public transport. They spend up to a quarter of their disposable income running a car and would find it hard to manage without one (DfT, 2003). However, there are ways to address this problem. If the charges were varied according to the level of congestion, then they would be much lower on rural roads that have less traffic than congested urban areas and motorways. As part of a national scheme, some of the money raised could be used to pay for the abolition of road tax, a fixed cost that falls heavily on low-income motorists (Foley and Ferguson, 2003).

If a revenue-raising charge were to be introduced in 2010, or soon after, it would not only help to reduce traffic and CO_2 emissions but also provide a much needed source of revenue. A revenue-raising charge introduced across England in 2010 could potentially raise an additional £16 billion per year, some of which should be used to pay for better roads and public transport improvements. To help make a revenue-raising charge more acceptable to motorists the Government should abolish Vehicle Excise Duty, which raised £4.5 billion in 2002/3 (Grayling, 2004).

The second challenge we mentioned above is to ensure access to transport as part of a wider social minimum. This should be seen as part of fulfilling our distributive principle. A significant minority of people do not have a car. Faced with declines in the provision of public transport and increased distances to shops, services and employment, this can represent a damaging form of social exclusion. What is needed is a new approach to transport policy that puts 'accessibility' centre stage. Spending on transport is regressive (SEU, 2003). We still focus too much on commuter trains and not enough on vital local bus services. There is a strong case both for an increase in the overall amount of spending on transport and for redistribution towards people on low incomes and poorer areas, so that the benefits of public spending on transport are spread more equitably.

Conclusion

Social justice should not be seen as standing at odds with environmental sustainability. In many areas, there are powerful synergies between the two. Thinking about policy challenges through the lens of the three principles identified in this chapter allows us to identify priorities for action.

Although preventing climate change is just one element of a socially just environmental policy, it provides a good illustration of how policy can be developed. There needs to be greater focus on providing energy efficient options appropriate for hard to treat homes and investment in low carbon industries. A revenue-raising national congestion charging system should be introduced with a large proportion of spending targeted at improving public transport. These two changes would greatly improve Britain's contribution to preventing climate change in a socially just way.

Yet climate change is far from the only environmental challenge. The three principles outlined in this chapter require action to be taken in many other areas. Although environmental sustainability is not sufficient for social justice, it is undoubtedly necessary.

References

Agyeman J and Evans B (2004) '"Just sustainability": the emerging discourse of environmental justice in Britain?' *The Geographical Journal* 170 (2), Oxford: Blackwells

Baer P (2004) *Honest about Dangerous Climate Change* Berkeley: Ecoequity. Available at http://www.ecoequity.org/ceo/ceo_8_2.htm

Beckett M (2003) 'A stitch in time' *New Economy* (10) 3, London: ippr

Bruntland G (ed) (1987) *Our Common Future: The World Commission on Environment and Development* Oxford: Oxford University Press

Cambridge Econometrics (2004) *UK Energy and Environment* Cambridge: Cambridge Econometrics

Danish Wind Power Industry Association (2003) *Danish Wind Power Industry* Information from the Danish Wind Power Industry website. Available at: www.windpower.org

Department for Environment, Food and Rural Affairs (DEFRA) (2004a) *Public Service Agreement 2005–2008* London: TSO

Department for Environment, Food and Rural Affairs (DEFRA) (2004b) *Review of UK Climate Change Programe:* London: TSO

Department for Environment, Food and Rural Affairs (DEFRA) (2004c) *Digest of Environmental Protection Statistics* London: TSO. Available at www.defra.gov.uk/environment/statistics/index.htm

Department for Trade and Industry (DTI) (2003) *UK Energy Sector Indicators. A Supplement to the Energy White Paper. Our Energy Future – Creating a Low Carbon Economy* London: TSO

Department for Trade and Industry DTI (2004) *Creating a Low Carbon Economy. First Annual Report on Implementation of the Energy White Paper* London: TSO

Department for Transport (DfT) (2003) *Managing Our Roads* London: TSO

Department for Transport (DfT) (2004a) *Transport Trends 2004 Edition* London: TSO. Available at http://www.dft.gov.uk/stellent/groups/dft_transstats/documents/page/dft_transstats_508294.hcsp

Department for Transport (DfT) (2004b) *The Future of Transport: a network for 2030* London: TSO

Department for Transport (DfT) (2004c) *Feasibility Study of Road Pricing in the UK: a report to the Secretary of State* London: TSO

Department of Health (DoH) (2003) *Tackling Health Inequalities* London: TSO

Dobson A (1998) *Justice and the environment – Conceptions of environmental sustainability and dimensions of social justice* Oxford: Oxford University Press

Duxbury (2004) 'Sustainable communities: regeneration and a just society' in Foley J (ed) *Sustainability and Social Justice* London: ippr

Ekins P and Dresner S (2004) *Green Taxes and Charges: reducing their impact on low-income households* London: Joseph Rowntree Foundation

Elliott P, Briggs D, Morris S, De Hoogh C, Hurt C, Kold Jensen T, Maitland I, Richardson S, Wakefield J and Jarup L (2001) *Birth Outcomes and Selected Cancers in Populations Living Near Landfill Sites* London: Imperial College Small Area Health Statistics Unit

Evans A (2002) *Fresh air? Options for the future architecture of international climate change policy* London: New Economics Foundation

Fabian Society (2000) *Paying for Progress: A new politics of tax for public spending* London: Fabian Society

Faculty of Public Health (2003) *Current Cold Snap Will Lead to Over 2,500 Unnecessary Deaths, Warn Public Health Doctors* London: Faculty of Public Health of the Royal Colleges of Physicians of the United Kingdom

Foley J (2001) *H₂: Driving the Future.* London: ippr

Foley J (2004a) 'The Problems of Success: reconciling economic growth and the quality of life in the South East' *Commission on Sustainable Development in the South East Working Paper Two* London: ippr

Foley J (2004b) *Sustainability and social justice* London: ippr

Foley J and Ferguson M (2003) *Putting the brakes on climate change* London: ippr

Grayling T (2004) 'Social justice in an upwardly mobile society' in Foley J (ed) *Sustainability and Social Justice* London: ippr

Hare W (2003) 'Assessment of knowledge on impacts of climate change – contribution to the specification of Article 2 of the UNFCCC: Impacts on ecosystems, food production, water and socioeconomic systems' *Paper for the German Advisory Council on Global Change* Available at http://www.wbgu.de/wbgu_sn2003_ex01.pdf

International Climate Change Taskforce (ICCT) (2005) *Meeting the climate challenge: recommendations of the International Climate Change Taskforce* London: ippr; Washington DC: the Center for American Progress; Canberra: The Australia Institute

Jacobs M (1997) 'The quality of life: social goods and the politics of consumption' in Jacobs M (ed) *Greening the Millennium – The New Politics of the Environment* London: Blackwell Press

Juniper T (2004) 'Strengthening the Link' in Foley J (ed) *Sustainability and social justice* London: ippr

Laslet P and Fishkin J (1992) *Justice Between Age Groups and Generations* New Haven: Yale University Press

Lynas M (2004) *High tide – news from a warming world* London: Flamingo

Metz D (2003) *Time Travel Constraints in Transport Policy* London: Population Ageing Associates

Meyer A (2000) *Contraction & Convergence: the global solution to climate change* Bristol: Green Books

Miller D (1999) 'Social Justice and environmental goods' in Dobson (ed) *Fairness and futurity – essays on environmental sustainability and social justice* Oxford: Oxford University Press

Mitchell C and Woodman B (2004) *The Burning Question: is the UK on course for a low carbon economy* London: ippr

Norton B (1991) *Toward unity among environmentalists* Oxford: Oxford University Press

Office of National Statistics (ONS) (2004) *Winter Mortality* London: TSO. Available at www.statistics.gov.uk/cci/nugget.asp?id=574

Office of the Deputy Prime Minister (ODPM) (2003) *Sustainable communities: building for the future* London: TSO

Retallack S (2005) 'Setting a long-term climate objective' *Paper for the International Climate Change Taskforce* London: ippr

Rio Declaration (1992) *Rio Declaration on environment and development* New York: United Nations

Royal Commission on Environmental Pollution (RCEP) (2000) *22nd report: Energy – the changing climate* London: TSO

Social Exclusion Unit (SEU) (2003) *Making Connections: social exclusion and transport* London: TSO

Stott, P, Stone D and Allen M (2004) 'Human contribution to the European heatwave of 2003' *Nature* 3089

Transport for London (TfL) (2005) *Central London Congestion Charging Scheme Impacts Monitoring: Summary Review: January 2005* London: TfL. Available at http://www.tfl.gov.uk/tfl/cclondon/pdfs/impacts-monitoring-report-january-2005.pdf

United Nations (1992) *United Nations Framework Convention on Climate Change* New York: United Nations

Urban Task Force (1999) 'Towards an Urban Renaissance' *Final Report to the Department for the Environment, Transport and the Regions* London: TSO

Walker G, Fairburn S and Mitchell (2003) 'Environmental quality and social deprivation' *R&D Technical Report E2-067/1/TR* London: TSO

World Bank (2004) *World Development Indicators 2004* Washington DC: World Bank. Available at http://www.worldbank.org/data/wdi2004/index.htm

Social Justice, Rights and Social Democracy

Raymond Plant[1]

> *Government requires] a large measure of equality in social rank and fortune, for otherwise equality of rights and authority could not long subsist.*

So wrote Jean Jacques Rousseau (1762) in his *Social Contract*, identifying an issue which is still at stake when thinking about rights in social democracy; what is the relationship between the protection afforded to civil and political rights in a liberal democratic state and the fact that social and economic life is marked by remaining large-scale inequalities?

Liberal thinkers have long made arguments, grounded in a sense of equality, for the protection of civil and political rights. Social democracy, however, was originally conceived in the 19th century as a way of extending these ideas about equality and the basic dignity of the person to the social and economic spheres. This was reflected in the growth of both democracy and extensive welfare states in western Europe. From its birth, then, social democracy made a link between the protection of civil and political equalities and liberties, and a commitment to greater social justice in social and economic terms. Indeed, it is doubtful whether social democracy would make sense as a political ideal without this commitment to social justice. Combined with a concern for rights, this might be seen as reflecting a deeper or more general set of values: respect,

---

[1] The author would like to record that he gained a great deal of insight into the issues discussed in this chapter during the preparation of the Report of the Joint Committee on Human Rights (of which he is a member) on The International Covenant on Economic, Social and Cultural Rights. This was the 21st Report of the 2003–4 Session of Parliament.

dignity, equality, personal autonomy and the possibility of fulfilling one's potential as an individual.

However, the relationship between rights, social democracy and social justice is not straightforward. The issues raised by Rousseau in 1762 are of growing contemporary relevance, largely because of the adoption, in 1998, of the Human Rights Act (HRA). This chapter explores one important tension and one question, both of which must be confronted by social democrats. The tension raised by the HRA and a rights-based approach is with democracy; do rights limit the power of an elected Parliament to legislate as it sees fit and should this be a concern? If so, how should we respond? The question is how far legally enshrining rights can be used to pursue social justice goals. Should the HRA, which largely covers 'negative' rights, be extended to 'positive' rights which guarantee access to things? These issues are addressed in turn before drawing out some policy implications.

This chapter argues that social and economic rights should not just be seen as matters of aspiration and policy; they should also be seen in more constitutional terms. Rights exist to protect the basic interests of citizens, including their freedom and autonomy; those which secure freedom from coercion are therefore crucial. However, we argue below that access to basic social and economic resources should be protected in a similar constitutional way.

This analysis implies a rethinking of the traditional social democratic approach to the politics of the state. The general assumption has been that the achievement of social justice is to be seen as a matter of policy and not of rights and that a successful social democratic government only requires a sufficiently large majority and the political will to implement social and public policies. It questions why a government with strong electoral support, and the legitimacy this entails, should be constrained by a set of rights which freeze the preferences of just one cohort of citizens into a special constitutional form. The issue has been well put by Tony Wright when he argues:

> *If British socialism was about using the state to achieve social and economic objectives, then the British constitution seemed to put the state at the disposal of majority parties. The left was instrumental in defining a 20th century theory and practice of the constitution that sustained this view, and in defending it against those who hankered after something else.* (Wright, 1993)

The HRA, the full implications of which have barely been felt, challenges this. One of the strongest arguments for the Act has been that it protects those rights which underpin the democratic process, making them part of the infrastructure of democracy. The HRA (and any newly enshrined social and economic rights) means (or will in the future mean) that the state is, to echo Wright's words, no longer quite so fully at the disposal of the majority. This should motivate an attempt to rethink the attitude of social democrats to constitutional issues and to consider how social justice can best be furthered in this new context.

This chapter concludes by arguing for a 'social democratic constitutional settlement', which would include legally enshrining social and economic rights of citizens.

Rights and democracy

Democratic equality is central to social democracy – understood as using the power of democratic procedures to achieve policies which will protect individual dignity and respect across a whole range of sectors in society (see Chapter 10). This suggests that there is a case for a protected sphere of rights, which sustain the democratic order that social democrats hope to be able to use to achieve socially just ends. Feldman makes the argument in the following way:

> Citizens must have certain guaranteed rights if an effective democratic structure is to be put in place and maintained. It is impossible to imagine a properly functioning democracy in a country where people by and large are not guaranteed freedom of expression, a free press, a right to vote, a right to petition Parliament, freedom of protest, and freedom from arbitrary arrest and detention by government agencies. Such rights are fundamental to the notion of democracy, and to the development of the very idea of citizenship. They should not be abrogated by democratic decision makers in the public sphere without undermining the very democracy which is said to legitimise public decision making. (Feldman, 2002)

This point of view implies that there can be no fundamental divergence between social democracy and a rights culture because of the constitutive democratic aspect of social democracy and the way rights underpin a democratic system, which in turn suggests there can be no fundamental tension between social justice and human rights.

Indeed, one could go further than this and say that without the protection for rights afforded by something like the HRA or the European Convention on Human Rights (ECHR), we would have a very fragile basis for our liberties. While we would be free to do whatever the law did not proscribe, this freedom would be vulnerable to the outlook of shifting majorities in Parliament. The only entrenched rights would be those which arose at common law out of contract and property.

So it looks, on the face of it, as though there is a good fit between human rights legislation and the democratic element of social democracy. Through the use of these democratic rights it may be possible eventually to secure the protection of social and economic rights, extending democratic values into the social and economic sphere, thereby protecting dignity, equality and respect here too. Certainly the Government seems to take this view. In the Foreign and Commonwealth Office Annual Report of 1999 it argued that: 'the achievement of social and economic rights is enhanced by progress in achieving civil and political rights.' (FCO, 1999)

The assumption that underpins this line of thought is that enshrining civil and political rights protects and enhances democracy. However, this assumption is not unproblematic. Considering the way in which the HRA has been incorporated in British legislation provides a useful way to think about the tensions between rights and democracy.

Parliamentary sovereignty and the Human Rights Act

The argument in favour of the HRA has been well put by Laws, who maintains that while Parliament has the duty to formulate public policy, nevertheless 'in its duty to the people, which is based on every individual's autonomy, Parliament will abide by a framework which gives pride of place to negative fundamental rights', and that:

> The good constitution has to recognise and entrench a bedrock of rights, based on the principle of minimal interference. Good government of any political colour must pursue its own vision of the morality of aspiration, which is itself a function of power held on trust. Where its vision cuts across the rule of minimal interference the courts have to say so . . . the rule of minimal interference and the morality of aspiration share the same roots in man's nature; the function of the courts and the government are

therefore complementary, and any tension between them should be creative and not destructive. (Laws, 2003)

This reflects an optimistic reading of the relationship between social justice and human rights, and between democracy and human rights. While a political movement like social democracy has a strong vision of the political good – the pursuit of social justice – this has to be undertaken in the context of a set of negative rights, defining freedom from interference and coercion as the protection of individual autonomy which, as Laws says, is the foundational value of democracy. Should it worry social democrats that the protection of these negative rights and the interpretation of the statutes are subject to judicial interpretation, adjudication and policing? It might be thought that this gives the courts power to determine what is meant at a fundamental level by a democracy. The answer depends on how parliamentary sovereignty is affected.

The constitutional aim of the HRA was to incorporate the provisions of the ECHR into UK law, and to do this in a way that did not compromise the sovereignty of Parliament. So the Act is not in any way entrenched and could in principle be repealed by any future Parliament. Nor do specific provisions of the Act infringe parliamentary sovereignty. This can be seen in the two respects in which the Act bears most directly on the powers of Parliament.

The first of these is that the secretary of state sponsoring any new Bill has to submit, on the title page of the Bill, a declaration that its provisions are compatible with the HRA. If they do not make such a submission then they are obliged to give a full explanation as to why it does not.

Second, the Act places an obligation on judges in the higher courts to interpret legislation in a way that is compatible with the provisions of the ECHR 'so far as it is possible to do so'. Only if this proves to be impossible is the court able to issue a statement of incompatibility between convention rights and the legislation under review. Even if they do issue a statement of incompatibility, government and Parliament are not under an obligation to bring forward legislation to rectify this.

So it looks, on the face of it, as though the Act is compatible with parliamentary sovereignty. However, two caveats have to be entered here, resulting from concerns about the role the Act implies for the judiciary. The first is in issuing statements of incompatibility. The second is the courts' role in interpreting legislation. These are discussed in turn below.

Incompatibility between legislation and the Human Rights Act

It has been argued that democratic participation is the master right, or as Waldron puts it, 'the right of rights' (Waldron, 1999). On this view, it is only through the sovereignty of the people as expressed through Parliament that we should pursue political aims and objectives. Sovereignty should not be shared with the courts as a situation in which the courts playing an increasingly active role in interpreting legislation would violate this master right.

The arguments set out by Feldman and Laws imply that the ECHR will create 'no go areas' for political action over time (Feldman, 2002; Laws, 2003). To take some not entirely hypothetical examples, the provisions of the ECHR might well protect a right to private education or to be educated in faith-based schools. If a radical government regarded removing these as essential to its social justice agenda then it is likely not to be able to do it because of the protection conferred by the ECHR, as Article 2 of Protocol 1 of the ECHR provides that 'the state shall respect the rights of parents to ensure such education and teaching in conformity with their own religious and philosophical convictions' (ECHR, 1954).

A real case comes from a different area of public policy. Under Section 55 of the Nationality Immigration and Asylum Act 2002 as it stands, those who are deemed not to have claimed asylum within a reasonable time of their arrival in the UK are denied benefits. The Court of Appeal ruled in the case of *SSHD v. Limbuela, Tesema, and Adam*, that Article 3 of the ECHR – the clause dealing with inhuman and degrading treatment – requires the state to provide support for those asylum seekers to whom Section 55 of the Act applies. In the judges' view, leaving asylum seekers destitute would be such an egregious breach of the Convention that, since Parliament has agreed that legislation should be compatible with Convention rights, it cannot be rational to allow Section 55 to stand.

We may have full sympathy with the judges' point of view here, but what we have to recognise is the extent to which the incorporation of the ECHR has placed a very clear and detailed constraint on majoritarian democracy and popular sovereignty expressed through Parliament. After all, Parliament did pass this Bill into law in the normal way, but the judges have found that one of its provisions infringes convention rights as protected by the HRA.

Interpretation and democratic legitimacy

The second cause of concern relates to the role of the courts in interpreting legislation in accordance with the HRA. The Government, at the time of the passage of the Bill, believed that an interpretive approach was to be preferred to issuing a statement of incompatibility. Jack Straw, then the Home Secretary, argued that:

> *We want the courts to strive to find an interpretation of the legislation that is consistent with Convention rights, so far as the plain words of the legislation allow, and only in the last resort conclude that the legislation is simply incompatible with them.* (Straw, 1998)

According to this view, interpretation would take place against a background in which the legislature is assumed only to want to legislate in a way that is compatible with Convention rights. That is why, after all, the Act exists and why the declaration of compatibility is made on the face of a Bill. However, it is arguable that as the cases stack up, the incremental effect of this interpretive approach will lead to a situation in which the interpreted statute may be a long way from the text that received the Royal Assent when it left Parliament. This is particularly true given some jurisprudential accounts of what judicial interpretation can mean, such as Campbell who argues that judges now place less weight on the actual text of the legislation than used to be the case (Campbell, 2001). Greater weight may be placed on the purposes of the legislation and the intent of Parliament in passing it and whether these are compatible with the Convention rights. This is a complex and subtle argument to which justice cannot be done here, but if there is plausibility in it, it clearly raises questions about democracy and the position of judges in a democratic society.

This sort of criticism is associated with the work of Ronald Dworkin. Many of his works, including *A Bill of Rights for Britain*, were influential in convincing the Government to incorporate the ECHR to the extent that the HRA does (Dworkin, 1986; Dworkin, 1990). With the ECHR as a standard in terms of which legislation has to be interpreted, it is difficult to think of judges in the higher courts simply applying legislation or adjudicating in any sort of mechanistic way. Furthermore, interpretation can be seen as part of adjudication (Campbell, 2001). Although most commentators believed that it was in the issuing of statements of incompatibility that the courts would come into a collision with a democratically elected government, it might well be the incremental effect of the scope for interpretation which the Act confers on the higher courts that leads to the greatest tension between democracy and human rights.

So, despite the arguments that human rights protection can be central to democracy, judicial interpretation does raise difficult questions about the scope that is being given to the courts. These difficulties are likely to be exacerbated if the EU Constitution is ratified. An integral part of the EU Constitution is a Charter of Fundamental Rights and Freedoms which member states will have to observe in their application of European Community Law. In effect, it would confer on citizens of the EU rights held in relation both to the EU itself and officials of national governments who are carrying out policies and directives set at the European level.

At the moment the Charter has only declaratory status, but if the Constitution was ratified it would become possible to enforce these rights in relation to the application of European Community laws and regulations. The Charter differs from the ECHR in that it includes some significant social and economic rights. These have been put into the Charter on the insistence of European social democratic parties, amongst others. Despite the current declaratory status of the Charter it has already been used by UK courts as an instrument to help in the consideration of domestic law and in particular the HRA. So, for example, in *R. v. East Sussex County Council and the Disability Rights Commission ex parte A, B, X and Y* were used by the Administrative Court. In doing so, Mr Justice Munby argued that:

> ...the Charter is not at present legally binding in our domestic law and is therefore not a source of law in the strict sense. But it can, in my judgment, properly be consulted insofar as it proclaims, reaffirms or elucidates the content of those human rights that are generally recognised throughout the European family of nations and in particular the nature and scope of those fundamental rights that are guaranteed by the Convention. (EHC, 2003)

This clearly supports concerns about interpretive creep. The Charter could be another constraint on majoritarian democracy in the EU as well as in individual nation states and social democratic theories of democracy will have to take account of this. Next though, we address more directly the relationship between social justice and rights.

Social justice and rights

The question we turn to now regards what might be thought of as the social justice side of social democracy. Should social democrats aim to develop a set of social and economic rights to secure legal protection for these forms of human dignity and equality, in addition to the negative civil and political rights of non-interference included in the HRA? Is the HRA one-sided in protecting negative rights and should there be some kind of legal recognition for positive rights to social and economic goods?

One reason to think that the HRA might be one-sided is that successive governments have not sought to highlight the distinction between positive and negative rights. Many of the conventions to which the UK is a signatory place obligations on the UK to protect economic, social and cultural rights. For example, the United Nations' International Covenant on Economic, Social and Cultural Rights gives binding legal force in international law to the social and economic rights contained in the UN Declaration of Human Rights of 1948, placing a requirement on the Government to make what are called 'Periodic Reports' dealing with its compliance with the human rights standards that the Covenant protects.[2] These are:

- equality between men and women;
- the right to work;
- the right to fair conditions of employment;
- the right to join and form a trade union;
- the right to social security;
- the right to the protection of the family;
- the right to an adequate standard of living (including the right to food, clothing and housing);
- the right to health;
- the right to education and the right to culture.

---

2 Other examples include 60 of the 72 social and economic rights in the European Social Charter of 1961 and several key ILO Conventions. The European Constitution also lays out a set of civil and political rights.

Given this plethora of protections to social and economic rights, it seems that successive governments have thought that declarations of rights in the social and economic field have been important in securing greater social justice by paralleling and supporting civil and political rights. Second, it might be thought that successive governments have not in practice claimed that there are categorical differences between civil and political rights and social and economic rights given that they have signed up to the use of the word 'rights' in these contexts. Indeed, they have signed up to both UN and European instruments which were designed to parallel similar instruments in relation to civil and political rights.

Furthermore, under the present state of the law in the UK, no clear line can be drawn between HRA rights and social and economic rights. As we have already seen, Article Three of the Convention against inhuman and degrading treatment has been construed by the courts as requiring government not to permit destitution. Rights to privacy, personal autonomy and integrity, of the sort secured under Article Eight, have been held to afford to individuals rights in relation to the adequacy and competence of health care. In addition, rights of access to education are guaranteed by the first protocol to the ECHR and incorporated into UK law by the HRA. These are clearly social rights rather than strictly negative civil and political rights and the current state of both politics and the law recognises this. We say 'politics', because the current draft Bill of Rights for Northern Ireland contains rights to healthcare, to protection from destitution, to shelter and to work. It is likely that there will be a political commitment to the statement of these rights in the final document.

It seems clear then that a number of economic and social rights have been thought to be derivable from the HRA/ECHR by the courts and from a plain reading of the clauses in the two texts. Yet despite this they are not explicitly enshrined in the HRA.

These remarks point to quite a large set of issues which have both constitutional and policy importance. The first is that if social and economic rights are genuine rights, it seems inconsistent that they are not thought to be as fundamental as the 'negative' rights set out in the ECHR and incorporated by means of the HRA. Indeed, when the State of the Nation poll in 2000 asked respondents which rights should be protected in a Bill of Rights, 94 per cent replied that there should be a right to hospital treatment on the NHS in a reasonable time and 76 per cent supported the right of the homeless to be housed (Dunleavy *et al*, 2001). A poll conducted in Northern Ireland by the Northern Ireland Human Rights Commission found that support for the inclusion of a right to healthcare and a right to an adequate standard of living ranged from between 87 and 91 per cent (NIHRC, 2001). If we believe that negative rights are essential constitutional protections for the exercise of autonomy, then it could be argued with some plausibility that a sense of physical security, shelter and education are as essential to the autonomous life of the citizen as their negative rights.

This raises two questions. First, are there any logical reasons for thinking that social rights are not genuine rights, as many academic commentators have argued? Second, is the pursuit of social rights an effective way of securing greater social justice or could this objective be better achieved with other policies? This section will take these questions in turn.

Is the idea of 'positive rights' defensible?

There are arguments that dispute the coherence of positive rights. This is important because if positive rights cannot be defended as coherent, then they cannot be enshrined in legislation to promote social justice in the same way that rights to civil and political liberties can be. However, these arguments are poor.

The first has to do with freedom and autonomy. As Laws argues, the idea of autonomy is an essential part of our understanding of democratic citizenship in a modern society (Laws, 2003). In company with many legal and political thinkers, he regards autonomy as being essentially negative; as being free from interference and coercion. On this view, freedom is essentially 'negative' freedom and fundamental rights are there to protect the core of such negative freedoms. The ECHR, for example, casts freedom in a negative way: to be free from being killed, free from torture and inhuman treatment, free from compulsion in respect of work, and free from interference in family life. So the absolutely fundamental question is, if constitutional rights are there to protect freedom, should freedom only be understood negatively or is there another legitimate understanding of freedom which sees it more in terms of access to resources and opportunities – 'positive' freedom?

Freedom can and should be interpreted in this latter way. Although some argue that 'freedom' and 'ability' are clearly separable – that freedom is merely the lack of constraint and does not include the capacity or ability to actually do something – this is a weak argument. Justice cannot be done to the reasons why here, but some of the main counter arguments can be outlined. First, a general ability or capability to do something is a necessary condition of determining whether someone is free or not. If there is no general ability of being able to sign a cheque in 1066 or to jump from London to New York, then it makes no sense to ask whether someone is free or not to do it. In forming public policy, we need to ask what generalised set of human capacities are necessary for people act as autonomous agents. Sometimes these will be negative, as people cannot live autonomously if they are subject to the coercion of another; but they will also be positive, as people cannot be autonomous without access to those resources – including health, education and social security – which are necessary to be free to do what others in society are generally able to do (Plant, 1991; Taylor, 1979)

Because autonomy is seen as a basic value in a liberal democracy, it might be argued that seeing it as underpinning both negative and positive rights can actually give us, at quite a deep moral level, a way of reconciling a concern with both the sorts of rights protected by the HRA and ECHR, so often defended by liberals, and social rights, which have more usually been seen to be the province of social democrats. The argument about the centrality of autonomy shows that they are both necessary.

However, there is a second reason why critics believe that social and economic rights are not genuine rights, which cuts quite deep. The argument has to do with scarcity. First of all, it is pointed out that negative rights – to be free from interferences of various sorts – place negative obligations on others. For example, my obligation in respect of your right to life is to abstain from killing you, or my obligation in respect of your right to be free from torture is to not torture you. These obligations require me to abstain from action and as such are not subject to scarcity (we cannot run out of people not doing things.) So these obligations can always be discharged. Since they can always be discharged, they can be made into requirements under a general and equally applicable rule of law such as those set out in the HRA. They are also compossible – that is to say, all rights to non-interference and all duties not to interfere can be realised simultaneously for the simple reason that these duties do not imply a need for resources.

It is argued that these features are not characteristic of social and economic rights. A right to health care, for example, cannot be made individually enforceable because of potential scarcity. Nor can such a right be asserted in a compossible way against a background of scarcity. Nor are the obligations connected to such rights categorical, since no individual has the duty to meet all the medical needs of others that he comes across. So, because of scarcity, critics argue there cannot be enforceable rights to social and economic goods. Indeed, they might go one step further and say that to constitutionalise social rights is to undermine politics because politics in modern societies is very much about the allocation of resources in the context of scarcity. This was a point that Rammell put before the Joint Committee on Human Rights recently when he argued that:

> *These are issues for which there is no absolute standard, and are rightly the business of governments and their electorates through general elections, to determine what standard we should achieve . . . There is a significant risk that if we were to incorporate [economic, social and cultural rights], and the courts were to look at one economic and social and cultural rights issue in isolation, that could potentially have profound and adverse consequences on expenditure in other areas.*
> (Joint Committee on Human Rights, 2004)

So, because of scarcity, critics argue that we should treat social and economic rights as distinct from any set of constitutional or legally enforceable rights. While it might be accepted that resources are necessary for the exercise of autonomy, the nature and extent of access to these resources should be settled by politics in a way that is not true of those rights to do with autonomy that are secured under the HRA.

In many respects this argument is also poor. It is just not possible to draw a distinction between negative rights and social and economic rights in the way described above. The reason is as follows. The motivation to forbear from action in the face of a negative right may in fact be scarce; perhaps people will be inclined to murder, rape, assault others or defraud from property. In these cases, the appropriate way of enforcing the right is to enforce the forbearance by preventive police or to impose penalties following an infringement. These require the police, a legal system, representation and prisons. It cannot be argued that these are somehow not implied directly by negative rights because the idea of the enforceability of a right is absolutely central to something being a right.

If a right is to be a right it has to be enforceable. This enforceability will involve costs, courts will have to make allocative decisions, and politicians will have to provide institutions which protect these negative rights. All of these will come up against the issue of scarcity. So from a negative rights point of view, the scarcity argument proves far too much. If scarcity militates against something being a right then that applies to the necessarily connected enforcement conditions of negative rights too (Plant, 2003).

One way of trying to make the scarcity argument work against positive rights is in terms of the nature of the obligation accorded to positive and negative rights. The idea is that in the case of a negative right the obligation is clear and categorical: to abstain from action, typically interference or coercion of some sort. In the case of a positive social right, say, to healthcare, the obligation is obscure and potentially open-ended. So if we thought that there was a right to healthcare, then scarcity would mean that not all rights would be capable of being met.

This would mean that positive rights are not categorical. It would also mean that consultants and managers in a rights-based health service would have to exercise discretion in respect of these rights. We would have moved from a rights-based culture to a more utilitarian one, since it will be likely to be calculations of costs and benefits that influence the exercise of discretion. However, if this argument is supposed to mark a fundamental difference between negative and positive rights then it is also clearly either mistaken or proves far too much. Compare the police service, which is part of the set of necessary enforceability conditions for negative rights, with the health service. The chief constable has a limited budget, but so does the NHS consultant or manager. The chief constable has a duty to police all areas of the law (otherwise the courts might impose a judgment of mandamus on him or her); but the Health Service Acts also require the secretary of state to provide a comprehensive health service. The chief constable has operating discretion to decide, within an overall responsibility to police all areas of the law, not to invest resources in detecting the perpetrator of a particular crime. Equally, an individual citizen does not have an individually enforceable right to the services of a police officer. In the same way, in the NHS, a particular consultant, given the overall responsibility to provide a comprehensive health service, may regard it as a misuse of resources to treat a specific individual. That individual does not have an enforceable right to the services of a doctor.

Given this point, either we have to say that in neither case do rights exist (whether negative or positive) because they are not individually enforceable. This though is to go much too far. More appropriately, the idea of a right in these contexts places a duty on government to provide services in the areas covered by the right, although not a generally enforceable individual right to those services. It is a right to general provision, rather than an individually enforceable right to whatever service it is. For this reason, it is not possible to argue that social and economic rights are not genuine, since they do share crucial features with so-called negative rights. Both imply a commitment of service provision from the government in a rights-based democracy. To see rights in this way preserves a proper role for politics in deciding the allocation of resources and the possibility of adaptation to dynamic and changing circumstances. Nevertheless, the existence of resource-implying rights of all sorts sets a very clear and categorical benchmark against which the service provision to match those rights can be judged.

Positive rights can promote social justice

So what are the implications of these arguments for social democracy? How do these points tie up into a social democratic view? First of all, if we take autonomy as the basic value of a liberal democratic society then that autonomy is going to have both a negative and positive side: a negative side of protection from interference; a positive side of provision of resources. If these forms of protection and provision are to be seen in terms of rights, then they are rights to the overall provision of a service. Because these services, whether for negative or positive rights, are going to involve scarcity considerations, it then follows that the degree and nature of service provision are going to have to be settled by politics rather than by large-scale allocative decisions by the courts (which are not equipped for that role and would not want it in any case).

For social democrats, those allocative decisions involve an appeal to social justice for a fair allocation of those resources arising out of a fair allocative mechanism to be decided by political dialogue and deliberation.

Yet it should not be thought that all of this makes rights evaporate. What it means is that the nature and scope of the provision of services have to be governed by values encapsulated in the idea of both negative and positive rights of autonomy. Government can be held to account in respect of the degree to which it meets its obligations in respect of those rights and a fair allocation of provision between particular types of rights.

The recognition of social and economic rights would mean that government could not just walk away from funding a range of services, nor could it dismantle those forms of social provision which are essential for meeting the positive and negative aspects of autonomy. It could also help protect important elements of the social minimum described in Chapter 1 by Miller and entrench progressive change. More positively, it could mean that the rights set out, for example, in the International Covenant on Economic, Social and Cultural Rights (ICESCR) could form part of the set of values which would frame government policy making so that its policies become compliant with the set of obligations which we regard as binding on the UK in international law.

It could also mean that the Human Rights Commission, which the Government is committed to establishing, could take the protection of this set of rights as part of its remit. At the moment what we have via the HRA is what has been called an 'unbalanced constitution' because it appears to secure a set of purely liberal rights to be free from certain forms of interference. This chapter has argued that such a reading of the HRA is too limited and social and economic rights do need to be made more directly visible. Incorporation of the ISESCR may be a political step too far at present, but the merits of such an approach should at least be recognised and discussed.

There are some links here to the argument in Chapter 10 which deals with the tension between setting national standards while allowing local variation. Social rights could play a role in setting a range of national basic standards but there could be a lot of leeway at the local level as to how these standards could be delivered. Within this framework, issues of democracy would arise at two levels. At the macro level, decisions would be needed about the level at which to set the social right. This would raise questions about a fair allocation of resources to one area of social rights, such as education. Equally, democratic deliberation and concerns about justice and fairness will also enter at the local or community level in terms of how these standards are to be delivered and any priorities within those standards, bearing in mind the local context.

In this way we would broaden the liberal constitution of the HRA further towards a social democratic one, while still recognising the autonomy of politics and the sovereignty of Parliament in the ways described above. Whether politicians like it or not, we shall have to engage in this debate since the Charter of Rights in the EU Constitution, to which the UK has signed up, includes highly visible social and economic rights and is in itself a reasonably social democratic document. This Constitution has to be turned into a Treaty, debated in Parliament and submitted to a referendum so to that extent the issues highlighted in this chapter will become increasingly politically salient.

Rights and obligations

The final source of tension between rights and social justice that needs drawing out is in terms of rights and obligations. We often hear it said that there can be no rights without responsibilities. In some respects this is true; in other respects quite false. It is true in the sense that to claim a justified right is to put an individual, a collection of people or a corporate body of some sort under an obligation in respect of that right (Raz, 1986). We could not make sense of the idea of a right without an obligation. Without the obligation, claiming the right would be whistling in the dark. In another sense, if what is meant is that the right-holder can only be the bearer of rights if she or he discharges other obligations, it is false. If we took this at its political rhetorical value then it would mean that small children, the mentally disabled, people with dementia and those in a persistent vegetative state would have no rights because they are not capable of fulfilling obligations. Surely in a mature democracy we should be able to have a rather more subtle account of the relation between rights and obligations?

Despite the complexity of these issues, some broad points can be made. If political, social and welfare rights are genuine rights then the government itself is under an obligation in respect of those rights to provide services to meet those rights. So too, it might well be argued on the basis of citizens' reciprocity or the avoidance of free riding that if political and social rights imply the provision of services then this implies a duty on the part of all citizens who are able to do so to work and thereby pay taxes for the provision and improvement of such services from which they themselves benefit. So instead of political and social rights being held directly against citizens, they are held against the state. However, those duties can only be discharged if the state has the resources to do so. This means tax (Holmes and Sunstein, 1999). Therefore the state has an obligation but it can only discharge this obligation if citizens in general pay taxes and there must be strong disincentives and sanctions to free riding of the form of tax avoidance, evasion and unwillingness to work when able to do so. These are part of the set of civic obligations which go hand in hand with the idea that we do possess rights to the provision of services. There are other views about this but it is not possible in the space available to go into detail about them. Let us just note here that arguments do exist in support of a civic minimum of income that is secured unconditionally to all citizens whether they are active or whether, as the literature sometimes has it, they are 'surfers' (Van Parijs, 1998).

The situation in respect of civil rights is rather different. These can be held as claims on the behaviour of identifiable other people, rather than the state. If we are part of a reciprocal system of civic rights recognition then again there should be sanctions against free riding: I cannot legitimately claim civil rights protection when I am not prepared to fulfill the duties which I have in respect of other people's civil rights. Sometimes the remedy in respect of infringements of some civil rights will be through civil action in the courts or even social pressure. There will, however, have to be politically provided systems of protection for civil rights when the sense of reciprocal obligation in respect of those rights has broken down – as, for example, in the case of anti-social behaviour orders.

Conclusion

Overall, this chapter has argued that it is possible to have a strongly rights-based form of social democracy with equal emphasis on both the social justice and the democratic aspects of the term. Although we should not be complacent about the role of judges and the possibility of a creeping role for their powers, there is a strong case for constitutionalising both rights to do with the exercise of political autonomy in the democratic process and those to do with social and economic autonomy. If rights are to protect autonomous individuals in a balanced constitution then we need to pay attention not only to the negative rights of autonomy but also to the positive ones. We need to pay attention to social and economic as well as political and civil forms of coercion. If rights are there to give effect to the basic terms of the contract between the state and the citizen, they cannot be just seen as the liberal rights of the HRA and ECHR.

There is a case for arguing for a social democratic constitution. Purists will say this is flawed; constitutions should be neutral between conceptions of the good. But this is to live in an unreal world of abstraction. Constitutions are intensely political, and although we do not have a codified constitution in the UK, left as it is, the HRA would be seen as such a political document as most of the essays in Campbell *et al* (2001). This would be the case even if it was left unchanged and only protected citizens from intentional coercion, without considering the other forms of basic goods we need to act as autonomous citizens, and from other forms of coercion, particularly in the social and economic fields, which would arise unless there were clear rights to social provision outside the market. A social democratic constitution would provide safeguards for both by protecting, in an indissoluble way, both sorts of rights.

References

Campbell T, Ewing K and Tomkins A (2001) *Sceptical Essays on Human Rights* Oxford: Oxford University Press

Campbell T (2001) 'Incorporation Through Interpretation' in Campbell T, Ewing K and Tomkins A (eds) *Sceptical essays on Human Rights* Oxford: Oxford University Press

Dunleavy P, Margetts H, Smith T and Weir S (2001) *Voices of the People: Popular Attitudes to Democratic Renewal in Britain* London: Politico's

Dworkin R (1990) *A Bill of Rights for Britain* London: Chatto and Windus

Dworkin R (1986) *Law's Empire* London: Fontana

ECHR (1954) *Protocol to the Convention for the Protection of Human Rights and Fundamental Freedoms, 213 U.N.T.S. 262* (entered into force 18 May 1954). Protocol 1, Article 8. University of Minnesota: Human Rights Library. Available at http://www1.umn.edu/humanrts/euro/z20prot1.html

EHC (2003) *The Queen (On the Application of (1) A (2) B (By their Litigation Friend the Official Solicitor) (3) X (4) Y) v. East Sussex County Council, The Disability Rights Commission CO/4843/2001 High Court of Justice Queens Bench Division Administrative Court QBD (Admin Ct)* Before: The Honourable Mr Justice Munby Tuesday 18th February, 2003. 167 paragraph 73. Available at http://www.drcgb.org/uploaded_files/documents/102_5_Case.doc

Foreign and Commonwealth Office (FCO) and Department of International Development (DFID) (1999) *Annual Report for 1999* London: TSO. Available online at http://www.fco.gov.uk/Files/kfile/HRPD_hrreport99.pdf.

Feldman D (2002) *Civil Liberties and Human Rights in England and Wales* Oxford: Oxford University Press

Holmes S and Sunstein C (1999) *The Cost of Rights: Why Liberty Depends on Taxes*. New York: W W Norton & Co

Joint Committee on Human Rights (2004) *Oral evidence: Taken before the Joint Committee on Human Rights on Monday 15 September 2003 Members present: Jean Corston, in the Chair Bowness, L Mr Shaun Woodward, Prashar, B Whitaker, B. Question 24.* Available online at http://www.publications.parliament.uk/pa/jt200203/jtselect/jtrights/uc1099/uc109902.htm

Laws (2003) in Griffith J A G 'The Brave New World of Sir John Laws' *Modern Law Review* Volume 63:2, Oxford: Blackwells

Northern Ireland Human Rights Commission (NIHRC) (2001). Available at http://www.nihrc.org/documents/BoR_RES_surveyOct01.pdf

Plant R (1991) *Modern Political Thought* Oxford: Blackwell

218   Social Justice

Plant R (2003) 'Social and Economic Rights Revisited' *King's College Law Journal* Vol 14:1, Oxford: Hart

Raz J (1986) *The Morality of Freedom* Clarendon: Oxford University Press

Rousseau J J (1762) *The Social Contract* London: Penguin

SSHD v Limbuela, Tesema and Adam [2004] EWCA Civ 540 OR Secretary of State for the Home Department (SSHD) (2004) *v.* Limbuela, Tesema and Adam, EWCA Civ 540, 2004.

Straw J (1998) *Hansard* Column 421 House of Commons Available online at http://www.publications.parliament.uk/pa/cm199798/cmhansrd/vo980603/debtext/80603-40.htm

Taylor C (1979) 'What's Wrong with Negative Liberty' in Ryan A (ed) *The Idea of Freedom* Oxford: Oxford University Press

The European Convention (2003) *The Secretariat. Draft Treaty establishing a constitution for Europe, Brussels 18 July 2003 CONV 850/03.* Available at http://european-convention.eu.int/docs/Treaty/cv00850.en03.pdf

Van Parijs P (1998) *Real Freedom for All: What (if Anything) Can Justify Capitalism?* Oxford: Oxford University Press

Waldron J (1999) *Law and Disagreement* Oxford: Oxford University Press

Wright T (1993) *Subjects and Citizens* London: Routledge

Democracy, Social Justice and the State

Will Paxton and Andrew Gamble

In this chapter we examine the relationship between strengthening democracy and achieving social justice. We focus particularly on the tensions raised by greater 'localisation' of the state. The chapter's central argument is that in an era characterised by falling trust in government and demands for greater personal autonomy, measures to improve Britain's democratic institutions, particularly at a local level, are not only compatible with social justice, but often necessary foundations for it.

In the UK, progressive governments have historically failed adequately to confront the relationship between social justice and democracy. One specific oversight has been the lack of serious debate on the thorny issue of when to accept devolution and local differences. Britain's Labour Government, in its third term, though, could be the exception. Indeed, it may have to be an exception.

One reason is that the genie is out of the bottle. Eighteen years at the wrong end of Britain's antiquated democratic structures led Labour to adopt an ambitious agenda for constitutional reform after 1997, with devolution to Scotland, Wales and London. Attempts to introduce regional assemblies in 2004, though unsuccessful, indicate a continued desire to develop a more devolved polity; a desire which also opens the door to reform in other areas – particularly local government. Though the constitutional implications of these changes have been much discussed, the fundamental questions that they raise for Britain's welfare state and for social justice have been largely ignored. It is untenable to continue to sweep these issues under the carpet.

The first few years since devolution may well come to be regarded as the easy ones. There are two main reasons for this. First, the same party has been in power – either alone or in coalition – in Wales, Scotland, Westminster and London. Second, we have seen sustained increases in public spending, and these have lessened opportunities for disputes over resource allocation. The result has been a relatively benign political environment. However, this situation is unlikely to last.

Devolution is not the only catalyst for this debate. Immediately after the 1997 election, with wide variations in performance in many public services, it was appropriate to steer improvements in poorly performing public services directly from Whitehall, with centrally set targets and rigorous inspection regimes. The experience of Germany after reunification shows the danger of localism when wide local variations demand a stronger centre. Its federal arrangements are proving quite a handicap in dealing with problems thrown up by reunification and it is far from achieving any national minimum standards, with the richest of the aastern regions, Brandenburg, still with only 75 per cent of the income of the old West Germany.

However, by 2005 in the UK the limitations of a centralist approach have become increasingly clear, and indeed accepted. In some of the key public services there are now active debates about the appropriate degree of local democratic control and about the functions and responsibilities of local government: foundation hospitals; Home Office proposals for local panels which give communities and individuals a greater say in setting local policing priorities and wider discussion about 'new localism', are all indicative of how lively this debate has become (Corry and Stoker, 2002; Walker, 2002; HMT, 2004).

This chapter proceeds as follows: the first section sets out two ways of thinking about the relationship between social justice and democracy. We start by arguing that in one sense democratic rights are components of social justice, but then move on to make the case that there are instrumental benefits to forging a more democratic state. In other words, we argue that a more democratic state will help achieve social justice in the social and economic spheres. But there are inevitably tensions. Perhaps the main one is when democracy means devolution of power and, with that, geographical differences in services provided. The second section discusses this tension, the history behind it and how it could be overcome. We argue that while some services must be provided at the national level because uniformity across the UK is important, in the case of others – indeed most areas of public policy – geographical differences in service provision are justifiable and compatible with social justice. The third section draws out the implications for policy: a radical empowerment of local government and further devolution to Scotland and Wales.

Democracy and social justice

Democracy as a component of social justice

Miller, in Chapter 1, argues that

> [One] aspect of equal citizenship is the right to influence government, something that goes beyond the right to vote in elections, important though that is. At present the distribution of political influence is heavily skewed in favour of those who have resources of other kinds – wealth, communicative skills, industrial muscle – and although it is unrealistic to think that we could ever achieve perfect equality in this area, there are ways in which we can try to redress the balance.

According to this definition, the basic rights of democracy – the right to vote and to associate freely – and the ability to take advantage of these rights, are themselves elements of social justice.

This argument has been made by social democratic political thinkers for some time. In the first half of the 20th century R H Tawney saw power as a central component of the type of equality he considered desirable. For other social democrats the state needs to be accountable and transparent, subject to the will of the people, and capable of promoting democracy and self-government throughout society. A long tradition of progressive thought from Tom Paine to GDH Cole, and from Harold Laski to William Morris, has insisted that a bottom-up self-governing society is the goal, not a top-down, centralised state.

Recently, drawing on the deep historical heritage provided by civic republican thinking, contemporary political philosophers such as Iris Young and Phillip Pettit have stressed the need to reduce 'domination' in order to achieve a more just society (Young, 1990; Pettit, 1997). Such domination, they argue, is a danger in a variety of spheres, from the family to the labour market, but it is crucial to understanding the relationship between citizens and the state. To ensure the state does not dominate citizens, all groups and individuals must have the ability and the inclination to engage and influence decisions that affect their lives. Chapter 11 draws similar implications by examining what determines subjective wellbeing. Although there has been some effort to engage with users, citizens and communities in the development of policies – initial community-based Sure Start programmes and the New Deal for communities being obvious examples – such participation has not been developed as far as is necessary.

Indeed, although in a formal sense people's basic democratic rights are in place – with the universal franchise and freedom of association – a striking trend in recent decades has been the increasing difference in their use by different classes and income groups. As Chapter 2 shows, participation – whether measured in terms of voting, people's interest in politics, political efficacy (the sense people have that they could influence decisions) or engagement in wider civic activities – shows sharp inequalities along class and income lines. More worryingly, trends in the nature of civil society and politics, if left unchecked, will widen this divide.

If self-government and democratic power are viewed as elements of equal citizenship, promoting a more equal democratic participation would be one part of a social justice agenda. Even if there were no link between democratic participation and wider social and economic injustices, there would be a case for action. Miller uses this line of logic in Chapter 1, suggesting that new forms of deliberative democracy should be explored. But the case for deepening democracy as part of achieving social justice may be stronger than this. Democracy could be instrumentally important too.

Democracy as instrumental in achieving social justice

At one time it was thought that the battle for democracy – albeit often in a narrow sense of securing the universal franchise – was the battle to turn the state from being a protector of existing privilege and established power into an instrument of the people for achieving redistribution and social justice. If democracy was secured, social justice would follow. Some evidence supports this: in most developed countries the decades after the full franchise had been gained were marked by narrowing of wealth and income inequalities. But that does not mean that social justice, at least when measured crudely through levels of income inequality, always follows democracy (Shapiro and Hacker-Cordon, 1999).

To the frustration of many on the centre-left, electorates have often tended to vote against what would appear to be their own interests: they have often not voted for greater equality. The explanation for this can be found, in part, in the nature of the electorate. There are a couple of intuitively attractive arguments here. When people are aspirational and think they will improve their lot, or when they are pragmatic and believe that economic efficiency demands high levels of inequality, they might vote against what might otherwise look like their interests. Another factor may be what Chapter 11 identifies as a 'framing effect': contemporary levels of income inequality and social divisions may be such that people come to hold views on the justness or otherwise of income inequality without being able to see the whole picture. Most people in their everyday lives usually see some others who are richer than themselves and some who are poorer; it is perhaps not surprising that social attitudes research finds people have very little understanding of the true nature of the income distribution. If asked where they think they fall in it, people invariably place themselves somewhere near the middle even if in reality they are either very rich or very poor (Hills, 2004). Shapiro has even suggested that as certain thresholds in income inequality are passed these framing effects increase in significance (Shapiro, 2004). Paradoxically then, as inequality increases, support for redistribution may actually fall.

So a straightforward equating of democracy and social justice is simplistic and does not account for the complexity of the relationship between the two. Even if a simple link between formal democratic rights and social justice measures, such as income inequality, does not exist, there may still be links between different forms of democracy and different measures of social justice.

If constitutional changes in addition to the universal franchise can make a society *more* democratic – allowing more citizens to use their rights, participate in decision-making, and make decision making more representative – then such changes should promote social justice. At a minimum, constitutional changes that make the state less elitist and more inclusive can create a climate in which it is harder for more disadvantaged people to be socially excluded. The argument then is not so much that democracy *per se* leads to wider social justice, but that some types of democracy may lead to more just societies. Though the research literature is by no means conclusive, a number of democratic reforms have been linked to more progressive social and economic outcomes:

- *Proportional representation* has been found by some to relate to higher levels of social spending and higher levels of redistribution (Alesina and Glaeser, 2004; Iversen and Soskice, 2003).

- *Direct democracy*, typically involving greater use of referendums, can lead to improvements in some measures of social justice (Frey and Stutzer, 2002). Again though, there are many varieties of direct democracy and some studies conclude that direct democracy as a whole leads to no consistent progressive bias (Bowler and Donovan, 1998).
- *Deliberative democracy*, involving the likes of citizens' juries or citizens' panels, may also have a moderating effect on more reactionary views. Theorists like James Fiskin would be cautiously in this camp, while others, like Roberto Unger, are more forthright (Unger, 1998). Some recent work in the UK has found some moderating effect on extreme views through deliberative democracy (White *et al*, 2005).

Democracy and devolution: progressive outcomes?

The degree to which there is localism is perhaps the most important way in which democratic states can vary. It is deliberately omitted from the list above because it is the focus of the remainder of this chapter. While a simple equating of a more democratic state with one which is more devolved and localised is problematic – local government can also be highly centralised and undemocratic – it is hard to imagine that a state can be fully open and democratic if it is entirely centralised. The UK – though not entirely centralised – gives no constitutional protection to lower tiers of government and consequently has tended to have weak local government. The gap between national election turnout and local government election turnout is high by international standards.

Rectifying this situation might be a goal for a number of reasons. Firstly, local autonomy and empowerment could be seen as goals in themselves. Secondly, it might just be more efficient to provide services at a local level. But thirdly localism could also be specifically beneficial for achieving social justice objectives. Countries such as Sweden, which have enviable records on key measures of social justice, also have devolved state institutions, albeit within a framework whereby resources are allocated to different areas in order to reflect different needs. This at least suggests that there is no necessary contradiction. More positively a devolved state may even benefit those who are disadvantaged in a number of ways:

Innovation at a sub-national level can push up overall standards
Allowing local government autonomy allows space for innovation. Where

this is successful ideas and approaches can be more widely adopted, pushing up overall standards. The same can be said of other levels of government. There has been some (limited) experience of the devolved administrations being used as 'policy laboratories' with differences occurring from the lessons that have been learnt. The introduction of a children's commissioner – first in Wales, followed by Northern Ireland, then Scotland and now England too – is an example (Keating, 2002). Similarly, road congestion charging first introduced in London may spread to other areas in the future. The problem, at a local and a regional level, is to enable better cross-UK learning. In regard to regions, for example, the 'centre' – Westminster and Whitehall – often has low awareness of any experimentation occurring in the devolved administrations.

Local interest is greater among the poor
There is some reason to believe that citizens who are disadvantaged are more likely to have an interest in their local area. They are likely to be less geographically mobile and survey evidence suggests that lower income groups do have a stronger sense of attachment to a local area (Parry *et al,* 1992; Home Office, 2004). At the same time, however, factors that have a negative impact on people's local quality of life – sometimes called liveability issues – disproportionately affect the poor. In 2000, 45 per cent of those in the 10 per cent of most deprived wards reported poor 'local facilities' compared to 23 per cent of those in the 10 per cent of least deprived areas (ONS, 2002). Across a wider range of different issues, from the quality of the local environment to low level crime and anti-social behaviour, it is those living in more deprived areas who perceive a greater problem (ODPM, 2001). Yet only 30 per cent of those from a low social class think they can influence decisions in their area at present, compared with over 47 per cent for higher classes (Home Office, 2004). UK research also suggests that higher levels of political and civic participation at the local level can have a positive effect on the performance of local services (Pattie *et al,* 2002).

Democratic innovation is possible at the local level
Forms of participation that can be made more attractive and conducive to engagement from all class and income groups are possible at the local level. At an extreme, community meetings can be held, local petitions signed and meetings between local elected officials and the public arranged. More ambitiously, an extension of deliberative and direct

forms of participation is more practical locally than nationally. In a similar vein, devolution allowed Scotland and, to a lesser extent Wales, to experiment with a 'new politics' – one which was more open and participative – and while not entirely successful, this has provided some important lessons (Paterson *et al*, 2001).

Devolution to cities and regions may act as a 'progressive brake' on future welfare state retrenchment

Although international comparisons tend to suggest that devolution has negative effects on levels of public spending and on levels of inequality, and that the price of devolution to regions is inevitably greater regional inequality (Pierson, 2001; Castles and Uhr, 2002; Banting, 1987; Swank, 2002), these findings need to be treated with caution. First, the impact is highly variable and will depend on the forms of devolution, particularly how resources are allocated (Obinger *et al*, 2005). Second, and more specifically to the UK, far from acting to undermine the welfare state, devolution may in fact act as a brake. Wales and Scotland can push for increased spending but only have limited responsibility for financing it: they have an incentive to free-ride.

The Scottish and Welsh administrations are both keen to demonstrate what they will provide in addition to that provided by Westminster. Indeed, demand for a Scottish Parliament has always been fed by a feeling that policies were being foisted on the Scots by an unsympathetic Conservative government, and had the Scots been granted their wish in the 1980s then the perceived attacks on the welfare state may have been avoided. In short, a more powerful Scottish Parliament could be both 'a route to a stronger welfare state in Scotland' (Paterson *et al*, 2001) and a brake on any future welfare state retrenchment in the UK as a whole. Devolution to cities, with London leading the way, could have a similar effect. Most large urban areas have progressive electorates, and this allows space for policy experimentation, which, as Ken Livingstone has shown in London with congestion charging and policing, may advance a number of social democratic agendas.

The danger presented by devolution to the existence of national minimums should not be exaggerated. Even when formal minimum standards are not set by the centre, in practice federal systems tend to lead only to small variations around common national standards (Banting, 2005). Public opinion data suggests that the people do not tend to want much regional difference. It might be expected that the language of choice and responsiveness would undermine public attachment to uniformity, yet if anything, such an attachment seems to have strengthened (Curtice, 2004; Wyn Jones and Scully, 2004). Simultaneous talk by politicians of 'national standards' and a failure to move public debate on from emotive concerns about 'postcode lotteries' and the North-South divide can outweigh the acceptance of difference.

Uniformity vs. difference

If greater devolution of decision making and power to a sub-national level were deemed desirable – either because it leads to more equal participation in Britain's democracy or, for the reasons outlined above, it actually helps achieve wider social justice objectives – this raises a long-standing tension for social democrats. Either the centralised power of the state is used as a ready-made instrument to achieve redistribution and universal provision of services for all citizens, or power is decentralised to let the people make their own decisions about matters that directly concern them.

Historically it is true that once the big issue of securing the universal democratic franchise was resolved, social democrats have often preferred to focus on delivery, rather than worry about constitutional reform of the state. The tradition represented by Laski and Cole never quite died with post-war centralism, but it is an opposing tradition which has remained, in most regards, dominant. This tradition maintains that achieving social justice and equality for all citizens wherever they live requires that common standards be enforced by strong central agencies. Otherwise there will be an unacceptable diversity of service provision and the loss of a sense of common citizenship: a loss of British citizenship. This tradition saw the way that the welfare state broke down the pervasive localism and randomness of previous welfare arrangements as a proud achievement. The National Health Service was conceived like the Royal Mail, a national service on which every citizen could rely. Whether you lived in Penzance or Basingstoke or Bradford, the central state undertook in principle to provide you with the same service.

The conception of democratic citizenship enshrined by this approach remained unchallenged for almost 30 years, and came to form part of the institutional framework within which all parties governed. It remains resilient. Whenever there are calls for the state to be made more demo-cratic and accountable by encouraging greater decentralisation, the counter-argument always surfaces: that to do so risks making it less efficient and less capable of delivering high quality and universal public services. Variations of Neil Kinnock's 1970s assertion that devolution 'could be an obituary notice for this movement' are still heard today.

However, from the outset there have been many problems with this traditional view. First, it has only been moderately successful at providing uniform national standards. In the NHS and the schools system the quality of services delivered remains highly variable. And in areas as diverse as social services and transport policy it is clear that having a plan and trying to deliver it centrally does not mean that a uniform service is actually delivered (Reid, 2003; Le Gales, 2005). Second, it has led to the adoption of hierarchical forms of organisation, often based on military models, which treat the public sector as a largely self-contained and expanding enclave within the capitalist economy, insulating it from competition and making it liable to capture by producer interests. Finally, it has tended to produce a rigidity and inflexibility in service provision that is poor at responding to changing circumstances and the desire for more choice in what is provided and when it is provided. This rigidity has also meant limited joining up at the local level and less learning capacity: learning, in organisations, comes from diversity rather than uniformity.

Recognising these problems – and the initial anti-state response to them by the Thatcher Government – a radical critique of previous models of social democracy and their conceptions of the state has begun to take shape. To legitimise the state and make it possible to pursue a new project for social justice, the left has recognised the need for an overhaul of the over-centralised, bureaucratic and paternalist character of the post-war state. In part this has meant changed thinking about the role of markets, but it has also kicked off debates about localism within the state.

A state that marries a concern for social justice with a concern for democracy would naturally be a hybrid. A state in which nothing was allowed to be done at any subordinate level without explicit authorisation from the centre would be unworkable and grim to experience. Uniformity would be at the expense of a loss of liberty. But at the other extreme, a purely decentralised model might see one local jurisdiction paying generous unemployment benefit and another no benefit at all. What this highlights is that there will always need to remain a strong common element and common standards in the provision of welfare. Even if it is deemed acceptable for decisions on any given service to be devolved, the centre can still play an important role in setting minimum floor standards which all localities have to achieve – the enabling or 'ensuring' state (Schuppert, 2003). The questions are: how much further variation around those standards is acceptable and in which policy areas? At what level – regional, sub-regional, local or neighbourhood – should decisions be made? And should sub-national jurisdictions be allowed to choose between different ways of delivering services?

When should we accept difference: a social justice test

In this section five questions are presented, the answers to which should help policy makers decide when it is desirable to devolve democratic decision making. We draw on the four dimensions of social justice, suggested by Miller in Chapter 1: equal citizenship, the social minimum, equality of opportunity and fair distribution. The questions presented seek to find areas where, from a social justice perspective, devolution of decision making, and the differences which potentially result, is desirable or acceptable. Other non-social justice factors may be important, not least at which level different services can most efficiently be provided. However, for social democrats the social justice test is paramount. The five questions are detailed below.

1. Is this policy area central to the definition of national citizenship?

Uniformity of citizenship within a single polity is desirable in the provision of fundamental legal and political rights that are the foundation of a free society and constitute large parts of equality. This includes basic rights, such as equality before the law and the right to vote, which provide the framework for a self-governing and a flourishing civil society. It would not be acceptable to limit these rights in one part of the country or to only some groups. The separate treatment of Northern Ireland in the past in respect of civil and legal rights only served to underline its separation from the rest of the UK. And proposals to depart from national standards with some categories of asylum seekers held in detention, naturally raise grave concerns for progressives.

Core public services such as health and education, and aspects of social security such as pensions, are also important as part of people's sense of national identity. A national minimum in these areas is undoubtedly an important component of citizenship, but it does not have to be interpreted as either a local maximum or requiring uniformity. Opportunities for devolution and for variations above any minimum set should still be explored.

2. Is this policy area central to a sense of regional or local identity?

One of the main reasons for accepting devolution of powers and a greater degree of variation in the provision of some public services is that to do so may satisfy particular regional or local identities (provision for particular languages or other cultural communities is an obvious example). Such identities have to be balanced within the overarching sense people have of their common citizenship and an acceptable compromise achieved. Yet as the devolution of powers to Scotland and Wales has demonstrated, it is possible for local jurisdictions to make different decisions on core components of the social minimum, such as the level of funding of care for the elderly, without imperilling the sense that there is still a national system of welfare. Indeed, if the 'progressive brake' argument above is accepted then satisfying local or regional identities in this way can even act to protect the welfare state. The strength of regional identity could make an erosion of core elements of the social minimum more difficult, rather than easier.

Furthermore, the danger presented by devolution to the existence of national minimums should not be exaggerated. Even when formal minimum standards are not set by the centre, in practice federal systems tend to lead only to small variations around common national standards (Banting, 2005).

3. Is demand for the service different across the country?

Where the demand is different, the case for devolution is stronger. There is likely, for example, to be greater demand for local variation in the case of primary and community healthcare services than in the provision of acute care. In schools too there may be some weak demand for local differences. Policy areas where there may be even greater variation in local preferences would be community safety and the quality of the local environment. Differences in demand are likely to be closely related to varying circumstances across the country. At an extreme, there may be some 'non-comparable' issues, such as the Welsh language in education policy, which arise as a result of local difference (Jeffrey, 2002).

4. Does justice demand a uniform social minimum or is a 'floor' below which provision will not fall acceptable?

Services which would provide an important part of Miller's social minimum – including core elements of the traditional welfare state such as social security, assistance to families and access to healthcare – and services which promote equality of opportunity, such as education and childcare, raise particularly difficult questions. Should they be uniform, or should a national minimum standard be set and guaranteed for all citizens, above which variation is allowed?

The dominant strand of thought outlined above would argue that provision in these areas should be uniform. In some cases this is right. It would obviously be undesirable if the state pension were worth less in Scotland than in Dorset. But in other cases it is less clear cut. There is a range of spending programmes, which although still very important, may safely be left to local jurisdictions to decide. A basic minimum of provision of such key services as health and education has to be guaranteed, but once that level has been achieved there may be scope for making choices about priorities and for allowing greater autonomy to schools and hospitals.

5. To what extent can improved overall outcomes result from experimentation?

Public service outcomes and processes can be better in areas where citizens are more engaged in democratic and civic activities. This may be because citizens play a role in holding public services to account and thereby drive improvements, or because the adoption of different approaches allows for experimentation at a sub-national level. Learning lessons from such experimentation will ultimately see an overall increase in the quality of provision across the country and an improvement in the social minimum. It is difficult though to have any *a priori* answers to the question of experimentation. It is likely that to an extent some element of local experimentation will always lead to improvements. But experimentation is perhaps likely to be most effective where we currently have a poor evidence base and understanding of the efficacy of different policy interventions. Community safety is perhaps one example where government knows less than it should about what actually works.

Will devolution make it harder to achieve distributive objectives?

If government sets out to ensure a fairer distribution of resources between different groups, it needs, in many cases, to retain control over tax and spending powers. The more that powers are ceded to local and regional jurisdictions the harder it will be to ensure that overall outcomes are just. It is for this reason that most policies influencing the distribution of income (be it overall macroeconomic management, tax and benefit policy or the setting of the minimum wage) tend to be national.

But even here there is scope for variation, provided that enough powers are retained at the national level to ensure the achievement of basic redistribution. Governments in the UK have been very cautious in granting tax-raising powers to subordinate bodies, and the powers local governments used to have through rates have been mostly removed in the last 20 years. One exception is the small tax-raising power that has been given to the Scottish Parliament. If at some point the Scots were to make use of this and increase the basic rate of income tax, one rationale might be to pursue a different and fairer distribution to that existing in other parts of the UK.

Table 10.1 suggests some initial implications of adopting this framework. A tick, cross or question mark is allocated alongside each criterion. The more ticks the stronger the case for local or regional democratic decision making. Care needs to be taken with the 'national identity' criteria where a cross indicates that the policy area is linked strongly to national identity and is therefore not a good candidate for the allowance of local difference.

Table 10.1: Devolution of democratic decision-making: the Social Justice test applied.

	National citizenship	Sub-national identity	Demand	Floor acceptable?	Experimentation	Overall distributive objectives
Health: Primary care	?	?	✓	✓	✓	✓
Health: Acute care	✗	✗	✗	✓	?	✓
Schools	?	✓	✓	✓	✓	✓
Social security	✗	?	✗	?	✗	✗
Local environment	✓	✓	✓	✓	✓	✓
Community safety	✓	✗	✓	?	✓	✓

This table only suggests how these questions could be answered. Ultimately, decisions on where difference is appropriate should only be taken after public and political debate, albeit informed by the questions outlined here. However, the most striking implication of Table 10.1 is that social justice appears to be compatible with significantly greater levels of local difference than currently allowed. Some policy areas, because they are crucial to national identity or are required to pursue nationwide distributive objectives, must be retained at the national level. In many others though, national minimum standards could be set and the advantages of allowing local decision making should be exploited more.

Given this, the move towards the use of 'floor standards' – something the Government has argued will 'ensure equity and minimum standards' – seems justified (HMT, 2004). Importantly though, the level of a floor standard can be more or less demanding; the tendency may always be for the centre to push up floor standards, squeezing the scope for local autonomy and difference. To gain the benefits from local empowerment, floor standards cannot simply be continually pushed up; there must be genuine space for local deliberation and decision making.

The analysis above also indicates that there is a series of services, such as those that relate to crime and those which affect the quality of the local environment, where the case for localism is relatively unambiguous. Decisions on many of these services are currently made locally though the degree of local public accountability is questionable. It is also questionable whether or not local government is the most appropriate level; new neighbourhood structures, below local government, could play an increasingly important role here (ODPM, 2005).

Policy implications

This chapter has made two central arguments. First, a more local devolved state is desirable partly because it should be considered an objective in itself, but also because localism can be used to help the worst off in society. The second argument is that the geographical differences which may be the result of greater local discretion can, in the case of many services and areas of policy, be reconciled with the goals of social justice. This final section outlines specific policy implications, for devolution and then for local government.

Devolution: unfinished business

Although the picture is complex, further devolution to the regional level can help protect the social minimum by embedding it as part of a regional identity as well as part of a common national citizenship.

However, we cannot ignore the looming challenges. Foremost among the constitutional issues that have to be faced is the need for the centre, in Westminster and Whitehall, to properly restructure itself and redefine its role *vis-à-vis* the devolved administrations. Imagine a future where policy divergence increased, particularly following changes in the political colour of different administrations. What would the role of the centre need to become in setting and enforcing minimum standards more formally? These issues have not been properly considered. Just one example comes with the National Health Service, where the UK government retains few responsibilities even though it is seen by many as a crucial element of the social minimum owed to each citizen. How could future divergence be managed? In other countries devolution to a regional level becomes formal federalism and there is a constitutional statement on the level of divergence around any social minimum allowed and on fiscal transfers. This can allow for greater regional autonomy but retains the ability to set clear minimum standards.

A similar concordat between the government and the devolved bodies is necessary in the UK. This could be accompanied by the creation of a Department of the Nations and Regions explicitly to manage the relationship between central government and the devolved administrations. A priority for this department would be to consider the future fiscal situation. To date, a benign financial situation has meant little tension on this front, but the honeymoon period will soon be over if it is not already. The current formula used – the Barnett formula – continues to serve Scotland well but is acting to squeeze public spending on Wales and Northern Ireland. To be effective and mature, devolved administrations need to be able to tax and spend with greater freedom. In the future the spending whims of Westminster could limit what Scotland and Wales can do for their citizens.

A new deal for local government

The discussion above indicates that a more empowered local democracy is compatible with social justice objectives. Bottom-up democratic control and experimentation can drive up overall standards only when some degree of difference is allowed, but the type of local government reform and 'localism' pursued is important.

One danger to democratic participation is a breed of 'localism' which seeks to bypass strategic, accountable local democracy. Whether it is diluting the role of Local Education Authorities and providing funding direct to schools, or raising the possibility of directly elected police boards (Blears, 2003), localism has sometimes been interpreted as something that happens outside of local government. This should be treated with caution. It is possible that decentralisation down existing service chains, for example to foundation hospitals, city academies, specialist schools and police basic command units, rather than to local government, may prevent effective local level collaboration.

Local government, for all the improvements which need to be made, does provide the primary site where politics at a local level – discussion and decision making about the allocation of resources and of the distribution of power – can occur. Local government will not always be the most appropriate site for greater localism, and sometimes taking services outside its boundaries is justified, but it should retain a central role. Indeed, the record of the new policies and partnerships that sit at least in part outside local government, from crime and disorder partnerships to local strategic partnerships, is mixed (Corry and Stoker, 2002). One of the upshots of government not having clearly stated that local government should retain a central role is a defensive and suspicious political debate. We need to move beyond such an unhelpful position.

The emasculation of local government must be reversed, but the *quid pro quo* is that local government must reform too. First, it is perfectly possible to have highly centralised local governance structures which can be injurious to increased democratic participation. An international example is Australian State governments, but it is a problem in the UK too. There is significant scope for radical reform with devolution from local government to neighbourhoods and communities. Pilots of neighbourhood councils and the use of neighbourhood citizen initiated referendums, or citizens' ballots should all be considered. Second, to ensure a higher calibre of councillors with clear roles the multi-member ward could be revisited and the number of councillors cut. Those who remain need to be better trained and rewarded. Third, in the short term, local authorities which are performing well should be given far greater freedoms and flexibilities and there should be swifter central intervention where there is failure or unacceptable performance. These changes should be seen as a prelude to achieving a historic legacy: the enshrining and protection of local government's position in the UK state.

However, no scheme of devolution and decentralisation will be meaningful unless there is also some serious financial devolution as well. In the longer term, only if local jurisdictions are responsible for raising their own finance will they also be responsible for outcomes. At one time local government in England was self-funding, but this has gradually diminished with the rise of the national welfare state, and under the Thatcher Government the financial independence of local authorities was finally destroyed. With the central exchequer contributing as much as 80 per cent of local revenues, the regimes of capping and direct administrative interference in local government, and where those failed the attempt to bypass local government, followed. The Thatcher Government's own solution to the impasse they had created for themselves was the Poll Tax. Its intention was to reconnect the voters with local government. It backfired disastrously on the Government, showing again the perils of, but also the necessity of, radical reform in this area.

Central government could do what it has done to local government in the last 30 years because under the uncodified British constitution local government has no constitutional right to exist, except through the will of the Westminster Parliament. One of the most far-reaching changes in Britain that is required if a different kind of state is to emerge is for the position of local authorities to be given a proper constitutional basis, rather than subject to the legislative whim of the government of the day at Westminster. Such a provision would require a written constitution, or at least a major Act of Parliament, entrenched in a manner similar to the bills which established the Scottish Parliament and the Welsh Assembly – legitimated by referendums. Among the powers which would need specifying would be the financial powers of the local jurisdictions, and the means for resolving disputes between the centre and the locality. All this should only come after the reforms discussed above have been implemented and local government has acquired clear tasks and functions which reconnect it to its electorate, but something like it must ultimately be attempted if a decentralised and more pluralist state is to work. The centre has to let go, and the only sure way of getting the centre to do this is to adopt a federal or quasi-federal constitution, where subordinate levels have a constitutional right to exist as well as defined powers, including financial powers.

Conclusion

A democracy in which all citizens participate is, in one sense, an important element of social justice. Even if constitutional reform that intended to fashion a more open, pluralistic and accountable state had no significant effect on some of the measures of social justice charted in Chapter 2, then it should still be a desirable objective. But this chapter has argued that a more democratic state, particularly a more local state, can be both compatible with and help embed wider social justice, not least through the flourishing of local initiatives and experiments with different policies.

The post-war universal welfare state with its universal provision was an ideal whose benefits to all citizens and consistency with people's sense of national citizenship were sufficient to grant it lasting support. The challenge is to set out a comparable ideal which can be easily communicated, can win majority support, and can provide the basis for active state intervention to promote social justice, in a context where trust is much lower than 50 years ago and where there is much greater resistance to central control and government paternalism. What is required is a democratic vision of a reformed British state – with a radically empowered local government at its core – which is less centralised and more responsive, but at the same time one that continues to ensure equal citizenship and a sense of national, British identity.

References

Alesina A and Glaeser E (2004) *Fighting Poverty in the US and Europe: a World of Difference* Oxford: Oxford University Press

Banting K (2005) 'Social Citizenship and Federalism: Is the federal welfare state a contradiction in terms?' in Greer S ed *Territory, Democracy and Justice: Territorial Politics in Advanced Industrial Democracies,* Basingstoke: Palgave Macmillan

Banting K (1987) *The Welfare state and Canadian Federalism* (Second edition) Montreal and Kingston: McGill-Queen's University Press.

Blears H (2003) *Communities in Control* London: Fabian Society

Bowler S and Donovan T (1998) *Demanding choices: Opinion and Voting in Direct democracy* Michigan: University of Michigan

Castles FG and Uhr J (2002) 'Australia: Federalism and the Welfare State' *Paper presented to conference on Welfare States and Federalism* Bremen June 2002

Corry D and Stoker G (2002) *New Localism: Refashioning the centre-local relationship* London: New Local Government Network

Curtice J (2004) 'Does England want evolution too?' in Park A, Curtice J, Thomson K, Bromley C and Phillips M (eds) *British Social Attitudes, the 21st Report* London: Sage

Frey B and Stutzer A (2002) 'What can economists learn from happiness research?' *Journal of Economic Literature* (40)2, Pittsburgh: American Economic Association

Hills J (2004) *Inequality and the State* Oxford: Oxford University Press

HM Treasury (HMT) (2004) *Devolved decision making* London: TSO

Home Office (2004) *2003 Home Office Citizenship Survey: People, Families and Communities* London: TSO. Available at http://www.homeoffice.gov.uk/rds/pdfs04/hors289.pdf

Iversen T and Soskice D (2003) 'Electoral systems and the politics of coalitions: Why some democracies redistribute more than others' *Paper prepared for presentation at the Juan March Institute November 2004*. Available at http://www.people.fas.harvard.edu/~iversen/Iversen-Soskice2003.pdf

Jeffrey (2002) 'Uniformity and Diversity in policy provision: insights from the US, Germany and Canada' in Adams J and Robinson P (eds) *Devolution in Practice: public policy differences within the UK* London: ippr

Keating M (2002) 'Devolution and public policy in the United Kingdom: divergence and convergence' in Adams J and Robinson P (eds) *Devolution in Practice: public policy differences within the UK* London: ippr

Le Gales P 'Decentralization, Civil Society and Public Policy' in Greer S ed *Territory, Democracy and Justice: Territorial Politics in Advanced Industrial Democracies* Basingstoke: Palgave Macmillan

Obinger H, Liebried S, Castels F (2005) *Federalism and the Welfare State: New World and European Experiences* Cambridge: Cambridge University Press

ODPM (2001) *English House Condition Survey* Wetherby: ODPM

ODPM (2005) *Sustainable Communities: People Places and Prosperity* London: TSO

ONS (2002) *People's perceptions of their neighbourhood and community involvement: Results from the social capital module of the General Household Survey 2000* London: TSO

Parry G, Moyser G and Day N (1992) *Political Participation and Democracy in Britain* Cambridge: Cambridge University Press

Paterson L, McCrone D, Curtis J, Brown A, Park A, Hinds K, Surridge P, Sproston K (2001) *New Scotland, New Politics* Edinburgh: Edinburgh University Press Available at http://www.shef.ac.uk/politics/citizenaudit/EPOP02.doc

Pattie C, Seyd P and Whitely P (2002) 'Does good citizenship make a difference?' *Paper presented to EPOP Annual Conference University of Salford* Available at www.shef.ac.uk/politics/citizenaudit/publications.htm

Pettit P (1997) *Republicanism* Oxford: Oxford University Press

Pierson P (2001) *The New Political Economy of the Welfare State* New York: Oxford University Press

Reid J (2003) *Localising the National Health Service: gaining greater equity through localism and diversity*, London: New Local Government Network

Schuppert F (2003) 'The ensuring state' in *Progressive futures: new ideas for the centre-left* London: Policy Network

Shapiro I (2004) *The State of Democratic Theory* Princeton and Oxford: Princeton University Press

Shapiro I and Hacker-Cordon C (1999) *Democracy's Value* Cambridge: Cambridge University Press

Stoker G (2003) 'New Labour needs local government' *Renewal* 14 March 2003, London: Lawrence and Wishart

Swank D (2002) *Global Capital, Political Institutions, and Policy Change in Developed Welfare States* Boston: Cambridge University Press

Unger R (1998) *Democracy Revitalized: a progressive alternative* London: Verso

Walker D (2002) *In praise of centralism* London: Central Books

White S, Lewis M and Paxton W (2005) 'Inheritance Tax: what do the people think?' in *The Citizens Stake: Exploring universal asset-based policies* Bristol: Policy Press

Wyn Jones R and Scully R (2004) 'Devolution in Wales: What Does the Public Think?' *Devolution Briefing Number 7* London: Economic and Social Research Council (ESRC) Devolution and Constitutional Change Programme

Young I (1990) *Justice and the Politics of Difference* Princeton: Princeton University Press

Just Happiness?
Subjective Wellbeing and Social Policy

Tania Burchardt

What has happiness to do with social justice?

The idea that a society should be arranged so as to ensure the greatest possible happiness of its members is likely to be met with derision in some quarters. Yet it is an idea which, in one form or another, dates back at least to the ancient Greeks and which provided the philosophical foundation for modern economics.[1] More recently, there has been a resurgence of interest in happiness in the fields of psychology, economics and sociology. However, it has received little attention in social policy; it seems too naive a concept to contribute to the discussion about problems as weighty as unemployment, child poverty and citizenship.

This chapter endeavours to assess the claims for happiness to be taken seriously as a component of social justice and provide some pointers for the kinds of policies which might be adopted if happiness were to be considered a significant social objective.[2] This chapter begins with a brief discussion of the role of happiness in political philosophy. Utilitarianism champions happiness as the key 'object of value' but it fails to provide guidance on how happiness should be distributed, and is therefore of limited use as a starting point for considerations of social justice. Other conceptions of social justice relegate happiness to a subsidiary or non-existent role.

Nevertheless, it is important to understand more about what promotes and detracts from happiness for two reasons, which will be looked at later in this chapter. First, even if happiness is relevant to only

---

1 Aristotle's *Politics* – see, for example, Keyt and Miller (1991); Adam Smith, see Cannan (1961).

2 Different meanings of 'happiness' are considered later in the chapter. For now, it is used inter-changeably with the general term 'subjective wellbeing'. These terms are distinct from 'objective wellbeing', which is used to refer to the levels of health, income, and other circumstances in which an individual finds him or herself.

some conceptions of social justice, it would feature prominently in most assessments of whether a society is a desirable society. Second, many of the inequalities with which theories of social justice do concern themselves (income inequality, lack of opportunity, and so on) turn out to have significant subjective as well as objective manifestations.

We then explore a circumstance in which objective and subjective inequalities are not so closely aligned, namely, where the phenomenon of adaptation is at work. Adaptation refers to the way in which an individual's own previous experience affects his or her subjective assessment of current circumstances; thus, for example, two individuals with the same income may feel very differently about it, depending on whether they were recently much richer or recently much poorer than their current state.

The chapter then goes on to illustrate the ways in which policies and policy making might change if the promotion of happiness were to be given greater priority.

Utilitarianism is the most obvious starting point for an examination of the role of happiness in social justice. Bentham (1789) famously argued that individual ethical judgements, and collective social decisions, should be made in order to secure the greatest happiness of the greatest number. This raises the question of what happiness is. How do we know whether a person in one set of circumstances is happier than the same person in different circumstances? Even more challengingly, how do we know whether one person is happier than another person? These are respectively the problems of unobservability and of interpersonal comparisons.

The response to unobservability, of which extensive use has been made in welfare economics, is to distance 'utility' from the concept of happiness as it is commonly understood. The argument runs as follows. Accept that we cannot observe happiness directly, but instead assume that people will choose what they prefer and that they will have higher utility if they get what they prefer. Then, 'revealed preferences' (the choices people make) can be used to order different states according to whether they produce more or less utility. From here, it is an easy step to using income as a proxy for utility; in a market economy, those with fewer resources are less likely to be able to secure what they prefer. Thus standard poverty indices can be derived and used to rank social states, while measures like GDP can be used to compare countries. The same reasoning leads to cost benefit analysis and techniques such as 'willingness to pay' to assess alternative policies, for example with respect to the location of airports.

One of the problems with this move is that it becomes less intuitively obvious why we should be concerned about happiness if it is interpreted as utility, and utility is inferred from preference satisfaction. Is preference satisfaction an appropriate goal for society to adopt? More specifically, considerable doubt has been cast on the validity of the chain of reasoning which leads to income as a proxy for utility and utility for happiness. People do not, it seems, consistently choose what they prefer, and getting what they prefer does not always make them happier, in the sense that they do not always express greater satisfaction with their lives or display a more positive mood as a result (Thaler, 1992). Moreover, how much happiness an individual gains from a given level of income depends on a whole range of things, including how he/she had to spend his/her time in order to acquire the income and his/her personal characteristics and circumstances. More recently, the assumptions which prompted the reliance on indicators of preference satisfaction rather than more direct measures of happiness (namely, that happiness is unobservable, and that interpersonal comparisons are impossible) have been challenged. This is discussed in more detail later in the chapter. For now, we can note that if happiness is observable, we would be better advised, in accordance with Bentham's stipulation, to assess social states directly by the sum of happiness they produce, rather than indirectly by measures based on income or revealed preference.

The resurgence of interest in happiness in social science is therefore welcome. However, aiming to maximise the total sum of happiness provides little guidance on the best distribution of happiness between people. The concept of Pareto optimality allows comparisons to be made between social states where one or more people can be made better off without anyone being made worse off – thereby increasing the total sum of happiness. However, it is silent on the more typical distributional questions where giving to one requires taking from another. Social welfare functions were developed to expand the range of social states which could be ordered, but Arrow showed that under a plausible set of minimal assumptions, it was impossible to find an ordering of social states based exclusively on the set of individual preference orderings – the only data which a utilitarian framework can accommodate, unless some way of measuring utility on a cardinal scale can be found (Sen, 1973).

The classical utilitarian position cannot distinguish between a society of 1000 citizens with one 'utility magnate' gobbling up 1000 utils and the remaining 999 citizens going without any, and a society of the same size in which everyone gets one until each, as the sum of happiness is the same. Of course, it may be that the utility magnate is distressed by seeing his/her fellow citizens starving and shivering in the cold, and if his/her distress is great enough, the total sum of happiness might be increased by a degree of redistribution. Similarly, it may be that there are diminishing marginal returns to wealth, so that a resource will increase the total sum of happiness more if it is distributed to the less well off. But these are purely instrumental reasons to be concerned with distribution; there is no fundamental motivation within a utilitarian framework for special attention to the worse off or to the gap between rich and poor. A separate distributional rule can be introduced (for example, by specifying the extent of trade-off between overall happiness and permissible inequality of happiness) but this has to be motivated by an egalitarian concern which is independent of utilitarianism.

This limitation is one of the reasons why a pure utilitarian conception has not been a leading contender in political philosophy for a long time (Rawls, 1971). Fortunately, alternatives are available which provide independent grounds for distributional concerns and broaden the informational base. Rawls' *A Theory of Justice*, for example, proposes the principle that inequalities should be arranged so as to maximise the welfare of the worst off. Here, welfare is understood not as a subjective state but as a function of 'primary goods' – those things which people require in order to pursue their individual conception of the 'good life'. The application of this so-called difference principle is constrained by other parts of the theory, such as the requirement for equal civil liberties. Many approaches move away from utility as the sole object of value. Sen advocates the evaluation of functionings (the activities individuals undertake and the states of being they achieve) and capabilities (the set of combinations of functionings individuals have the opportunity to achieve), while Dworkin developed an account of equality of opportunity based on equal access to resources (Sen, 1980; Dworkin, 1981).

This overview shows that utilitarianism, the philosophy which places happiness at its core, is the foundation for modern welfare economics and for traditional measures of poverty and development. However, its reticence on distributional issues makes it an unattractive starting point for theories of social justice. To enable distributional judgements to be made, alternative political philosophies have expanded the range of information and values which can be taken into account. Some, for example the capabilities framework, retain subjective wellbeing as one among other valuable ends. Others, such as Rawlsianism, regard subjective wellbeing as strictly irrelevant to the evaluation of social justice.

Even where happiness is not considered an important value, if two equally just policies were to be devised, one of which promoted the subjective wellbeing of the population and the other of which detracted from it, it seems reasonable to assume that the former should be adopted. Happiness is in that case relevant to the construction of a good or desirable society and even if it is not, it is central to the evaluation of social justice. This provides one reason for seeking to understand the determinants of subjective wellbeing – the subject of the next section. A second reason is that many of the inequalities with which theories of social justice directly concern themselves, such as income inequality, or inequality of opportunity, turn out to have significant effects on subjective wellbeing. An appreciation of that relationship can help to reinforce the priority accorded to questions of equality.

What promotes subjective wellbeing?

The decision about how to measure subjective wellbeing depends on the underlying concept. The traditional economists' interpretation is desire or preference satisfaction, but this is more a product of epistemological caution (we might be able to observe, or at least infer, preference satisfaction, but we can't observe happiness) than it is of an argument about what is truly valuable. Some psychologists have promoted the idea that what we ideally want to measure is the sum of momentary moods (positive and negative 'effect'). They have developed a survey instrument that involves giving each sample member a buzzer, which sounds at random times during the course of a day and asks them to record their mood at the moment the buzzer sounds (Kahneman, 1999). Proponents argue that this is conceptually clearer and more scientifically robust than the alternatives. Experiments by people such as Davidson have shown that changes in mood correspond to alterations in brain activity (Layard, 2005). However, this interpretation of the meaning of happiness falls foul of what may be called the *Brave New World* objection; if all we are concerned about is mood, we should simply strive for a world with free and plentiful access to soma.[3] Most people's intuition is that true

---

3 Soma is the drug taken by inhabitants of Aldous Huxley's (1932) fictional *Brave New World*, which soothes anxiety, gets you high, and does not have any unpleasant side-effects (though it may eventually kill you). Some commentators do not find this such an abhorrent idea; most, however, would prefer to aim for a world in which personal fulfilment is a reality, not a chemically induced illusion.

happiness – that is to say, the kind of happiness which a good society would promote – is more reflexive; a product of our cognitive as well as our affective faculties, and that it requires us to actually do and be things in the world.[4]

At the other end of the spectrum, the ancient Greek concept of eudemonia meant something like 'flourishing' or 'fulfilment of human potential'. The opportunity to pursue eudemonia may seem a more attractive concept for considerations of social justice, but unfortunately there is no straightforward way to measure it. Instead, a commonly used survey question asks respondents to consider 'How satisfied are you with your life overall?' with responses recorded on an ordinal scale. This invites a more reflective response than simply current mood, and thus gets closer to an idea of personal fulfilment, although it is clearly possible to express satisfaction without having fully explored all aspects of your potential. Similar questions are used to assess satisfaction with various domains of life, such as job, family and leisure.

Survey questions like these have now been exposed to intensive scrutiny, and on the whole they stand up well. Survey respondents have no difficulty in making sense of questions like, 'Overall, how happy are you with your life?' and their answers show a reasonable degree of test-retest reliability over the short term, with variations corresponding to life events which theory predicts to be significant. Precisely how people interpret the questions is of course not known, but the responses also correlate well with other people's observations of the individual, both people who know them well and strangers who have to rely on how happy the person looks. More objective measures like frequency of smiling or laughing, health, and likelihood of committing suicide also turn out to be correlated in the expected direction with self-reported subjective wellbeing. One of the pre-eminent researchers in the field concluded in a review of measurement issues that 'self-report measures of well-being appear to possess adequate psychometric properties.' (Diener, 1994).

Other questions ask respondents to rate how happy they are, a formulation which probably lies somewhere between mood and life satisfaction in terms of the degree of reflection on life as a whole. In the summary of evidence which follows, the general term subjective wellbeing (SWB) is used unless the results are particular to one specification of the concept.

---

4 See also Nozick's (1974) discussion of the experience machine.

The summary is selective, with an eye to those contributors to SWB which are most relevant from a policy perspective.[5] The policy implications are drawn out later in the chapter.

National income and average SWB
Comparisons between countries show a positive correlation between average SWB and GNP per capita, but with diminishing marginal returns to GNP, such that over about $10,000 per capita (in 1995 US dollar Purchasing Power Parities), SWB increases little (Frey and Stutzer, 2002a). The implication is that after basic needs have been met, a development strategy based solely on GNP growth will not reap rewards in terms of SWB.

Some of the earliest economic studies of SWB were concerned with the apparent anomaly that within a country at a point in time, the rich were happier than the poor, but that a time series over a period with strong GDP growth showed no overall upward trend in happiness (Easterlin, 1974). This has been confirmed for a number of different countries and with controls to allow for the changing composition of populations and for macro-economic conditions (Alesina *et al*, 2001). One possible explanation is that rising expectations and aspirations reduce the subjective returns to increases in national income – a process of changing social reference groups and individual habituation, which is returned to below.

Personal income, income inequality and unemployment
At a given place and time, richer people are, on the whole, happier than poorer people. Money does buy you happiness – but only up to a point[6] and taking the following into account: (i) while the cross-sectional correlation between income and SWB is consistently found to be positive and significant, it is relatively weak; (ii) there are strongly diminishing marginal returns to income; and (iii) relative income matters more than absolute income (debate continues about 'relative to whom' – society as a whole, the rich, the individual's own previous income, other family members, or others with similar characteristics).

Greater income inequality in society as a whole is generally associated with lower SWB in European countries (Alesina *et al*, 2001). Similar

---

5 General reviews of the determinants of SWB can be found in Frey and Stutzer (2002a), Kahneman, Diener and Schwarz (1999), and Strategy Unit (2002).

6 A summary of the research on income and happiness can be found in Frey and Stutzer, (2002b).

results have been found for different communities in Israel (Morawetz, 1977). The US appears to be different, however; some suggest this may be because Americans perceive there to be greater social mobility and hence worry less about cross-sectional inequality although whether this perception is accurate or not is another question (Alesina *et al,* 2001).

Being unemployed is unequivocally bad for SWB (and is worse than economic inactivity), and the association is independent of level of income or change in income (Frey and Stutzer, 2002a). Moreover, panel studies have shown that the causation runs mainly from unemployment to low SWB rather than vice versa. There are, clearly, psychological and social costs to unemployment over and above the financial costs. High levels of unemployment in society lower SWB generally, even for those not currently unemployed. In fact, the negative effect on an individual of being unemployed is reduced if the regional rate of unemployment is high (Kelvin and Jarrett, 1985).

Conversely, being in rewarding employment is associated with higher SWB. Job satisfaction itself is influenced by many factors including increases in wages, security, personal autonomy and opportunities for interacting with others (Warr, 1999). Self-employment is generally associated with higher SWB, possibly because of the degree of control (perceived or actual) which individuals have over their working hours and conditions (Benz and Frey, 2003). The significance of non-monetary factors is supported by evidence that people who undertake voluntary work are happier than those who do not and that the causation runs at least in part from the volunteering to higher SWB (Meier and Stutzer, 2004).

State institutions and local conditions

A large cross-country study (Veenhoven, 2000) found that three indices of freedom – political (democratic process and civil rights), economic (conditions of exchange of goods, services and labour) and personal (religious freedom) – were each strongly positively correlated with SWB. Economic freedom was especially important in poor countries while political freedom was more important in rich countries (perhaps due to there being less variation in economic freedom in more developed countries).

Focusing on political freedom, Frey and Stutzer used differences between the 26 Swiss cantons as a natural experiment to assess the effect of direct democracy on SWB. They found that individuals in cantons with more referendums had significantly higher SWB, even after controlling for socio-demographic and other characteristics. This can be interpreted as showing that referendums are an effective way of aligning local policy with what makes the population happy, or that the opportunity to participate in decision making is itself highly valued. The latter interpretation is supported by the fact that it is the right to participate rather than actual individual participation which appears to make the difference (Frey and Stutzer, 2000a).

Surprisingly little research has been done on the extent to which local conditions affect overall life satisfaction. Various indicators of crime (perceived and actual) and housing and neighbourhood conditions contribute significantly to people's satisfaction with their neighbourhood, but these tend to disappear when controls are introduced for socio-demographic characteristics or when overall life satisfaction is considered (Michalos and Zumbo, 2000). Part of the explanation may be that being a victim of crime and living in a poor neighbourhood are strongly associated with characteristics which in themselves are associated with low life satisfaction, such as living on a low income. However, this is a topic which merits further research in the UK context.

Individual characteristics and life events

Personality traits have an important, though not overwhelming, role in explaining variations in SWB. For example, those with an optimistic disposition, and those who have an 'internal locus of control' (that is, they believe they are in command of their own fate to a greater extent), tend to have higher levels of SWB (Lachman and Weaver, 1998). It also appears to be the case that actually having greater control over your circumstances is associated with higher SWB, although the evidence for this is drawn from a rather narrow base. In the Whitehall studies, civil servants in jobs with greater autonomy were found to have higher self-esteem and better health. In another study, volunteers exposed to noise levels which they themselves controlled tolerated longer and louder exposure than those who could not regulate the input (Frederick and Lowenstein, 1999).

Significant changes occur in an individual's SWB in association with a range of life events. There is selection into marriage (happy people are more likely to get married), and getting married itself increases SWB, at least for a while. Controlling for income and other explanatory variables, Frey and Stutzer use German panel data to show that the 'honeymoon effect' pre-dates the marriage by up to two years and lasts for a similar period afterwards (Stutzer and Frey, 2003). The birth of a child exhibits a similar relationship with SWB, for both men and women, while divorce is preceded for both sexes with a diminution in SWB but followed by an increase in SWB only for women (Clark *et al*, 2003).

Social reference groups

Cantril's classic study in thirteen countries across the world concluded that the relationship between material circumstances and SWB was determined by 'the psychological context, the frame of reference within which ratings are made' (Cantril, 1965). He found that the priorities which featured prominently for people in India were a water well, a bicycle and being able to secure the marriage of their daughters, while in the US they were a Cadillac, being able to travel and putting children through college. This can be read as showing a surprising degree of consistency in human concerns: material wellbeing, expansion of opportunities, and promoting the wellbeing of the next generation, or it can be seen as showing the inflation of desires that accompanies economic development.[7]

The phenomenon of individuals evaluating their situation, especially their standard of living, in relative terms is often described in derogatory terms as the politics of envy. In fact there is little evidence that the emotion of envy plays a significant role. More sophisticated psychological and sociological research has revealed that the identification of an individual's social reference group is considerably more complex than simply aspiring to acquire the standard of living of the next social stratum up the scale. Rather it would appear that self-identity, self-esteem and a sense of belonging are important factors and that they lead to social reference groups defined in a range of different ways (Atkinson, 1983). Adam Smith made the same point when he observed that 'custom has rendered leather shoes a necessary of life in England. The poorest creditable person of either sex would be ashamed to appear in public without them.' (Smith, 1776) The person is not envious of the well-shod, but his self-esteem is imperilled by a lack of proper shoes.

Moreover, rising material aspirations and the generation of desires for new products and services are essential to the functioning of capitalism

---

7 The process of changing social reference groups is akin to adaptation, discussed below.

(Galbraith, 1969). Economic development would not have got far if US citizens today were wholly satisfied with a well for a water supply and a bicycle for transport. By equating the relative evaluation of standard of living with the politics of envy, the critics are perversely castigating those at the bottom of the heap for responding in precisely the way that is required to generate the wealth for those at the top.

The problem of adaptation

The possibility that people become used to the situation they find themselves in, and subsequently assess their wellbeing in relation to that situation, is particularly problematic for the use of measures of subjective wellbeing in the context of social justice. Two illustrations may serve to make the point. Someone who is accustomed to three foreign holidays a year, fine wine with every meal and a fast car may feel very deprived if he/she is suddenly required to live on an average income (the so-called expensive tastes problem). Conversely, someone who has never known anything other than a lower standard of living may not be especially unhappy or dissatisfied with his/her circumstances (conditioned expectations). Sen summarises the problem as follows:

> *The battered slave, the broken unemployed, the hopeless destitute, the tamed housewife, may have the courage to desire little, but the fulfilment of those disciplined desires is not a sign of great success and cannot be treated in the same way as the fulfilment of the confident and demanding desires of the better placed.* (Sen, 1987)

If SWB alone is used as the metric for assessing the relative position of different individuals, the 'broken unemployed' could be at the same point in the distribution as the erstwhile jet-setter.

One response to the problem is to deny that the kind of adaptation to wealth or deprivation described in these hypothetical examples is widespread in the real world. A number of cross-sectional studies are highly suggestive of a process of adaptation being at work. For example, individuals with higher income also report higher values for the 'absolute minimum income required to make ends meet' (Stutzer, 2004), and income aspirations are higher for people with higher incomes (although satisfaction is also higher (van Praag and Kapteyn, 1973). Recent perceived improvements in financial circumstances are positively correlated with satisfaction (Ingelhart and Rabier, 1986; Davis, 1984; Graham and Pettinato, 2002), and in some cases, perceived change is more strongly correlated with satisfaction than current level of income. However, there are methodological drawbacks to data on perceived changes in income.

Conclusive evidence for or against adaptation requires longitudinal data. Job satisfaction seems to be related to changes in wages more strongly than levels of wages (Clark *et al*, 1998; Clark, 1999; Grund and Sliwka, 2003). The implication is that wage rises bring increases in SWB but as the workers become accustomed to the new wage rate, the effect on SWB does not endure. Evidence on adaptation to changes in household income is mixed. Diener *et al* for the US find no effect on SWB of moving from one income band to another, controlling for income level, but studies in other countries (Singapore, Taiwan and Russia) find change in income is independently and strongly associated with subjective assessments of income adequacy (Diener *et al*, 1993; Chan *et al*, 2002; Ravallion and Lokshin, 2001). Burchardt for the UK does not find evidence of adaptation to changes in income in the short term, but over a longer period (nine years) adaptation to increases in income can be observed (Burchardt, 2004).

So it appears that adaptation needs to be taken seriously as a phenomenon in the real world. It offers a way to reconcile the cross-sectional evidence that wealthier people are happier and the time series evidence that average happiness does not increase over time in developed countries, despite GDP growth. But the existence of adaptation is bad news for the use of SWB in evaluations of equality and social justice. Of course, one can insist that subjective wellbeing is indeed the only relevant information – that if an individual does not feel unhappy or dissatisfied, then there is nothing wrong. This is a consistent position although it leads to some unpalatable conclusions; a rational policy-maker should seek to restrict access to education and institute a rigid caste system, in order to avoid raising expectations and to limit awareness of alternatives. The ruling elite could then be confident of maintaining a happy, ignorant population.

An alternative response is to conclude that in cases where adaptation is suspected, subjective wellbeing should not be the sole basis on which equality or social justice is judged. Although further research is needed on the exact timings and mechanisms of adaptation in different circumstances, it is clear that attention should be given to the conditions in which an individual's 'baseline' SWB was established: for example, whether their childhood experience was one of plenty or poverty, of freedom or constraint, and whether they have recent or long-term experience of unemployment or of living in a deprived area. The individual's subjective assessment of his or her current circumstances then needs to be adjusted to take this frame of reference into account, to avoid biasing the assessment of need in favour of the recently-poor and against the long-term poor. SWB measurements can also be supplemented with information on objective conditions, such as the extent to which basic functionings are fulfilled or the scope of the individual's capability set.

Pointers for policy and policy-making

In the context of social justice, a concern with subjective wellbeing – though not an exclusive concern – can be securely theoretically grounded. There is an accumulating body of evidence about what promotes SWB and what damages it, and also in what circumstances subjective assessments may need to be treated with caution. So what does this imply for practical social policy?

Wellbeing is multi-dimensional
It has become customary to assert the multi-dimensionality of poverty, not to mention of deprivation or social exclusion. This has generated a multitude of indicators, but in the final analysis the objective is often still to identify those who are disadvantaged by a lack of material resources. Happiness research points in a different direction; there are several distinct domains which contribute to, or detract from, overall life satisfaction and they cannot be reduced to a single dimension of material wellbeing. These include family relationships, work, health, income and leisure (Frey and Stutzer, 2002b).

This implies, first of all, that more imaginative policy tools need to be developed to address the non-material domains, and second, that the potential interaction between different domains needs to be considered. Financial hardship often contributes to difficulties in other areas (health, for example) and tried and tested methods of redistribution can and should be used to mitigate that. On the other hand, a policy which reduces financial hardship (improving satisfaction with income) by giving the poor access to jobs which involve long hours and poor conditions, is likely to have off-setting effects in the domains of satisfaction with work, health, friends and family relationships. The overall effect on SWB could be negative.

Moreover, the strongly diminishing marginal returns to income indicate that the deficit in SWB of, for example, fraught family relationships, cannot be easily made up with financial transfers. So policies which directly promote loving and supportive relationships within and between generations (not at all the same thing as promoting so-called traditional family values) should be given higher priority. Statutory paternity leave is a good start, but two weeks is hardly sufficient to allow bonding between father and child, let alone provide the basis for equal shares of parenting in the early years. Better support for carers, whether through facilitating breaks in their paid employment, offering respite care services, or simply providing adequate social services in the first place, would be another area for reform.

Inequality matters, not just levels

There are two sources of evidence that inequality matters for SWB. The first is that high overall income inequality is associated with lower average SWB, at least in Europe. The second is that individuals evaluate their income, and indeed other aspects of their situation, relative to a social reference group, defined in various different ways. As noted above, this cannot be lightly dismissed as the politics of envy but is instead indicative of basic human needs for self-respect and group membership.

These observations have led some commentators to argue that taxation should be made more progressive and additional taxes introduced on items of conspicuous consumption (Frank, 1997).[8] Increases in income or expenditure impose negative externalities on others, by shifting everyone's frame of reference (or at least the frame of reference of a peer group) and a standard response to externalities in economic theory is taxation. A further argument for progressive income tax relates to adaptation; individuals anticipate greater subjective gains from an increase in income than actually occurs, because once they have obtained the new income level they adapt to it. Taxation, in principle, reduces the incentive to increase income at the margin and thus helps to protect indi-

---

8 In the UK, although income tax is progressive, the burden of indirect taxes and National Insurance is such that overall, the bottom income quintile group pays a higher proportion of their gross income in tax (37.9 per cent) than the top income quintile group (35.0 per cent) (ONS 2004: Table 3).

viduals from the consequences of misjudging their own expected utility (Layard, 2005). However, behavioural responses to changes in incentives are notoriously difficult to predict from theory, and subjective responses are possibly even harder to foresee.

Whether the best tools are restructuring and regulation of the labour market, or redistributive benefits and taxation, there is a strong argument from SWB for tackling the historically high levels of income inequality in the UK (see Chapter 2)

Combining a concern with inequality with the previous point about multi-dimensionality leads to the suggestion that inequality in other domains also need to be addressed. There is strong evidence that inequalities in social status – for example in terms of employment and occupation – matter subjectively. The narrowing of social class differences is therefore important, not just the narrowing of income inequality. This means confronting inter-generational transfers of financial, human and social capital, as well as short-term mobility (Piachaud, 2002).

There is rather less evidence of a concern with inequality for other domains of SWB: Do we assess our satisfaction with leisure time relative to a reference group? (Very likely). Do we assess our satisfaction with family relationships relative to a reference group? (Less likely).

Once again, care needs to be taken not to stretch the argument based on SWB too far. If it is the case that social reference groups dominate people's assessment of, for example, their health, and if social reference groups are delineated partly by class, health inequalities between classes would not be a problem from a happiness perspective. Most people would find that an unacceptable conclusion – a reminder that SWB cannot serve as a sole guide to policy formation, especially when it comes to distributional issues.

Hope, expectation and lifetime dynamics
Several pieces of evidence point to the importance of hope in promoting subjective wellbeing. One interpretation of the fact that younger people are consistently found to have higher SWB (even after controlling for other characteristics) is that they tend to be optimistic about the future. Optimism itself is associated with SWB at all ages. Similarly, the anticipation of a desirable event (marriage, birth of a child) clearly contributes to SWB. From a SWB perspective then, it is important not only that there are routes to securing a better life, but

also that the individuals concerned believe these routes are open to them. Young people may:

a. Have opportunities and believe they exist;
b. Have opportunities but not believe they exist;
c. Not have opportunities but believe they exist;
d. Not have opportunities and not believe they exist.

Group d) is the usual focus for policy ('disaffected youth'), but groups b) and c) may also need attention because their beliefs are not in line with reality. The SWB of group b) is likely to be unnecessarily low and they are not likely to take advantage of such opportunities as there are.[9] An example might be academically able young people from less well-educated family backgrounds. Group c) are fine in the short term from a SWB perspective, but are unlikely to make optimal decisions for the longer term, possibly resulting in a discrepancy between expectation and outcome which is definitely harmful to SWB.

The current Government's emphasis on policy interventions in childhood and young adulthood is therefore right, but continuing obstacles, failures and pure bad luck in adulthood merit attention too. Even if a level playing field were to have been created for all school-leavers (a goal which we are a very long way from having achieved), subsequent events can restrict both the objective and subjective opportunities available to an individual. If the policy referee blows the whistle at the start of the game and then leaves the pitch, fair play is not likely to ensue, the injured will go untended and morale will quickly slump.

Repeated opportunities to recover from set-backs are needed, recognising the complexity of situations in which individuals find themselves, to ensure the maintenance of hope. This means, for example, significant investment in adult education and grants for mature students, and perhaps a reconsideration of a human capital approach to welfare to work for the long-term unemployed and others with additional needs. It means intensive programmes for ex-offenders. It means greater emphasis on rehabilitation services within the NHS, focusing on rebuilding aspirations, especially for patients with mental health problems. What these interventions have in common is the attempt to expand people's capa-

---

9 It is worth noting that not all opportunities are good opportunities; in these cases, the individual may be better off remaining ignorant of them.

bilities, to set them on a different track from that which they were previously following – an approach John Hills has termed 'propulsion' (Hills, 2002). These are often seen as expensive policy options, but long-term gains reduce the net costs and the potential benefits in terms of social justice and are considerable.

Lack of hope is often accompanied by low expectations; a process of subjective adaptation. If you have had to wait two hours to be seen in a benefit office on the previous five occasions, you are unlikely to expect to be seen straight away this time (even when the benefit office is re-branded Jobcentre Plus!). This presents a problem for policy-makers both in collecting information about how services are performing and in attempting to improve service delivery. The ubiquitous customer satisfaction survey, for example, fails to take into account that relative to low expectations, even a poor service can appear to perform well (Duffy, 2000). In many contexts this is translated into fewer resources for the services used by those with low expectations because the pressure from users is weak or absent. The mechanism of 'voice', identified by Hirschman, to prompt improvements in the service is missing. Raising expectations which have been conditioned by long experience of poor services takes more than publishing targets or customer charters (Hirschman, 1970). It requires mechanisms by which individuals can at least sample a better kind of service – a politically risky but perhaps necessary strategy.

Participation, agency and autonomy

A number of findings point to the importance of active participation and autonomy: a perception of being in control increases SWB, at work and in other environments; volunteering and self-employment are associated with higher SWB; opportunities for political participation are valued subjectively. Individuals will not always want to take the responsibility of decision making directly, but having the opportunity to decide whether or not to delegate their choice to some other authority is important.

This has implications for policy-making and implementation as well as for policy content. First, it favours a model of policy development where the subjects of the policy are actively involved rather than passive recipients of a pre-formulated strategy. Area regeneration programmes under New Labour have been progressive in this respect, making greater efforts to involve local residents in decision making from an early stage. Other area-based policies, such as Sure Start and Health Action Zones, have made moves in a similar direction though sometimes only in a half-hearted fashion. The tension between, on the one hand, targets and overall policy goals set by central government, and participative policy development on the other, has not been entirely resolved. Are residents to have discretion over the ends as well as the means? How can this be reconciled with the nature of funding streams and the need for accountability? Other policy areas have paid lip-service to individuals taking an active role in formulating a programme. For example, many of the New Deals incorporate an element of choice for participants, but this is more often nominal than actual. For the SWB of participants, it is possible that offering pseudochoices is more alienating than giving a realistic assessment of limited employment opportunities (Mitchell, 2003).

Second, the ability to be in control of one's own life, or to contribute collectively to policy formulation and implementation, is something which needs to be nurtured and developed. This is especially true in the context of expectations conditioned by long-term, possibly intergenerational, disadvantage. There are general and specific ways to encourage autonomy in this sense. Specifically, citizens' juries are a tried and tested method of exploring complex policy problems, providing non-experts with the information, facilitation and time for deliberation which are needed to reach a considered collective opinion. The use of citizens' juries could be expanded greatly. More generally, the pressure on school and higher education to concentrate solely on skills which the labour market rewards should be resisted. Education must retain as its central objective the development of individual agency, of critical thinking and reflection.

Conclusion

The pursuit of happiness is not the same as the pursuit of social justice. For a start, the maximisation of happiness is indifferent to the distribution of happiness between people, or, at best, takes account of distribution only in instrumental terms. An independent normative principle, such as maximising the wellbeing of the worst off, or equality of opportunity, must be combined with happiness as the 'object of value' if it is to be a plausible candidate as a metric for social justice.

Moreover, it is not clear that happiness is the right object of value to select. In its narrowest interpretation as 'positive mood', it does not allow us to distinguish between chemically-induced ecstasy and deeper personal fulfilment. In its broader interpretations, for example as life satisfaction, sole reliance on happiness as a guide to policy formation, because of the phenomenon of adaptation, leads to some counter-intuitive results. Long-term deprivation may be subjectively less painful, but should that mean it is given lower policy priority than protecting the well-off against shocks to their living standard? Subjective assessments are often relative to expectations and the justice or injustice of the circumstances which conditioned those expectations need to be taken into account.

Despite these limitations, attention to subjective wellbeing can provide a useful corrective to more narrowly materially-based conceptions of wellbeing. For too long, social policy has relied almost exclusively on income poverty as an indicator of disadvantage – crucially important, but not the only domain which registers in people's own assessments of their lives. Careful study of the evidence on happiness can also help to unblock some of the ideological opposition to thinking about inequality, revealing, as it does, the relationships between equality, self-esteem and group membership. Finally, considering happiness alongside other values reminds us of the importance of what might be called subjective dynamics – hope, expectation and disappointment – and of the need to promote individual and collective autonomy. In itself, happiness is neither just nor unjust, but nor should it be lightly dismissed – as those concerned with social policy are sometimes tempted to do – as just happiness.

References

Alesina A, Di Tella R and MacCulloch R (2001) 'Inequality and Happiness: are Europeans and Americans different?' *NBER working paper 8198* Cambridge MA: National Bureau of Economic Research (NBER)

Atkinson M (1983) 'The perception of social categories: implications for the social comparison process' in Olson J, Herman C, and Zanna M (eds) *Relative Deprivation and Social Comparison: the Ontario symposium,* volume 4 Hillsdale NJ: Lawrence Erlbaum Associates

Bentham J (1789) *An Introduction to the Principles of Morals and Legislation* (Re-published 1907) Oxford: Clarendon Press

Benz M and Frey B (2003) 'The Value of Autonomy: evidence from the self-employed in 23 countries' *Institute for Empirical Research in Economics Working Paper 173* Zurich: University of Zurich

Burchardt T (2004) *One man's rags are another man's riches: identifying adaptive preferences using panel data* London: London School of Economics Centre for Analysis of Social Exclusion (CASE)

Cannan E (ed) (1961) *Adam Smith: An Inquiry into the Nature and Causes of the Wealth of Nations* London: Methuen

Cantril H (1965) *The Pattern of Human Concerns* New Brunswick: Rutgers University Press

Chan A, Ofstedal M, Hermalin A (2002) 'Changes in subjective and objective measures of economic well-being and their interrelationship among the elderly in Singapore and Taiwan' *Social Indicators Research* 57, London: Kluwer

Clark A (1999) 'Are wages habit-forming? Evidence from micro-data' *Journal of Economic Behavior and Organization* 39, London: Elsevier

Clark A, Diener E, Georgellis Y and Lucas R (2003) 'Lags and Leads in Life Satisfaction: a test of the baseline hypothesis' *DIW Berlin Discussion Paper 371* Berlin: German Institute for Economic Research

Clark A, Georgellis Y and Sanfey P (1998) 'Job satisfaction, wage changes and quits: evidence from Germany' in Polachek S (ed) *Research in Labor Economics* 17 London: JAI Press

Davis J (1984) 'New money, an old man/lady and 'two's company': subjective welfare in the NORC general social surveys, 1972-1092' *Social Indicators Research* 15, London: Kluwer

Diener E (1994) 'Assessing subjective well-being: progress and opportunities' *Social Indicators Research* 31, London: Kluwer

Diener E, Sandvik E, Siedlitz L and Diener M (1993) 'The relationship between income and subjective well-being: relative or absolute?' *Social Indicators Research* 28, London: Kluwer

Duffy B (2000) *Satisfaction and Expectations: attitudes to public services in deprived areas* London: London School of Economics Centre for Analysis of Social Exclusion (CASE)

Dworkin R (1981) 'What is Equality? Part I: Equality of welfare' *Philosophy and Public Affairs* 10 (3), Oxford: Blackwells

Easterlin R (1974) 'Does economic growth improve the human lot? Some empirical evidence' in David P and Reder M (eds) *Nations and Households in Economic Growth* New York: Academic Press

Frank R (1997) 'The frame of reference as a public good' *The Economic Journal* 107, Oxford: Blackwells

Frederick S and Lowenstein G (1999) 'Hedonic adaptation' in Kahneman D, Diener E and Schwarz N (eds) *Well-Being: the foundations of hedonic psychology* New York: Russell Sage Foundation

Frey B and Stutzer A (2002a) 'What can economists learn from happiness research?' *Journal of Economic Literature* XL, Pittsburgh: American Economics Association

Frey B and Stutzer A (2002b) *Happiness and Economics: how the economy and institutions affect human well-being* Princeton: Princeton University Press

Galbraith G (1969) *The Affluent Society* London: Andre Deutsch

Graham C and Pettinato S (2002) 'Frustrated achievers: winners, losers and subjective well-being in new market economies' *Journal of Development Studies* 38 (4), London: Routledge

Grund C and Sliwka D (2003) 'The Further we Stretch, the Higher the Sky: on the impact of wage increases on job satisfaction' *Bonn Econ Discussion Paper 1/2003* Bonn: University of Bonn

Hills J (2002) 'Does a focus on social exclusion change the policy response?' in Hills J, LeGrand J and Piachaud D (eds) *Understanding Social Exclusion* Oxford: Oxford University Press

Hirschman A (1970) *Exit, voice, and loyalty: responses to decline in firms, organizations, and States* Cambridge MA: Harvard University Press

Huxley A (1932) *Brave New World* London: Chatto and Windus

Inglehart R and Rabier J-R (1986) 'Aspirations adapt to situations – but why are the Belgians so much happier than the French? A cross-cultural analysis of the subjective quality of life' In Andrews F (ed) *Research on the Quality of Life* Flint: University of Michigan, Institute for Social Research

Kahneman D (1999) 'Objective happiness' in Kahneman D, Diener E and Schwarz N (eds) *Well-Being: the foundations of hedonic psychology* New York: Russell Sage Foundation

Kahneman D, Diener E, and Schwarz N (eds) (1999) *Well-Being: the foundations of hedonic psychology* New York: Russell Sage Foundation

Kelvin P and Jarrett J (1985) *The Social Psychological Effects of Unemployment* Cambridge: Cambridge University Press

Keyt D and Miller F (eds) (1991) *A Companion to Aristotle's Politics* Oxford: Oxford University Press

Lachman M. and Weaver S (1998) 'The sense of control as a moderator of social class differences in health and well-being' *Journal of Personality and Social Psychology* 74 (3), Washington: American Psychological Association

Layard R (2005) *Happiness: lessons from a new science* London: Penguin

Meier S and Stutzer A (2004) 'Is volunteering rewarding in itself?' *Institute for Empirical Research in Economics Working Paper 180* Zurich: University of Zurich

Michalos A and Zumbo B (2000) 'Criminal victimization and the quality of life' *Social Indicators Research* 50, London: Kluwer

Mitchell G (2003) 'Choice, volunteering and employability: evaluating delivery of the New Deal for Young People's voluntary sector option' *Benefits* 11 (2)

Morawetz D (1977) 'Income distribution and self-rated happiness: some empirical evidence' *The Economic Journal* 87, Oxford: Blackwell

Nozick R (1974) *Anarchy, State and Utopia* Oxford: Blackwell

Office of National Statistics (ONS) (2004) 'The effects of taxes and benefits on household income, 2002-3' *Economic Trends* 607, London: ONS

Piachaud D (2002) 'Capital and the Determinants of Poverty and Social Exclusion' *CASEpaper 60* London: London School of Economics Centre for Analysis of Social Exclusion (CASE)

Ravallion M and Lokshin M (2001) 'Identifying welfare effects from subjective questions' *Economica* 68, Oxford: Blackwell

Rawls J (1971) *A Theory of Justice* Cambridge MA: Harvard University Press

Sen A (1973) *On Economic Inequality* Oxford: Oxford University Press

Sen A (1980) 'Equality of what?' in Mcmurrin S (ed) *The Tanner Lectures on Human Values*. Cambridge: Cambridge University Press

Sen A (1987) *The Standard of Living* Cambridge: Cambridge University Press

Smith A (1776) *An Inquiry into the Nature And Causes of the Wealth of Nations* London: Methuen

Strategy Unit (2002) *Life Satisfaction: the state of knowledge and implications for government* London: TSO

Stutzer A (2004) 'The role of income aspirations in individual happiness' *Journal of Economic Behavior and Organization* 54 (1) London: Elsevier

Stutzer A and Frey B (2003) 'Does Marriage make People Happy, or do Happy People get Married?' *Institute for Empirical Research in Economics Working Paper 143* Zurich: University of Zurich

Thaler R (1992) *The Winner's Curse: paradoxes and anomalies of economic life* New York: Free Press

Veenhoven R (2000) 'Freedom and happiness: a comparative study in forty-four nations in the early 1990s' in Diener E and Suh E (eds) *Culture and Subjective Well-Being* Cambridge MA: MIT Press

van Praag B and Kapteyn A (1973) 'Further evidence on the individual welfare function of income: an empirical investigation in the Netherlands' *European Economic Review* 4 (1) London: Elsevier

Warr P (1999) 'Well-being and the workplace' in Kahneman D, Diener E and Schwarz N (eds) *Wellbeing: the foundations of hedonic psychology* New York: Russell Sage

Section 3

Achieving Social Justice in Britain

A 21st Century Welfare State

Lisa Harker

The 1994 Commission on Social Justice left a clear imprint on Labour's welfare policy. Its recommendations for reform were echoed in the introduction of a National Minimum Wage, welfare to work policies and pension reform. The Commission's view that the welfare state must 'offer a hand up, not just a hand-out', and that social justice and economic success should not be competing priorities, found expression in Labour's determination to put access to paid work at the heart of its welfare policy. The modernisation of the Beveridge welfare system has continued since 1997, in much the way the Commission envisaged. In one important respect, however, reform has been out of step with the Commission's recommendations, in failing to place a revitalised social insurance system at the centre of the modern welfare state.

The result of Labour's changes is a system of tax and benefits and welfare-to-work policies which are making a greater difference to the pursuit of social justice than their most recent predecessors. Labour has developed a system more effective at reducing poverty and increasing opportunities by helping individuals to enter the labour market. In some ways reform has gone beyond what was envisaged ten years ago, with a new emphasis on supporting asset accumulation from birth.

But the renewal of Britain's welfare system remains incomplete, in both meeting the Commission's original vision and achieving social justice. When tested against a broad definition of social justice (see Chapter 1) its inadequacies become apparent: it fails to provide an adequate minimum income for everyone, an important part of Miller's social minimum; it increasingly rests on a notion of citizenship that is not open to all; and, while it has made some contribution to holding down the growth in income inequality, whether it can continue to do this in the future or even reverse current levels of inequality is far from clear. Chapter 3 notes that the approach of the Government since 1997 has been to largely accept market generated income inequality and to attempt to use the tax and benefit system to redistribute, but it is by no means certain how sustainable this approach is.

What's more, these challenges need to be addressed in the context of limited public commitment to reform. While public support for the welfare state as a whole remains strong, attitudes towards some aspects of social security policy have been hardening (see Chapter 5).

This chapter first considers the main elements of Labour's approach to welfare reform and then sets out two key challenges – one presented by the decline of the contributory principle and one presented by continued high levels of original income inequality. It asks what a new welfare contract between citizens and the state might look like and concludes by suggesting that the tax and benefit system will continue to play an important role in achieving social justice objectives, but that to gain popular support a broader notion of participation needs to underpin welfare policy.

Labour's welfare policy: three stories

Although Labour has described its approach as 'work for those who can, security for those who cannot', its welfare policy can not be captured in as simple a phrase. Labour's policy can in fact be characterised in three welfare stories: of active welfare, selective welfare and asset-based welfare. The first two stories have dominated; it is only in recent years that we have witnessed the emergence of asset-based welfare.

Active welfare

Labour has placed paid work at the centre of its welfare policy, reflecting the view that employment is the most effective route to social inclusion. Increasing labour market participation has become one of the most important goals of the welfare system and, while policies do not easily fit into an active/passive dichotomy, 'active' welfare has been used to describe those policies which are principally orientated towards this goal.

Active welfare has consisted of two main elements: help with finding a suitable job and improvements to the financial incentives to take paid employment. The former has been principally delivered through New Deal programmes, which have largely consisted of personalised job search support for the unemployed and, crucially, the economically

allocated to health spending. More people have been 'credited in' to contributory benefits despite having little or no contribution record, some contributory benefits (incapacity and bereavement benefits) have been made less generous for new claimants and there appears to be no long-term plan to substantially increase the value of the basic state pension, which accounts for the biggest share of National Insurance spending on benefits. What's more, the case is now being made for a Citizens' Pension which would break the link between contributions and pension entitlement altogether.

To some extent, further weakening of the link between contributions and benefits entitlement has reflected an attempt to ensure that the welfare system meets individuals' needs in the context of a more flexible labour market. It has also been a consequence of targeting resources according to the current circumstances of claimants rather than their past contributions. There has been a further shift towards means-testing. The principal mechanism for greater income-testing has been the introduction of tax credits, which account for more than half of the total increase in social security spending since 1998. Some regard the shift towards greater means-testing as 'one of the hallmarks of new Labour's social security policy.' (Brewer *et al*, 2002a).

Largely because of the state pension, contributory benefits still make up a substantial proportion of welfare spending. In 2005/6 contributory benefits are projected to amount to 44.8 per cent of total social security spending, down from 46.4 per cent in 1996/7 (Brewer *et al*, 2002a). Yet at their peak in the 1960s and 1970s contributory benefits accounted for 70 per cent of all social security spending.

What is the likely impact of the further demise of the contributory principle? In the UK the link between contributions and benefits has always been weaker than in countries such as Germany, Austria and France where both contributions and benefits are earnings-related. Nevertheless the contributory principle has been seen in the UK as important in manifesting social solidarity through the pooling of risk, lowering stigma because benefits are paid as of right to those who have made contributions (thereby increasing take-up) and minimising disincentives to additional self-provision since benefits are contingent on circumstances (old age, unemployment) rather than means. Its hypothecated nature has also been seen to be likely to be more popular than a tax-based system, something that opinion surveys seem to bear out (Commission on Taxation and Citizenship, 2000). But if the decline in the contributory principle continues in its present form, as it seems certain to do so, what are the implications for welfare policy?

Tackling poverty and inequality

The second key challenge lies in the wider social and economic drivers shaping modern Britain and, in particular, continued high levels of income inequality.

While the impact of economic globalisation has often been overstated, other changes over the coming decades will mean that the state must play an increasingly influential role in addressing inequality (see Chapter 4). One of the most important of these is demographic change. People are living longer and having fewer children, later in their lives. By 2030 it is predicted that older people will outnumber working-age adults by a fifth and providing an adequate level of support is going to become an even more significant challenge. Without increases in tax rates, savings rates or average retirement ages, pensioners will on average suffer about a 30 per cent decline in their incomes relative to average incomes between now and 2035. Maintaining the current standard of living for pensioners would require the percentage of GDP transferred to normal retirement age pensioners to rise from 9.9 per cent today to 17.5 per cent in 2050 if there is no change in retirement ages (Pensions Commission, 2004).

Another source of pressure on the British welfare state is the rapid pace of technological change and the related shift in demand for skilled labour. This has contributed to a continued polarisation of the British labour market, with growth being strongest in well-paid high-skill jobs and low-paid low-skill ones (Wilson *et al*, 2004). Many workers who had skilled manufacturing jobs have been unable or unwilling to move into service occupations which often offer lower wages than their previous employment and require different skills. The effects of this have been particularly concentrated in regions which had particularly strong manufacturing production, such as the North East of England and some areas of Wales. Although government has provided incentives for some service industries to relocate in these areas, a significant challenge remains in re-skilling many former manufacturing workers and providing protection from disadvantage as they do so (Rowthorn, 2004). Overall these pressures point towards greater or at least continued high levels of income inequality.

But how far can the UK government seek to influence original market income inequality? Or will it have to continue to rely on the tax and benefit system to tackle poverty and put a lid on high income disparities? The answer, of course, is both, but where should the emphasis be?

One way to influence original income inequality might be to encourage greater corporatism, collective bargaining and employee protection. Yet, in contrast to some other European countries, the UK has not favoured this route. The reliance on flexible labour markets to maintain high employment rates has discouraged the revitalisation of collective bargaining and led to a relatively cautious approach to minimum wage and working hours' protection. There seems little scope for a significant shift in policy direction here.

A second response is to raise spending on education and training, improving the skill levels of the workforce, with a particular focus on those with low skills. This was a central theme of the Commission on Social Justice and has since been developed in the thinking about the 'Social Investment State' (Lister, 2004; Giddens, 1998). It is particularly tempting in Britain since the UK lags behind many of its continental neighbours in workforce skill levels, especially at Level Two, which partly explains its lower productivity in many sectors (DfES, 2004). Improving post-sixteen staying on rates and vocational courses are key. But it is important to be realistic about the timescale involved and the amount of difference this will make. In the short term such a strategy will have relatively little impact. And although in the longer term achieving social justice depends as much, if not more, on improving education and skills, supporting easier access to the labour market and reducing inequalities in earnings, this will never remove the need for redistributive tax and benefit policies.

It seems likely then, that at least in the short and medium-term, government will continue to seek to constrain inequality through the tax and benefit system. This should come as little surprise. Looking at how much redistribution goes on in different countries shows how important social transfers are in creating a more equal society. In Sweden, which had a very low disposable income Gini coefficient of 0.24 in 2000, transfers changed the original income Gini coefficient by 38.9 per cent, compared to 22.7 per cent in the UK in 1999 and just 7.1 per cent in the US in 2000 (Kenworthy, 2004). As Hills points out, Britain's experience during the 1980s was not typical of other industrialised countries, in that while other countries experienced rising income inequality no country experienced as large a change as the UK (Hills, 2004a). Part of the reason for this was that the welfare systems of other countries were more effective in tempering the rise in inequality. Since income from benefits accounts for 60 per cent of the income of the poorest fifth, the relative value of these benefits strongly affects income inequality. With general living standards rising, those on price-indexed benefits have inevitably fallen behind the rest of the population, which has contributed towards rising levels of poverty and inequality.

Yet using the tax and benefit system to reduce income inequality is not unproblematic. There are at least three challenges. First, although resources can be targeted at those in the most need, it is still likely to be costly. It is clear that the value of benefits and tax credits will need to increase at a faster rate than earnings if relative poverty levels are to fall and income inequality reduced. Substantial rises to benefits for families with children have resulted in clear dividends in terms of reductions in child poverty, but support will need to be increased further if child poverty is to be significantly reduced. The scale of the task this requires of the social security system is now huge; it would cost around £2 billion a year by 2007/8 to keep the Government on track to meet its target for child poverty in 2010 (Brewer, 2005), for example.

Second, attention will also need to be paid to those groups who have hitherto been less favoured in Labour's welfare policy. An anti-poverty strategy that concentrates on the old and young has considerable appeal – it is these groups who have fared worst in recent decades and, in the case of children, where most long-term difference can be made to life opportunities. But the inadequacy of benefit support for single childless people of working age who are not in employment (particularly those under the age of 25) remains a major driver of high levels of poverty.

Improvements to the support for those of working age need to be accompanied by an obligation to participate in society as an active citizen; there has never been a 'something for nothing' welfare state. In some ways the Government has sought to return to some of the principles that underlie the Beveridge Report, with its emphasis on reciprocity and an obligation-based view of citizenship, with work a major component of citizenship (Plant, 2003). But conditionality has been extended further by explicitly linking benefit entitlement to participation in a work programme (in the case of young people and long-term unemployed), attendance at a Jobcentre interview for those who would previously have been regarded as economically inactive rather than unemployed (as in the case of lone parents and those claiming incapacity benefit) and, even going beyond that by, for example, making receipt of a maternity grant dependent on consulting a health advisor.

Some have argued that increased conditionality in the benefit system has not been in keeping with the pursuit of social justice, nor helped to increase public support for the welfare system. On the other hand, the assertion of obligation in the welfare system reflects a more active notion of citizenship and may actually help legitimise welfare spending. There is evidence that the public supports some conditionality in the benefit system, but only up to a point (Taylor-Gooby, 2004). For social democrats there appears to be no easy answers to the question of when welfare conditionality is justified and when it is not (White, 2004).

If work is to be the passport to citizenship then some work tests are clearly necessary. But whether work should be seen as the passport to economic and social citizenship without the guarantee of a job for all is a moot point. Despite overall improvements in employment rates, labour market participation remains relatively low for some groups including people with disabilities, those from minority ethnic groups and the low-skilled. It is far from apparent that genuine barriers to employment have been removed for such groups. Indeed there will always be some for whom work is not possible or appropriate. Social justice, built on a notion of equal citizenship (see Chapter 1), is threatened unless the definition of citizenship is broad enough to account for their circumstances. What's more, the tendency to 'fetish' paid work as the route to citizenship serves to undermine other forms of work, such as care work and community or voluntary work (Lister, 2001).

While there are good grounds for having a certain amount of conditionality attached to benefits for people of working age, there seems little justification for further reform to begin here. Evidence that 'active' welfare has been less successful in supporting people from ethnic minorities and disabled people into work (Platt, 2002; Stanley and Regan, 2003) suggests that it would be more effective to ensure that welfare-to-work policy becomes more responsive to their needs before resorting to greater conditionality. The development of rehabilitation support for people with disabilities, for example, would be a necessary pre-requisite to the introduction of tougher sanctions.

Third, and more fundamentally, the most difficult issue is the potential conflict between maintaining public confidence and support for the social security system through universal participation, and continuing to target resources towards the most disadvantaged groups. It is to this issue that this chapter turns next.

A new welfare contract

What effect have changes to the welfare system in recent years had on the 'welfare contract' between the state and citizen? On the one hand we might expect the success of 'active' welfare policies to have boosted the legitimacy of the system. On the other hand the emphasis on the undesirability of welfare 'dependency' may be contributing to hardening attitudes to social security support. Furthermore, the continuing decline of the contributory principle threatens to undermine the welfare contract because the link between the benefits individuals receive and the contributions they make is weaker than ever. Can a modern progressive welfare system be built on such crumbling foundations?

There is certainly evidence that collective support for welfare has eroded. Despite survey findings that the public believes that levels of poverty and inequality are too high, and supports government action to tackle them, people's view of welfare, and of welfare recipients in particular, have hardened in recent years (Taylor-Gooby, 2004). This may be, in part, a consequence of the success of employment policies. Bryson has noted that attitudes have tended to be more pro-welfare in times of high unemployment (Bryson, 1997). But the trends nevertheless suggest that public support for welfare is on the slide; younger generations, in particular, are least likely to expect the state to provide for them (Sefton, 2003).

There is also evidence that the decrease in public support for welfare is by no means inevitable. Other countries have retained stronger buy-in and the UK public's commitment to fairness and support for the worst off is low by EU standards (see Chapter 5). Interestingly. the biggest attitudinal shift in recent years has been among traditional Labour supporters who have become more circumspect about the desirability of generous welfare provision largely (it appears) because of concerns about fraud, rather than benefit generosity (Taylor-Gooby, 2004). Labour has been accused of wooing, rather than seeking to lead, the electorate, and of assuming public opinion to be conservative and reactionary (Lister, 2001). But the change in attitudes among Labour supporters may well have been led by political debate, rather than vice versa, particularly since political debate around the time of the 1997 election focused heavily on fraud and the need to curtail social security spending. The most significant shift in public opinion seemed to occur around the same time as the Labour Party was shifting its stance away from income distribution (Sefton, 2003). Had Labour taken a different route and promoted a more positive image of welfare, public opinion may well have shifted in its favour.

If government were to provide the leadership to create a new welfare contract, what would that contract be built around? Public perceptions of the welfare system are often ill-informed and the principles on which it is based are no longer well understood. If a new welfare contract is to be built which binds people into a collective system of mutual support, the principles which underpin the welfare system must be articulated more clearly.

More progressive universalism?

One route to a stronger welfare contract might be to build on the principle of progressive universalism. This phrase started to become part of Labour's lexicon in 2000 (Brown, 2000) and describes the aspiration that welfare support should be open to (almost) all, but with the poorest benefiting most. Through progressive universalism it is hoped that social solidarity and public support for the welfare system may be enhanced, while greatest help remains targeted on the poorest.

In practice, the application of progressive universalism has been selective, relating primarily to the total package of benefit and tax credit support now in place for families with children. The Child Trust Fund, as a universal benefit that has a means-test built into it, perhaps best embodies what is meant by progressive universalism. Moves towards progressive universalism in other areas of welfare policy have been very limited. Indeed, pension policy has largely comprised of a move away from universalism, despite the introduction of some universal payments (winter fuel allowance, free TV licences). The basic state pension has been falling in relative value pretty much continually since 1979, usually only being increased in line with prices. By contrast, means-tested support has been made more generous and has been extended higher up the income scale.

Is there a case for extending progressive universalism? In terms of pension policy a shift towards universalism would be desirable given the low take-up of means-tested benefits. But there are also clear arguments for avoiding targeting altogether, even within a progressive universal structure. The best way to reduce pensioner poverty and meet other objectives such as affordability, clarity and simplicity, would be simply to raise the universal basic state pension and index it in line with earnings (Brooks *et al,* 2002).

Nevertheless it might be possible to apply the principle of progressive universalism to a wider range of support for those of working age. Arguably, progressive universalism should be the principle behind the allocation of support for childcare costs, for example. Whether support is delivered via the benefit system, or by subsidising services directly, some help with childcare costs should be universally available in order to guarantee affordable provision, even if the least well off still benefit most. There might also be merit in bringing support for carers of elderly and disabled people closer into line with support for parents, by aligning tax credit eligibility and providing a more generous carer's benefit with a value that is progressively targeted. Such moves towards progressive universalism would seem to be desirable, even if there is still some element of income targeting, since it would bind more people into a similar welfare system and might attract higher levels of public support.

Yet given that progressive universalism would seem least appropriate for pension policy, which makes up the vast majority of welfare spending, it would not seem to provide enough of an answer to the problem of a weakening welfare contract.

From contribution to participation
The decline of the contributory principle poses a challenge for those concerned about the pursuit of social justice. Can, and should, the link between contributions and benefit entitlement be saved and, if not, is there a worthy replacement for a system which helps to pool risk, foster social solidarity and galvanise public support?

In some ways, with its emphasis on reciprocity, you might expect Labour's welfare system to retain the contributory principle as the ultimate embodiment of rights being matched by responsibilities. And despite obvious signs of its decline it is important not to predict the death of the contributory principle prematurely. There is still a widely held notion, especially in relation to pensions, that claimants are 'entitled' to support, even if this is based on the erroneous notion of having saved funds. This may be partly a generational attitude but it is still very much in evidence and, as Hills has noted, it has been argued that this is a useful myth for the population to believe in because it continues to provide the basis for public support for the welfare system (Hills, 2004b).

Nevertheless, full resurrection of the contributory principle now seems difficult to justify. Beveridge's welfare system was built on the foundations of a more certain labour market where regular contributions could be made through paid employment. Even with the prospect of full employment, the comparative insecurity of today's labour market requires individuals to be 'credited in' to the system, a process which continues to erode the contribution-benefits link.

There is also the question of adequacy. As Clasen notes, contributors are being asked to devote more and more resources to a system which is increasingly failing recipients in terms of providing social protection comprehensively and adequately, despite the fact that the National Insurance fund runs a surplus (Clasen, 2001). At current levels contributory benefits are currently too low to avoid the means-test. A complex system of entitlements supplemented by means-tested payments is unlikely to foster the kind of social solidarity we hope for.

The dilution of the contributory principle does not necessarily mark the death knell for the social insurance model, not least because of already accrued state pension rights. Some, including the Commission on Social Justice, have argued that a revitalised social insurance system needs to break the link between contributions and entitlement, accepting that in today's society there is a more complex set of risks that citizens need to be insured against than originally anticipated by Beveridge. The Commission proposed, for example, that eligibility for unemployment insurance should be determined by whether or not someone has recently been in paid employment. The House of Commons Social Security Select Committee similarly proposed in 2000 that eligibility for National Insurance benefits should rest on a record of previous earnings rather than contributions.

There may indeed be merit in binding more people into a social insurance model that does not restrict entitlement to contribution record. But what then would replace the contributory principle as the glue that binds people into a welfare system? It is clear that the next stage for welfare reform ought to be a move away from a principally paid work-focused model towards one that acknowledges a wider range of activities that society believes to be valuable, including caring for dependants, education and training, and voluntary work as well as paid employment. This would imply a system built around participation rather than paid employment. Indeed, it is possible to envisage a reinvigorated National Insurance funded benefit system for people of working age with entitlement based on participation rather than contributions, alongside a citizens' pension, based on age rather than contribution record.

Given the increasing fetishism of work in our welfare system, a move towards participation would have considerable appeal. It would endorse a wider definition of citizenship than the 'citizen worker' model (Lewis, 2001) that currently underpins the system. And it would help foster the legitimacy of a modern welfare system by embodying a broader principle of reciprocity, emphasising that our responsibilities as citizens extend beyond developing a work ethic.

A welfare system built around a notion of participation might eventually bring us closer to a participation income. The case for a participation income has often been made; indeed, the Commission on Social Justice saw some merit in one that would complement, rather than replace, social insurance benefits. This would involve a universal flat-rate payment in recognition of 'active citizenship', desirable activities deemed to reflect a valuable contribution to society, including paid employment, caring for dependants and voluntary work. It could help reduce the need for means-tested support, as well as recognising the value of unpaid caring work. If set at a high enough level, a participation income could allow greater choice over hours of work and, as benefit paid to individuals rather than households, would encourage independent choices for men and women. A participation income of this sort, financed by the abolition of certain tax allowances and rises in National Insurance contributions, would be highly progressive (Oppenheim, 2001).

In some ways the conditions for introducing a participation income seem more favourable than a decade ago. Indeed, it has been suggested that a significant extension of in-work benefits might lead to a strong case for introducing a flat rate participation income, in order to avoid the accumulation of high marginal tax rates that are caused by income-related payments (Atkinson, 2002). In fact, with child benefit (essentially a basic income for children) and the child tax credit (which is targeted but paid higher up the income scale than most income-related benefits) we are now closer than ever to approaching a kind of participation income for families with children.

However, there would still be considerable obstacles that would need to be overcome before the introduction of a participation income. There would be administrative and political challenges associated with such a substantial change to the tax and benefit system. The cost of a universal payment might still be considered politically unfeasible. And, since a participation income would increase replacement ratios, there could also be a detrimental impact on incentives to take up paid work.

We have yet to reach the point when the introduction of a participation income appears feasible. But in the short term there is much that could be done to move further towards a participation-based welfare system. Central to this might be a revitalised social insurance system built around the principle of participation. There would also be grounds for underpinning means-tested benefits with a broader conception of participation by, for example, ensuring that those who are not in paid work but undertake voluntary work remain eligible for support.

Conclusion

Although government can affect the distribution of original income, it can only realistically do this over the long term. It will therefore need to continue to rely on the tax and benefit system to meet its poverty targets and to reduce income inequality. In the context of challenges facing society, and with the decline of the contributory principle, there is demand for a new welfare contract between state and citizen which harnesses popular support. A welfare contract built around the notion of participation offers an alternative approach.

Building a new welfare contract around participation would require strong political leadership and a willingness to foster changes in public attitudes towards the welfare system. It will not be possible to pursue social justice with tinkering to the welfare system, nor through reform by stealth. But there are strong grounds for re-orientating our welfare system to the needs of today's society and to prepare for the challenges that lie ahead. The goal is not only a welfare system that is fit for purpose but one that fosters social solidarity and has public support. The future of the welfare system will ultimately rest on whether the welfare contract can be rebuilt.

References

Agulnik P and Legrand J (1998) 'Tax Relief and Partnership Pensions' in *Fiscal Studies* (19) 4, London: Institute for Fiscal Studies

Atkinson A (2002) 'How basic income is moving up the policy agenda: news from the future' *Paper prepared for Basic Income European Network 9th International Congress* September 2002, Geneva

Brewer M (2005) 'Maintaining momentum in tackling child poverty' in Reed J and Robinson R (eds) *Promoting Social Mobility and Life Chances: maintaining momentum* London: ippr

Brewer M, Clark T and Wakefield M (2002a) 'Social security in the UK under New Labour: What did the Third Way mean for welfare reform?' *Fiscal Studies* 23 (4), London: Institute for Fiscal Studies

Brewer M, Clark T and Goodman A (2002b) 'The Government's child poverty target: how much progress has been made?' *Institute for Fiscal Studies Commentary* 88 London: Institute for Fiscal Studies

Brooks R, Regan S and Robinson P (2002) *A new contract for retirement* London: ippr

Brown G (2000) *Speech to East London Partnership* 29 February 2000

Bryson C (1997) 'Benefit claimants: villains or victims?' in Jowell R, Curtis J, Park A, Brook L, Thomson K and Bryson C (eds) *British Social Attitudes 14th Report* Aldershot: Ashgate

Clark T, Myck M and Oldfield Z(2001) *Fiscal reforms affecting households, 1997-2001* London: Institute for Fiscal Studies

Clasen, J (2001) 'Social insurance and the contributory principle: a paradox in contemporary British social policy' *Social Policy and Administration* 35 (6), Oxford: Blackwell

Commission on Taxation and Citizenship (2000) *Paying for Progress: a new politics of tax for public spending* London: Fabian Society.

Department for Education and Skills (DfES) (2004) *Five Year Strategy for Children and Learners* London: TSO

Gamble A (2004) 'New Directions in the British Welfare State' *Paper presented at the 2004 Annual Meeting of the American Political Science Association* September 2004

Giddens A (1998) *The Third Way* London: Polity Press

Glennerster H and McKnight A (2004) 'A Capital Start: but how far do we go?' *Paper presented at Department of Politics and International Relations Oxford University New Politics of Ownership Seminar: Financing the citizen's stake*, 4 June 2004 London: Centre for Analysis of Social Exclusion

Goodman A and Oldfield Z (2004) *Permanent differences? Income and expenditure inequalities in the 1990s and 2000s* London: Institute for Fiscal Studies. Available at http://www.ifs.org.uk/inequalityindex.shtml

Goodman A, Johnson P and Webb S (1997) *Inequality in the UK* Oxford: Oxford University Press

Goodman A, Shaw J and Shephard A (2004) 'Understanding recent trends in income inequality' *Paper prepared for IPPR social mobility and life chances forum, 3 and 4 December 2004* London: Institute for Fiscal Studies

Hills J (2004a) *Inequality and the State* Oxford: Oxford University Press.

Hills J (2004b) 'Heading for retirement? National insurance, state pensions and the future of the contributory principle in the UK' *Journal of Social Policy* 33 (3), Cambridge: Cambridge University Press

Hills J and Stewart K (2005) *A More Equal Society? New Labour, Poverty, inequality and exclusion* Bristol: Policy Press

HM Treasury (2001) *Savings and Assets for all. The modernisation of Britain's tax and benefit system* London: TSO

HM Treasury (2004) *Child Poverty Review* London: TSO

House of Commons Social Security Select Committee (HCSSSC) (2000) *The contributory principle, Fifth Report, 1999-2000* London: TSO

Kenworthy L (2004) *Calculations based on the Luxembourg Income Study* (Unpublished)

Lewis J (2001) 'The decline of the male breadwinner model: implications for work and care' *Social Politics* (8), Oxford: Oxford University Press

Lister R (2001) 'New Labour: a study in ambiguity from a position of ambivalence' *Critical Social Policy* 21 (4), London: Sage

Lister R (2004) 'Creating responsible citizens of the future in the 'social investment state' *Paper presented to ESPANet 2004 conference*. Available at http://www.apsoc.ox.ac.uk/Espanet/espanetconference/papers/ppr.15A.RL.pdf

Oppenheim C (2001) 'Enabling participation? New Labour's Welfare-to-Work policies' in White S (ed) *New Labour: the progressive future?* Basingstoke: Palgrave Macmillan

Palmer G, Carr E and Kenway P (2004) *Monitoring Poverty and Social Exclusion* York: Joseph Rowntree Foundation

Paxton W and White S (2005) *A Citizens' Stake: policy options and public opinion* London: Policy Press

Pensions Commission (2004) *The First Report of the Pensions Commission* London: TSO

Plant R (2003) 'Citizenship and Social Security' *Fiscal Studies* 24 (2), London: Institute for Fiscal Studies

Platt L (2002) *Parallel Lives? Poverty among ethnic minority groups in Britain* London: Child Poverty Action Group (CPAG)

Rowthorn R (2004) 'The Impact on Advanced Economies of North-South Trade in Manufacturing and Services' *Paper presented at the First Annual International Forum for Development* New York: 18 October 2004

Sefton T (2003) 'What we want from the welfare state' in Park A, Curtice J, Thomson K, Jarvis L and Bromley C (eds) *British Social Attitudes: Continuity and change over two decades, 20th Report, 2003/04* London: Sage Publications

Stanley K and Regan S (2003) *The Missing Million: supporting disabled people into work* London: ippr

Taylor-Gooby P (2004) 'The work-centred welfare state' in Park A, Curtice J, Thomson K, Jarvis L and Bromley C (eds) *British Social Attitudes, 21st Report, 2004/05* London: Sage Publications

White S (2004) 'A Social Democratic Approach to Welfare Conditionality: Finding a Framework for Evaluation' in Stanley K and Lohde L A (eds) *Sanctions and Sweeteners: Rights and Responsibilities in the Benefits System* London: ippr

Wilson R, Homenidou K and Dickerson A (2004) *Working Futures: National Report 2003-4* Warwick: Institute of Employment Research

From Social Mobility to Equal Life Chances: Maintaining the Momentum

Jodie Reed and Peter Robinson

Governments have always had to prioritise, but policy-makers will be faced with some particularly tough choices as we move into the second half of this decade. In its first three years, the current Government kept a relatively tight fiscal reign, but over the period 2000 to 2005 it has been firing on many fronts to achieve social justice. To improve and equalise life chances during the first stage of life, it has expanded early years provision, ensuring all three and four year olds have access to publicly funded high quality part-time nursery places and putting resources into innovative policies such as the Sure Start Children's Centres. It has put more resources into mainstream schooling and further and higher education to maintain the momentum towards improved life chances. It has financed generous increases in benefits and tax credits especially for families with children to tackle child poverty directly. Most of the mainstream public services, and especially the NHS, have seen handsome increases in resources.

From 2006, however, the fiscal situation will not allow for such generous increases in public spending across the board if only modest tax increases are made. The NHS and early years provision will remain relatively favoured, but the Government will have to make some difficult choices about how to allocate public resources across other areas.

One useful way of forcing us to think about these choices is by asking: where should we spend the 'marginal pound' in order to increase social mobility? In other words, in the context of public spending allocations that depend to a large extent on existing commitments, where can we best deploy the limited extra resources that are available in a way that would most cost-effectively achieve the maximum impact in improving life chances and enhancing upward mobility through the class and income distribution for the largest number of people? Does the evidence base exist to enable us to make relatively finely-tuned judgements about where best to deploy extra resources and is there any consensus on what this evidence base might tell us? In the context of more binding constraints on the growth of future public spending, finding some answers to these questions is a particularly pressing matter.

'Social mobility' has long provided a helpful looking-glass through which to view fluidity of movements between social classes and occupational groups and has often been seen as a proxy for openness and equality of opportunity. Yet while traditionally the centre-left have used lack of mobility to highlight injustice, the notion of improved social mobility as an objective in itself has often met with suspicion. Critics have questioned the loaded notion of 'merit' with its implicit acceptance of particular kinds of 'effort' as more worthy of reward than others. This criticism has been reinforced in the past by the common failure to acknowledge all the factors which might predispose an individual toward such efforts; the role of social upbringing and perceptions of opportunity and their impact on aspiration are often overlooked by meritocrats. Indeed, as Miller argues in Chapter 1, there may be good reasons why we should not aim to achieve pure equality of opportunity.

Taking this on board, we do not seek to argue that 'social mobility' should be prioritised over, for example, social inclusion or poverty reduction as a policy objective as this might produce skewed outcomes for public policy. There is no single objective that defines social justice. We should instead think of social mobility as just one objective which must be balanced with a number of others.

In order to answer our marginal pound question properly however, we must not only acknowledge the value and limits of the concept of social mobility overall, but also give some consideration to the type of mobility policy-makers should be aiming for. There are a number of debates here regarding, for example, whether the mobility of individuals relative to one another should be prioritised above overall (or absolute) levels of mobility; whether more attention should be paid to improving intergenerational mobility (between parents and their children) or intragenerational mobility (over the course of individual lifetimes); and even over what we should consider as the prime mobility variable. While economists prefer to use income, sociologists prefer to use occupational status though it has been argued these two approaches may be seen as two sides of the same coin (Esping-Andersen *et al*, 2002).

Prioritising levels of absolute mobility through creating more 'room at the top' initially seems to have strong appeal. Increases in the total proportion of a social class who move into another social class has, in the past, improved life chances all round while creating few losers. Indeed, the belief that an expansion of the middle classes is achievable within a fairly short timescale seems implicit when Blair argues simply that his Government's mission must be 'to break down the barriers that hold people back, to create real upward mobility' (Blair, 2001). However, it is doubtful whether the policies of any national government alone can significantly alter the overall shape of social class and income structures which are largely fashioned by wider global trends.

The alternative is to put the focus on relative mobility. As highlighted in Chapter 2, looking across rates of relative mobility internationally it seems the UK's experience of a slowdown is by no means inevitable. Differences across countries indicate that rates of relative mobility are far more amenable to change through policy intervention than absolute rates.

Clearly, improving relative rates of social mobility does not sit so comfortably in the rhetoric of politicians as it means accepting that upward mobility has a flipside. If the size of the upper socio-economic stratum is not increasing so quickly, but the aim is for a greater number to elevate themselves, others must move downward; it is at least in part a zero-sum game. Trade-offs may be particularly painful as current literature seems to highlight that upward mobility from the bottom is more likely than downward mobility from the top. Of course, this is easier to argue for if they have less far to fall. This is the case in the country with the greatest levels of relative social mobility, Sweden. Not only does Sweden have the flattest income distribution but more equal outcomes in terms of educational attainment, occupational mobility and cognitive development. The political feasibility of governments actually pushing for more downward mobility may well depend on our ability to create these conditions in the UK over time.

It is important for social justice that public policy improves outcomes both in terms of intragenerational and intergenerational relative mobility. Ways in which we might increase the scope for individuals to be mobile over the course of their lifetimes are largely dealt with elsewhere in this publication (see Chapter 16 which deals with policy on progression and participation in the labour market). However, turning the spotlight to breaking the link between parents' socio-economic background and the outcomes for their children's socio-economic status exposes one of the greatest identifiable social injustices currently pervading our society.

Longitudinal studies focusing on economic status have indicated that relative intergenerational mobility has reduced substantially between cohorts growing up in the 1980s and 1990s as against those who grew up in the 1970s and 1980s (Machin and Gregg, 2003). It seems the middle-classes have consolidated their position. Measuring the cognitive abilities of the 1970 birth cohort, Leon Feinstein shows that the magnitude of the link between a child's status and that of its parents is such that 'high early achievers from disadvantaged backgrounds are overtaken between the ages of five and ten by poor early achievers from advantaged backgrounds' (Feinstein, 2003a; Feinstein, 2003b). A similar trend is reflected in terms of educational attainment in work by Stephen Machin and Anna Vignoles who find early ability to be an increasingly poorer predictor of higher education outcomes relative to parents' social class and income when comparing the 1958 and 1970 birth cohorts (Machin and Vignoles, 2004). In order to turn these trends around, policy-makers need to aim to increase access to what Miller earlier referred to as 'ladders of opportunity' or, as others have referred to them, 'life chances'.

Sweden and some other Northern European countries seem to offer models that appeal to those on the left who would like to see more equal access to life chances and improved relative social mobility. However, all these models have in common much higher levels of public spending and taxation than the UK, so while specific policy instruments and attractive policy outcomes rightly generate interest, they do not help us with the question of where best to spend the marginal pound in the UK in the immediate term. Their experience has, however, helped to generate some consensus on at least one part of the policy agenda and gives strong pause for thought about whether we would want to move towards a high tax and spend model in the future.

The early years: building on consensus?

For some time a clear consensus seems to have been emerging amongst academics over one policy area where we should be spending a large proportion of our extra resources in order to break the link between a parent's social and economic status and that of their child.

Alongside direct financial support for families with children, there appears to be widespread agreement that achieving equal life chances means recognising the early years as a critical opportunity for a variety of social policy interventions. A wide range of evidence tells us that intellectual, psychological and health differences established at this stage have a strong and persistent impact forming the basis of divergent life courses (Stipek and Ryan, 1997). In their life cycle analysis of human capital accumulation and policy in the US, Carneiro and Heckman go so far as to challenge the dominant thesis that the high cost of tuition and a decline in the earnings of families headed by low-skilled workers act as barriers to university admission. They find that at most only 8 per cent of children face financial constraints to entering university. A far greater proportion fail to reach university because they do not develop the necessary cognitive abilities nor crucially the necessary attitudes and social skills in early childhood due to a lack of resources and a poor home environment (Caneiro and Heckman, 2003). The evidence for the UK is consistent with this argument: the key problem is that far too few individuals from lower socio-economic backgrounds obtain the A-level results at eighteen that would allow access to higher education and the roots of that relative lack of success are to be found earlier in childhood (Piatt and Robinson, 2001). Findings of this kind mark out the value of early childhood interventions over other areas.

Fortunately, a great deal is now known about the relative effectiveness of different early years interventions and this is leading to some clear conclusions about the precise kinds of social policy we should be implementing in this area. We know for example that the formation of a stable adult attachment in the first eighteen months is crucial for child development and has an array of positive long-term impacts which may affect life chances (Harker and Kendal, 2003). Extending the period of paid parental leave (rather than simply job-protected leave) for as long as possible within this timeframe is necessary for ensuring all parents have the same option to spend significant amounts of time with their infants (Tanaka, 2004). The long-term consequences would also be reaped through better health outcomes for mothers and children (Chatterji and Markowitz, 2004; Ruhm, 2000).

We also know that long-term, part-time, formal, quality early-years provision can have a significant impact for two to five year olds, especially for those from disadvantaged backgrounds. There are strong signs that this can have effects significantly over and above increases in family income. Importantly for policy, no additional benefit was detected from full-time provision. Indeed, some research shows negative behavioural impacts from maternal full-time employment if children are in poor quality care (Brooks-Gunn *et al*, 2002). Childcare has already been branded as 'the new frontier of the welfare state' (Blair, 2004), but in order to help create more equal life chances a concerted push would need to be made towards training a 'quality' childcare workforce to provide highly professional, fully integrated education and care.

A couple of thorny issues remain. First, guidance on parenting is seen as a tempting investment by policy-makers. We know, for example, that the simple things that make up the home learning environment such as reading with your child have a large impact. These things tend to be more present in advantaged homes but higher socio-economic status is by no means a precondition for developing them (Smith *et al*, 1997). Yet how successfully parenting behaviour can be modified by policy interventions is not clear.

The success of any parenting intervention is largely dependent on parents being able to give time and cooperation. Ensuring that these things happen can be very costly, especially when it comes to reaching the parents who may most need support (Magnuson, 2004). Making such support compulsory might be the only way of ensuring buy-in, but this would not only run the risk of alienating parents thereby undermining the whole programme but might also prove politically unacceptable, leading to charges of the 'nanny state'.

There are questions too about effectiveness. US research shows little evidence of parental education or training programmes providing long-lasting positive effects on children's achievement or behaviour (Duncan and Magnuson, 2003). Meanwhile, in the UK, the Government's Sure Start local programmes have aimed at a broader concept of parental support. This initiative has seen substantial sums spent on offering families combined early education, childcare, health and family support with advice on employment opportunities. However, preliminary evaluation findings show limited positive effects so far. Out of eight criteria measured across 150 programmes, on average the only significant positive impact detected was that mothers/principal carers were observed to treat the child in a warmer and more accepting manner than in comparison areas (NESS, 2004). While this is clearly important it is perhaps disappointing that no overall impact has yet been detected in terms of father involvement, home learning environment, parent/child conflict, parent–child closeness, home chaos, maternal responsiveness or parental discipline. Other effects may become evident in the longer term as both the programmes and programme recipients mature but this does raise some initial doubts about further investment here for now.

The most notable lack of consensus on all of these early years issues is the extent to which services should be provided on a universal, publicly funded basis or in a more targeted manner with contributions from better off parents. Esping-Andersen specifically argued in 2002 from a social mobility point of view 'the pressing need for a new family policy' with a universal offer of largely tax funded quality childcare pointing out that the period when inequality in children's cognitive attainment decreased in countries such as Sweden roughly corresponds with the time when universal childcare came into place (Esping-Andersen *et al*, 2002). Adopting this approach would certainly avoid the pitfalls of area-based targeting. Yet would this be the most efficient use of government funds from a social justice perspective? Jane Waldfogel argues for a more careful individually targeted provision such as cash grants for families with children aged between one and two which could be more generous for the most disadvantaged. This approach could require a larger degree of co-payment from better off parents who choose more formal care and allow parents more scope and flexibility (Waldfogel, 2004).

With constraints on resources and Scandinavian levels of taxation and spending out of sight for now, this might seem the most feasible option. However, a more universal approach to the provision of early years services would be worth working towards in the long term, if we are clear about what we mean by universal. Paid leave entitlements that all parents could choose to take advantage of when their infants are aged up to twelve months, or eventually eighteen months, combined with universal high quality part-time education and care for all two to four year olds funded by the state could be the package to roll out. If parents want to extend the part-time to full-time, this wrap-around childcare could be the means-tested element with user charges for some. This would not only allow a shift from area-based targeting to individual targeting of resources, but it could also be one way that the state could encourage social mix within early years provision. In the context of years of research on the importance of pupil-mix for school age children (discussed below) and borne out for early years by another Institute of Education finding, this should be a real priority.

Schooling: maintaining the momentum

While it is possible to argue that some consensus has emerged that justifies the extra resources made available for early years, it is critical to recognise that even a shift from equal at birth to equal at five years would not be enough. We know from longitudinal research into cognitive and behavioural outcomes that if the benefits brought about by early years interventions are to be prevented from fading away, or a resilience against persistent environmental factors installed, policy-makers must maintain momentum into later childhood (Feinstein and Bynner, 2004). Without continued impetus, early interventions could be rendered meaningless from a life chances perspective (Ramey and Ramey, 2000). In addition, accepting that early interventions will never completely equal out all advantages and disadvantages means acknowledging that more than a simple consolidation on earlier gains is needed. Constructing ladders of opportunity throughout the life cycle is essential. However, there seems less consensus on how best to deploy resources to maximum effect during the period of compulsory schooling to either of these ends.

Does education still matter?

Is 'education, education, education' the key to equality of opportunity we once supposed it to be? There is an ongoing debate about the impact of education on life chances. Cognitive abilities and social and cultural capital have been shown to affect life chances independently of educational attainment (Bowles *et al*, 2001). Using an analysis of newspaper job adverts, Jackson, Goldthorpe and Mills put forward the argument that education is less important than previously because the relative weight employers give in their recruitment decisions to qualifications is on the decline. They point to the increasing number of graduates, arguing that it is forcing employers to look for other distinguishing characteristics. The combination of this and the rise of service industries is leading employers to be interested in qualities that tend to be nurtured in the middle-class home such as confidence and articulacy (Jackson *et al*, 2003). This might lead one to believe that the Government has got it wrong in prioritising schools. Yet formal educational attainment does still matter a great deal. A large body of research shows that the wage premiums attached to qualifications, after falling modestly in the 1970s and rising sharply in the 1980s, have since the early 1990s been broadly stable. Sianesi presents up-to-date estimates drawn from the Labour Force Survey (2003). This is in spite of a sharp rise in the supply of more highly qualified labour following on from significant increases in enrolment and attainment in the formal education system from the late 1980s. There are many more graduates, but on average their qualifications still command a healthy wage premium in the labour market, as do many other traditional qualifications.

It is important therefore to stress that while family background may have a large impact on later labour market success, this impact is still principally working through educational attainment and early cognitive ability rather than being a direct association (Machin and Vignoles, 2004). We also have some direct evidence on the kinds of specific skills which are valued by employers. One important piece of empirical work is that of Francis Green and his colleagues using data from workforce surveys conducted in 1997 and 2001, which allows us to measure the wage premiums attached to particular skills rather than just qualifications. High-level communication skills and planning skills carry a substantial positive independent premium, as do computer skills. Other 'soft' skills, like routine communication skills, do not. Neither, surprisingly, does 'technical know-how' (Green *et al,* 2002).

So the link between class origins and class destinations remains strong and indeed may have grown. However, this is not because the link between educational attainment and class/labour market destinations has lost its strength; it is because the link between class origins/family income and cognitive ability and educational attainment remains strong and may have grown. This is backed up by the Programme for International Student Assessment (PISA) study which shows that the English education system simultaneously has amongst the highest levels of achievement for fifteen year olds in standard literacy, mathematics and science tests but also one of the strongest relationships between pupils' socio-economic status and test scores. Of the twelve countries scoring above average for literacy, six also manage low levels of inequality in scores, while England is one of three with above average inequality. So, while English schools do well for top achievers they are not equally meeting the needs of those at the other end of the scale who tend to be from lower socio-economic groups.

Despite these findings, education remains an excellent 'ladder' with enormous transformational capacity if we can get it right, as some other countries may be doing. Relative improvement during the school years brings substantial and long-lasting benefits. Focusing again on the 1970 cohort, Feinstein highlights this, showing that escaping from the bottom quartile of cognitive ability into a higher cognitive range between the ages of five and ten has significant impacts on later outcomes in adulthood and can have an effect over and above what may have happened in early years. He finds also the converse to be true. A relative decline in cognitive outcomes during the later years of schooling can count against earlier gains (Feinstein, 2003a; Feinstein, 2003b).

Funding schools

While it is intuitive that more spending directed at schools will improve life chances overall and secure more equal life chances for the most disadvantaged, the dispute about the extent to which funding influences outcomes is very complicated and largely unresolved through research (Vignoles *et al*, 2000). Any discussion on what the most effective schools funding policies for life chances might be must be undertaken on the basis that, while a fair amount of research indicates that resources do have a significant effect on outcomes, it is not possible to make any water-tight evidence-based claims (West *et al*, 2001).

However, thinking in terms of more equal life chances, there are some important questions to answer regarding how resources are allocated. Roemer and Betts have made an attempt to fully cost what spending in education for equal life chances might look like. Looking at differences by race in the US, they find that using educational finance as the sole instrument for equal life chances would require spending nine times as much on black students, per capita, as on white students (Betts and Roemer, 1999). In England, the official funding formula for schools is based on the calculation that the mean additional costs of meeting pupils' additional educational needs, including those arising from social need, amount to one-and-a-half times the mean funding per pupil (Johnson, 2003).

Yet there is reason to question the efficacy of the number of provisions bolted on to the standard funding formula to redress the regressive impacts of a simple per pupil funding model. These provisions have been made through extra funds distributed via outside school agencies in specifically targeted areas (via initiatives such as Education Action Zones and Excellence in Cities) and also given directly to schools (via the 'Additional Educational Needs' element of the local educational authorities' funding formula, the Ethnic Minorities Achievement Grant and latterly the Vulnerable Children's Grant). The first concern is whether these funds have in fact had any significant redistributive impact. There is evidence that the most deprived local authorities are often more constrained in the priority they are able to give education and have a clear tendency to spend less overall on education relative to other central allocations (Sefton, 2004). Even with ring-fenced education budgets, we know that other pressures mean that the way LEAs distribute funding between schools does not clearly reflect need, either as measured by the proportion of ethnic minority pupils or by those eligible for free school meals (Johnson, 2003).

However, what is the impact of cutting the LEA out of the equation for more schools? In an age when it is hoped that schools can be cast as key players within the community, this strategy would remove decisions on school spending from the local democratic process and would thereby risk setting schools up in opposition to the very communities they serve. And further, how can we ensure that the distribution of resources at the level of the individual school is any more progressive? There is plenty of anecdotal evidence from the chalkface that pressure from the national targets' regime to focus on borderline grade C/D pupils at GCSE may well work in the opposite direction, encouraging schools to concentrate on 'middling' pupils rather than the most disadvantaged. Perhaps more troublingly, there are grave uncertainties about the assumptions that underpin our methods for deriving funding formulae. While funding is generally distributed on the basis of eligibility to free school meals and the number of black and ethnic minority pupils, some areas which score highly on these measures offer more favourable environments for schooling than areas with smaller populations eligible for free school meals but with large white, working-class populations (Lupton, 2004). It may be that the current bases for allocating funding progressively are too crude. Either better measures of context are required, or we may need a new type of funding assessment, based on an appraisal of the roles and activities needed to achieve certain outcomes for different types of pupils rather than on the status of a school's intake.

Choice and admissions

There is an argument that while schools do matter, most of the effective policy changes that could be made do not require further significant growth in spending. Those who follow the ongoing debate about school choice and methods of admissions might certainly suspect this to be true.

Unlike with funding, there is a robust evidence base indicating what the optimum outcome for school admissions might look like: an even socially mixed pupil intake in each school. The OECD have stated that 'in almost all countries, and for all students, there appears to be a clear advantage in attending a school whose students are, on average, from more advantaged family backgrounds' (OECD, 2001). Moreover, they show that the average socio-economic make-up of a school's intake has a stronger relationship with performance than students' socio-economic status itself, especially for pupils from families with lower socio-economic status (Feinstein, 1998). All this seems unsurprising considering the evidence on the strong tendency for advantaged intakes to bring benefits such as more aspirational peer group influences, greater levels of parental involvement with children's learning, higher expectations of teachers and more effective use of resources (OECD, 2001; Desforge, 2003). Yet the most effective methods for achieving pupil mix and the extent to which greater pupil mix is possible are matters of some dispute. 'Choice' has been the guiding principle for admissions in England since 1988. Part of the rationale for sustaining this under the Labour Government has been the drive to reduce the weight given to geographical catchment area as a determinant of access to the best state schools, thereby breaking the so-called postcode lottery which unavoidably reinforces neighbourhood segregation in schools. Indeed, international comparisons show segregation by parental occupation to be lower in countries allocating places at school through elements of choice rather than use of rigid catchment areas or school selection (Gorard and Smith, 2003). Overall, however, there has been no significant change in social segregation of schools since choice policies were first introduced in the UK (Gorard, 2003). Schools were before, and now remain, relatively socially segregated. Gorard shows that in any given year, around one third of students in England and Wales would have had to change schools in order for there to be an even spread of 'poor' children between schools. This is in part a reflection of a preservation of the status quo in policy on admissions since 1997. Most parents continue to choose the local school for reasons of convenience. Levels of selection have increased slightly as a result of increases in grammar school places and there is no plan for any significant change in public policy in this area. Furthermore, in some cities oversubscription has meant it is not only the selective schools that are able to choose their pupils. Popular schools have been able to tighten up their eligibility according to catchment criteria, reinforcing the neighbourhood effect and even impacting upon house prices (Gibbons and Machin, 2002). Overall admissions appeals have risen 50 per cent since 1997 to around 9,200 for 2002/3, reflecting the level of public disquiet. So, is it worth pursuing 'perfect choice' or is there a better means for achieving pupil mix? Attempts to increase diversity of provision of local state-funded schools aim to broaden the list of options available to individual parents, though it is unclear whether this will increase overall satisfaction. The idea that the benefits of 'good' schools can be shared through school collaboration may have limited success in the face of the quasi-market, with many successful schools reluctant to collaborate in a meaningful way. And the proposal that good schools can simply expand to meet all 'choices' seems to ignore the fact that schools are different from private companies. There is no price mechanism to balance supply and demand. Indeed, supply is highly inelastic and proposals to expand schools are impractical or very expensive. Moreover, they may not want to expand. Many schools feel that to expand would alter the character and ethos of the school and for this reason have not done so thus far. So, if good schools simply cannot expand exponentially to meet demand, in this restricted market there will always be losers.

Abandoning choice altogether and going back to the days of allocating places or setting quotas based on attainment level and/or US style pupil bussing would not be politically feasible. So perhaps it is time to take one step back and think more seriously about how the catchment area can be used more positively – after all, opinion polls consistently show that the main thing parents want is a good local school. Without a fully integrated housing market, a catchment area approach may never be able to provide a perfect social mix but if combined with careful thought about how catchment boundaries are set (perhaps with annual border reviews carried out by one overall admissions authority) some progress could be made. Is it time to give up on the pure choice ideal and consider how re-introducing an element of compulsion in admissions could be made politically marketable? If so, perhaps priority should be given to considering more limited versions of school choice.

A framework that required schools to join together in collegiates so that pupils and parents could choose a group of schools to apply to, rather than an individual school, would be one way of doing this. Collegiates may consist of about six schools, all with different characteristics, ethos and levels of independence from the state. In addition to sharing good practice and leadership, they would share a single ranking in performance tables (Johnson, 2003). In practice this would take the Government's recommendations for groups of schools to take collective responsibility for managing and admitting excluded and seriously disruptive pupils one step further so that schools would be taking collective responsibility for educating and meeting the needs of all pupils within their locality.

Teaching and learning

It is important not to overplay the potential of changes to school admissions as a way of impacting on life chances. While it seems to be an irresistible issue for the London elite (who send their children to school in the most ferocious market of all), the fact remains that in the UK differences within schools are far more significant to student outcomes than differences between schools. Taking literacy for example, the OECD shows that 82 per cent of the variation in student performance nationally is down to pupil performance differences within schools. Focusing efforts more on the choices and opportunities for pupils within schools may be a far more effective option and may not always require further significant growth in spending.

The year-on-year rise in the number of pupils gaining five A*-Cs at GCSE over the past two decades should be celebrated, as should the evident impact of strategies such as the literacy hour and Excellence in Cities. Nonetheless, some trends might lead us to question from a life chances perspective whether the standards agenda in its current incarnation has reached its limits. The plateau in attainment by eleven year olds in end-of-Key Stage Two tests of literacy and numeracy is well known. The proportion of sixteen year olds attaining five or more A*-Gs at GCSE including English and mathematics did not improve between 2000 and 2003, despite an official target being set and subsequently abandoned for attainment at this level. Perhaps most worryingly, the percentage of pupils staying on in post-compulsory education has not risen significantly in a decade. This leaves 13 per cent of sixteen year olds out of education and training in 2003 and 8 per cent out of education, training and employment.

As mentioned above, one possible explanation is that many teachers, even within socially mixed comprehensives, have felt encouraged to concentrate efforts on those C/D grade borderline pupils. This may have led to the skewing of teacher time and resources at pupil level. Yet if this was the only driving factor it would appear to invite a simple solution – broaden the targets. Such attempts have indeed been made, including the A-G grade target introduced in 2000 but subsequently dropped as noted above, and the inclusion of points scores for GCSE and Key Stage Two results so that all results and all children count. These initiatives have not had the desired impact; it seems that either the incentives were not strong enough or the culture of focusing on the A-C target was already too ingrained in schools (Reed and Hallgarten, 2003). Interrogating 'the culture' brought into schools by the standards agenda is perhaps a more meaningful place to start than tinkering with the targets. Teachers complain that curricula and pedagogies have been narrowed to focus on the measurements that performance tables have chosen to value, and that the bureaucracy that goes with accountability has left them with little chance to focus on broader learning (Earl *et al*, 2003). This culture may be reinforcing what is essentially a very traditional, academic curriculum. At Key Stage Two for example, there has been anxiety, not only that non-core subjects have been marginalised, but that areas within the core subjects, for instance drama in English, or enquiry and practical experiments in science, have also suffered. These are often the subjects which impart wider thinking skills and may encourage inclination toward staying on post-sixteen. If indeed we have come to the end of the current phase of the standards agenda, which direction should schools policy in England take next? For primary schools, there are already a number of shifts such as the return of target-setting powers to the teachers themselves and efforts to broaden the curriculum. But perhaps we should be asking more radical questions. Should we, for example, be drawing lessons from findings on pre-school provision and providing an experience for five to seven year olds based far more on an integrated care and education package? Should we fashion a primary school workforce far more closely on the Scandinavian pedagogue model? Or indeed, should children really be starting school at five years old? The alternative in Scandinavian countries is to start compulsory schooling at seven with an option to start at six. Radical reforms to the fouteen to nineteen curriculum are being mooted. The challenge will be to ensure that the greater choices on offer to students do not end up replicating the traditional splits between the academic and the vocational along social class lines. And for all the rhetoric, does personalised learning have the potential to rejuvenate the standards agenda for a new era or would personalising education around the needs of the user involve unrealistic spending outlays?

Beyond schools

Finally, it is imperative that we also consider the possibility that improving educational outcomes for those with the lowest levels of attainment will not come from within schools at all (or at least not from within the traditional remit of schools). What happens out of school hours, not just in early years but throughout childhood, can have a crucial impact on both outcomes in school and in other areas that affect life chances.

The new 'joined-up' children's services that are promised in England offer a real opportunity to think in preventative terms to address those out of school factors that impact on attainment. However, beside the practical obstacles the danger is that we will shift to a preventative model for the early years and for young children, but that interventions focused on older children will continue to prioritise young people deemed at risk. Support here might continue to be triggered only after problems have reached crisis point.

If we are to avoid reproducing a deficit model in youth services, it is crucial that policies for equal life chances fully recognise moments of risk. Crime, school exclusion, anti-social behaviour, substance abuse and teenage pregnancy are all recognised and to some extent reacted to in policy. However, a number of more subtle, but widely known, warning signs, which do not relate directly to the child but to the parent, do not trigger any emergency response. These include long-term parental unemployment and family breakdown. By their nature such events are impossible for service providers to predict so it may be that consideration needs be given to rolling out some kind of universal parenting support. Judging from ippr research such an initiative would be popular but in the context of such tightly competing claims on resources the case would have to be watertight (Edwards, 2004).

Conclusion

It is clear that the answer to the question of where most effectively to commit extra resources at the margins may be far easier to come by in the early years than when thinking about the years of compulsory schooling that follow. What we do know about this phase is that justifying further significant increases in spending on schools would be incredibly difficult, not least because there should be a greater capacity to distribute the resources already in the system more effectively to improve life chances, and because there are other no or low cost improvements that could be made to this end. In the context of tight resources the agenda relating to choice and schools admissions policies will rightly continue to receive attention. Even more importantly we need to find out how to change the incentives structure that individual schools face in deciding how to allocate priority to different pupils within the school. Both agendas require looking at the way we measure school performance.

The real question for education spending during the compulsory school years is: what will be the cost of change in teaching and learning? If we are to build a society where access to life chances is more equal, there is a clear need for reform in this area and we can assume this will come with a price tag attached. Yet until we have decided the scope and form of change it is impossible to know the resource costs.

It is apparent then that the battle for resources within the education budget will continue to rage, and this chapter can reach that conclusion without looking at the claims that would be made by higher education and adult further education. Future research may help us to better understand how to deploy resources to best effect in the school years to deliver more even outcomes in terms of educational attainment as a contribution to achieving more equal life chances. At the moment the evidence base outside of the early years seems too fragile to reach any definite conclusions. This does not mean though that there is not a fruitful debate to be had about the school choice agenda and the possibility of schools joining together in collegiates, as well as discussion on the reform of the curriculum and pedagogy within schools.

References

Betts J and Roemer J (1999) 'Equalizing Opportunity Through Educational Finance Reform' Public Policy Institute of California February 1999

Blair T (2001) *Tony Blair's speech on the Government's agenda for the future* 8 February 2001. Available at http://www.number10.gov.uk/output/Page1579.asp

Bowles S, Gintis H, and Osborne M (2001) 'The determinants of earnings: a behavioural approach' *Journal of Economic Literature* XXXIX, Pittsburgh: American Economic Association

Brooks-Gunn J, Wen-Jui H, and Waldfogel J (2002) 'Maternal Employment and Child Cognitive Outcomes in the First Three Years of Life: The NICHD Study of Early Child Care.' *Child Development* 73(4), Oxford: Blackwell

Caneiro P and Heckman J (2003) 'Human Capital Policy' *IZA Discussion Paper Number 821.* Available online at www.iza.org

Chatterji P and Markowitz S (2004) 'Does the Length of Maternity Leave Affect Maternal Health?' *National Bureau of Economic Research (NBER) Working Paper Number W10206* Cambridge MA: National Bureau of Economic Research

Desforge C (2003) *The impact of parental involvement, parental support and family education on pupil achievement and adjustment: A review of the literature* London: TSO

Duncan G and Magnuson K (2003) *Individual and Parent-based Intervention Strategies for Promoting Human Capital and Positive Behaviour.* Available at http://www.northwestern.edu/ipr/publications/papers/2004/duncan/17jacobsconference.pdf

Earl L, Watson N, Levin B, Leithwood K, Fullan M and Torrance N (2003) *Watching and Learning 3: Final Report of the External Evaluation of England's National Literacy and Numeracy Strategies* University of Toronto: Ontario Institute for Studies in Education.

Edwards L (2004) *Lever Faberge Family Report* 2004 London: ippr

Esping-Andersen G, Gallie D, Hemerijck A and Myles J (2002) *Why We Need a New Welfare State* Oxford: Oxford University Press

Feinstein L (1998) 'Which children succeed and why: What the keys are to success for British School Children?' *New Economy* 5 (2), London: ippr

Feinstein L (2003a) 'Inequality in the early cognitive development of British Children in the 1970 cohort' *Economica* 70 (277), Oxford: Blackwell

Feinstein L (2003b) 'Not just the early years' *New Economy* 10 (4), London: ippr

Feinstein L and Bynner J (2004) 'The Importance of Cognitive Development in Middle Childhood for Adulthood Socioeconomic Status, Mental Health and Problem Behaviour' *Child Development* 75 (5), Oxford: Blackwell

Gibbons S and Machin S (2003b) 'Valuing English Primary Schools' *Journal of Urban Economics* 53 (2), London: Sage

Gorard S and Smith E (2003) 'What does PISA tell us about equity in education systems?' *Comparative Education* 40 (1): 16-28. Available at http://www.cf.ac.uk/socsi/equity

Gorard S (2003) *School Choice Policies and Social Integration: The Experience of England and Wales* Cardiff: Cardiff University School of Social Sciences. Available at http://www.ippr.org/socialmobility

Green F, Gallie D and Felstead A (2002) *Work Skills in Britain 1986–2001* Nottingham: DfES Publications

Harker L and Kendal L (2003) *An Equal Start, improving support during pregnancy and the first twelve months* London: ippr

Jackson M, Goldthorpe J and Mills C (2003) *Education, Employers and Class Mobility* London: Institute for Public Policy Research (ippr). Available at http://www.ippr.org/socialmobility

Johnson, M. (2003) *Fairer Funding for Schools?* London: ippr. Available at www.ippr.org/education

Johnson M (2003) *Not choice but champion* London: ippr. Available at www.ippr.org/education.

Lupton R (2004) 'Schools in Disadvantaged Areas: Recognising Context and Raising Quality' *CASE paper 76* London: Centre for Analysis of Social Exclusion (CASE)

Machin S and Gregg P (2003) 'A lesson for education: University expansion and falling income mobility' *New Economy* 10 (4), London: ippr

Machin S and Vignoles A (2004) 'Educational inequality: the widening socio-economic gap' *Fiscal Studies* 25 (2), London: Institute for Fiscal Sudies

Magnuson K (2004) 'Parenting interventions: How to spend the marginal dollar?' *Paper prepared for ippr/HM Treasury Conference on Social Mobility* 30 March 2004

The National Evaluation of Sure Start (NESS) (2004) *The Impact of Sure Start Local Programmes on Child Development and Familiy Functioning: A Report on Preliminary Findings* London: Institute for the Study of Children, Families and Social Issues, Birkbeck, University of London

Organisation for Economic Co-operation and Development (OECD) (2001) *Knowledge and Skills for Life: First results from the OECD programme for international student assessment (PISA) 200* Paris: OECD

Patterson J, Mockford C, Barlow J, Pyper C and Stewart-Brown S (2002) 'Need and demand for parenting programmes in general practice' *Archives of Disease in Childhood* 87, London: BMJ Journals

Piatt W and Robinson P (2001) *Opportunity for whom? Options for funding and structure of post-16 education* London: ippr

PISA (2001) *Knowledge and Skills forLife: First Results from PISA 2000* Paris: OECD Publishing

Ramey C and Ramey S (2000) 'Persistent effects of early childhood education on high risk children and their mothers' in *Applied Developmental Science* 4(1),Mahwah: Lawrence Erlbaum Associates

Reed J and Hallgarten J (2003) *Time to Say Goodbye? The future of school performance tables.* London: ippr

Ruhn C (1998) 'The Economic Consequences of Parental Leave Mandates: Lessons from Europe' *Quarterly Journal of Economics* 113 (1), Harvard: MIT Press

Ruhm C (2000) 'Parental Leave and Child Health' *Journal of Health Economics* 19 (6), London: Elsevier

Sefton T (2004) 'A Fair Share of Welfare: Public Spending on Children in England' *Case Report 25* Leeds: Save the Children.

Sianesi B (2003) *Returns to Education: A Non-Technical Summary of CEE Work and Policy Discussion*, London: Institute for Fiscal Studies and Centre for the Economics of Education

Smith J R, Brooks-Gunn J and Klebanov P K (1997) 'The consequences of living in poverty for young children's cognitive and verbal ability and early school achievement' in Duncan G J and Brooks-Gunn J (eds) (1999) *Consequences of growing up poor* New York: Russell Sage Foundation Press.

Stipek D J and Ryan R H (1997) 'Economically disadvantaged preschoolers: Ready to learn but further to go' *Developmental Psychology* (33), Washington: American Psychological Association

Tanaka S (2004) *Parental Leave and Child health across OECD countries* New York: Columbia University

Vignoles A, Levacic R, Walker J, Machin S and Reynolds D (2000) 'The relationship between resource allocation and pupil attainment: a review' *DfEE Research Report 228* London: TSO

Waldfogel J (2004) 'Social Mobility and the Early Years' in Eds Robinson, Reed and Delorenzi Eds *Promoting Social Mobility and Life Chances: Maintaining Momentum* London: ippr

West A, West R, Pennell H and Travers T (2001) 'Financing School-based Education in England: Poverty, Examination Results and Expenditure' *Environment and Planning C: Government and Policy* 19 (3), London: Pion

Is Britain Pulling Apart?
Area Disparities in Employment, Education and Crime

Stephen Gibbons, Anne Green, Paul Gregg
and Stephen Machin

Geographic disparities in economic and social outcomes, from the broad regional to the community level, have been a concern to those seeking social justice for centuries. The heavy geographic imbalance associated with the early 1980s' recession and subsequent recovery only heightened these concerns ahead of the Commission on Social Justice's report. In essence, the concerns have two components. The first is a simple sense of territorial equity, namely that people should not be disadvantaged by where they live. The second, deeper, concern is that spatial imbalances can have substantial economic and social costs. The key costs are:

- The economic costs from congestion in areas of intense economic activity.
- The costs resulting from the need for economic tools, such as higher interest rates, to be required to ease inflationary pressures generated in boom areas while other areas are characterised by excess non-employment. (Clearly a single, national interest rate cannot take account of such regional differences).
- The costs arising from the effect of concentrated deprivation on employment, crime, education and other outcomes for residents.

This last grouping is usually called 'neighbourhood effects'. These are highly localised community level concerns, whereas the first two groups above impact at a regional, city-regions or local labour market area levels.

There is no single agreed definition of 'neighbourhoods', but often micro areas such as wards have been used as a proxy.[1]

This chapter focuses on policy issues around spatial imbalances in outcomes both at the regional or city level and the neighbourhood or community level. At the more aggregate level we consider only employment or its absence while at neighbourhood level we explore three issues: employment, crime and education. To make the exercise tractable we have to leave other interesting topics such as incomes, productivity and health to one side.

The chapter opens by assessing recent trends in the geography of economic activity and asks why persistent differences in employment exist at sub-national levels. In particular we seek to assess why migration of people to jobs – or jobs to people – does not even out broad level disparities. At the more micro 'community' level, we assess the evidence of how disparities in levels of deprivation develop through the sorting of certain population groups into certain areas and whether this concentrated deprivation does in itself affect the economic and social outcomes of their residents. Here we focus on whether or not there are substantive 'neighbourhood effects' in employment, crime and education. The final section of the chapter makes policy recommendations based on these findings.

Changes in employment at the regional and city level

Population changes within England and Wales in the 1990s were marked by a number of trends. At the regional level a population drift to the South and East of England continued, while at a sub-regional level the picture was one of counter-urbanisation, with city decline, movement toward small town and more rural settings, and greater commuting to work. This offers a prima facie case for regional imbalances creating and reinforcing congestion costs. While population growth has been more marked in the South and East, the recent recovery in employment rates

---

1 There are more than 10,000 wards in the UK, and these vary markedly in size; from populations of less than 1,000 to over 30,000. For the 2001 Census of Population, the finest level of spatial disaggregation is the output area, with an average working-age population of around 335. Local labour market areas also vary considerably in size; the minimum working population size of a Travel-to-Work Area (TTWA) is 3,500, while in metropolitan areas TTWAs can have working populations of over 500,000 and well over a million in the case of London. For further details of UK 'geographies' see http://www.statistics.gov.uk/geography/

has been less clearly focused. Unemployment rates have converged markedly across regions in the last decade, but this in part reflects increasing differences in inactivity across regions, with levels of disability showing a particular skew. Hence overall employment (and non-employment rates) form a better guide to regional labour market performance. Table 14.1 shows that the regional employment situation through the 1990s has been far more balanced than for a very long time (Jackman and Savori, 1999). While all regions show increases of over 2.5 per cent, the pattern of the best and worst performers bears little relation to any North-South divide. London, the North East and East Midlands have performed the least well and Wales, Scotland, the West Midlands and the South West the best.[2] Yet the bigger picture is one of a wide-spread improvement in the employment situation overall, but no reversal of the regional imbalances which were so obvious in the early 1990s. While the situation is far better than at the height of the 1980s boom, large cross-sectional regional imbalances remain intact.

Table 14.1: Percentage of working age population in employment by region, 1993-2003

	1993	1997	2003	Change 1993-2003
North East	65.4	66.8	68.1	2.7
London	67.5	70.3	70.3	2.8
East Midlands	72.9	75.3	75.9	3.0
Yorkshire & Humber	70.7	70.5	74.1	3.4
Eastern	74.4	75.9	78.7	4.3
South East	74.8	77.9	79.5	4.7
North West	68.4	69.9	73.4	5.0
South West	73.2	77.1	78.4	5.2
West Midlands	68.8	72.7	74.0	5.2
Scotland	69.0	70.3	74.3	5.3
Wales	65.6	68.2	72.6	7.0

Source: ONS (2004) Labour Force Survey

2 A regression of the regional change in employment against the initial level has almost no predictive power (an r-squared of just 0.003) and the coefficient on the initial level is an insignificant 0.0209. This suggests no convergence or divergence in employment rates over this period.

Why are employment differences across regions so persistent?
Standard labour economics suggests that regional imbalances in employment should be eroded, either by the migration of people to jobs or, attracted by lower labour costs, the movement of jobs to depressed regions. This process of adjustment is either not happening at all, or is glacial in pace in the UK. This stands in marked contrast to the situation in the US, where state differences in unemployment are fairly short lived (Blanchard and Katz, 1992).

One should, however, note that the question needs defining carefully. Regional differences in employment are almost non-existent for graduate labour and extremely marked for those with no formal education qualifications. Figure 14.1 shows this picture for the regions, with the major metropolitan areas split out to show the major cities in detail. While employment rates for men with no formal qualifications differ by more than 25 points, from the depressed areas to the affluent East Anglia and South East, for graduates the maximum difference is just eight points (Gregg *et al*, 2004). What is more, there is barely any relationship between employment rates for the least and most qualified across regions. So the real question is: why are there such persistent differences in employment among low-skilled labour, which are almost completely absent for educated labour?

Figure 14.1: Comparison of working age male employment rates by region, spring 2003

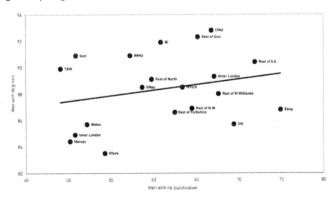

Source: ONS (2004) Labour Force Survey
Note: excludes full-time students

Moving the low skilled to jobs?

So how can we explain these patterns? One possible explanation could be patterns of residential mobility. Overall such mobility is quite high in the UK compared to other European countries and strongly pro-cyclical; that is, regional mobility occurs mainly in periods of strong growth and job creation (Gregg *et al*, 2004). This research also highlights that regional mobility is only marginally higher among the unemployed than the employed, but it is much higher (two to three times) among the better educated than the least qualified. This evidence combines to suggest that people migrate across regions in response to job openings, rather than due to concentrated regional unemployment, and that the better educated are far more prone to move region in response to available job openings.

The same work also suggests that most job-related mobility is due to people securing a job and then moving, rather than speculative moves followed by attempts to secure employment (ibid). But this is harder for the lower skilled. While national newspaper adverts or specialist business magazines create easy opportunities for graduates to locate openings in other regions prior to moving, for the lower skilled this is less the case. For these groups most recruitment occurs via word of mouth, adverts in windows or local job centres. In short, an inability to secure knowledge of job opportunities outside their local area presents hurdles to migration by the lower skilled.

At the same time, large differentials in regional housing costs and the high cost of housing as a share of income in the UK make speculative moves to boom areas very risky. Indeed, the high differentials in regional housing costs restrict moves to boom areas for the low skilled even if a job is secured in advance. Graduates can trade down house size in moves, but there is little for the less skilled to trade down into (in the US trailer parks may serve this purpose).

An argument often made is that social housing may also restrict the mobility of the least educated. Social housing tenants receive a housing subsidy (the lower rent available to social renters relative to other tenure types) and it is very difficult to take this subsidy on moving to a new local authority. So it is argued that the potential loss of this subsidy discourages tenants from moving to areas with more job openings. However, this lower mobility among those in social housing is common to those in receipt of the subsidy and those, mainly offspring, who are not (ibid). This suggests other barriers to mobility (including non-economic factors such as family connections and cultural factors) are probably more important (Kitching, 1990; Hollywood, 2002).

Moving low-skilled jobs to low demand areas?

If low-skilled labour is close to being geographically fixed, then it is important to ask why low-skilled jobs are not moving to low demand areas. In theory this would happen only if the wages are substantially lower and the potential jobs are producing goods and services that can be traded over a wider geographic area. Manufacturing jobs have traditionally met these criteria for the less skilled, but they have grown more and more scarce. While there has been substantial growth in jobs in low wage occupations, such as the personal service occupations, and there are new job opportunities for the less skilled, most of these are in services directly related to consumption in the local area (Goos and Manning, 2003).[3] This means that many low-skill jobs are servicing increased consumption of retail and leisure goods for more affluent consumers, and as a result are located in the same areas as the expanding managerial and professional opportunities.[4]

As a consequence there is little opportunity for the less skilled to migrate to boom areas and relatively few mobile low-skilled jobs to migrate to depressed regions. Hence, taking account of both economic and non-economic factors, immobility of the less skilled is often the result of rational choice given the constraints that exist in Britain.

When do employment rates for the low skilled recover?

The argument above suggests that when an area experiences a downturn, many of the better educated (including new school leavers) migrate to areas offering job opportunities, while the less skilled do not. This can leave a residue of high worklessness concentrated on the less qualified in deprived areas. Equally, and more positively, it would suggest that if an area sees a marked upturn, a tightening labour market and inwards migration (or lower outwards migration) of the well educated will create opportunities for the less skilled (Gregg and Wadsworth, 2003).

---

3 The expansion of call centres is an exception to this pattern, although these jobs have potential for outsourcing at a global scale.

4 Looking to the other end of the labour market: because there is no excess of graduate labour even in depressed areas/regions there is no downward pressure on graduate wages.

However, the picture is more complicated. In the early part of a recovery the intermediate education grouping (below degree level but not among the least educated third of the country) benefit most from the increased employment opportunities and the gap between the least skilled and the rest actually widens. This continues until employment rates among the intermediate group start to approach the levels observed for graduates and only then does job creation benefit the least skilled disproportionately, as shown in Table 14.2 below.

Table 14.2: Area economic performance and employment rates of less skilled

	High Employment Areas			Middle Employment Areas			Low Employment Areas		
	1993	2002	% chg	1993	2002	% chg	1993	2002	% chg
Area Employment Rate	76.6	81.1	+3.5	70.9	73.5	+3.6	64.6	70.3	+5.7
Men									
Low qualifications	73.9	79.5	+5.6	61.6	62.4	+0.8	52.8	51.6	-1.2
Low qual's 25-49	79.6	84.9	+4.7	69.8	70.6	+0.8	58.9	53.5	-5.4
Low qual's social housing	57.6	65.0	+7.4	38.7	35.7	-3.0	32.2	25.3	-6.9
Women									
Low qualifications	59.1	64.8	+5.7	52.4	50.8	-1.6	46.1	50.3	+4.2
Low qual's 25-49	61.8	64.5	+2.2	55.7	53.7	-2.0	47.8	50.2	+2.4
Low qual's social housing	41.7	45.5	+3.8	32.0	29.1	-2.9	29.8	32.9	+3.1

Source: Gregg and Wadsworth (2003). Low qualifications comprise bottom 30 per cent of education qualifications in each year. Social housing includes both council housing and housing associations.

Table 14.2 shows employment change between 1993 and 2002 for three groups of areas. The first group includes those where employment was already high in 1993 (the South East, excluding London and East Anglia); the second is an intermediate group (the North of England, excluding Tyne and Wear, North Yorkshire and Greater Manchester); and the third covers 'depressed' areas where employment was very low in 1993 (Tyne and Wear, Merseyside and Strathclyde). Employment growth was strong across all these areas and, in this time period, was actually strongest in those which were most depressed in 1993. What is crucial though is what happened to employment amongst the 30 per cent of the population with the lowest qualifications. In depressed and intermediate areas employment rates in this group fell, or saw very little change – except for the case of women in depressed areas. In contrast, in areas where the labour market was already tight in 1993, employment growth was very strong among the less qualified, even outperforming the average. This means that the employment gap between the less skilled and the rest closed in these tight labour markets. A little further investigation suggests this occurred when employment in the area reached around 75 per cent. The Government has recently stated an aim to reach an 80 per cent employment rate nationally (DWP, 2005). However, a rate close to this will be needed in every region in order for a disproportionate rise in employment for the low skilled.

Neighbourhood deprivation

What shapes the geography of neighbourhood deprivation?
Regional differences in employment rates are marked. Yet there is often more variation between local areas within a region than between regions themselves. What is the evidence that this neighbourhood level of geographic concentration of deprivation is changing? Do such concentrations make any difference to the key outcomes for the residents? In this section we consider employment but also broaden our focus to education and crime.

While differences in these outcomes do clearly vary by people's residential area, robust evidence of causal relationships between community and individuals is difficult enough to identify, in even the simplest of cases. McCulloch suggests that 'neighbourhood' does have a statistical association with poverty, unemployment and other characteristics associated with social exclusion, albeit there are equally or more important influences at individual and household levels (McCulloch, 2001). The problem is that group and individual characteristics are intertwined, even without causal influences. The selection mechanisms just described mean that adults choose their neighbourhood and community (or have it chosen for them on the basis of criteria related to their circumstances) and children choose their friends, based on income, preferences, talents and personality; a child is placed in a class or school alongside children of similar characteristics and ability.

At the heart of the issue then is whether the observed differences in outcomes across areas reflect the influence of our neighbours and peers on our outcomes, and whether local public services accentuate or fail to diminish such patterns. So in what follows we assess the evidence that area sorting is strengthening or weakening over time and whether such sorting has any independent influence on employment, education or crime victimisation outcomes. We also discuss the likely routes that such influences are taking as this will influence any policy response.

There are (at least) two powerful selection mechanisms that create concentrations of deprivation at this community level. The first is the transmission of inequalities of work and wages, operating via house prices and rents, into patterns of housing and neighbourhood demand. People can be thought of as 'consumers' of their local environment, from the population mix to social problems experienced, and from the natural beauty to the quality of services. Where the local environment is good people pay a premium to live there (Gibbons and Machin, 2003). By contrast, neighbourhoods with negative intrinsic characteristics tend to lose out in the process of residential sorting, and in turn concentrations of poverty can acquire further problems (Lupton and Power, 2002). Wider income inequalities across the population tend to widen price differentials and are likely to make segregation more extreme (Cheshire *et al*, 2003).

The second selection mechanism particularly applies to the more deprived communities. This is rationed access to social housing through local authorities' allocation rules. Because of right-to-buy legislation and lower levels of new building, social housing has declined as a share of the housing stock for the past two decades. This trend has continued since 1997. As a result, rationing for new entrants to social housing has become ever more restrictive. These restrictions mean that only those with the most acute housing need – especially workless or low-income families with children – get housed.

Neighbourhood employment
Figure 14.2 summarises the changing extent of variation in employment rates for working-age men at ward level. It uses census data to rank, in ascending order, all the wards in Great Britain (England, Wales and Scotland) in terms of their employment rate and then records the median employment rate for each decile group in 1981, 1991 and 2001. So as an example, the bar furthest to the left shows that the median employ-

ment rate for the lowest decile of wards in 1981 was slightly less than 70 per cent.

Employment rates for males of working age between 1981 and 1991 fell sharply, but this decline was concentrated in low employment wards. The first decile of wards saw employment rates drop by 10 per cent, whereas in the top decile group there was a decline of less than half this. The bottom two deciles experienced notably worse outcomes than the rest of the distribution. The overall decline in male employment has continued, albeit to a less marked extent, between 1991 and 2001, with the decline being slightly more focused on the lower half of the distribution (though not especially focused on the bottom two deciles).

Figure 14.2: Employment rate by ward decile group for males of working age, 1981, 1991 and 2001

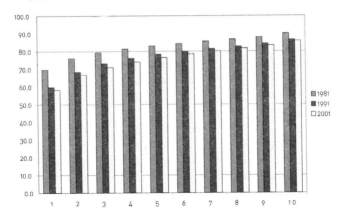

Note: There are around 10,000 wards, but they are not the same in the three census years.

Figure 14.3 presents similar information, but for women of working age.[5] Contrary to the experience for men, women's employment rates increased between 1981 and 1991, and then again between 1991 and 2001. As with men, the change was more marked between 1981 and 1991 than in the

---

5   It is not necessarily the same wards that have low male and female employment rates. However, the correlation between male and female employment rates at ward level has increased from 0.75 in 1991 to 0.87 in 2001.

later period, but unlike with men, the gain in employment was pretty even with only a slight hump around the third and fourth deciles. Looking to the lower deciles, the increase in the female employment rate between 1991 and 2001 was smaller in the first decile than everywhere else.

Figure 14.3: Employment rate by ward decile group for females of working age, 1981, 1991 and 2001

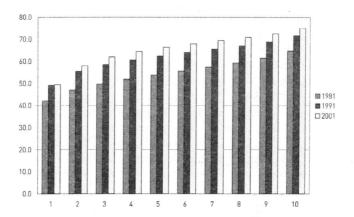

A comparison of the two charts shows that employment rates for males and females have converged; there has been a gradual decline in employment rates for men over time and an increase in employment rates for women from each census year to the next. But for both sexes there is a marked step between the worst performing 10 per cent of wards and the next tenth. Over time the size of this gap between the very worst and the rest has increased markedly. This suggests that, at least in terms of employment, the worst 10 per cent of wards may be deserving of special attention.

The most deprived 10 per cent of wards form a key government target population under the National Strategy for Neighbourhood Renewal and hence we have a lot of information about them.[6] They house nearly 15 per cent of the population (or around eight million people), have a

---

6 These wards are identified using the index of multiple deprivation (IMD), which covers domains such as income, housing and health as well as employment.

disproportionate number of children, are predominantly urban, have high housing densities and a high incidence of social housing – as we saw in Chapter 2 (Figure 2.15).

Neighbourhood employment effects?

A key social justice question is whether this concentration of deprivation has an impact on the employment chances of residents. As many residents of deprived areas have very localised outlooks and often lack the confidence and means to travel far from their home area (Green *et al*, 2005) and most low-skilled jobs come by word of mouth or adverts in windows (Gregg and Wadsworth, 1996), being in an area with low employment rates may damage a person's chances of finding employment as informal information networks for gaining intelligence about employment openings are restricted. It is also possible that employers exercise postcode discrimination, choosing not to hire from certain areas. However, evidence on such neighbourhood effects is difficult to identify. This is because of the selection issues described above; the people in the worst areas are not there by chance and hence whatever has led them to reside in these communities may also drive their poor employment outcomes.

The best evidence comes from US experimental studies, especially the recent Moving to Opportunity Program carried out in a number of major US cities (Orr *et al*, 2003). This randomised experiment moved families from acutely deprived neighbourhoods into better neighbourhoods. The families received help finding accommodation and were given financial support to pay for the higher housing costs. The findings across all the studies are that there are no substantive impacts on welfare rolls, employment or earnings (ibid; Goering, 2003). These results strongly suggest that the low employment problems of those in the most deprived wards would be broadly the same if they lived in somewhat better wards in the same city area.

This is reasonably intuitive as most deprived wards in cities are close to the central business district where work is plentiful but largely filled by people commuting in from sub-urban areas. For more geographically isolated deprived wards in old mining areas or city fringes this will not hold so strongly. It suggests the major focus on raising employment among people in deprived city areas should be about helping the individual. Of course, as individuals secure employment they may well leave these deprived areas if the areas are very unattractive to live in. Individuals' situations may be therefore be improved without necessarily leading to an improvement in the concentration of deprivation. We will return to this crucial point later.

Neighbourhood and education

We now turn to area disparities in terms of the human capital that gives individuals the skills and capabilities, which in turn affect individual earnings, employability, health and other correlates of happy and successful lives. As is standard, we consider educational attainment as our measure of human capital, since we know that educational attainments are good predictors of individual adult outcomes. Looking at education shifts the issue of neighbourhood effects firmly to look at children, for whom the potential influence of neighbourhood services (schools) and peer groups seems intuitively stronger than for adults.

Three key themes

Three key issues arise when thinking about the geographical concentration of educational attainment.

First, the educational composition of the population is a building block of area advantage and disadvantage, and increasingly seen as a key factor in economic development at the regional level. So it is important to know how much places differ in terms of the educational characteristics. We also want to know how this is changing; are places becoming increasingly disparate, with the uneducated concentrated in some places and the educated in others, or are our communities becoming more educationally mixed? Accepted wisdom seems to be that places have become increasingly segregated along socioeconomic lines; this is one of the justifications for area-based policy initiatives.

Second, environmental factors in the neighbourhood, or social interactions amongst peers and within the community, may well be influential in the formation of children's knowledge, understanding and the attainment of educational goals. Again, this is often taken for granted, and neighbourhood-based policy is to some extent predicated on the assumption that tackling problems at the neighbourhood-community level is an effective way of tackling individual disadvantage. We review the evidence on such 'neighbourhood effects', drawing on UK data, but also recent experimental evidence from the US.

Third, geographical factors are linked to education because of the nature of school admissions in the state sector. In general, school choice is tantamount to residential choice, because admission is restricted to those who live close by. The implications of this for house prices are well known, through anecdote and through media coverage. There is also an emerging body of harder evidence that these patterns of demand for neighbourhood schools are important in the housing market. We argue that this is where the constraints of geographical space might play their most important role in the process of education, by rationing access to good schooling to those who can afford it.

Patterns and changes in Britain

There is no question that neighbourhoods differ markedly in terms of the mix of educational qualifications held by their residents. This will be news to nobody, but what is remarkable is the magnitude of these differences. Figure 14.4 shows the latest snapshot of how highly qualified people are distributed across different areas. It uses similar techniques to the employment graphs in Figure 14.2. In this case, the chart ranks census wards in terms of the proportions of working-age highly qualified men and women in 1981, 1991 and 2001. The mean proportion of 'highly qualified' men in census wards in each census year, for each 5 per cent of the distribution (semi-decile) is presented.

Figure 14.4: Distribution of the highly qualified at census ward level, men 1981-2001

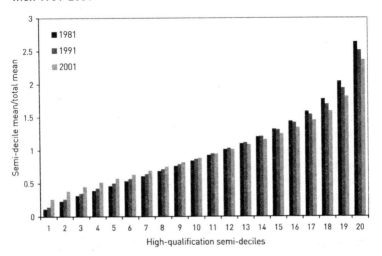

The chart shows that there are very wide disparities between the wards with the most educated and the least educated populations. It is commonly thought that this kind of segregation has increased over the past decades, with places becoming increasingly polarised along income, demographic and human capital lines. Such changes have been documented in the US (Jargowsky, 1996; Kremer, 1997), but there is no strong evidence for this in the UK (Hills, 1995; SEU, 2000). Local authorities with higher proportions of higher-educated residents in 1991 gained more educated residents over the 1990s than areas with few educated residents initially (Dorling and Thomas, 2004), but these changes can be explained by general educational upgrading throughout the country. As Figure 14.4 shows, the changes in the relative status of neighbourhoods is somewhat different. In 1981 the proportion of qualified male residents in the top 5 per cent wards was 24 times higher than the proportion in the bottom 5 per cent wards. In 1991 this figure fell to eighteen. In 2001 the ratio fell to just nine.[7] Though we do not present the data, the story for women is very similar. This reduction in inequality may be due to changes in ward definitions, changes in the classification of qualifications, or because no further segregation is feasible at the top end once all residents are qualified. But the majority of the reduction must reflect a genuine decrease in the extent to which neighbourhoods are segregated along educational lines. Wards seem to have become more educationally mixed over the past two decades.

Perhaps area differences in child, rather than adult, educational attainment might be more telling. Children are considered the most vulnerable to neighbourhood and community influences, so intuitively there could be stronger patterns in the distribution of their achievements. Figure 14.5 summarises the achievements of eleven year old boys at Key Stage Two (tests taken at ages ten or eleven). It charts the distribution of school-average point scores for tests in 1996, 1999 and 2002. Again, though the data is not shown, the picture for girls is almost identical. Since primary schools serve quite localised communities, we can visualise the geographical distribution through these school-level patterns.

Again we see marked inequality, but again the general trend (albeit at a slow pace) is towards slightly greater equality; primary schools seem to have become somewhat less segregated in terms of the attainments of children at the ages of ten and eleven. Part of this may be due to the fact

---

7   The coefficient of variation (standard deviation/mean) falls from 0.64 to 0.60 to 0.51 over these years.

that there is an upper limit to how high the best schools can go. Yet, only 0.2 per cent of schools had reached this upper limit by 2002.

Figure 14.5: Distribution of school-average Key Stage Two point scores, boys, 1996-2002

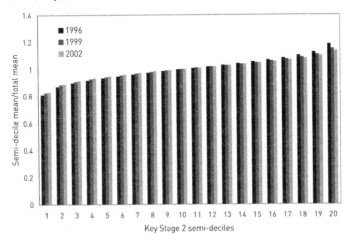

Government policy over this period has been towards greater choice for parents. This policy has been argued to increase inter-school segregation. But admissions policies which tie school intake to the specific disadvantages of a school's geographic location can be more conducive to high levels of segregation than policies which allow schools to admit from a wider geographical area. We explore this more later.

Does neighbourhood matter anyway?
Our description of the patterns and changes in the educational attainment by area suggests that the disparities are wide, but narrowing slightly. Still, we should be concerned if these differences in place and community context have an important role to play in shaping children's life opportunities and outcomes. Indeed, it is partly this thinking that motivates area-related regeneration schemes and school improvement schemes such as Excellence in Cities (Machin *et al,* 2004). The reasoning is that it is more effective to tackle educational disadvantages at the area level, because improvements in the group as a whole have knock-on effects to the individual. Given this, it is worth reviewing what evidence we have on these processes.

There are many ways in which we could imagine that people, especially children, are influenced by their neighbourhood or community. These fall into two broad categories: mechanisms related to the social interaction between children and their friends, class mates or neighbours; or alternatively mechanisms related to actual physical location, like accessibility of schools or environmental quality. Most interest, at least as far as schooling is concerned, has been in the first category. Empirical studies with evidence for these sorts of neighbourhood and peer-group effects, on education and other outcomes, have appeared thick and fast in the US since the early 1990s. In most cases the objective is simply to measure whether any causal relationship exists between some neighbourhood or school class-mates' characteristics and child achievements. Yet studies using traditional statistical techniques struggle to disentangle the influence of group characteristics from the child's own attributes and those of her family. Taken as a whole, this older evidence from the US is suggestive of some neighbourhood or school peer-group influences, but is certainly not conclusive (Jencks and Mayer, 1990; Brooks-Gunn *et al*, 1997; Ellen and Turner, 1997; Sampson *et al*, 2002). The same could be said of neighbourhood studies for the UK that takes a similar approach (Garner and Raudenbush, 1991; Gibbons, 2001; McCulloch and Joshi, 2001). Children from more educated or less deprived neighbourhoods in Britain seem to do better at school and gain higher qualifications, even taking into account observable differences such as family background. But it is hard to be sure that this is not just because families living in rich neighbourhoods differ from similar families living in poor neighbourhoods in ways that are hard to observe.

Because of these problems, recent research in the US has tried to find situations where the group in which an individual finds herself is unrelated to her own characteristics, or where neighbourhood or school change happens because of some policy intervention. Some of these 'quasi-natural' and policy experiments have proved useful, such as bussing of black pupils to out-of-town schools (Angrist and Lang, 2002), random assignment of pupils to schools (Cullen *et al*, 2003), allocation of college freshmen to dormitories (Sacerdote, 2000), the destruction of housing projects (Jacob, 2004), and the Moving to Opportunity (MTO) programme already described.

The overall story these studies tell is, however, one of weak or non-existent neighbourhood effects on children's attainments. For example, the opportunity to move to a better neighbourhood under the MTO programme produced little or no improvement in reading and mathematics test scores (Sanbonmatsu *et al*, 2004). Perhaps this is because not all those given the opportunity actually moved and because some of the children that moved did not change school. Perhaps it is the school or classroom peer-group that really matters.

How about school peer-group?

Other well-executed research from the US that looks specifically at school peer groups does find some effects, but the results are mixed. For example, boys and girls in Texas seem to do slightly better in classes with more girls (Hoxby, 2000) and peers' achievements seem to matter too (Hanushek *et al*, 2003; Lefgren, 2004). However, pupils who won lotteries to attend better, sought after high schools in Chicago gained no advantage in terms of test-scores and other traditional educational outcomes (Cullen *et al*, 2003). Even here, the overriding message is that there is probably an impact on education attainment from peer groups, but this is of fairly modest importance relative to aspects of the family background.

How does this evidence square with the common belief that peer-group and class room composition makes a big difference to our children's success at school? It is well known, for example, that the average pupil attainment in a school declines rapidly as the proportion of pupils from disadvantaged backgrounds increases (typically measured by free-school meal eligibility). This is undeniable, but is largely due to each child's own family background; children from poorer family backgrounds have, on average, lower attainments. But these children begin with lower attainments and end up with lower attainments, and there is only fragile evidence that school 'context' – that is the characteristics of the pupils with which a child shares the class or school – really matters much for that child's progress. An extensive 'school effectiveness' literature in Britain (and elsewhere) is scattered with examples that seem to show school-based 'contextual' effects, especially related to free school meal entitlement. But most take little account of the fact that children educated amongst low-income peers will also tend to be from low-income families (even if they are personally ineligible for free meals). This happens because the housing market sorts individuals geographically according to incomes, and because schools draw their intake from geographically defined neighbourhoods.

A simple story about peer effects on primary school pupil attainments in England can be told by looking at progress through Key Stage Two in the

National Curriculum, using the 2002 Pupil Level Annual Census carried out by the DfES. On average, pupils in community schools who were ineligible for free school meals scored 45.4 points in the tests at the end of Key Stage One, when they were six or seven years old (total points in reading, writing and mathematics). These pupils increased their overall scores by an average 38.0 points between ages of six or seven and ten or eleven at Key Stage Two. Pupils who were eligible for free school meals – the more income-disadvantaged – achieved 38.4 points in their age six or seven tests and a 36.9 point increase by age ten or eleven. Clearly background makes a big difference to baseline achievements – 7.4 points at the end of Key Stage One – and a small (but significant) difference to progress through primary school.

However, as Figure 14.6 shows, the mix of free school meal entitlement in a child's cohort makes very little difference to the academic progress of poor children through Key Stage Two. The figure charts the mean Key Stage One to Key Stage Two increase in point score for income-disadvantaged children, as school cohort income disadvantage increases. The column on the left represents the mean point increase for the 10 per cent of pupils with the lowest proportion of their school cohort eligible for free-school meals. The column on the right represents the mean point increase for the 10 per cent of pupils with the highest proportion of their cohort eligible for free school meals. There is no obvious systematic trend in achievement as pupil cohort composition changes (and statistical analysis would confirm that there is no significant trend). Poor pupils in a wealthier classroom context progress no better than poor pupils in poor classes through Key Stage Two. Evidence elsewhere indicates that school average free school meal entitlement may have more relevance to progress before Key Stage One, but even here the effects are relatively weak (Strand, 2002).

None of what has been said should be taken to imply that peer groups and neighbourhoods never matter. Some aspects of peer and neighbourhood groups will matter sometimes for some groups of the population, and some studies find quite general effects for Britain (Gibbons, 2001; Robertson and Symons, 2003). Recent international evidence on peer groups is also supportive of small school-related peer effects (OECD, 2003; Fertig, 2003). But any reading of the literature would surely concur that if neighbourhood and peer group effects exist, their role in the development of traditional educational outcomes is relatively minor in comparison with personal family background factors and individual attributes.

Figure 14.6: Peer group income disadvantage and progress through Key Stage Two, free-school meal eligible children, age 10/11 in Community schools in 2002

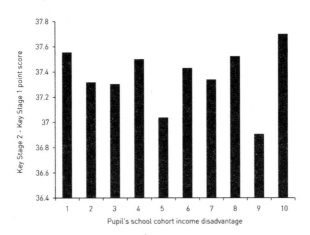

Source: DfES (2002) Pupil level annual census

For instance, if neighbourhood of origin is an important influence on educational attainments, we would expect to see strong correlations between the education of adults raised in the same neighbourhood (wherever they are later on in life). But in 1991, the correlation between years spent in education for adults who were teenagers in the same ward in the 1970s was only 0.16, and as low as 0.07 once family background differences are taken into account (Gibbons, 2001). This result suggests that neighbourhood factors account for only a very modest proportion of the inequality that exists in educational attainment.

Access and opportunity

Taken as a whole then, this body of evidence indicates a possible role for the attributes and behaviours of neighbours and peers in fostering or hindering personal educational development. But the role seems to be a minor one. A recent survey of the effects of spatial disadvantage draws similar conclusion about a much wider range of outcomes (Buck and Gordon, 2004).

Should we conclude that geography is largely irrelevant for education? This would certainly be too hasty. Schools differ in many ways, and some schools are clearly more desirable and popular than others. At least part of the reason for a school's popularity must be the effectiveness of the education it offers. Yet schooling choices are still heavily restricted by where a family lives and the most effective schools are not available to everyone. Yes, preferences take precedence in non-selective schools. But as soon as applications exceed the number of places available, it is how close a family lives that counts. Numerous US studies and a handful for England have shown that this type of admissions policy leads to higher house prices nearer better, more popular schools, particularly at primary school level (Gibbons and Machin, 2003; Cheshire and Sheppard, 2004). It is not hard to see that this reduces opportunities for poorer families to access more effective schools. One study for England showed that the annual housing price premium for the highest performing primary schools could be as high as the fees for a private preparatory school education (Gibbons and Machin, 2003). Anyone concerned about equity in education provision should be concerned about the continuing, strong importance of geography in the school admissions systems (see Chapter 13). Systems of school admissions based more on parental choice or ability (selective LEAs) than on residence result in lower neighbourhood segregation (Burgess *et al*, 2004). However, it doesn't follow that parental choice results in lower school segregation. Burgess *et al* compare segregation at a neighbourhood and school level. They show that there is a strong positive correlation between the feasibility of school choice and the extent of school segregation, controlling for residential segregation. They find this for segregation along the lines of both ability and income (ibid).

Neighbourhoods and crime

Crime and fear of crime are highly concentrated into particular areas, often featuring hot spots in highly localised places (see Chapter 2). Figure 14.7 shows the distribution of property crime rates (defined as numbers of burglaries or thefts per 1000 population across 376 areas of England and Wales in 2003-4. The chart shows that the range across areas is wide, going from 2.9 crimes per 1000 people a year up to a huge 78.8 crimes per 1000 people, with the average being 24.6 per 1000 people. It is also the case that particular areas remain high or low crime areas over long periods of time; Hansen and Machin give an analysis of crime persistence over time in the 43 police force areas of England and

Wales (Hansen and Machin, 2003). So, for people who have concerns about area disparities, it is important to establish which areas have high crime rates, and which factors are important in determining this.

Figure 14.7: The distribution of property crimes by Crime and Disorder Reduction Partnership (CRDP) (expressed as rate per 1000 population)

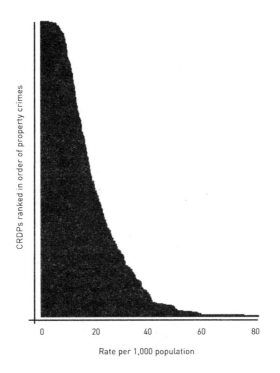

Source: Home Office (2004)

Standard economic models of crime postulate that the crime participation decision of individuals is formed by weighing up the expected costs and benefits of committing a crime relative to engaging in legal work, taking into account the probability of being caught and the sanction associated with being caught (Becker, 1968). In this framework, individuals are predicted to commit a crime if the expected benefits outweigh the expected costs. As such there will be individual variations in the propensity to engage in crime, which will be influenced by the willingness to take risks and empathy toward the victim (especially for personal crime). Researchers have used area-level data to try to test the predictions of the economic model, namely that crime should be higher in places where earnings from crime are higher, where earnings from the legal labour market are lower and where sanctions and deterrence are less tough.

Area modelling of crime is relatively new in the UK, despite there being a huge literature on the development of macroeconomic models of crime. However, the work that exists is useful in shedding light on which areas are more likely to be characterised by higher crime rates. Machin and Meghir focus on the relationship between crime and the low wage labour market in the 43 police force areas of England and Wales (Machin and Meghir, 2004). This research looked at cross-area changes in crime and changes in the 25th percentile of the area wage distribution between 1975 and 1996 (the 25th percentile wage is the wage of a person one-quarter from the bottom of the area wage distribution and can thus be viewed as an index of relatively low pay). The research reports a strong, negative correlation between the types of crime they examine (theft and handling, burglary, vehicle crime and total property crime) and low wages, even after controlling for other variables including demographic change and measures of deterrence. Hansen and Machin approach the link between crime and the low wage labour market in a different way, asking what happened to crime rates in areas where more people were beneficiaries of wage increases due to the introduction of the national minimum wage in April 1999, as compared to areas where fewer people received a wage boost (Hansen and Machin, 2002). Their findings show that crime rates fell by more in relative terms in areas with more people who benefited from the minimum wage. Importantly this research compares what happened before the minimum wage was introduced and shows that the relationship between crime and the low wage labour market that existed in the period surrounding minimum wage introduction was not present before.

The finding that low wages matter for crime is now widely accepted by researchers. In contrast, the huge amount of research looking at connections between crime and unemployment conclude that evidence of an association is fragile at best (Freeman, 1999). Other evidence based upon area analysis of crime rates is supportive of the notion that economic incentives matter for crime. For example, Feinstein and Sabates (2004) find that the financial incentive to stay in full-time education at the age of sixteen under the Educational Maintenance Allowance programme reduced both theft and burglary by male youths in pilot areas compared to similar areas not operating the programme.

Thus there are significant spatial variations in crime rates, and crime is concentrated in certain areas with high levels of persistence through time. This reveals the presence of important place and neighbourhood influences on criminal activity. It is also evident that the spatial incidence of property crime is linked to the economic opportunities available in particular places.

These findings based on data for England and Wales are in line with findings from the US. For example, the Moving to Opportunity programme confirms that moving to different, more affluent neighbourhoods leads to reductions in the chances of being a victim of crime for adults (Duncan et al, 2004). Girls (though not boys) of families who moved to a better neighbourhood also reported lower witnessing of criminal activity. Likewise there were differences in reported engagement in risky behaviour, with girls reporting improvements but boys, if anything, going the other way. Furthermore, girls experienced far fewer arrests for violent offences but boys showed higher arrest rates for property crimes. So there is a mixed picture on adolescent behaviour and criminal activity, but clear differences in adult victimisation and areas with high crime rates reflect poor economic opportunities, mostly in terms of wages rather than unemployment.

Discussion and policy

How should these findings be translated into policy? It is clear that regional inequalities and neighbourhood effects represent a substantial social injustice. At a regional or city/travel to work area level there are large and highly persistent differences in employment levels focused heavily on the least educated. The evidence presented above suggests these differences will not be dissipated through mobility of the low-skilled to areas of job creation or of low-skilled jobs to deprived areas. Most economic migration is undertaken by people securing a job in a new area and then moving to that location. Graduates are highly mobile in this way with a well functioning national labour market and area variations in employment are rapidly evened out. Low-skilled labour is less mobile because information on opportunities is hard to access and the high cost of housing in growth areas prohibits such moves. Social housing subsidies, which are not transferable across areas, are probably a minor additional restriction rather than a major factor in this low mobility. Low-skilled jobs are not flowing to low-wage areas because most growth areas of low-skilled employment are locally servicing consumption and leisure activities of the affluent. Once the employment rate in an area rises above 75 per cent, however, the low-skilled start to benefit disproportionately from further jobs growth. This suggests that the Government's stated ambition to secure an 80 per cent employment rate will be needed to be nearly achieved in every region to reabsorb the lowest skilled.

So the solutions to employment differentials at the city/regional level probably lie less in trying to move low-skill jobs to deprived regions through relocation grants and so on, but in seeking the high value-added economic activity usually associated with well-educated labour. The spending power of these people will generate jobs for others. It is notable that strategies of urban regeneration aimed at making cities vibrant and attractive places to live have produced some clear success in this way. Government can support this agenda by encouraging university-based research activity and central government functions to move out of London and the South East. Supporting migration by the less skilled through national vacancies data in job centres and making social housing subsidies mobile would provide some additional support to reducing regional employment differentials by encouraging some (even short range) mobility – this is discussed more below.

At the community level there are sometimes huge degrees of spatial segregation along the lines of employment, education and crime. These patterns are also highly persistent across time. While the picture for employment segregation is of some further widening at ward level, spatial inequalities in education are diminishing for adults. These conflicting trends reflect the sharp increase in the employment differences across education groups which have been sufficient to offset the minor lessening of the extent of educational segregation at ward level. Spatial differences in educational attainment amongst children are also slightly narrowing over time.

This spatial segregation is partly due to the more affluent seeking to purchase desirable neighbourhoods with low crime rates and high quality public services, raising house prices in these areas. Restricted entry in social housing to those in the most desperate circumstances also drives concentration of the poorest into certain neighbourhoods. There is no evidence that this special segregation has any effect on employment. That is, it seems that moving a person to a more affluent neighbourhood in the same broader area would have little on impact on their employment prospects.

For education, the available evidence is that peer group effects – who children attend school with – make only a modest difference to attainment, certainly when compared to the importance of the child's family. But families will pay substantially over the odds for higher school quality. Access to good schools is one of a number of ways that the affluent use their financial clout to advantage their offspring and this in part drives spatial segregation.

Being a victim of crime is strongly related to where you live and crime is concentrated heavily in certain areas. There is also some modest evidence that peer group in the neighbourhood influences the propensity to engage in crime or risky behaviour (including teenage pregnancy) for girls. There is clear evidence, however, that criminal activity is related to wage opportunities in the area.

This is important for policy-makers because it suggests that at the community level employment issues are about helping individuals into work, as there is no evidence for neighbourhood employment effects. Indeed, improving economic opportunities for the less skilled in an area may not reduce spatial inequalities in employment if the gainers use their improved incomes to move out of the deprived areas. In contrast, for crime and risky behaviour there is evidence of modest neighbourhood/peer group effects for children and substantial spatial aspects to being a victim of crime.

While most educational disadvantage does not seem to come from the peer group, delivering resources to the child still may be best done through the school when it is more cost effective to do so or when the intervention requires group delivery; school resources and high quality teachers do not operate on just the individual child. Targeting resources on poor communities is therefore advantageous both as a cost effective way of reaching disadvantaged children and because of the spillover effects of concentrated deprivation. The Excellence in Cities programme has had modest effects in raising attainment in deprived areas, but is cost effective given the relatively low level of resources injected (Machin, McNally and Meghir, 2004). Likewise the Street Crime Initiative, which puts greater policing resources in the most deprived areas, seems to have had a significant impact in reducing robberies (Machin and Marie,

2005). Furthermore, the very act of improving the schools and reducing crime (and similar neighbourhood regeneration issues) will make these areas more attractive to live in, lessening incentives for people to leave if their personal circumstances improve. This addresses the very heart of the problem. Hence schools and crime reduction initiatives can be important elements of area regeneration.

This suggests that large amounts of extra funding for schools, and policing in deprived communities, should be a key component of a social justice agenda. The maze of local funding currently makes this approach very difficult. There are government funding streams given to local authorities which take account of area deprivation but the LEA does not have to transmit this to the schools serving poor children, and schools do not have to address the extra needs of deprived children (see Chapter 13). Likewise, police funding is to the local police authority, not the policing of the most deprived wards. To address these problems the main approach of the Government has been to set targets to reduce gaps between the most deprived areas and the national average under the National Strategy for Neighbourhood Renewal. National and local public services are then required to meet these targets and local strategic partnerships are supposed to act as coordinating bodies to achieve these ends. In addition though there are two further approaches. The first is hypothecated resources given to agencies to deliver area-based improvements in services and outcomes; Excellence in Cities and an array of Action Zones or the Street Crime Initiative reflect this. The second additional approach is the New Deal for Communities, which also delivers resources to an area but differs in that local residents are engaged in choosing priorities and even aspects of delivery.

A more direct transmission of resources for deprived families and communities has obvious benefits for the delivery of the public services they receive. It would also be desirable if institutional blockages could be eased. For example, offering appropriate incentives to encourage good teachers to teach deprived children (who tend to engage in more disruptive behaviour) in disadvantaged schools serving deprived communities seems desirable. If these schools could pay more they would have a good chance to recruit and hold such teachers. Residence-based schools admission policies generate neighbourhood segregation and create a direct link between neighbourhood and school segregation. Selective education and parental choice based systems reduce neighbourhood segregation, but appear to raise school segregation given the lower level of neighbourhood segregation. Parental choice can only improve on residence selection where the best schools cannot choose the pupil (as the school is oversubscribed another selection mechanism comes into play), as the school will choose the most able and least difficult pupils. Furthermore, a simple choice system is less than ideal where the power to exercise meaningful choice is constrained by income. low-income families can only choose local schools because they have less access to transport. None of these currently widely used systems is really effective at tackling educational segregation.

Yet policy can make a difference here; access to high quality public services and low crime neighbourhoods substantially influences patterns of spatial segregation. There is then the potential for improved public services (such as schools, policing and transport) in deprived areas, helping to reduce the crowding of the poor into a minority of wards by making these areas more attractive. This is not an argument for gentrification, which is the almost complete replacement of poor populations by affluent ones in an area, but an argument in favour of creating more mixed populations in the areas currently in the most deprived 10 per cent of wards and of making inner city areas more attractive places for people to live. In the case of schools, this could involve further weakening the link between where children live and the schools they attend, so that schools do not perpetuate geographical patterns of disadvantage and advantage. This requires choice backed by access and support (such as better bus services and informing and engaging with parents) and a blind selection mechanism for oversubscribed places. A form of clearing system that matches choices and available places as with higher education (but here without an attainment pre-requisite) seems a clear way forward and is under trial in London. If a deprived child comes with substantial extra resources, any residual discretion schools have may be biased to taking and supporting deprived children rather than the affluent. New funding mechanisms to deliver resources to the schools teaching deprived pupils and policing of deprived areas are required with substantially higher rates of funding than the national average.

Social housing reform can also play a role in creating more mixed communities (as well as enabling greater mobility as discussed above). Currently social housing subsidies are rationed to those who are in acute housing need (which is in turn strongly related to poverty and poor employment) and can only be secured through residence in social housing in one local authority. An local authority has no duty to offer housing to those already housed in another local authoriy and so shifting tenure type or moving across local authority boundaries normally results in loss of the subsidy – it is embedded in the bricks and mortar. As social housing units, with only some exceptions, are concentrated in certain communities, this exacerbates the concentration of deprivation. This issue has been recognised and most new build social housing is in smaller units often dotted around towns and cities. However, there is very little new build and this does not address these issues for the existing stock. A possible solution is to make the subsidy a long-term housing cost reduction for any family being assessed as having long-term need. It would then no longer be attached to one LEA and could be taken with the tenant when they move area or even into buying a house (although, unlike the right-to-buy scheme, not restricted to the current property). Housing associations would be able to rent to anyone at full cost but those eligible to the subsidy would pay a lower rent. This would reduce the concentration of deprivation on social housing, creating more mixed communities while also supporting more mobility.

Conclusion

Neighbourhood segregation is shaped by income inequalities translating into the better off securing more attractive neighbourhoods, which includes good schools and low crime levels. Social housing allocation mechanisms and school admissions policies also create greater patterns of segregation in Britain. Whether the degree of segregation is worsening depends on the measure used but there clearly is no substantive recent improvement. These neighbourhood disparities have wider social consequences for their residents, which are commonly called neighbourhood effects. These are large for crime, modest for child education and non-existent for adult employment except in geographically isolated areas. Addressing these neighbourhood effects through increased funding for schools, crime reduction and wider neighbourhood renewal would help create a virtuous circle as these are factors that make neighbourhoods attractive. Addressing the way that social housing allocation and schools admissions policies create segregation would be of further substantive benefit.

References

Angrist J and Lang K (2002) 'How Important are Classroom Peer GroupEffects: Evidence from Boston's METCO Program', *NBER Working Paper 9263*, New York: National Bureau of Economic Research

330   Social Justice

Becker G (1968) 'Crime and Punishment: An Economic Approach' *Journal of Political Economy*, 76, , Chicago: University of Chicago Press

Blanchard O and Katz L (1992) 'Regional Evolutions' *Brookings Papers on Economic Activity*, Issue No. 1, Washington: Brookings Institution

Brroks-Gunn J, Duncan GJ and Aber JL (1997) *Neighbourhood Poverty: Context and Conseqwuences for Children* New York: Russell Sage Foundation

Buck N and Gordon I (2004) 'Does Spatial Concentration of Disadvantage Contribute to Social Exclusion?' in Boddy M and Parkinson M (eds) *City Matters* Bristol: Policy Press.

Burgess S, McConnell B, Propper, C and Wilson, D (2004) *Sorting and choice in English secondary schools*. CMPO Discussion Paper 04/#

Cheshire P and Sheppard S (2004) 'Capitalizing the Value of Free Schools: The Impact of Land Supply Constraints' *Economic Journal*, 114(499), F397-F424, Oxford: Blackwell

Cheshire P, Monastiriotis V and Sheppard S (2003) 'Income inequality and iresidual segregation' in Martin R and Morrison P (eds) *Geographies of Labour Market Inequaliry* London: Routledge

Cullen J, Jacob J and Levitt S (2003) 'The Effects of School Choice on Student Outcomes: Evidence from Randomised Lotteries', *NBER Working Paper 10113*, New York: National Bureau of Economic Research

Department of Work and Pensions (DWP) (2005) *Five Year Strategy: opportunity and security throughout life* London: TSO

Dorling D and Thomas B (2004) *People and Places: a 2001 census atlas of the UK* London: Policy Press

Duncan, G, Clark-Kauffman E and Snell E (2004) *Residential Mobility Interventions as Treatments for the Sequelae of Neighbourhood Violence*, Chicago: Northwestern University

Ellen I G and Turner M A (1997) 'Does Neighbourhood Matter? Assessing Recent Evidence', *Housing Policy Debate*, 8 (4), Washington: Fannie Mae Foundation

Fertig, M (2003) 'Educational Production, Endogenous Peer Group Formation and Class Composition' – *Evidence from the PISA 2000 Study, IZA Discussion Paper 714*, Institute for Study of Labour: Bonn

Feinstein L and Sabates R. (2004) 'Crime and Education: Evaluating Externalities Using the Education Maintenance Allowance Programme', *Wider Benefits of Learning Research Report* London: Institute of Education

Freeman R (1999) 'The Economics of Crime' in Ashenfelter O and Card D (eds) *Handbook of Labor Economics*, Elsevier Science: Amsterdam.

Garner C L and Raudenbush S W (1991) 'Neighbourhood Effects on Educational Attainment', *Sociology of Education*, 64 (4), Washington: American Sociological Association

Gibbons S (2001) 'Neighbourhood Effects on Educational Achievement', *Centre for Economics of Education Discussion Paper no. 18*, London: LSE

Gibbons S and Machin S (2003) 'Valuing English Primary Schools', *Journal of Urban Economics*, 53 (2), London: Elsevier

Goering, J (2003) 'The Impacts of New Neighbourhoods on Poor Families: Evaluating the policy implications of the moving to Opportunity Demonstration' *FRBNY Economic Policy Review*, June 2003, New York: Federal Reserve Bank of New York

Goos M. and Manning A (2003) 'McJobs and MacJobs: The Growing polarisation of jobs in the UK' in Dickens R, Gregg P and Wadsworth J (eds) *The Labour Market Under New Labour ; The State of Working Britain,* London: Palgrave

Green A E, Shuttleworth I. and Lavery, S (2005) 'Young people, job search and labour markets: the example of Belfast' *Urban Studies*, 42 (2) , Glasgow: University of Glasgow

Gregg P, Machin S, and Manning A (2004) 'Mobility and Joblessness' in Card D, Blundell R. and Freeman R. (eds) *Seeking A Premier League Economy* Chicago: University of Chicago Press

Gregg P and Wadsworth J (1996) 'How Effective are State Employment Agencies? Job Centre Use and Job Matching in Britain' *Oxford Bulletin of Economics and Statistics* 58, Oxford: Blackwell

Gregg P and Wadsworth J (2003) 'Labour Market Prospects of the Low Skilled over the recovery' in

Dickens R, Gregg P and Wadsworth J (eds) *The Labour Market Under New Labour ; The State of Working Britain* London: Palgrave

Hansen K and Machin S (2002) 'Spatial Crime Patterns and the Introduction of the UK National Minimum Wage', *Oxford Bulletin of Economic and Social Statistics* 64, Oxford: Blackwell

Hansen K and Machin S (2003) 'Modelling Crime at Police Force Area Level, in *Modelling Crime and Offending, Recent Developments in England and Wales, Home Office Occasional Paper 80*, London: Home Office

Hanushek E, Kain A J, Markman J M and Rivkin S G (2003) 'Does Peer Ability Affect Student Achievement?' *Journal of Applied Econometrics* 18(5), Chichester: John Wiley

Hills J (1995) *Income and Wealth: Report of the JRF Inquiry Group* York: Joseph Rowntree Foundation

Hollywood E (2002) 'Mining, Migration and Mobility: Towards an understanding of the relationship between migration and occupation in the context of the UK mining industry' *International Journal of Population Geography* 8, Chichester: John Wiley

Home Office (2004) *CRDP Crime Rates*. Original analysis supplied to the authors

Hoxby C (2000) 'Peer Effects in the Classroom: Learning from Gender and Race Variation' *National Bureau of Economic Research Working Paper 7867*, New York: National Bureau of Economic Research

Jackman R and Savori S (1999) 'Has Britain Solved the 'Regional Problem'?' in Gregg P and Wadsworth J (eds) *The State of Working Britain* Manchester: Manchester University Press

Jacob B (2004) 'Public Housing, Housing Voucher, and Student Achievement: Evidence from Public Housing Demolitions in Chicago' *American Economic Review* 94(1), Nashville: American Economic Association

Jargowsky PA (1996) 'Take the Money and Run: Economic Segregation in U.S. Metropolitan Areas' *American Sociological Review* 61(6), Washington: American Sociological Society

Jencks C and Mayer S E (1990) 'The Social Consequences Of Growing Up In A Poor Neighbourhood' in Lynn Jr L E and Mcgeary M G H (eds) *Inner-City Poverty In The United States* Washington DC: National Academy Press

Kitching R. (1990) 'Migration Behaviour Among the Unemployed and Low-Skilled' in Johnson J H and Salt J (eds) *Labour Migration*, London: David Fulton

Kremer M (1997) 'How much does sorting increase inequality?' *The Quarterly Journal of Economics* vol 112, pp. 115–39 Cambridge MA: MIT Press

Lefgren L (2004) 'Educational Peer Effects and the Chicago Public Schools' *Journal of Urban Economics*, 56, London: Elsevier

Lupton R and Power A (2002) 'Social exclusion and neighbourhoods' in Hills J. (ed) *Understanding Social Exclusion* Oxford: Oxford University Press

McCulloch A (2001) 'Ward-level deprivation and individual social and economic outcomes in the British Household Panel Study' *Environment and Planning A* 33(4), London: Pion

McCulloch A and Joshi H (2001) 'Neighbourhood and family influences on the cognitive ability of children in the British National Child Development Study' *Social Science and Medicine* 53,5, London: Elsevier

Machin S, McNally S and Meghir C (2004) 'Improving Pupil Performance in English Secondary Schools: Excellence in Cities' *Journal of the European Economic Association* 2, , Harvard: MIT Press

Machin S. and Meghir C (2004) 'Crime and Economic Incentives' *Journal of Human Resources*, 39(4), Madison: University of Wisconsin Press

Machin S and Marie O (2005) 'Crime and Police Resources: The Street Crime Initiative', forthcoming *CEP Discussion Paper*

OECD (2003) *Learning for Tomorrow's World; First Results from PISA 2003* Paris: Organisation for Economic Cooperation and Development

Orr L, Feins J, Jacob R, Beecroft E, Sansbonmatsu L, Katz L, Leiman J and Kling J (2003) *Moving To Opportunity: Interim Impacts Evaluation* Washington: US Department of Housing and Urban Development and Research

Robertson D and Symons J (2003) 'Do Peer Groups Matter? Peer Group versus Schooling Effects on Academic Attainment' *Economica* 70, Oxford: Blackwell

Sacerdote B (2000) 'Peer Effects with Random Assignment: Evidence from Dartmouth Roommates', *NBER Working Paper 7469*, New York: National Bureau of Economic Research

Sampson R J, Morenoff J D and Gannon-Rowley T (2002) 'Assessing "Neighbourhood Effects": Social Processes and New Directions in Research' *Annual Review of Sociology* 28, Palo Alto: Annual Reviews

Sanbonmatsu L, Brooks-Gunn J, Duncan G and Kling J (2004) *Neighborhoods and academic acheivement: Result from the Moving to Opportunity Experiment* Princeton NJ: Princeto University Press

Social Exclusion Unit (2000) *National Strategy for Neighbourhood Renewal: A Framework for Consultation* London: Cabinet Office

Strand S (2002) 'Pupil Mobility, Attainment and Progress During Keys Stage 1: a cautious interpretation' *British Education Research Journal* 28, 1, London: Routledge

The Economy: Achieving Full Employment

Peter Robinson

> *Employment opportunity for all is a precondition of a fair society. Social justice and full employment go hand in hand* (DWP, 2004).

The central role of full employment in achieving social justice was recognised long before the Commission on Social Justice emphasised in 1994 that 'Paid work for a fair wage is the most secure and sustainable way out of poverty' (CSJ, 1994). Unsurprisingly, given the background of the 1930s, the post-war consensus placed the maintenance of full employment at the centre of economic and social policy. It was the failure of governments after the mid-1970s to keep unemployment down that led many to the pessimistic conclusion that full employment as an aspiration was dead. It is the steady downward trend in unemployment since the early 1990s that has allowed policy makers to talk meaningfully again about getting back to full employment.

Indeed, the labour market has changed in two significant ways since the Commission reported in 1994. First, employment has risen and unemployment has fallen steadily since the end of the recession in 1993. Second, a less well noticed change, that occurred at around the time of the Commission's report, is the ending of the sharp rise in wage inequality that took place from the late 1970s to the early 1990s. Labour market outcomes look much less threatening than they were in 1994. However, significant problems remain and economic inactivity is still high and although wage inequality is no longer rising so sharply, it is not falling either.

Why do we care about full employment? Clearly, worklessness is highly correlated with income poverty in the UK. Two thirds of working-age adults living in workless households had incomes below 60 per cent of the median (after housing costs) in 2002/3 compared with just 7 per cent of adults in households where all the adults were in work (DWP and ONS, 2004). Of course this is in part due to the low levels of income replacement offered by the British benefits system; more generous out-of-work benefits could lift a higher proportion of workless households out of poverty.

However, we care about involuntary unemployment for reasons other than just the effect on income. As Chapter 11 shows, involuntary unemployment and the fear of unemployment have one of the biggest adverse impacts on self-reported measures of wellbeing and objective indicators of physical and mental health, as emphasised most recently by the research on happiness (Di Tella *et al*, 2002). This adverse effect becomes more severe the longer a person is out of work and the various scarring effects of unemployment can impact significantly on an individual's life chances. Although we need to know more about the impact of long periods of economic inactivity, as opposed to unemployment, on wellbeing, anyone familiar with a century's worth of literature would not doubt the impact of worklessness. It is useful that more rigorous analysis has demonstrated that Orwell and Steinbeck retain some relevance and that unemployment continues to impact significantly on wellbeing today, despite dramatic improvements in overall living standards since the 1930s.

New Labour – a new definition of full employment?

Since 1997 the Government's approach to the labour market has emphasised four explicit policy objectives and one implicit political objective.

Reducing unemployment and economic inactivity
Labour inherited an economy in 1997 where employment and unemployment rates had already been moving in the right direction since the end of the early 1990s recession (see Figures 15.1 and 15.2 below). The New Deal, as one of the Government's early flagship initiatives, emphasised the importance of reducing youth unemployment, but was soon joined by a range of other 'new deals' aimed at different target groups. Policy increasingly emphasised those who were economically inactive as well as those who counted as unemployed under international definitions because they were actively looking for work. By the end of its first term the Government had formalised explicit public service agreement

targets aimed at raising employment overall and for a number of key target groups. What it had not done was set out a measurable target for what it would mean to achieve full employment.

Figure 15.1. Unemployment rates 1971–2004

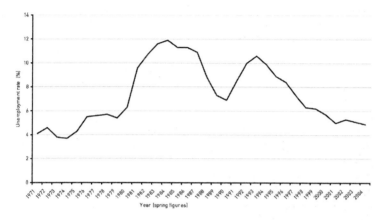

Source ONS (2003) Labour Market Trends Vol 111, No 9, and ONS (2004a) Labour Market Trends Vol 112, No 9.

Figure 15.2. Employment rates 1971–2004

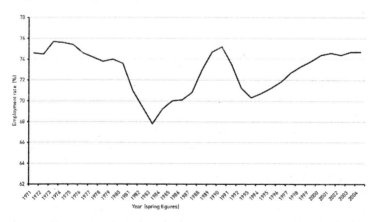

Source ONS (2003) Labour Market Trends Vol 111, No 9, and ONS (2004a) Labour Market Trends Vol 112, No 9.

Improving retention and progression in the labour market
From an early point, one criticism of the New Deals was that they were too focused on getting participants into a job – any job – regardless of how long that job was likely to last or whether it offered any chance of progression to a better position in the labour market. This led to some focus in policy debates on how the state might improve both retention in employment and further progression in the labour market.

Securing 'fairer outcomes' in the labour market
The Government's best response to the allegation that it was too focused on securing any kind of job for the unemployed was the strong emphasis it placed on eliminating the worst aspects of low pay and reducing in-work poverty. It was also committed to tackling various forms of discrimination in the labour market. It was not, however, obviously committed to reducing the high levels of wage inequality it had inherited or tackling the gender pay gap.

Improving the quality of working life
The Government was interested in what went on in the workplace, in terms of the quality of day-to-day working life as experienced by employees. It was also very interested in the range of issues relating to work-life balance that had risen up the political agenda during the 1990s.

Keeping business sweet and satisfying the labour movement
It is important not to forget the political context facing the Labour Government. It had invested a great deal of capital in establishing and maintaining a good working relationship with business. Indeed, the ippr's other pre-1997 Commission – on Public Policy and British Business – was explicitly geared to this political end. At the same time, the Government had to satisfy the expectations of a labour movement battered by two severe recessions and a raft of legislation that had placed restrictions on the role of the trade unions. Squaring this political circle was always going to be tough.

If the wording used to describe some of these objectives seems a little vague, this is in part a reflection on how genuinely difficult it is to define a subjective concept like the 'quality of working life' in a rigorous and measurable manner (Edwards and Burkitt, 2001). However, defining full employment in a measurable way is something policy-makers should be able to do. One such attempt managed to encompass prospects for progression in work and the elimination of in-work poverty, as well as the aspiration that 'everyone who wants to work can quickly find a job [and] no groups are excluded from the labour market' (Mulgan, 2000). This formulation echoes that of economists in recognising that in a dynamic labour market you will always have a minimum level of 'frictional' unemployment reflecting people changing jobs and spending the optimal time searching for their next best employment opportunity.[1] However, it also adds an important focus on the exclusion of groups from the labour market.

What this Government has not done is tell us what actual unemployment and employment rates would constitute full employment. It uses the excuse that the labour market has changed so much since the postwar period of full employment that old measures have been rendered redundant, an assertion that should be questioned. Fortunately, statisticians have recreated time-series of unemployment and employment based on current definitions (Figures 15.1 and 15.2) which show that in the early to mid-1970s the unemployment rate was about 4 per cent. This seems a reasonable benchmark for full employment. Nearly 76 per cent of the working-age population was in employment at this time. In mid-2004 the employment-population ratio was a little under 75 per cent and the unemployment rate a little under 5 per cent, leading to the important conclusion that Britain was still some way off full employment and still below previous post-war peaks. Moreover, some other OECD economies sustained employment: rates approaching 80 per cent in the early 2000s as did tighter labour markets in the south of England. Making significant inroads into economic inactivity would seem to require aiming for a similar employment rate for the UK as a whole. An employment rate of at least 75 per cent in each region would also seem to be the minimum necessary to pull less advantaged groups back into the labour market in significant numbers.

The Government would also claim that it had a very clear assignment of policy instruments to achieve the objectives set out above.

---

1 One interesting issue for the child poverty debate is whether there might be an analogous 'frictional' level of child poverty that would reflect the temporary movement of households into and out of poverty. This would be the minimum level of child poverty at which the Government's flagship target could aim, reflecting the commonsense notion that a zero child poverty rate is as unrealistic as a zero unemployment rate.

Macroeconomic policy geared to stability

One of the Government's proudest boasts is the generally good performance of the UK economy relative both to Britain's recent past and to other major OECD economies. They would ascribe this to the monetary and fiscal policy framework put in place after 1997, though it really takes nothing away from the Government's achievement to note that this has been built on a framework put in place by the previous government after 1992.

Active labour market policies

The various New Deals are heralded as great success stories, and their impact is discussed further below. Key features were built on successful programmes that were running before 1997, as well as borrowing from both US and Scandinavian experience. It is the setting up of an integrated employment service in the form of Jobcentre Plus that, looking ahead, might be one of the Government's most significant achievements. The New Deals have been inexpensive, with gross annual costs of just £600 million in 2003–04 and, in an international context, the UK spends less on such policies than most other OECD countries, though of course this tells us nothing about their effectiveness.

Education and training

Famously the Prime Minister's top three priorities, in practice training programmes specifically aimed at disadvantaged jobseekers, have played less of a role than active labour market policies geared to helping people move directly into work. This tension between a 'job first' approach and a 'human capital' approach has been a source of policy debate, here and in the US. In particular, the elimination of in-work poverty would seem to require measures that help improve participants' hourly earnings and not just move them into work of any kind. However, the effectiveness of these different approaches is in the end an empirical matter.

Financial incentives

More generous in-work and out-of-work benefits and tax credits aimed primarily at families with children have served the dual purpose of directly redistributing income to lower-income households, while also sharpening incentives to work. The national minimum wage was consciously introduced at a modest level to remove the worst features of low pay and further sharpen incentives to work without causing significant job loss.

Labour market regulation

The Government also consciously strove to strike a balance in its approach to regulating the labour market between providing more rights and security for employees, and maintaining those elements of flexibility in the labour market that were seen as desirable. Needless to say, striking the balance here and with respect to the minimum wage was central to holding the political ring between business and the labour movement.

A notable absence from this list of policy instruments is any mention of a regional policy designed to raise employment in the less advantaged regions, a point we will come back to.

Of course, setting out the Government's policy objectives and instruments in this rational way might suggest the unfolding of a grand plan that was clear to all in 1997. In practice, any government's detailed approach to any major issue evolves pragmatically, even if based on some notion of what is to be achieved and how. The key questions are whether, since 1997, this strategy has contributed to a more socially just set of labour market outcomes and, equally important, where policy might go next.

The Government has always faced some strategic choices, most importantly in relation to the emphasis to be given to the four different objectives for the labour market outlined above. The successful introduction of the minimum wage has allowed the Government to dismiss the crudest exposition of the trade-off between the level of wages and levels of employment at the bottom end of the labour market, even if at some point that trade-off must exist. Importantly, the capacity of Jobcentre Plus to implement more than one key objective at a time has set up a further potential trade-off between the 'tackling inactivity' and 'promoting progression' agendas that would not have been identified in 1997. This strategic choice faces the Government as acutely now as it did in 2001. It is this potential strategic choice that we primarily focus on in this chapter, with only some limited discussion of the objectives of securing fairer outcomes in the labour market and a better quality of working life.

The evolving labour market

An alien looking at the trends in employment and unemployment in Figures 15.1 and 15.2 might struggle to see an obvious break after 1997 associated with a change in government. Labour inherited a recovering economy in 1997 and that recovery has continued and matured. The key challenge for analysts as always is to establish the counter-factual; what would have happened without the specific policies introduced by this Government and how much impact have they had? This is not straightforward, though an attempt is made below.

It is worth setting out some further context in terms of the structure of the labour market and how it has been evolving. Looking at employment patterns by household should give us a better indication of how changes in employment might impact on household incomes (See Figure 15.3 below). The proportion of all working-age households where no adults are in work has fallen by about 2.5 percentage points over the decade since 1994, though the proportion of households where all adults are in work has risen by 5.5 percentage points over the same period. The proportion of children living in workless households has fallen by a fifth over the decade, but still stood at 16 per cent in 2004. This is one aspect of the polarisation of labour market opportunities that is of concern to those worried about the labour market's contribution to poverty, inequality and the achievement of social justice (Gregg and Wadsworth, 2003a).

Figure 15.3 Working and workless households 1990–2004

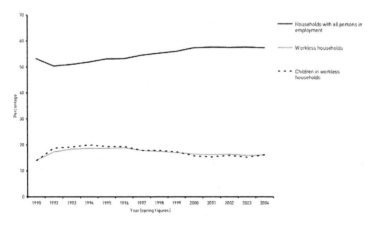

Source: ONS (2004b) Labour Force Survey
Note: Percentages refer to proportion of total working-age households. A workless household is one with at least one person of working age where no one is in employment. Percentages of children refer to proportion of total children under sixteen.

Another aspect of the polarisation debate focuses on the declining share of skilled manual jobs through the 1980s and 1990s and clerical and secretarial jobs in the 1990s. As Table 15.1 below shows, less skilled operative and elementary jobs have also seen their share decline. Net growth in employment has come at both ends of the labour market, with a significant increase in managerial, professional and technical jobs but also a rising share of the less well paid personal service and sales occupations. However, overall, two-thirds of the net increase has come in the form of well-paid jobs requiring significant qualifications and experience – the British labour market has not been generating disproportionately low-skilled, low-paid work.

Table 15.1: Changes in the occupational structure of employment in the UK, 1982-2002

Occupation	per cent of total employment		
	1982	1992	2002
Managers and senior officials	10.7	12.6	14.9
Professional	8.0	9.4	11.3
Associate professional & technical	9.6	11.3	14.0
'Higher occupations'	**28.3**	**33.3**	**40.2**
Admin/clerical/secretarial	15.5	15.8	13.2
Skilled trades	17.0	14.6	11.4
'Intermediate occupations'	**32.5**	**30.4**	**24.6**
Personal services	3.7	4.9	7.3
Sales/customer services	6.1	6.7	7.9
Transport and machine operatives	11.8	9.7	8.4
Elementary occupations	17.7	15.0	11.6
'Lower occupations'	**39.3**	**36.3**	**35.2**

Source: Wilson *et al* (2004), SOC (2000)

In terms of the impact of these changes on people's life chances over the generations, the sons and daughters of clerical and skilled manual workers appear to be going off to higher education to fill the growing ranks of those at the top end of the labour market. The continuing worries relate to the bottom end of the labour market and the changes in the skills required and the attractiveness of jobs in the personal services compared with less skilled manual jobs. There is, however, one puzzle to resolve; this polarisation in the labour market was associated with widening wage inequality in the 1980s and early 1990s, but the same broad pattern of polarisation continued through the rest of the 1990s when the growth in wage inequality slowed down significantly.

Clearly, the trends in wage inequality are of critical importance to debates on social justice. There are a number of data sources to draw on with different strengths and weaknesses, but Figure 15.4 below uses data on hourly wages from the New Earnings Survey, focusing on the trends for women, though the trends for men are not wholly dissimilar (Machin, 2003). Wage inequality in the UK labour market rose sharply from the late 1970s to the early 1990s. However, since the mid-1990s this growth has been much tempered. Data from the Labour Force Survey also shows a great deal of stability between 1996 and 2001 in the wage premiums attached to the holding of particular qualifications following a period in the 1980s when the better qualified pulled ahead in terms of their wages (Sianesi, 2003). These trends mirror those discussed in Chapter 2 showing no significant movement in the distribution of original or market household income since the mid-1990s.

Figure 15.4. Changes to overall female wage inequality, Gini coefficients,[2] 1975–2001

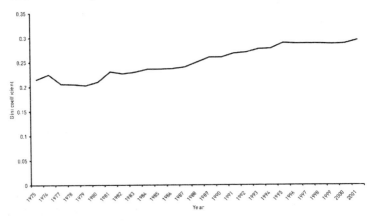

Source: ONS (2004c) New Earnings Survey (NES)

---

2 The Gini coefficient is a number between 0 and 1 , where 0 means perfect equality and 1 means perfect inequality (that is, one person has everything and no one else has anything).

It is worth emphasising these contrasts between the experience of the 1990s and the 1980s. Much comment on the labour market – including that contained in the 1994 Commission on Social Justice – has a decidedly Trotskyist feel to it, asserting that the labour market is in the grip of some form of permanent revolution. In part this is based on false notions of what the labour market was supposed to have looked like in the post-war period when female labour force participation and part-time employment were already rising rapidly and most people did not have access to jobs for life.

The break in trend from the early 1990s – that is the steady improvement in employment and the slowing down of the growth in wage inequality – poses a real challenge to labour market analysts. The adverse trends in wage inequality from the late 1970s to the early 1990s were put down to a range of interwoven factors: the shock of two sharp recessions in the early 1980s and early 1990s; the shift in demand away from the less skilled as a result of technological change and greater international competition; institutional changes, including the decline of the trade unions and collective bargaining, the end of incomes policies and the phasing out of minimum wage protection; and, at the risk of sounding like a soft sociologist, attitudinal changes that made very high pay awards at the top end of the labour market more acceptable and supported the institutional changes that undermined wages at the bottom end.

By the time of the 1994 Commission on Social Justice there was no wholly convincing or complete explanation of the trends towards more unequal rewards in the labour market. Unfortunately, this uncertainty was not reflected in the Commission's report. The fact that no one predicted the break in trend from about that point on and that indeed the existence of that break in trend is only just being fully recognised should humble us further.

Looking back at the factors listed above, the first obvious puzzle is why continuous technological change and further globalisation have been associated with one set of outcomes for market inequality in the 1980s and a different set from the mid-1990s. The avoidance of further catastrophic shocks to employment after the early 1990s recession must count for something. The decline in coverage of the unions and collective bargaining in the UK slowed down from the mid-1990s, but on the other hand, the wage premium that results from trade union membership still appears to have declined over the 1990s and especially for the less well qualified. We now have a national minimum wage, but the change in trend pre-dates its introduction and it is set at too modest a level to make much of a contribution. Sharp improvements in educational attainment have gradually fed through to improve the stock of qualifications in the labour market and this must help explain some of the change in trend. However, it is not obvious that attitudes have changed to render further increases in inequality somehow less acceptable. In short, we still do not have a wholly convincing or complete explanation of these trends. Of course, this makes public policy-making all the more difficult.

Reducing unemployment and inactivity

A great deal had been learned before 1997 about the kinds of interventions that appeared to be most cost-effective in helping the workless to move into employment. Drawing on UK experience and some lessons from the US and Scandinavia, the emphasis has been on creating a unified employment and benefit service for the working-age population. At the heart of Jobcentre Plus is the model of the personal adviser helping individuals to search more effectively for work and offering incentives and removing barriers to help ease the path into employment – very consciously a work-first model. It should be stressed that evaluations of the effectiveness of different active labour market programmes available at the time would have pushed policy in this direction (Robinson, 2000).

Although the original headline target group for the New Deal was the young long-term unemployed, the Government had, by 2000, moved clearly towards targeting key groups suffering not just from high unemployment, but from high levels of economic inactivity. A rising economic tide tends to lift most boats, so the steady economic recovery from the early 1990s would have been expected to raise employment rates even for these relatively excluded groups. Figure 15.5 below shows employment rates for the over 50s and for lone parents rising steadily from 1993 and at a faster rate than the overall rate, so that the gap between the employment rates of these groups and the overall employment rate has narrowed. A shorter but consistent time series for people with disabilities shows their employment rate rising since 1998 and also at a faster rate than the overall rate. However, more people are identifying themselves as having a disability so the overall size of this excluded group continues to pose concerns (Stanley and Regan, 2003). The employment rate for ethnic minority people has also risen since 1994, but at a pace similar to the overall rate. However, employment rates for the lowest qualified have not recovered, though this partly reflects a compositional effect as this group has gradually got older on average. This makes the point of course that these different groups overlap significantly. Older people with a disability and lacking qualifications, for example, might be expected to face some of the most significant barriers to employment.

Figure 15.5. Employment rates of disadvantaged groups

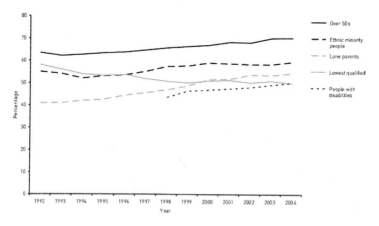

Source: ONS (2004b) Labour Force Survey (LFS)
Note: Data from 1998 for ethnic minority people not comparable with earlier years.

Taking each group separately, people with disabilities and the lowest qualified constitute the largest single categories with worklessness amongst both groups very strongly concentrated regionally (Adams *et al*, 2003). An overall employment rate in excess of 75 per cent appears to be required in a labour market to lift the demand for the less skilled (Gregg and Wadsworth, 2003b). This reinforces the concern that the spatial dimension of employment is largely neglected by current policy. Issues relating to gender are also rather hidden within these excluded groups: lone parents are of course disproportionately women; employment rates are especially low for women from some Asian communities; rates of reported disability amongst women of working age are similar to rates amongst men.

To give an indication of the scale of the challenge that remains in tackling unemployment and inactivity, employment rates for all of these excluded groups still lag between 5 and 25 percentage points behind the overall rate. Raising the employment rate of people with disabilities to the overall employment rate would require an increase in employment of 1.8 million, about equivalent to the entire increase in employment from 1997 to 2004. It is worth emphasising this point because in some circles, including for example the DTI, one sometimes hears musing along the lines of 'employment – been there, solved that', with the implication that policy-makers can move onto other agendas relating to productivity or quality of working life. The scale of the challenge is also worth emphasising as background to the strategic choices that still face the Government.

What has been learned from evaluations of the New Deals and the tax and benefit changes introduced to sharpen work incentives? The evaluation literature is voluminous, and summarising it in a paragraph or two is not easy. The combination of the New Deal for lone parents and tax/benefit changes may have increased the employment rate of lone parents by about 5 percentage points or by 80,000 between 1998 and 2002 (Gregg and Harkness, 2003). As the authors emphasise, this was in the context of a programme where participation was voluntary and despite generous increases in benefits for those families where the lone parent is not in employment. They also point out, however, that the remaining population of non-employed lone parents is less skilled and concentrated in rented housing, suggesting further significant gains in employment might be more difficult.

The aggregate impact of the flagship New Deal for young people has been to raise employment amongst the target group by about 17,000 a year, though the impact may be bigger if the programme has reduced wage pressure by turning unemployed outsiders into insiders (Blundell *et al,* 2003). As the authors emphasise, this impact does not amount to a dramatic transformation of the youth labour market, though given the modest gross costs of the scheme, it offers reasonably good value for money. The New Deal for the Over Fifties has not been evaluated in the same rigorous fashion, but has probably played little role in the significant increase in employment that has taken place for this group (Disney and Hawkes, 2003).

Overall then, the Government's active labour market policies and its tax and benefit changes have made a contribution to reducing unemployment and increasing employment for the target groups and in the overall labour market. Contrary to Government propaganda, the scale of the effects is to be measured in the tens of thousands rather than the hundreds of thousands but, in contrast to opposition propaganda, these policies have definitely not been a waste of resources.

In terms of going forward, as already indicated, the scale of the challenge remains significant. In this context the observation that the

Jobcentre Plus network, first launched in October 2001, will not be fully in place until 2006 is germane. It is a useful rule of thumb that if policy-makers advocate significant administrative changes as a necessary component of any policy, they should factor in half a decade for those changes to bed down. The staff in jobcentres are having to concentrate more and more of their attention on inactive groups that have not tradi-tionally been the main clients for their services, focusing attention on the balance of skills and staffing within the agency. In many ways Jobcentre Plus exemplifies the challenges facing the public services, of how to offer more personalised services and the workforce implications this involves, how to make funding more sensitive to variations in need across the country, and how to reconcile local managerial autonomy with the need to meet national targets.

The approach of Jobcentre Plus so far has been primarily based on the work-first model, with limited attempts to build up participants' 'human capital'. Given that this approach was based in part on the experience of US programmes, a comprehensive review of the impact of US welfare-to-work programmes published in 2004 is salutary (Greenberg *et al*, 2004). This found that the positive impact of such programmes could persist for up to five to six years, but that the impact of the work-first approach was much greater than the human capital approach even after this period of time. The UK Government does appear to have been 'doing what works' based on the evaluation evidence available in 1997 and in 2004. The impact of training programmes emphasising the human capital approach in the UK is discussed below.

Improving retention and progression
The perceived lack of attention to helping people secure jobs that may last for a reasonable period of time and helping people to progress to better positions in the labour market will remain a persistent criticism of current policy. Policy-makers in 1997 were aware of the problem of a substantial minority of the British workforce – around 5 to 10 per cent – who spent their entire lives in a cycle of disadvantage moving between low paid jobs, often with spells of unemployment and inactivity in between (Meadows, 1999). These repeated returns to benefit were known to have 'scarring effects' on individuals' future employment prospects. The problem was that, unlike the experience with active labour market policies that the New Deals might build on, the evidence on what worked in improving retention and progression was sparse.

Post-employment support services can build on the services already offered to participants in existing employment programmes, effectively offering a follow-up service to help people keep the jobs the employment services have helped them secure and also perhaps to progress to better jobs. They can also target people already in low paid employment. These services can offer help with childcare, transport or specific financial incentives to keep people in work. They can also offer training programmes designed to enhance participants' human capital to help them gain a better job. At the heart of such interventions is the same personal adviser model that has been at the centre of existing employment programmes, the idea being of course that the same adviser can continue to maintain contact with those they have placed in work.

There are examples of post-employment services in North America that have been evaluated, but not often in the same rigorous fashion as mainstream employment programmes (Kellard *et al*, 2002). The evaluation evidence suggests that financial incentives may improve job retention rates at least in the short-run, with limited, less robust evidence that assistance with transport, employer-provided childcare, financial assistance to help deal with domestic emergencies, job coaching,mentoring programmes and skills training may also help. A key pointer as to why such programmes might face difficulties lies in the observation that personal advisers are often overwhelmed by their caseload and that the pressure to help those clients still looking for a job limits the time and resources available for post-employment support.

The response of the UK Government has been to launch an ambitious Employment Retention and Advancement (ERA) Demonstration project that will be evaluated using the rigorous random assignment methods characteristic of the best US evaluations. It is targeted at those eligible for the New Deal for the Over Twenty-fives and those volunteering for the New Deal for Lone Parents, as well as lone parents on Working Tax Credit (WTC) working part-time in low-paid jobs. For these two New Deal groups, help will start before they enter employment; for the WTC group after they have started working. There will be one-to-one support for each participant from a dedicated Advancement Support Adviser for up to two years after someone has entered employment, with financial incentives to encourage retention in full-time work and to support approved education or training. Quite consciously, the ERA Demonstration is being piloted with up to 27,000 individuals and with no plans at the outset to roll it out on a national scale before the results of the evaluation are known, which will be from about 2006/7 onwards. Indeed, for a government notorious for announcing every single initiative many times over, the almost subliminal status of this initiative is striking.

If this really is the ultimate demonstration of evidence-based policy-making, the Government has effectively given itself most of the period of a third term in office to see whether such post-employment services are effective, before any attempt to roll them out. This may be based on a conscious calculation that Jobcentre Plus will in the meantime have its hands full with reducing inactivity amongst the key target groups. Faced with the strategic choice of using the limited capacity of the employment services to deal with either inactivity on the one hand or retention and progression on the other, the Government has prioritised the former.

The evidence base on the effectiveness of training programmes for the adult workless may or may not have influenced this decision. Of the three types of training offered under the Work-Based Learning for Adults (WBLA) programme, one had no impact on employment, a second accelerated entry into work but had no long-term effects on employment, and the third significantly increased the chances of working 30 hours or more (Anderson *et al,* 2004). None of the types of training had any impact on wages, suggesting no enhancement of human capital. These conclusions mirror the results of a set of disappointing evaluations of such training programmes going back to the 1980s (Robinson, 2000). We have some idea then of what appears not to work and the results of these UK evaluations are no more favourable to the human capital approach than the US evaluations.

One of the Government's key flagship skills initiatives, the Employer Training Pilots (ETPs), offer incentives for workplace-based training aimed at getting participants their first Level Two qualification, seen as the minimum level necessary for people to be able to make some progression in the labour market. Initial evaluation suggests good take-up but with a heavy concentration in certain sectors and especially the care sector (Hillage and Mitchell, 2003). However, take-up is only a preliminary indication of programme success. The qualifications attained and most importantly the progression made in the labour market as measured by earnings will be the key indicators of success. Participants are almost all working towards Level Two NVQs, which is a little worrying as research has suggested these qualifications have at best no impact on earnings and may even have a negative impact. However, the most recent research suggests that for women working in the health and social care sector, obtaining a Level Two NVQ does yield a significantly higher wage (Dearden *et al*, 2004). This makes the important point that the type of qualification attained by participants on training programmes matters as does the role played by those qualifications in particular sectors of the economy. Not all qualifications are the same in terms of their purchase in the labour market. It will be interesting to see if the ETPs prove to be an example of evidence-based policy-making or whether they are extended nationwide before we know much about their impact on participants' earnings.

Fairer outcomes

The successful introduction of the national minimum wage (at a relatively modest level) was one of the significant early achievements of the Government, not least because employers were brought around to support its introduction. Its value relative to average earnings has been increased modestly since its introduction and its coverage is to be extended to sixteen and seventeen year olds. And importantly, employers remain on board, even if parts of the labour movement and some other observers believe the Government remains too cautious. The other pressure requiring this Government to act, in much the same way as the previous Government, comes from the need to meet EU Directives relating to employment rights, especially in relation to working time and in relation to countering discrimination.

The Government therefore faces three sets of pressures: from employers, the labour movement and the EU. To a significant extent its approach to employment regulation reflects how it balances those pressures. There has been some loose talk about renewed forms of 'social partnership'. At a practical level this has involved some useful, modest, initiatives such as the Union Learning Fund. However, there can be no pretence that what is envisaged is anything along the lines of Northern European forms of partnership. More cynically it might be viewed as a strategy of 'wine and canapés' to replace 'beer and sandwiches' as a device for squaring competing political interests.

If the Government has a strategy to secure fairer outcomes then it relies on many of the same instruments designed to reduce unemployment and inactivity: benefits, tax credits and the minimum wage to sharpen incentives and reduce in-work poverty; measures to tackle discrimination; and education and training to improve human capital. As already discussed, the term 'fairer outcomes' does not encompass an explicit objective of tackling overall wage inequality or the gender wage gap, other than through the contribution made by the policy instruments discussed above. If the comparatively high levels of wage inequality and the large gender pay gap in the UK are in some large part a function of institutional factors including relatively low levels of unionisation and collective bargaining, it is definitely not part of the Government's agenda to borrow this aspect of the Scandinavian model.

Quality of working life

A random sample of the speeches, seminars or publications of the policy-making establishment might lead one to believe that excessive working hours, childcare costs and general unhappiness amongst the professional classes were some of the most pressing problems facing the UK. Clearly the Government believes that quality of working life issues are bound to rise up the political agenda in the context of a broadly affluent population in a labour market closer to full employment. The challenge for progressives is to balance this set of issues against the unresolved problems of high levels of economic inactivity, poor opportunities for progression at the lower end of the labour market and continued inequality.

One obvious way forward for those committed to social justice is to view quality of working life issues from the point of view of those at the lower end of the labour market. This could help us to think through our priorities in relation, for example, to the issue of employees not working the hours they would like. In autumn 2001, almost three million workers would have accepted less pay to be able to work fewer hours with 2.4 million workers wanting to work longer hours. If everyone had been working the hours they wanted, the total volume of hours worked would have been little altered (Simic, 2002a; Simic, 2002b). The contrast between the two groups lies in their distribution; over-employment disproportionately affects managerial and professional workers and the well paid while under-employment disproportionately affects the lowest occupational groups and the lowest paid. Policy debates on the other hand, even among progressives, seem to concentrate on the former group.

This is one in a series of issues where there appears to be a need for a significant rebalancing of policy debate. Others include whether we spend too much time worrying about childcare issues and not enough time worrying about working adults caring for their spouses or other disabled or elderly relatives. In the early years and childcare debates it is often unclear whether the key policy outcome being pursued is the better development of children or higher (female) labour force participation rates. In contrast to the policy deliberations around unemployment and inactivity, the poor quality of evidence-based thinking in this area is striking. This seems to be the reason why there is so little discussion of whether the modest downward trend in working hours in evidence since around 1997–98 might signal a reversion back to traditional post-war trends. Another interesting issue is why the trend to greater work intensity over the 1980s and 1990s appeared to level off between 1997 and 2001 (Green, 2003).

Conclusion

A commitment to social justice should always lead policy-makers to focus on those excluded from the labour market and those at the lower end of the labour market. However, the passion or anger that continuing exclusion and inequality should engender needs to be balanced by a dispassionate assessment of the effectiveness of different policy instruments. One key observation for progressives to mull over is that there will always be some jobs at the lower end of the labour market that demand modest skills and offer lower pay and limited progression. Jobs in the care sector are not going to be displaced anytime soon by technology or foreign competition (though migrants might fill some of them).

There are two key research challenges. First, to understand better the trends in wage inequality and that break in trend in the early 1990s. Second, to understand what combination of policy instruments will help bring about a significant reduction in inactivity, especially amongst those with disabilities. What might have worked for the unemployed or lone parents may not work so well for the disabled. Current initiatives such as the pathways to work pilots may give us some further clues, but again the evaluations of these pilots will not become available until around 2006.

The Government faces four key policy challenges in employment policy now it has secured a third term.

1. It has already made the choice to give priority to tackling inactivity rather than promoting retention and/or progression. This is the right choice, given limitations on the capacity of Jobcentre Plus and the

scale of the problem of inactivity, but the challenge, referred to above, of finding out what works, is acute.

2. Further reductions in relative poverty, in-work and out-of-work, will continue to prove expensive, whatever combination of policy instruments is chosen. The Government may be a little less cautious in pushing up the minimum wage, but tax credits and benefits will remain the main instrument for improving incomes and sharpening incentives. However, after 2005–06, the rate of growth in public spending will fall significantly outside of health (and international development). The Chancellor has previously found the extra resources for increases in credits and benefits at the time of each Budget and Pre-Budget report, but the scope for such pragmatism will be limited in a harsher fiscal environment.

3. Those who advocate more of a human capital approach need to be clear about what skills/qualifications they think will give participants greater purchase in the labour market. The current emphasis in policy on securing Level Two NVQs is very problematic. There is a fundamental difference between a system driven by the choices of individual adults, with those choices supported by adequate funding, and a system driven by planning bodies with funding going via the employer, which discussion about a vague 'New Deal for Skills' completely fails to address.

4. The Government's political capital with employers will need to be used up in advancing further leave entitlements for parents and carers of adults after 2006, which means avoiding conflict in other areas. This will leave the Government subject to criticism from the unions that it is not doing enough to compel employers in other areas such as training.

The past decade has seen significant improvements in labour market outcomes, but in the next decade we will need to see further inroads into inactivity and poverty if the goals of social justice are to be further advanced.

References

Adams J, Robinson P and Vigor A (2003) *A new regional policy for the UK* London: ippr

Anderson T, Dorsett R, Hales J, Lissenburgh S, Pires C and Smeaton D (2004) *Work-based learning for adults: an evaluation of labour market effects* London: TSO

Blundell R, Reed H, Van Reenen J and Shephard A (2003) 'The impact of the new deal on the labour market: a four-year assessment' in Dickens R, Gregg P and Wadsworth J (eds) *The labour market under new labour* Basingstoke: Palgrave Macmillan.

Commission on Social Justice (CSJ) (1994) *Social Justice: strategies for national renewal* London: ippr

Dearden L, McGranahan L and Sianesi B (2004) *An in-depth analysis of the returns to national vocational qualifications obtained at level 2* London: Centre for the Economics of Education

Department for Work and Pensions (DWP) (2004) *Building on New Deal: Local solutions meeting
individual needs* London: TSO

Department for Work and Pensions and Office for National Statistics (2004) *Households below average
income, 1994/95 – 2002/03* London: TSO

Disney R and Hawkes D (2003) 'Why has employment recently risen among older workers in
Britain?' in Dickens R, Gregg P and Wadsworth J (eds) *The labour market under new labour*
Basingstoke: Palgrave Macmillan

Di Tella R, MacCulloch R J and Oswald A J (2002) 'The Macroeconomics of Happiness' *Centre for Economic
Performance/Oxford University Discussion Paper* London: Centre for Economic Performance (CEP)

Edwards L and Burkitt N (2001) 'Wanting more from work? Aspirations and expectations of work' in
Burkitt N (ed) *A life's work: Achieving full and fulfilling employment* London: ippr

Green F (2003) 'The demands of work' in Dickens R, Gregg P and Wadsworth J (eds) *The labour
market under new labour* Basingstoke: Palgrave Macmillan

Greenberg D, Ashworth K, Cebulla A and Walker R (2004), 'Do welfare to work programmes work
for long' *Fiscal Studies* 25 (1), London: Institute for Fiscal Studies

Gregg P and Harkness S (2003) 'Welfare reform and the employment of lone parents' in Dickens R,
Gregg P and Wadsworth J (eds) *The labour market under new labour* Basingstoke: Palgrave Macmillan

Gregg P and Wadsworth J (2003a) 'Workless households and the recovery' in Dickens R, Gregg P and
Wadsworth J (eds) *The labour market under new labour* Basingstoke: Palgrave Macmillan

Gregg P and Wadsworth J (2003b) 'Labour market prospects of less skilled workers over the recovery'
in Dickens R, Gregg P and Wadsworth J (eds) *The labour market under new labour* Basingstoke:
Palgrave Macmillan

Hillage J and Mitchell H (2003) *Employer training pilots: first year evaluation report* London: Institute
for Employment Studies

Kellard K, Adelman L, Cebulla A and Heaver C (2002) *From job seekers to job keepers: job retention,
advancement and the role of in-work support programmes* Loughborough: Loughborough University
Centre for Research on Social Policy

Machin S (2003) 'Wage inequality since 1975' in Dickens R, Gregg P and Wadsworth J (eds) *The
labour market under new labour* Basingstoke: Palgrave Macmillan

Meadows P (1999) *The flexible labour market: implications for pension provision* London: National
Association of Pension Funds

Mulgan G (2000) 'Full employment: the UK' in Muet P A, Pisani-Ferry J, Mulgan G and Layard R
(eds) *Achieving full employment* London: Policy Network

Office of National Statistics (ONS) (2003) *Labour Market Trends* (111) 9, London: ONS

Office of National Statistics (ONS) (2004a) *Labour Market Trends* (112) 9, London: ONS

Office of National Statistics (ONS) (2004b) *Labour Force Survey* London: TSO

Office of National Statistics (ONS) (2004c) *New Earnings Survey* London: TSO

Robinson P (2000) 'Active labour market policies: a case of evidence based policy making?' *Oxford
Review of Economic Policy* 16 (1) Oxford: Oxford University Press

Sianesi B (2003) 'Returns to education: a non-technical summary of CEE work and policy discussion'
London: Institute for Fiscal Studies (IFS) and Centre for the Economics of Education (CEE)

Simic M (2002a) 'Underemployment and overemployment in the UK' *Labour Market Trends* 110 (8) ,
London: ONS

Simic M (2002b) ''Volume of underemployment and overemployment in the UK' *Labour Market
Trends* 110 (10), London: ONS

Stanley K and Regan S (2003) *The missing million: supporting disabled people into work* London: ippr

Wilson R, Homenidov K and Dickerson A (2004) *Working Futures: New Projections of Employment by
Sector and Region: Volume 1, National Report* London SSDA

Foundations for a Progressive Century

Will Paxton, Nick Pearce and Howard Reed

The social justice gap

Progressives should be optimistic about the ability of politics and public policy to improve Britain. It is one of the great successes of the current Government that public action is now seen as a part of the solution to social injustice, in stark contrast to the prevailing view at the time of the original Commission on Social Justice report in 1994, when the state was too often seen as part of the problem. After two terms of Labour Government, Britain is well placed to make continued progress towards a socially just society. Fundamental to this is Britain's evolving 'Anglo-social' welfare state, which combines an economic framework designed to encourage stability, flexibility, entrepreneurship and improvements to our skills base with a social framework of strong support for universal public services and a redistributive tax and benefit system.

However, a significant social justice gap still remains. Some of the earlier chapters of this book revisit themes central to the original report including lifelong learning, work and the labour market, taxation and the future of the welfare state and communities and citizenship. Others have addressed issues which were largely absent from social justice discourse at that time. In particular, we need to respond coherently to increased migration and to clarify Britain's obligations in seeking global justice. At the same time the relationship between social justice and other goals valuable to progressives, such as democracy and environmental sustainability, needs clarifying. Taken as a whole, this book is a starting point for explaining how a progressive 21st century can be forged.

This final chapter returns us to the central theme of building a fairer Britain by mapping out a practical but ambitious strategy to achieve social justice in the key areas of domestic economic and social policy. The chapter is divided into two sections. In the first we identify three social justice priorities for Britain. These are as follows:

1. Developing a high quality and affordable system of early years education and child care.
2. Increasing the skills of all adults and the opportunities for progression within the labour market.
3. Continuing the fight against poverty by ensuring security in retirement and reducing child poverty further.

Mapped onto Miller's four principles of social justice discussed in Chapter 1, the first two priorities are primarily about equality of opportunity and fairness in outcomes, while the third can be understood as part of developing the social minimum.

The second section asks how much bridging the social justice gap might cost. While to an extent our priorities can be achieved by changing current policies and spending existing revenue differently, to bridge the social justice gap will require an overall increase in public spending. In the second section we discuss the demands on public finances in the period covered by the Government's most recent spending review and Budget Statements (up to 2007/8) and present options for modest tax rises that could be implemented in the first part of Labour's third term. We then examine the longer-term pressures on public spending and suggest more radical reforms to the tax system which can achieve a progressive and fair tax settlement, and how this package might be sold to the electorate.

Care and life chances

Why early years care is a priority: labour market changes and child development
In Chapter 3, Pearce and Dixon detailed the growing pressures placed on all welfare states as a result of what has been described as a 'crisis of care' (Daly, 2002). Recent decades have seen far-reaching social and economic changes. On the one hand, prevailing family structures in Britain have been changing, with increased rates of divorce and larger numbers of lone parents and cohabiting couples than in previous decades. At the same time, the number of women in employment has increased dramatically, with profound impacts on the labour market.

The trend of increased female employment looks set to continue. This is for a number of reasons. Increasing rates have been actively encouraged by government, and active welfare policies in the UK that do not discriminate between women and men and increased female employ-

reducing the number of single and zero-earner households – will need to be an important element of any future anti-poverty strategy (Brewer, 2005). Furthermore, while balancing work and care responsibilities is difficult for women – time-use surveys show that men have only increased their contribution to the unpaid work of care and household labour to a small extent (Gershuny, 2000) – as Chapter 3 pointed out, there is demand amongst women for even higher levels of labour market participation (Crompton *et al,* 2004).

Some have argued that because of the fundamental social and economic trends which developed countries have experienced, the (non) availability of early years care has effectively become a 'new social risk' to which welfare states must respond (Bonoli, 2005; Taylor-Gooby, 2004). With women less likely to be able and willing to provide the requisite informal care for children and other relatives, and men in the family unable or unwilling to redefine their traditional roles to include greater caring responsibilities, the state will face growing economic and political demands for extending provision.

At the same time as increased female employment rates place additional pressure and demands on modern welfare states, evidence is mounting that it is the early years – usually taken to refer to the first five or six years of a child's life – which are of overriding importance in influencing later life outcomes. These years are crucial in breaking, or at least mitigating, the links that currently exist between the position of a child's family of origin and his or her eventual life position (Esping-Andersen, 2005). Chapters 2 and 13 detailed some of the evidence in this field. A recent summary of the literature summed up the findings well when it stated that:

> *It is widely agreed that the early years are a particularly important time for efforts to increase social mobility, because a good deal of inequality is already apparent by the time children start school, and because children's development may be less amenable to change after they enter school.* (Waldfogel, 2005)

Evidence suggests that the most important factors driving unequal child development are variations in levels of parental interest among different families, and other aspects of children's home environments. The Sure Start programme, which aims to focus on a wider range of interventions in addition to childcare and early years education (for example, health and emotional development, and parental relationship counselling), attempts to provide a more holistic package of support for children in particularly disadvantaged circumstances. However, across society as a whole it would be very hard – and prohibitively expensive – for government to influence parental interest and the home environment directly. Instead it is in the development of preschool education and non-parental care where the state can make the most practical difference and has the most potential to reduce the development of inequalities so early in people's lives (ibid).

There are three reasons why tackling the early years care crisis is a social justice priority:

1. The need to respond to recent labour-market changes in a progressive way, in particular by enabling women to re-enter the labour market after having children.
2. The need to promote child development, with a particular emphasis on breaking the link between parental background, child development and later life outcomes.
3. The need to promote gender equity, in reducing discrimination in the labour market and barriers to women's labour market progression, where these exist.

In the next section, we examine whether there are trade-offs and tensions between these three objectives.

Key policy objectives

The scale of any trade-off between child development, mothers' employment and gender equity should not be overstated; it is possible to develop policies which help meet all three. Good evidence for this comes from Scandinavia, where childcare policy has been credited with helping to break the link between parental social class and income and children's outcomes, while at the same time allowing greater choice for parents, especially mothers. Without high-quality childcare, children from low-income households may be doubly disadvantaged. They are more likely to live in poverty if their parents cannot work – which may reduce the resources available for children in the home – and at the same time they will not receive forms of childcare which can prepare them for school and improve cognitive development.

Internationally, countries with high levels of social protection, good state childcare provision and flexible working allowances tend also to have the highest female participation rates, while those with low social protection where a significant responsibility for care is taken up by women have much lower rates on average. The exception is the US, which has high levels of female participation in the labour force but very low levels of state provision of childcare. The drawbacks with the US system are that many children attend unregistered day-care and that a larger proportion of women work in low-wage jobs which offer greater flexibility. We argue that Sweden represents a better model for the future of the UK childcare market than does the US. Moving closer to the Swedish system of provision would enable the Government to respond to changes in the labour market, promote more equal child development, and give women better choices about the type of work they want to do.

There are also good economic grounds for an expansion of state intervention in the childcare market. Economic efficiency is increased if childcare makes children better able to benefit from subsequent education, and if increased availability of childcare means parents have the opportunity to spend more time in work, should they wish to do so. In addition, parents may be poorly informed about the long-term benefits to their children of high-quality pre-school care and so may 'under-invest' in childcare if provision is left to the market (Sylva *et al*, 2004). Universal childcare provision also enhances equity, in that high-quality pre-school education can be made available to all children, regardless of parental income. There is also strong evidence that supporting child development in the early years can improve children's economic prospects at lower cost than intervening when the children are older (Carneiro and Heckman, 2003).

However, this does not mean that trade-offs between responding to labour market change and promoting child development are totally absent. At the extreme, labour market participation would be best supported by services that are open 24 hours a day, seven days a week, but these would not be in the best interests of children. Recent policy in the UK has placed the objective of labour market participation and the associated gains in household income above the objective of enhancing child development. The current system of tax credits is weighted in terms of encouraging full-time work, even though research suggests that in the early years of a child's life, spending long hours in institutional childcare provision is not the best environment to enhance children's development

(Belsky and Fearon, 2002; Chatterji and Markowitz, 2004; Tanaka, 2005).

There may also be important implications of the childcare system for the status of women in the labour market. Higher levels of provision of good quality public services for the care of children, and cash transfers in respect of parental leave, could mean that higher proportions of women are able to work, which would mean that the gap between women's overall employment rate and that of men may narrow further. However, if the women entering work do so predominantly in low-paid jobs at part-time hours and in the service sector, then overall the impact may be to increase, rather than reduce, the gender pay gap. Once again evidence from Sweden is informative here. In Sweden, the labour market is one of the most gender segregated in the western world, with most women working in the public sector. Swedish women have more choice about combining work and care, but at the expense of low levels of participation in some parts of the economy. To the extent that gender segregation of occupations increases the probability of discrimination against women in pay and conditions, and makes progression through the labour market more difficult for women, policy should seek to avoid it where possible.

We believe that policy-makers should place the life chances of children, and the contribution that early years support can make to breaking the link between parental income, social class and children's life outcomes, at the centre of their pursuit of social justice. At the same time, securing equity between men and women in their work and home lives, and providing more labour market opportunities for mothers, are also vital objectives which should drive policy wherever possible. Below we discuss how the existing system of state support for childcare and early years provision can be improved to secure all three of our objectives.

Four problems with the existing system

The existing system of childcare and early years education has four considerable drawbacks: poor quality, inadequate supply, a lack of affordability and limited flexibility. All these will need addressing as part of any reform package.

Quality is perhaps the most fundamental problem. There are isolated examples of very good provision and there have been some improvements since 1997, but generally quality remains poor (NAO, 2004), although a survey by Ofsted in 2005 showed improvements during 2004. The UK has developed childcare 'on the cheap', characterised by poor levels of pay for staff and low levels of training. Minimal qualifications are required to work in childcare and workers earn an average of £5 an hour – less than the average for supermarket workers, for example. As a result, many working in the sector are untrained and very young. This compares poorly with most other developed countries, particularly the Scandinavian countries, where early years workers study for a three-and-a-half year degree. Recent years have witnessed some progress in introducing quality assurance mechanisms for providers themselves; yet even now, fewer than 40 per cent of providers are accredited to one of the 67 quality assurance schemes currently in operation in the sector.

The supply of childcare and early years education places, though it has increased recently, still lags far behind levels which could be considered optimal. At present there is only one formal childcare place, delivered by a registered provider, for every four children (NAO, 2004). Though more than half of parents of pre-school children in 2003 now use some form of formal childcare or early education regularly (largely as a result of an increase in the availability of part-time nursery education which is now a near-universal experience for three and four year olds), in 2002, 30 per cent were still not using any form of formal childcare (NAO, 2004). Many parents still rely on informal care from relatives. Despite a government focus on deprived areas and a narrowing of the gap, it remains true that there is less early years provision in the 20 per cent most deprived wards in England than in other areas (NAO, 2004). Additionally, particular groups are less likely to use registered childcare, including parents on low incomes, parents who work atypical hours, parents of disabled children and parents from some ethnic minority groups such as Bangladeshi parents (Dex, 2003). This is largely because of difficulties in accessing care (although in the case of ethnic minority parents this may be the result of prevailing cultural practices).

Price remains a considerable barrier for many people (NAO, 2004). The most recent Daycare Trust childcare survey, at the end of 2004, found that the average increase in the cost to parents of nursery places was 5.2 per cent per annum – over three times the rate of inflation. This leaves the typical cost of a nursery place for a child under the age of two years at £141 a week, up from £134 last year. For a child aged over two years, the typical cost in England is £132, a 7.3 per cent rise from £123 last year. London and the South East have faired particularly badly with inner London boroughs seeing nursery place costs soar by more than 17 per cent (Daycare Trust, 2005).

Flexibility – the ability of parents to choose according to their different circumstances and demands – is also limited under the current system. In the first two to three years of a child's life there is a need for a more flexible package of support for parents, to give them a better set of choices. Not all families want to use centre-based care for children under the age of three and, for some children, less intensive forms of provision might be more suitable, particularly during the period between their first and second birthday. Parents may also want greater choice about when to take parental leave. Using it all in the first year of a child's life may not fit with many families' needs and circumstances.

The policy vision

The Government has already indicated the scale of its ambitions in its ten-year childcare strategy (HMT, 2004a) and there is a growing consensus that we should move towards a high-quality and affordable system of childcare and early years education. But what should the details of the policy be? Below, four elements of reform are suggested.

Extended parental leave

The evidence suggests that there is a positive relationship between parental leave and children's outcomes. Where both parents return to work within the first year of their child's life, there is some evidence of negative effects on both behaviour and cognitive development, particularly if mothers work full-time and the childcare available is of low quality (Gregg *et al*, forthcoming; Tanaka, forthcoming; Ruhm, 2000). The immediate policy objective should be that all parents can choose to take paid leave when their infants are aged up to twelve months. In time, parents could be offered greater choice between continued leave and use of affordable high-quality care after their youngest child turns one year old. This could be achieved by allowing a further six months paid leave when children are at any age between one and five.

It is important for parental leave policy to encourage the role of fathers as carers, as well as mothers. So long as the division of labour in the domestic sphere is so unequal, women will be entering the public sphere of the economy and politics with one hand tied behind their back. In the words of Taylor-Gooby in Chapter 5, women face a 'double bind'. At the same time, fathers taking paternity leave can improve future relationships with their children, something which in turn can be good for child development. Ideally Britain should move towards what Nancy Fraser has described as a 'universal caregiver' model in which men increasingly combine obligations and responsibilities for paid work and care (Fraser, 1997).

Ultimately this will require cultural change, but public policy can help. In Norway in 1992, only 2.3 per cent of fathers took up their right to paid paternity leave, so in 1993 a 'use it or lose it' quota was introduced. Most of the 52 weeks of parental leave is transferable between the father and mother. However, four weeks are allocated specifically to fathers and nine weeks specifically to mothers. This means that if fathers do not use their right to four weeks leave, that allocation is lost. After the Norwegian reform, the proportion of fathers taking paternity leave rose to 45 per cent in 1994 and 80 per cent in 1998 (Brandth and Kvande, 2001).

Unfortunately, recent policy changes in the UK appear to have been less successful. Only approximately one in five new fathers has taken advantage of the right to two weeks paid paternity leave, which was introduced in April 2003. One option is to consider something along the lines of the Norwegian scheme of 'use it or lose it' paternity leave. Allocating four weeks specifically to fathers along these lines would be a positive start. It should also be possible for all but nine weeks of the paid maternity leave to be transferable to fathers from mothers.

Improved quality of childcare

It is crucial to increase the quality of care if maternal employment is not to have adverse effects on child development and the incidence of anti-social behaviour. Research suggests that if mothers with children between one and two work there is no necessary impact on their child's development, but if only low-quality care is available then there could be negative impacts, especially on behaviour (Brooks-Gunn *et al*, 2002; NICHD Early Childcare Research Network, 2002; Ruhm, 2004). Furthermore, high-quality care can actually have beneficial impacts on cognitive development, while having no corrosive effect on behaviour (Currie, 2001).

Improved regulation and inspection will help, but the most important determinant of the quality of childcare in the long run is the quality of staff running the services. Given the continuing pressures on many areas of public spending, it is tempting for the Government to seek to make changes to the funding of childcare but to continue to seek to contain costs by accepting low quality provision. This would be a huge mistake. The size of the work force must be expanded, and at the same time there must be a significant increase in the number of graduates and higher skilled workers. Improvement in the quality of provision must underpin any other reforms.

An integrated early years service

The system of care provided when children are between the ages of one and five needs to become far better integrated and coherent. Too often, families bear the burden of having to piece together different provision, in different locations. The false divide between 'education' and 'care' needs to end. This means ending the distinction between 'nursery education' and 'wrap-around childcare'; the same standards should apply to both. It also means ending the perceived difference between childcare/education for three and four year olds and childcare for the under threes. The early years are when all kinds of learning takes place: socialisation, behavioural, emotional, as well as cognitive. Early years services need to reflect all these.

While there is some logic in the state funding a 'dosage' of high quality early learning (as it currently does for three and four year olds), if the distinction between education and care is dropped then it would be questionable whether such a policy is appropriate. Indeed, the Government has already announced its intention to extend free part-time care for other age groups. The long-term ambition should be for free part-time provision to be available to all children between the age of two and when they start school. If all parents have non-means-tested access to some element of childcare then public support for expanded provision of services is likely to be greater.

As suggested in Chapter 13, any additional care required beyond part-time hours should be means-tested. Parents could extend part-time provision to full-time if they so chose, but user charges for some on higher incomes would be levied. Even in countries with universal provision, parents contribute towards childcare. In other words, 'universal' provision means services that are available and affordable for all parents, not free at the point of use for all parents.

It is difficult to say the precise level parental contributions to the cost of care should be set at. There is no exact consensus among other countries on the particular percentage that parents should be expected to pay. For example, it has taken Denmark thirty years to reach a stage where parents pay a maximum of 33 per cent of the cost of the service. But the overall thrust that policy should take is clear. The Government should implement a fairer sharing of the costs of childcare between state and parents.

Raise the school starting age

Many of the new services provided will be based around schools, but it is important that early years services are not seen as a downward extension of primary education. Indeed, as Chapter 13 suggests, there may be a case for raising the school starting age to six so that a coherent service can emerge for children aged five and under. This would put the UK in line with most other developed countries. In the Nordic countries the starting age is seven (apart from Norway which recently reduced it to six) and in the US it varies between five and seven (Moss, 2001). An increase would also be consistent with evidence which suggests that five year olds will benefit more from a rounded early years provision than being moved into a formal education setting (Sharpe, 2002; Woodhead, 1989; Schweinhart and Weikart, 1998). It would be valuable to establish a pilot scheme for raising the school starting age, perhaps in a particular regional area, which could then be rigorously evaluated before committing to raising the school starting age on a nationwide basis.

Supply through a government-subsidised mixed market

To date in the UK we have predominantly adopted a market model for both the provision and funding of childcare. The state is only a minor player in delivering childcare services and the UK remains unusual by international standards, even among English-speaking countries, in having a very high proportion, possibly as much as 90 per cent, of provision that is organised on a for-profit basis. Only in recent years has government invested in some services directly in areas of deprivation, for example with Neighbourhood Nurseries, Early Excellence Centres and some of the childcare provision in the Sure Start programme.

Yet outside of this direct spending on provision in deprived areas, current policy has continued to favour using the market – through demand subsidies – to provide the necessary services. The childcare element in the Working Tax Credit is set to remain as the main vehicle through which policy is seeking to stimulate providers of childcare places (HMT, 2004a). While measures like this are effective in channelling resources to low-income parents who would otherwise be unable to afford childcare, they are probably not the best long-term solution. The current market is not delivering high quality, affordable provision for parents and is operating inefficiently and inequitably in some areas. Many groups, including those in rural areas, some minority ethnic groups and people working non-standard or irregular hours, continue not to have their needs met. Furthermore, 16.7 per cent of providers close annually and a proportion of the public money channelled through the childcare tax credit is being 'wasted' because services are subsequently closing down (NAO, 2004). Reliance on demand side measures is not enough to achieve long-term sustainability; payments to providers can be unreliable and there is a danger that providers increase prices in response to any increase in the generosity of tax credits (Daycare Trust, 2004). This is particularly a problem in rural areas where the childcare market is thin with little competition, as well as in areas where the market is dominated by larger-scale childcare providers.

International comparisons show that high-quality, universal provision is difficult to achieve via reliance on a market model of childcare using demand subsidies (OECD, 2001; McQuail *et al*, 2003). There are strong grounds for moving towards an alternative system with more supply-side intervention, where the state block-purchases childcare places from a range of providers and sets the tariff that parents can be charged to ensure that they are affordable. Though a private sector would still exist, a diversity of providers would be desirable to meet the different needs of parents and children; private, cooperative, parent-run, public and voluntary services could exist alongside each other. The proposed duty on local authorities to secure sufficient provision to meet local childcare needs is the obvious route through which to secure this (HMT, 2004a). In this way, early years services could be considered more of a public service. This should be the case even if funding for the service is shared between the state and parents.

The package of reforms that the UK should aspire to includes:

- Extensions of paid leave entitlements to twelve months with a further six months paid flexible parental leave beyond this.
- Policies to encourage fathers to take more leave, including four weeks of 'use it or lose it' paternity leave which cannot be transferred to mothers.
- An integrated early years service with no rigid distinction between education and care.
- Improved quality of care, achieved through more rigorous inspection, but more fundamentally improved training for early years staff.

- Free part-time education/care as an entitlement for all children.
- Means-tested full-time provision.
- Raising the school starting age from five to six.
- Supplying services through a government-subsidised mixed market and moving away from sole reliance on demand-side measures.

It will take time and money to implement this package of reforms. This is a challenge that the British people face over the long term, the direct result of being thirty years behind other countries – in particular Scandinavian countries – where the new social risk represented by care was anticipated. In 2004/5 the UK Government will spend around £6.5 billion or 0.54 per cent of GDP on early years provision (covering maternity pay and the maternity allowance, nursery education for three and four year olds, Sure Start and the Childcare Tax Credit) (Daycare Trust, 2004). By way of contrast, Denmark now spends approximately 2.5 per cent of GDP on early years provision. In Sweden, the cost of an early years place is twice that of a primary school place, such is the level of support that is deemed necessary in the early years. Clearly, moving from the current system of childcare provision to something a lot more like the Danish or Swedish system, as we recommend in this book, is a costly undertaking. The second section of this chapter contains full details of the investment necessary to achieve this new childcare settlement and how we recommend that it be paid for, as far forward as reliable projections can be made.

Employment skills and labour market progression

Social justice cannot just be about equality of opportunity at the starting gates of life. As Miller argues in Chapter 1, we must create 'multiple ladders of opportunity'. This means, first and foremost, recasting education and training policy to create an economy where all children and young adults can fulfil their potential by acquiring valuable skills and qualifications at school, further education, higher education and on entry into work. This needs to be supplemented by effective policies to promote lifelong adult learning. A second requirement is full employment in every region (as argued in Chapters 14 and 15), which will only be achieved through measures to assist inactive disabled people who are capable of work back to the labour market. Third, in response to structural changes in the UK's labour market which have removed many 'stepping stone' jobs which lead from low-skilled employment to higher wages, as discussed in Chapter 3 (Goos and Manning, 2004) the Government needs to turn its attention to policies which will improve people's ability to progress into better paid and more rewarding jobs once they have entered the labour market.

Education and training for fourteen to nineteen year olds

Although participation rates in post-sixteen education and training rose in the late 1980s and early 1990s following the introduction of the GCSE, this growth tailed off after 1994 and participation has now stalled at around 75 per cent of sixteen to nineteen year olds. This is below the OECD average and compares badly with the majority of European Union countries. Social class and ethnicity are still powerful predictors of whether a young person will stay on in education and what qualifications he or she will achieve. Of persistent concern is the large proportion of sixteen to eighteen year olds that does not participate in education, training or employment at all.

Some 16 per cent of sixteen to nineteen year olds were in jobs without training in 2004 (ONS, 2005). Many are in routine unskilled jobs such as food processing or packing. Although the Government has legislated to provide such young people with the right to request time off for study, little evidence exists which suggests that this entitlement has proved effective. These years in the youth labour market add little if anything to their educational achievements; just 25 per cent of eighteen to nineteen year olds in full time work, 30 per cent of those in part-time work and 17 per cent of those in government-supported training had achieved Level Three qualifications in 2004, compared to 67 per cent of those in full-time education (ONS, 2004).

Although the Government did not accept the main proposals of the Tomlinson Report, we believe that substantial reform of the curriculum and fourteen to nineteen qualifications would provide renewed impetus to post-school achievement (Tomlinson, 2004). A unified fourteen to nineteen qualifications and curriculum structure, from initial entry to A Level and vocational equivalents, would improve progression opportunities at different levels of education and ensure that all young people achieve a core of basic education in mathematics, literacy and ICT alongside broader learning programmes as well as help raise education standards, particularly in vocational studies. A divided system in which the links between different levels and types of study are weak is unlikely to achieve these aims.

Financial support for young people should be neutral between different modes of learning but provide clear disincentives to dropping out of education or taking work without training. In recent years, the Government has taken important steps towards the extension and simplification of financial support for young adults in learning, in accordance with these principles. Education Maintenance Allowances have been rolled out nationwide and from 2006 entitlements to Child Benefit and Child Tax Credit will be extended to the families of unwaged trainees. New Activity and Learning Agreements will be piloted for those who have dropped out of learning and those in jobs without training. In the long term, these forms of financial support should be consolidated into a Single Youth Allowance, modelled on the Australian system, to provide a unified and potentially less complex system of allowances, geared to learning participation but equitable between the levels and types of education and training chosen by young people (Pearce and Hillman, 1998; SEU, 1999; HMT and DWP and DfES, 2005). Higher allowances would be paid to those from lower-income families, with additional resources provided to those with particular social needs.

As resources allow, financial support for study should also be progressively extended beyond the age of nineteen, so that those who drop out, take longer to complete courses or simply experience interruption in their studies do not face a sharp 'cliff edge' end to their entitlements. Those entering higher education do not currently face this cut-off and age restrictions on apprenticeships have also recently been relaxed.

Skills and life-long learning

The Commission on Social Justice proposed a system of Individual Learning Accounts (ILAs) held with a national 'learning bank'. While problems with fraud led to the abrupt curtailment of the ILA programme subsequently introduced by the Government, the objectives of the Commission's proposals – equitable funding of adult learning regardless of the level or type of study, flexibility and choice in learning programmes, and the promotion of funding partnerships between individuals, the state and employers – remain absolutely valid.

In particular, the further development of equitable entitlements to study, linked to credit frameworks for qualifications, is an essential goal. The national rollout of free tuition for Level Two courses should be accompanied in due course by a system of maintenance allowances set at a higher level than the current £30 per week, which is insufficient to allow full-time study, particularly for those seeking to come off social security benefits. Income-contingent loans are not appropriate for Level Two courses, where the disincentive effects of borrowing are likely to be higher and wage returns lower than in higher education. However, for Level Three courses for adults, equivalent to A Level study, there is a role for subsidised loans. Improved childcare, as we discuss above, will also facilitate 'return-to-learn' opportunities for adults with young families.

Social justice also demands a rebalancing of state support for students towards further education and away from higher education. Many thousands more adults study in further education colleges and community centres than in universities, and improving their skills, particularly those who lack basic literacy and numeracy, is central to the achievement of a fairer society. Even after the introduction of top-up fees of £3,000 for university students, the UK funding system remains weighted towards those in higher education rather than adult learners in further education.

Another important dimension of support for training and skills acquisition is the Employer Training Pilots (ETPs) scheme. The ETPs offer employees paid time off to train for a Level Two vocational qualification or a basic skills qualification, with free or heavily subsidised tuition. By the end of the second year of the pilots, almost 12,000 workplaces were involved. The latest evaluation evidence from the scheme shows that take-up has been very good, particularly amongst workers in businesses with less than 50 employees. The scheme has had positive effects on training but there is a degree of 'deadweight' in the pilots, in that many of the employers who signed up for the scheme would have delivered some training even in its absence (Hillage *et al,* 2005). As yet it is too early to say whether the scheme has had longer-term positive effects on the earnings and labour market progression of the employees who have taken part. The Government announced in the 2004 Pre-Budget report that the ETPs will be rolled out nationally in 2008.

The qualifications framework is a vital part of the credibility and effectiveness of skills acquisition and lifelong learning policy. The late 1980s and early 1990s saw substantial reform of vocational qualifications, with the creation of National Vocational Qualifications (NVQs) and General National Vocational Qualifications (GNVQs). This new framework has been persistently criticised for creating a confused and complex system of vocational certification at the same time as failing to add real value to training and skill development for individuals or employers (see Chapter

12). Reform of vocational qualifications is therefore imperative if government policies to promote skills acquisition at Level Two are to achieve the goals of enabling workplace progression and improving productivity. As new individual entitlements to Level Two study and the ETPs are rolled out nationally, the focus should be on the achievement of vocational qualifications that add to earnings power.

Employment services for inactive and disabled people

Employment services and welfare-to-work schemes will continue to play a key role in achieving full employment. In the short term, as Chapter 15 argues, there will be a policy trade-off between helping those who are economically inactive into work on the one hand, and supporting employment retention and progression for those already placed into jobs on the other. In situations where both types of service are offered, the evidence suggests that personal advisers at the sharp end of delivery struggle to meet their commitments to those in work (Johnson, 2002).

With International Labour Organisation (ILO) unemployment measures on a downward trend since 1993, and claimant count unemployment at its lowest level for 30 years in 2004, the focus of welfare-to-work policy has shifted towards the challenge of reducing the numbers of economically inactive, particularly those with long-term health problems or a disability. The reform of disability benefits, including Incapacity Benefit (IB) and Disability Living Allowance (DLA), is a social justice issue and must be driven by the aims of increasing the employment rate and decreasing poverty for claimants and their dependants. Though reform of IB is only one part of a wider picture, it is undoubtedly necessary. As the Government has recognised, the current policy is not fit for purpose as it stands (DWP, 2005). It fails to provide a decent standard of living for those for whom work is not possible while simultaneously failing to provide swift and effective routes back to work for people experiencing work-limiting health problems or disability. The essential problem is that it is implicitly assumed that people on IB are incapable of work, despite the fact that one million people in receipt of the benefit say that they do want to work (Stanley and Regan, 2003).

The Government's proposals to end IB – replacing it with a new benefit structure, setting the new benefit at a flat rate, and introducing mandatory action plans tailored to individuals' needs and aspirations – are very welcome, but problems still remain with the proposals as they stand. We believe that IB should not be replaced by two separate benefits, one for people with more serious conditions and one for those who are expected to take steps towards work. There is a real danger that the new benefit for people who cannot work – the Disability and Sickness Allowance (DSA) – will become the IB of the future. Considerable energy and resources could be expended patrolling the border between the DSA and the other benefit, Rehabilitation Allowance (RA). Having two separate benefits fails to recognise the reality that people's conditions may change over time and that such distinctions are fraught with difficulties.

Our recommended solution is to replace IB with a single benefit, Earnings Replacement Allowance, available to everyone satisfying the Personal Capability Assessment (PCA) eligibility of having a disability or sickness which significantly limits a person's ability to work (Stanley and Maxwell, 2004). All claimants would then negotiate action agreements with personal advisers which would increase opportunities for employment and social and economic inclusion. This could be linked to the national rollout of the Pathways to Work pilots (DWP, 2005). Rather than making cut-and-dried distinctions which categorise people too rigidly, such a system would be responsive to the reality of people's experiences of sickness and disability.

Promoting progression in the labour market
Efforts to improve workplace retention and progression – the extent to which entrants into the labour market can stay in work for long periods of time, and move on to jobs with higher pay and better working conditions – are a vital part of a socially just labour market policy. Improving retention and progression can alleviate 'churn' in the benefits and tax credits system, whereby benefit claimants tend to 'cycle' between work and unemployment or inactivity. Evaluations of welfare-to-work programmes in the US show that retention and advancement can be improved if intermediary advisers are, as far as possible, selective about the jobs into which they place clients (Strawn and Martinson, 2001; Johnson, 2002). People are more likely to stay in jobs and improve their incomes if they obtain work in higher wage sectors, larger firms with career structures, low turnover firms, and those that offer training opportunities (Holzer, 2004). Those who switch jobs voluntarily also appear to achieve higher income mobility, while tailored services for jobseekers that combine job search, training and careers advice may also be more effective than those that prioritise work first or basic education and training (Poppe *et al*, 2003).

In the medium term, government policy should start to focus more on progression in the labour market. The Employment Retention and Advancement scheme (ERA), currently at the pilot stage, is a potential vehicle for achieving this. ERA is directed at individuals in three different low-income groups known to have difficulty retaining jobs or advancing to better positions in the labour market: those eligible for the New Deal for the Long-Term Unemployed (aged 25 and over), volunteers for the New Deal for Lone Parents, and lone parents claiming the Working Tax Credit but currently working part-time. Once in ERA, all participants have access to a combination of work-related services and financial incentives for a substantial period after employment commences.

The ERA is currently being rigorously evaluated, but because of the length of the assistance provided in the scheme, full evidence of its effectiveness will not be available until 2007. While this will create a frustrating delay in rolling out the scheme nationally if it is successful, we would argue that is essential to wait to be sure before proceeding with a roll-out. This is because the current evidence base on what works in encouraging provision is patchy at best. Even in the US and Canada, where there have been far more trials and evaluations of pilot ERA-type schemes than in Europe, there is little consensus on their effectiveness in the long run. A national commitment to an ERA scheme which failed to deliver would be an expensive white elephant which would damage the prospects for getting better-designed schemes off the drawing board in the future.

If ERA proves to be a successful policy, there are other possible extensions which could help encourage progression on a wider basis. For example, Jobcentre Plus could set clear targets for retention and wage progression, over a much broader category of clients than those who are eligible for ERA. The targets could be included in measures to improve career plans for those who no longer claim benefit, with personal advisers to back the agreed measures up. Once again, this policy should be piloted and evaluated to make sure it is actually effective before the Government commits to it on a national basis.

In the short term, better information, advice and guidance should be made available to jobseekers and workers who are currently low paid. The DWP and DfES should encourage closer links between learndirect and the Sector Skills Councils in developing structured career plans for low-skilled entrants to industries. And partnerships with the private sector could be encouraged (building on the success of the Employment Zones scheme) to provide continuing support to those who have entered employment.

Poverty: security in retirement and reducing child poverty

The third element of the social justice gap is the continued high level of relative poverty in the UK. Social justice demands that all citizens have some basic minimum floor of material provision below which they do not fall. In this section we focus on the two most vulnerable groups on which the Government has concentrated its anti-poverty strategy: pensioners and families with children. As Chapter 2 indicated, despite progress, the challenge remains significant. We also consider to what extent other groups of people on low incomes, such as childless people of working age, should be made a higher priority.

Security in retirement

Ensuring adequate income for retirees will be even more of a challenge in the future. One of the upward pressures on state spending outlined in Chapter 3 is demographic change and the ageing society to which it is giving rise. Though the UK is not as badly positioned as some other countries, the pressures on some areas of welfare spending are very real. Some of these pressures will affect public services, particularly the NHS. But it is in relation to pensions and long-term care that demographic change is most significant. In both of these areas significant reform is necessary.

The Government's current policy priority with pensions, to tackle pensioner poverty as a key element of social justice, is to be supported. Its current policy approach is not credible, however. Take-up of the means-tested pension credit remains lower than is required to lift all of the poorest pensioners out of poverty. The role of the State Second Pension (which since April 2002 has started to replace SERPS) is unclear and its efficacy as an anti-poverty policy is uncertain. At the same time, the incentive effects created by means-testing are acute. The Pension Credit does not solve this problem but instead spreads it over a larger group of the population. Estimates from the Institute for Fiscal Studies suggest that by 2050, up to 73 per cent of pensioners will be eligible for means-tested benefits, a significant increase from the 2003 figure of 52 per cent (Brewer and Emmerson, 2003).

In the past few years a growing consensus has emerged amongst opposition politicians, the financial services industry, academics and policy makers that the complexity of the current system of state pension provision is a key obstacle to reducing pensioner poverty. The interim report from the Pension Commission highlighted the tough choices which need to be made. It outlined four options, all with significant drawbacks. These were: for pensioners to become poorer relative to the rest of society, for taxes to increase, for people to start to save significant amounts more, or for average retirement ages to increase (Pension Commission, 2004).

Our recommended answer is a combination of people saving more and working longer (Brooks *et al*, 2002a). In order to achieve the first objective the most effective response would be a radical simplification of the state system. This could be achieved by once again returning the Basic State Pension to the heart of the state pensions system. It should be up-rated to the level of the Pension Credit Guarantee and then indexed with earnings, not prices, to ensure it maintains its value *vis-à-vis* wider living standards. Setting the Basic State Pension at the Pension Credit Guarantee level – £109.45 per week for a single pensioner from April 2005 – would ensure that all people with full contribution records have an income around the 'low cost but acceptable' benchmark and above the quasi-official pensioner poverty line which is 60 per cent of median household income after housing costs.

Such an approach would also provide a bedrock onto which individuals could add, confident than any saving they make will increase their retirement income. Some people may save less, in the knowledge that they would receive a more generous, though hardly overly generous, state pension, but many of the current incentive problems would simply fall away.

This reform would not require tax increases. It would be paid for in part by the savings from phasing out other parts of the current pensions system. The Pension Credit would become redundant, the State Second Pension could be closed and the contracting out rebates currently paid into the private or occupational pensions of those who opt out of the Second State Pension, would be abolished. But over the longer term the tough decision which must be made is on the state pension age. This should be increased slightly to 67, in a gradual way in the decade between 2020 and 2030. Ensuring affordability for the system is not the only justification for this increase; average life expectancy has been increasing for many years and is projected to continue its increase. For men at 65 it has grown from twelve years in 1950 to an estimated nineteen years today, and is projected to rise to 21 years by 2030 (Pension Commission, 2004). Retiring two years later than at present would still leave around 20 years of retirement for most men and women. We might also expect a higher official retirement age to increase labour force participation rates among older workers (Disney and Johnson, 2001). The difficult issue here from a social justice perspective is the differential effect that this dragging up of employment rates may have on different classes (Sefton and Van de Ven, 2004).

Some means-testing issues will remain as long as entitlement to a full Basic State Pension depends on a full National Insurance Contributions record. In the longer term, one option to consider is the introduction of a Citizens' Pension, to which all pensioners are eligible on the grounds of citizenship rather than contribution. By bypassing any means-testing issues it would essentially be a simpler way to reach the same outcome and achieve the same core objective – abolition of pensioner poverty (NAPF, 2002; PPI, 2004). However, the Citizens' Pension would raise the issue of how citizenship is defined. For instance, old people might have to have been resident in the UK for a certain number of years to qualify, as is the case in New Zealand. For this reason, we do not recommend it unconditionally, but as an option for further study.

Guaranteeing minimum incomes for pensioners is vital. A 'new contract for retirement' must also cover other risks, the most salient of which in many older people's minds is the funding of long-term care. Here too, despite some progress, further reform is required. Much care is means-tested which is often both unfair (because of sometimes arbitrary boundaries being drawn between acute health care and long-term health care and between 'nursing' and 'personal' care) and unpopular. It is particularly unpopular with home owners forced to run down housing assets to pay for the cost of their care.

The devolved administration in Scotland has opted to take a different route and has made personal care free at the point of use. The difficulty for the Westminster government is that the future cost implications of adopting such a policy nationwide are highly unpredictable – more so than is the case with pensions. Modelling work by ippr projects the additional cost of making personal care free at some 0.3 per cent of GDP by

2050 (Brooks *et al,* 2002b). This is a significant sum, but as we show in the second section of this chapter, it is affordable. A proportion of the added revenue we raise through the tax changes recommended below would be used to meet the costs.

Child poverty

The Government's target for reducing child poverty represents perhaps its clearest social justice objective, and the objective where it has made most progress so far (Brewer, 2004). Continuing to make progress will be difficult, largely because the Government must continue to find additional resources to do so (Brewer, 2005). It is also inevitable that other difficult decisions will need to be taken. Further reductions in child poverty can be achieved through a combination of more generous benefits and tax credits and increased employment rates among parents, particularly lone mothers. Although the employment rate of lone mothers has increased from 45.6 per cent in 1997 to 53.4 per cent in 2003, there is still some way to go to meet the Government's long-run target of a 70 per cent lone parent employment rate. Given the large increase in resources going to lone parent families through the tax credit system, we believe that once the reforms to the childcare system which we recommend are rolled out, it would be appropriate to extend benefit conditionality to lone parents of children over the age of eleven. Such a move would be in sympathy with the majority of public opinion as presented in the analysis of attitudinal data in Chapter 5, and would help to build a sense of reciprocity into the welfare system – something which research evidence suggests people do not think is provided by the National Insurance system any longer (Stafford, 1998; Hedges and Bromley, 2001).

As things currently stand, the UK has a different approach from most other countries to conditionality with lone parents. They are required to attend a Work Focused Interview, but do not have to take any action following this. While there are dangers in imposing conditionality on parents with young children, we feel that once the new framework which we recommend for childcare provision is in place, lone parents whose youngest child is over the age of eleven should be required not only to attend a series of such Work Focused Interviews, but also to carry out the activities in an action plan and accept a job should they be offered one. Failure to comply would result in benefit sanctions, just as with Jobseekers Allowance at present.

Other groups

Reducing child poverty may also require a continued prioritisation of households with children over able-bodied working-age childless adults. Chapter 2 and Chapter 12 highlighted the position of these relatively unfavoured groups. While we should certainly maintain the safety net of Jobseekers Allowance at a financially adequate level for childless people of working age who are capable of work but for whom work is hard to find, the priorities for this group should be to increase the effectiveness of programmes which can support them into work, to reduce in-work poverty through the National Minimum Wage and the Working Tax Credit for childless people, and to ensure a stable and prosperous macro-economic environment in which it is possible to move into a job and progress up the labour market as easily as possible.

However, there are two key groups of people who have not been prioritised thus far under Labour for whom benefit increases are a vital component of an anti-poverty strategy. The first group is pregnant women. Mothers who are healthier and/or have higher incomes during pregnancy tend to have children with higher birth weights and better subsequent outcomes (Blair *et al,* 1996; Kehrer and Wolin, 1979). A pregnancy premium, attached to Jobseekers Allowance and Income Support, paid from the 20th or 30th week of pregnancy, should be considered alongside other measures to improve support for pregnant women (Harker and Kendall, 2003).

The second group of people who should be prioritised is people who are unable to work due to chronic illness or severe disablement. It is vital that the planned set of reforms to Incapacity Benefit do not disadvantage this vulnerable group. The combination of the Government's proposed Disability and Sickness Allowance, which would replace IB for people who are incapable of work, and Disability Living Allowance, which meets the extra mobility and care costs associated with disability, should be set at a high enough level so that disabled people can avoid poverty and social exclusion (Burchardt, 2003).

Delivering social justice

Upward cost pressures on the welfare state

The task of delivering social justice and making progress on the three priorities listed above needs to be seen in a wider context. All modern welfare states, including the 'Anglo-social' model into which Chapter 3 argues the UK is evolving, face long-term upward cost pressures. The cost of an ageing population is one such pressure that will increase over the coming decade. With regard to pensions policy, taking difficult (but justifiable) decisions about the state pension age can ameliorate the impact, but demographic change will also impact considerably – though often unpredictably – on the costs of the NHS and long-term care.

Furthermore, there are good reasons to think that this is indicative of a wider trend; governments will come under increasing budgetary pressures in many policy areas. The fact that governments around the world have actually found it hard to reduce taxation is mainly due to the constantly increasing expectations of electorates who expect to see year-on-year improvement in public service delivery, at the same time as cutting edge services become ever more expensive. In healthcare, for example, the quality of new equipment, drugs and infrastructure is rising rapidly but with a price tag to match, outstripping the general rate of price inflation. The main driver behind enhanced public expectations is increasing affluence: as people get richer they tend to spend more of their income on healthcare and education and consequently are more demanding of the services supplied by the state (Hills, 2004). Another factor is the comparisons people naturally make with the private sector, which is providing increasingly tailored, professional and personal services, particularly as political rhetoric shifts in the direction of citizen-consumers.

More specifically for the UK, Chapter 12 points out that designing a future welfare system around the principle of 'participation' while continuing to make progress on child poverty will also necessitate increases in spending. The Anglo-social model will continue to rely heavily on tax and benefit policy to counter high levels of original income inequality.

These fiscal pressures are generally not new, but the responses available to governments have become more limited. From the end of the Second World War until the OPEC crises in the mid-1970s, strong growth meant that the state could rely on steadily increasing revenues to fund public service expansion in Britain, as in most other developed countries. In the 1980s, there was a realisation that this expansion had placed too much pressure on state spending and there was 'a retreat to the core' as the state cut spending in areas where it could afford to, such as support for industry and earnings related pensions, and (arguably) in areas in which it could not, such as housing, pensions, benefits and social services (Glennerster, 1998). In the late 1980s and 1990s, there was a focus on doing things more efficiently, through public–private partnerships, targets, audits, restructuring and drives to reduce 'waste'. This continues today, but the ability to squeeze more out of existing funding is likely to be more and more limited. Given the focus since the late 1980s on cutting waste in the public sector, it would be surprising if chronic inefficiencies still remained by this stage. Certainly the Government believes that some further cost-cutting is possible, as evidenced by the Gershon review of public sector efficiency (HMT, 2004c). But it is debatable whether further state reform should be primarily about achieving cost efficiencies; some argue now that a wider objective of improving the quality of the service provided should underpin future public administration (Kelly *et al*, 2000). It is doubtful, therefore, whether there is the practical possibility of much greater efficiency gains being made or services cut and it is questionable whether doing so would be a wise long-term strategy in achieving greater social justice.

This legacy makes for a particularly tough set of choices facing governments in 2005 (Robinson, 2004). This is especially true given the existing commitments made by the UK Government. Some of these are the result of strategic choices, such as the commitments to eradicate child poverty and to increase expenditure on the NHS from 5.5 per cent of GDP in 1996/7 to 7.9 per cent in 2007/8 (HMT, 2004b). These decisions are to be welcomed, but at the same time it needs to be recognised that they make meeting future social justice priorities even more challenging. All the pressures discussed thus far in this chapter will be present before policy-makers even start to consider the new social challenges outlined above, the most costly of which is the need to develop a universal system of high quality and affordable childcare.

Social justice: paying for progress

It is important to address the question of how to secure public support for the programme of reforms that we are recommending in this chapter. There are three key components: universal childcare, ending child poverty and free long-term care for the elderly. The analysis in Chapter 3 and at the beginning of this chapter clearly points to childcare as the new frontier in the welfare state, and it is clear that childcare reform should be presented as the centre piece of social policy over the next few years. There is good reason to believe that this would be a politically popular move. Chapter 5 reported support from all groups, including the middle class, for increasingly generous early years provision. One advantage of a universal service is that most people in society will in some way or another benefit. Even for those without children, the positive spillovers for wider society that greater investment in childcare can bring would help make a powerful political case. There are clear parallels with the language of the 'social investment state'; language which, at least in part, has been developed as a way of bolstering the legitimacy of modern welfare states (Lister, 2003).

Likewise, there are good reasons to believe that the introduction of free long-term care for the elderly would be a politically popular policy, provided that the public can be convinced that it is affordable. As argued in the first section of this chapter, previous research by ippr suggests that free long-term care can indeed be introduced with only modest implications for the tax burden.

Although Taylor-Gooby's analysis in Chapter 5 indicates that the public do not regard 'the poor' as a universally needy group, support for alleviating poverty amongst families with children is much stronger than it is for single adults or couples without children. To this extent, our proposals for extra spending to reduce child poverty still further are in line with the public's priorities and should ensure maximum support for a socially just anti-poverty strategy.

This package of priorities, combined with the longer-term cost pressures on the welfare state identified in the previous section, presents political parties and the people of Britain with one fundamental question: if we want to continue to improve public services, respond to new risks like demand for childcare and forge a fairer Britain, are we willing to pay for it? This is the fundamental issue which will decide whether Britain becomes a fairer society.

The remainder of this final chapter is structured as follows. First, we discuss the short-term costs of the key reforms we recommend over the next three tax years, up to 2007/8. We present a carefully costed package of tax reforms designed to meet these costs. We then attempt to estimate the costs of achieving social justice over a much longer timeframe, to the year 2020. Finally, we suggest some progressive guiding principles that should inform the design of the tax system into 2020 and beyond.

Tax increases required by 2007/8

The Government only gives its spending commitments three years into the future. Currently, spending projections are available up to the 2007/8 tax year, as detailed in the latest Spending Review (SR2004) which was published in July 2004 (HM Treasury, 2004d). The next Spending Review is not due until summer 2006. Ideally we would like to assess the size of the social justice gap over the entire next Parliament – probably a period of four to five years – but this is not possible because we do not have detailed figures going beyond 2007/8.

Our estimates of the social justice 'spending gap' up to and including 2007/8 are calculated as follows:

- Extensions to state funding for childcare provision. Our spending estimates for this research are based on a report for the Daycare Trust by John Hawksworth of PriceWaterhouseCoopers who models a broadly similar package of reforms to that presented in this chapter: twelve months paid parental leave with additional support after this, free part-time care for all two, three and four year olds, additional 'wrap-around' care for one, two, three and four year olds from 8am to 6pm and significant development of the early years workforce (Daycare Trust, 2004). Hawksworth's analysis suggests that, taking into account the predicted costs and benefits of the full package of reforms,[1] the cost of the childcare policies by 2010 over and above planned childcare expenditure in the Government's current spending review plans, factoring in the benefits to the Exchequer from increased female employment,[2] will be £5.6 billion.[3] We estimate that to be on course to expand childcare according to Hawksworth's recommendations, the Government would need to be spending around £4 billion extra on childcare in the 2007/8 tax year. This is because it is likely that there will need to be some 'front-loading' – a relatively heavy investment in terms of training staff, expanding the number of childcare places, and so on, in the early years of the strategy – to make it maximally effective.
- The introduction of free long-term care for the elderly in England and Wales. Previous work by ippr (Brooks *et al*, 2002b) suggested that the total cost of long-term care will amount to an extra 0.3 per

---

1 Hawksworth's analysis takes into account the direct costs to the Government of expanding childcare provision but also estimates the benefits that accrue to the Exchequer from the policy. These comprise: (a) increased employment for women with children; (b) higher lifetime earnings for children who benefit from additional early years education and care; (c) any long-term increases in the earnings of mothers who are able to avoid a prolonged career break as a result of additional childcare provision.

2 But not the longer-term benefits in terms of children's increased earning power and women's increased earnings from not taking a career break. These benefits are more likely to accrue after 2010 as it takes a few years for them to build up.

3 This estimate includes the £600 million of additional childcare spending allocated by the Chancellor in the 2004 Pre-Budget report, on top of the spending plans in SR2004.

cent of GDP – £4 billion in current prices – but this full cost will only be payable in the year 2050. The initial cost is £1.2 billion and the costs will rise only slowly to the year 2050 as the population ages. We have therefore taken £1.2 billion as our estimate for Table 16.1.

- The reforms which we recommend to the pensions system are self-financing, as detailed earlier in the chapter.
- Additional spending to keep the Government on course to meet its targets for reducing child poverty. As calculated by Brewer, at least £2 billion extra spending on the Child Tax Credit will be required by 2007/8 to stay on course to meet the targets (Brewer, 2005). However, the Government allocated £600 million additional spending on the Child Tax Credit in Budget 2005, and so we have adjusted Brewer's estimate of the required extra spending down to £1.4 billion.

We give our estimates for the spending commitments in billions of pounds in 2005/6 prices and also as percentages of Gross Domestic Product (GDP). For 2004, the most recent year for which end-year figures are available, GDP was around £1,100 billion.

Table 16.1: The 'social justice spending gap' – spending commitments by 2007/08, costs in 2005 prices and as percentages of GDP

	£bn	%GDP
Extensions of affordable, available and high-quality childcare	4.0	0.36
Reducing child poverty in line with government targets	1.4	0.13
Reforms to pensions	0.0	0.0
Free long-term care	1.2	0.11
TOTAL	6.6	0.60

Sources: Daycare Trust 2004; Brewer 2005; Brooks *et al*, 2002

Note: These figures assume the Government's own predictions that they will hit their two self-imposed fiscal rules; the 'golden rule' and the 'sustainable investment rule'. The golden rule states that on average over the economic cycle, the Government will borrow only to fund investment spending, and not to fund current (non-investment) spending. The sustainable investment rule states that public sector debt should always be below 40 per cent of national income, a limit the Chancellor has defined as 'stable and prudent'. There is currently some dispute between expert commentators and the Government as to whether the fiscal rules will be hit over the current economic cycle (Chote *et al*, 2005; NIESR, 2005). As such the figures presented here should be read as the minimum spending increase that would be necessary to achieve the objectives we set out. Any deterioration in the public finances – due to low growth in the economy, or lower than predicted tax receipts, for example – would make the Government's task harder.

Which taxes should be raised?

Our argument in this chapter is that higher taxes are required by 2007/8 to meet spending programmes that are core parts of a socially just society: universal childcare provision, an end to child poverty, and free long-term care.

There are a number of different taxes that could be reformed to raise the necessary £6.6 billion. This section assesses the role that different taxes might play in contributing towards the total that needs to be raised. Below we outline our key recommendations. Five key criteria should guide policy makers in considering tax changes. These are as follows:

- *Progressivity* – Overall the package of tax changes should raise money in a progressive way. In general terms this means that the rich should pay more than the poor as a proportion of their incomes. As shown in Chapter 12, although the tax and benefit system as a whole is progressive, the tax system taken on its own is at best neutral and possibly mildly regressive (Hills, 2004).
- *Relative efficiency* – Many taxes create inefficiency by distorting economic incentives relative to what they would be in the absence of the tax. It is best if taxes are designed so as to keep efficiency losses to a minimum, while raising adequate revenue to fund spending plans. Where possible taxes should increase economic efficiency, for example in the case of environmental taxes which correct existing distortions due to what economists call 'externalities' – costs of economic activity which are not fully borne by the participants in the activity.
- *Simplicity* – As far as is possible it is best to make tax changes simple, and indeed the taxes themselves simple. However, sometimes the most efficient tax instruments are highly complex due to the way they are expected to operate. An example is the road charging scheme proposed in earlier ippr work (Foley and Ferguson, 2004). There is thus sometimes a trade-off between simplicity and efficiency.
- *Openness* – To have a proper debate about the appropriate level of spending on public services necessary to promote social justice, it is best if any tax increases necessary to pay for increased spending are announced openly and transparently – as was the case with the increases in National Insurance Contributions announced in the 2002 Budget.
- *Inclusiveness* – One option is for a package of tax changes to impact largely on just a small group of the very well off. To rely solely on this

approach is dangerous though. It gives credence to the myth that Britain can pay for an expanded welfare state and the services that people need and demand just by asking the rich to pay more – a dangerous strategy. It also weakens the link between tax and citizenship (Fabian Society, 2000).

In addition, the Government ruled out raising the basic or higher rates of income tax in its election manifesto. Hence in this section, we assume that increases in income tax rates during the third term are ruled out by the manifesto commitment. Later on we discuss the case for and against specific pledges on taxation of this kind.

A package of tax changes also needs to carry popular support or, at a minimum, popular acceptance. In part, tax changes can be justified simply on the grounds of fairness. This, Chapter 5 suggests, is the case with increasing the proportion of tax paid by people on relatively high incomes. But more importantly a clear link between any tax change and 'what people will get in return' must be made. This chapter argues that in the coming years, the Government should make a clear link between a timetable on delivering improvements in childcare and parental leave and a package of moderate tax changes as detailed in the next section.

The recommended reforms: direct taxation
The changes to direct taxation suggested below would meet the criteria above. They would be simple and clear, both because they would be easy for taxpayers to understand and because they would rationalise some elements of the current system; they would be progressive, asking those on higher incomes – above the upper earnings limit for National Insurance contributions – to pay a larger increase than other tax payers, while at the same time inclusive because all tax payers would be asked to pay a little more; and they would be a relatively efficient means of raising the money. The changes would have four main elements:

1. An increase in the Upper Earnings Limit for employee National Insurance Contributions
The structure of employee National Insurance Contributions (NICs) is responsible for a long-standing anomaly in the schedule of marginal tax rates faced by UK taxpayers. Presently, for an employee taxpayer of working age who earns the same amount each week throughout the course of a tax year, the reduction in the rate of employee NICs from 11 per cent to 1 per

cent above the NICs Upper Earnings Limit creates a 'kink' in the combined
marginal rate. Effective rates of income tax and employee NICs paid on
each pound of additional weekly income are as shown in Figure 16.1 below.

**Figure 16.1: Current income tax, employee NICs and combined
marginal rate schedules**

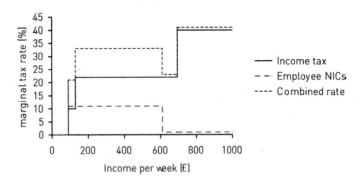

This is an anomaly in the tax system. There is no obvious economic
case on efficiency or equity grounds for having a tax schedule where the
marginal rate falls, then rises, as income increases. This kink can be
ironed out by raising the Upper Earnings Limit for NICs from £630 to
£715 per week – the weekly equivalent of the income tax higher rate
threshold. This rationalisation would raise about £1.2 billion according
to projections from the Institute for Fiscal Studies (Adam and Reed,
2004). The reform goes with the thrust of Government policy, as it is
effectively the logical culmination of a long gradualist process whereby
successive Governments have reduced the size of the kink by either
increasing the NICs UEL by more than the rate of price inflation (as
occurred in 2000 and 2001, for example) or freezing the Higher Rate
Threshold in nominal terms (as occurred in 2003).

*2. A 2 per cent increase in employee National Insurance Contributions
above the Upper Earnings Limit*
After raising the Upper Earnings Limit for National Insurance
Contributions, employee NICs will be paid at a rate of 1 per cent for
weekly incomes above £715 per week – which equates to £37,000 per year
for someone with regular earnings. There is a strong social justice case for

increasing this rate, so that men and women on high incomes pay a greater share of the cost of funding essential public services. We propose a 2 per cent increase in NICs for employees and the self-employed above the Upper Earnings Limit, to 3 per cent in total. This reform would raise around £1.7 billion.[4] Raising the higher rate of income tax would be a more transparent tax increase with similar distributional effects, but the Government ruled this out in its 2005 election manifesto.

3. A 0.5 per cent increase in employee National Insurance Contributions (between the Primary Threshold and Upper Earnings Limit)

It is not possible to raise all of the revenue necessary to bridge the social justice gap from top earners, nor is it desirable. The link between the main spending commitments – universal childcare and long-term care – which will be used by large swathes of the population and the notion that the majority of the population need to contribute something towards the tax going to pay for those services must be maintained. This was certainly the case in 2003 when NICs were increased to pay for extra spending on the NHS. Therefore we propose a 0.5 per cent increase in employee NICs between the Primary Threshold (£94 per week) and the Upper Earnings Limit (£715 per week). This would raise about £1.9 billion.[5]

4. A 0.5 per cent increase in employer National Insurance Contributions

As in 2002, we recommend that employee NICs and employer NICs are both raised. We propose a 0.5 per cent increase in employer NICs, which would raise about £2.1 billion. Thus we split the burden of the National Insurance increase between employees and employers, although as both types of NICs are effectively a tax on labour costs, there is good reason to think that in the long run the burden of an increase in NICs will fall on employees rather than employers.

The overall package

The overall effects of our package of direct tax reforms are shown in Figure 16.2 below. The reforms raise around £6.9 billion – slightly more than is necessary to meet our extra spending commitments in 2007/8. The full line shows the present marginal rates schedule and the dotted line shows

---

4 Source: HM Treasury (2004e). The Treasury estimate has been modified to take account of the fact that our reform raises the value of the National Insurance Upper Earnings Limit.

5 Source: HM Treasury (2004e).

that after the changes we recommend (including the increase in employer NICs as if it were an increase in the employee's marginal tax rate, for consistency). The tax system would be simplified and rationalised. The removal of the kink and greater alignment of income tax and National Insurance meets the simplicity criteria outlined above. Furthermore, overall the marginal rate schedule resulting from the reforms is more steeply progressive. Taking the increase in employer NICs into account as well as employee NICs, combined marginal rates range from 22 per cent just above the income tax personal allowance (and the National Insurance Earnings Threshold) to 43.5 per cent above £37,295 per year. The distributional effects will be very progressive, with those on higher incomes paying more. No one who does not pay NICs would lose out from our proposals. But we have explicitly sought to ensure that all employees and self-employed people above the National Insurance threshold pay something, mainly to meet the cost of expanding childcare.

Figure 16.2: Effects of proposed direct tax changes on combined marginal rates schedule (including increase in employer NICs)

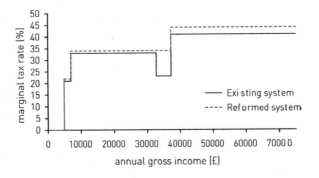

In magnitude, these tax changes are smaller, but more progressive, than the changes the Government announced in the 2002 Budget to provide extra funding for the health service (which came into effect in April 2003). Chapter 5 reports no perceptible backlash in terms of public attitudes from the 2003 tax rises, which indicates that when there is a clear rationale for tax increases and when the taxes are perceived as being fair they stand a good chance of being supported by the public. Employers will tend to complain that the burden of employer National Insurance increases (which make up about a third of the fiscal weight of the package) fall on them, but in fact, the economic effects of a rise in employer NICs are likely to be very similar to the impact of a rise in employee NICs of a similar magnitude; both forms of NICs are a tax on the same cost base.[6] To the extent that the reforms raise more than is necessary to meet our spending commitments (£6.9 billion raised compared with £6.6 billion spending required), we recommend that the surplus be used to increase the income tax higher rate threshold slightly. This would help reduce the burden on taxpayers who lose out from the closure of the National Insurance 'kink' and the increase in employee NICs above the higher rate threshold.

Achieving social justice in the longer run

Although the tax increases necessary to meet our short-term social justice objectives by 2007/8 are relatively modest, at £6.9 billion or 0.6 per cent of GDP, in the longer run – out to 2020, and beyond – the costs are larger. In this section we assess the magnitude of these costs. This is not a straightforward process for any of our key objectives. Spending projections get more uncertain the further we look into the future because there are so many factors that might impact on public spending – the rate of growth and structure of the economy, mortality and fertility rates, household formation and dissolution, immigration and emigration and so on. Below we attempt to take a 'best guess' at the long-term costs of achieving social justice for each of our priority spending areas.[7]

- As noted above, our spending estimates for extensions in childcare provision are taken from a report for the Daycare Trust by John Hawksworth of PriceWaterhouseCoopers. His analysis suggests that, taking into account the predicted costs and benefits of the full package of reforms, the net additional cost of the childcare package to the Exchequer by 2020 would be £10.8 billion in today's prices.
- The introduction of free long-term care in England and Wales would amount to 0.3 per cent of GDP – about £4 billion in current prices

---

6   With the exception that jobs employing people aged 60 and over are subject to employer NICs but not employee NICs.

7   Note that these costs are estimated relative to the Government's planned spending for 2007/08, not relative to our suggested short-run spending increases of £6.6 billion by 2007/08. Hence the estimates below *include* the £6.6 billion detailed above as a component of our long-run spending recommendations.

in 2050. The initial cost is £1.2 billion and the costs would rise only slowly to the year 2050 as the population ages. Given that there is a large margin of error on these figures, we take £4 billion per year as a sensible upper estimate for the cost of providing free long-term care through 2020 and beyond (Brooks *et al*, 2002).

- Unfortunately, no publicly available projections for what it would cost to stay on course to reduce child poverty beyond 2007/8 exist at the time of writing. As noted above, Brewer suggests that over the three years between 2004/5 and 2007/8, spending of around £2 billion per year on the per child element of the Child Tax Credit would achieve a reduction in line with a halving of child poverty rates between 1999 and 2010, which is the Government's target (Brewer, 2005). But it is impossible to say with any precision how much it would cost to continue reducing child poverty with a view to eliminating it (as defined by the Government) by 2020. A crude extrapolation of the increase in costs required between 2004 and 2007 would suggest a figure of around £12 billion in total by 2020.

Table 16.2 below puts these estimates of long-run social justice costs together to derive an overall price tag. These are very much our best approximations given unavoidable uncertainties about economic performance, demographic change and so on. They should not be considered definitive estimates.

Table 16.2. The 'social justice spending gap' - estimates of spending commitments by 2020, costs in 2005 prices and percentages of GDP

	£bn	%GDP
Extensions of affordable, available and high-quality childcare	11.0	1.0
Reducing child poverty in line with government targets	12.0	1.1
Free long-term care	4.0	0.3
TOTAL	27.0	2.4

Sources: Daycare Trust 2004, ippr extrapolation based on Brewer (2005), Brooks *et al* (2002b). Figures should be taken as indicative only.

The upshot of Table 16.2 is that in the long run, we are looking at an increase in tax (and public spending) as a share of GDP of around 2.5

per cent to achieve social justice. To put this in perspective, HM Treasury figures indicate that on current Government spending plans, it is predicted that Total Managed Expenditure will be 42.1 per cent of GDP (HM Treasury, 2005). On this particular measure, the kind of long-run increases in tax which we are envisaging would raise this to around 44.5 per cent of GDP. In the next section we ask if increases in taxation as a share of GDP of this magnitude can be squared with the need to ensure an efficient and prosperous economy in the future.

Combining social justice with economic efficiency and prosperity
Data from HM Treasury show that UK Total Managed Expenditure will rise from 39.0 per cent of GDP in 1997/8 to a forecast 42.1 per cent in 2007/8. Would a further rise of 2.5 per cent in spending (and tax) as a share of GDP, however defined, make it difficult or impossible to maintain the strong economic performance that the British economy has enjoyed since the early 1990s?

To get an initial perspective on this question, we examine data on public spending and economic growth from the OECD. OECD produces data for public expenditure as a share of GDP under a consistent definition for a wide range of countries. Figure 16.3 below uses this data for a number of developed economies over the last decade (1995–2004) to examine the relationship between the annual growth rate of a country's GDP and public spending as a share of GDP in that country.

If it were always the case – or even often the case – that relatively high levels of public spending produced low rates of economic growth, we should expect to see a negative relationship between the two, in which case the points on the graph would tend to lie on or around a downward sloping line. In fact, with the exception of Ireland, which achieved 8 per cent growth over the period, there is little obvious relationship. Sweden, with public expenditure averaging 60.5 per cent of GDP over this period,[8] had an average growth rate per year of 2.9 per cent – around the same as the UK, which had public expenditure averaging 41.8 per cent of GDP over the period. Obviously this is a crude and simplistic analysis

---

8 Note that the OECD's definition of public expenditure –general government outlays – is consistantly a few percentage points higher than the UK government's preferred measure, Total Managed Expenditure (TME). So, for example, in 2004/5 the OECD measure was 44.4 per cent, wheras TME is 41.2 per cent. We are forced to use OECD's prefeRred measure in this section as comparable figures are not available for other European countries.

and there will be many factors other than the share of public expenditure in GDP that have affected growth rates in each of the OECD countries shown here in the last decade. But certainly there is no evidence to be had here that a 2.5 per cent rise in public spending as a share of GDP would damage the UK's economic prospects.

Figure 16.3: Growth 1995–2004 and public spending 2004, selected OECD countries

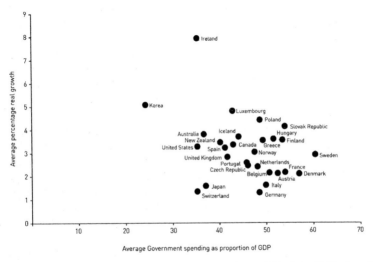

Source: OECD (2004) Economic Outlook No. 76 – Statistical Annex Tables Paris: OECD. General government total outlays data is derived from Annex Table 25. Real GDP growth rate data is derived from Annex Table 1.

The argument for reducing the size of the state and the associated burden of funding it was the mantra of the 'New Right' during the 1980s and 1990s. Conservative thinkers present two main reasons why a large share of the state in the economy's resources might be damaging for economic prosperity. First, the high levels of taxation needed to finance spending are claimed to create disincentives to work and high burdens on business which tend to lower national output and make the economy less competitive. Second, the public sector is often held to be less efficient than the private sector, because the private sector is subject to competitive pressures which the public sector is insulated from.

Even if we did accept the right's critique that economies where public expenditure consumes a relatively large percentage of national income are less efficient than economies where the state's share is small, there would still be a strong case for government intervention to redistribute incomes through the tax and benefit system on equity grounds. Certainly, the distribution of resources, and the social minimum, are two of the key principles of social justice identified earlier in this book. However, we do not accept the right's argument in the first place, because it suffers from a simplistic and false view of government's role in developed economies. A large percentage of the additional expenditure we have recommended in this chapter is for the expansion of low-cost, readily available childcare and early years education. As argued earlier in the chapter, we believe that investing in children in this way can improve equity and enhance efficiency in the economy – by allowing mothers more opportunity to enter work, and by improving the earnings and employability of children when they enter the labour market later in their lives. We believe that there is a potential for prudent and well-targeted government spending to enhance economic efficiency as well as equity in several key public service areas – education, health and public transport, for example. Our belief is that in the long run, the Government should increase public expenditure to around 45 per cent of GDP and spend the extra money on our highest priorities for social justice. But this has to be combined with a continued focus on the economic reforms which have produced high growth in Britain in the last fifteen years, namely: a macroeconomic policy framework designed to maintain low and stable inflation; a flexible labour market to maintain high employment levels (and raise them further if possible); a business regulatory regime which promotes entrepreneurship; and improvements to our skills base and research and development capabilities. This combination of increased spending and economic reform is no barrier to economic success. On the contrary, it is a precondition for the continued prosperity of British society as a whole.

Towards a fairer tax system in the long run

If, as we believe, tax as a share of GDP will need to rise by around 2.5 per cent of GDP in the long run, what is the best way to raise this money? While we believe that the guiding principles of tax reform listed earlier – progressivity, efficiency, simplicity, openness and inclusiveness – are as important in the long run as they are in the short run, there is more flexibility in the design of the tax system in the long run. This is because the

Government made a specific pledge not to raise the basic or higher rates of income tax in its 2005 general election manifesto, which limits it for this Parliament. Hence our suggested package of tax changes for the coming Parliament relies largely on increases in National Insurance Contributions to raise the extra money. In the longer term, however, choosing a socially just tax system for Britain in 2020 will require a much more holistic debate about who should pay taxes, and about the balance between different forms of taxation. This should involve mature consideration of taxation as a whole, including the basic and top rates of income tax.

We make no attempt here to provide a specific package of reforms. In part, this is because, as explained above, there is such a wide margin or error in our projections for what our recommended policies will cost in the long run that it would be disingenuous to suggest that we can identify the precise level of taxation that would need to be set by 2020. However, we would like to advance four main principles which we believe should underline long-term tax reform, before suggesting a strategy to achieve this.

Lower taxes on the lowest paid
Where possible, tax cuts should seek to reduce the burden of taxation on the lowest paid workers. Currently the income tax personal allowance for a man or woman below state retirement age is £4,895 per year. The National Insurance Lower Earnings Limit is set at the weekly equivalent – of £94 per week. An employee earning the National Minimum Wage of £5.05 per hour (which will be the rate as from October 2005) and working a 37-hour week earns approximately £187 per week, equivalent to an annual salary of £9,700 per year, almost double the personal allowances for income tax and National Insurance. Even someone working a 20 hour week at minimum wage pays income tax and NICs. Given that the National Minimum Wage is designed to avoid 'poverty pay', it is perhaps unfortunate that under the current tax system, 33p of every £1 increase in gross pay arising from an increase in the minimum wage goes to the Exchequer. Of course, low-income families with children can claim the Working Tax Credit to boost their in-work incomes. But for childless working people on low incomes the WTC is far less generous. The tax system also interacts with the income tapers on Council Tax Benefit and Housing Benefit (for employees in rented accommodation), which increases effective marginal tax rates and reduces the incentives to work. To have the highest chance of maximising

employment rates in the UK it would be best if a long-term objective of taking low-paid workers out of income tax liability entirely could be set. Although this would be hugely expensive to introduce in one fell swoop (HM Treasury estimates suggest that a £100 increase in the value of the personal allowance over and above the rate of inflation costs about £600 million) it could be achieved over a 20 or 30 year period via progressive over-indexation of allowances. We would argue that this should be a higher priority than reductions in the basic rate of income tax, for example.

Higher taxes on the very top earners

Along with lower taxes on low earners, we argue that a socially just tax system should impose higher taxes on top earners than is the case in the UK at present. Hills shows that the tax system, taken as a whole, is not progressive: it does not take a higher share of income from people on high incomes than it does from people on low incomes (Hills, 2004). Rather, it is roughly proportional as a share of income over most of the income range, but regressive at the bottom, largely due to council tax and VAT. At the same time, Chapter 2 shows that the incomes of people at the very top of the income distribution have risen by far more than the increase in average incomes over the last 25 years.

Currently, the highest income tax rate in the UK is 40 per cent, paid by individuals earning more than £37,295 per year. In addition to this, individuals pay 1 per cent employee NICs, resulting in a combined rate of 41 per cent. We propose that top earners – say, those on the equivalent of £100,000 in today's prices – should pay a combined income tax and NICs top rate of 50 per cent, as proposed by the Liberal Democrats in the last election campaign. If enacted on top of our NI increases recommended earlier in this chapter, this reform would increase the new effective top tax rate from 43 per cent to 50 per cent and would raise around an additional £3.5 billion per year. If top incomes continue to escalate up at a much faster rate than the growth at the middle of the income distribution, the 50 per cent rate has the potential to raise far more in future decades. It could play a vital role in financing the extra spending which the UK needs in the long run. There would also be scope for raising the current higher rate threshold (i.e. the point at which individuals start paying 40 per cent income tax) by more than the rate of inflation, to offset the process of fiscal drag whereby high earnings growth over the last two decades has pushed a greater proportion of taxpayers into the 40 per cent tax band.

Concern is often raised about the work incentive effects of hikes in the rate of income tax on top earners, but the predictions of economic theory on this point are ambiguous – under some scenarios, an increase in marginal tax rates actually increases work effort. The balance of research evidence shows that over the range of 40 to 50 per cent marginal tax rates for top earners there is little evidence of much change in hours worked resulting from a change in taxes (Blundell, 1992; Blundell and MaCurdy, 1999). Also, the 50 per cent top rate, is reasonably in line with combined top rates in most other OECD countries (Saxton, 2004).

Integrating tax and National Insurance

The tax changes above raise an important question about the direction of long-term reform. What should the future of the National Insurance system be? The kink described above is an artefact of the dual system of direct personal taxation which the UK has, where income tax and employee NICs are levied on reasonably similar tax bases. Recent changes by the Government to the thresholds of employee NICs have already made the two taxes appear more similar. Closing the kink would go a long way to fully aligning the two. While the revenues from National Insurance are nominally assigned to paying pensions and other National Insurance benefits, and to a lesser extent for the NHS, in reality this is a very casual form of hypothecation as there is no strict actuarial relationship between the size of National Insurance receipts and spending on the earmarked items of public expenditure – in practice National Insurance operates as a general tax, just like income tax. Chapter 12 suggested that National Insurance in its present form no longer legitimates the welfare system in the way previously envisaged.

In the long run we believe it would be desirable to merge income tax and employee National Insurance into a single tax. This would create administrative savings as well as increase the simplicity of the overall tax system. To be sure, such a bold step is not without its difficulties. The Government would need to move carefully before introducing such a radical reform of the tax system and significant public debate would be required. In particular it would need to be linked to any proposed pension reforms after the publication of the final report of the Pension Commission in the autumn of 2005. The link – real and perceived –

between the contributory principle and the basic state pension is a key issue that needs to be addressed.

But a complete overhaul of the existing income tax and National Insurance systems would provide an ideal new starting point for the tax debate, allowing the Government to sidestep the increasingly sterile debate over pledges on individual income tax rates and move towards a new, simpler, fairer and more progressive system. It could also produce administrative savings, as indicated in a recent review of the possibilities for amalgamating employee NICs and income tax (British Chambers of Commerce, 2004). Given the current upward pressures on public spending analysed in this chapter, even modest administrative savings and reductions in the tax compliance burden on businesses and employees would be most welcome.

Harmonising the tax system with environmental and democratic objectives
Creating a simpler and fairer income tax system is a vital long-term goal for tax policy but it is not enough by itself. The tax system also needs to do much more to support other aspects of social justice. Foremost among these are progressive and sustainable environmental policies and a renewal of democratic participation in the UK. Taking the environment first, Chapter 8 argues for a national road user charging scheme to be introduced in 2010, or soon after. This would help reduce traffic congestion and carbon dioxide emissions while raising substantial additional sums of revenue. This would allow badly needed investments in public transport to make employment and key services more accessible to people on low incomes and in poorer areas – which is itself a key component of social justice.

Likewise, a well-functioning and open democracy demands a higher degree of fiscal decentralisation than exists in Britain (and particularly in England) at present. Cities, regions and localities in Britain should have the power to vary tax rates and the level and mix of public spending, within clearly set parameters (as occurs in the devolved Scottish administration at the moment, for example). This would give increased legitimacy and weight to local and regional democracy. In Chapter 10, Paxton and Gamble argue that the experience of Scotland and Wales shows that devolving elements of taxation and public spending to cities and regions in this way will help safeguard and extrench progressive policy measures, without endangering standards of public service provision. Indeed, local autonomy in policy-making allows more scope for innovation in the provision of local services, which should help drive up standards and ensure that policies are tailored to local needs.

Social justice – leading from the front

Britain faces a long-term challenge. Most pressures on the welfare state – demographic change, increased demand from the public and technological change – are pushing in the same direction: upwards. At the same time this chapter has identified three key components of a 'social justice gap': the need to reduce child poverty and increase security of income in retirement; a demand for greater progression within the labour market; and, most significantly, a need to respond to the emerging crisis of care. These are challenges for the country as a whole. They do not all necessarily demand immediate action, but must be faced up to over the coming decade.

Britain can continue to prosper as a dynamic economy and become a fairer, more cohesive country. Social justice and economic efficiency can go hand in hand. But the people of Britain must give their support to building a fairer Britain and show a willingness to pay for it. Our ambitions have run ahead of the means to achieve them. We must close the gap.

References

Adam S and Reed H (2004), 'Income Tax and National Insurance Contributions', Chapter 5 in Chote R, Emmerson C and Simpson H (eds), *The IFS Green Budget: January 2003*, London: IFS

Belsky J and Fearon R M P (2002) 'Early attachment security, subsequent maternal sensitivity, and later child development: Does continuity in development depend upon continuity of care giving?' *Attachment and Human Development*, 4(3), London: Taylor and Francis

Blair P, Fleming P and Bensley D (1996), 'Smoking and the sudden infant death syndrome', *British Medical Journal*, 313, 195-198.

Blundell, R (1992), 'Labour Supply and Taxation: A Survey', *Fiscal Studies*, 13(3), 15-40.

Blundell, R and MaCurdy, T (1999), 'Labor Supply: A Review of Alternative Approaches', Chapter 27 in Ashenfelter, O and Layard, R (eds), *Handbook of Labor Economics*, Vol 3A, North-Holland.

Bonoli, G (2005) 'The politics of new social risks and policies', in Armingeon K and Bonoli G (eds.) *The Politics of Post-Industrial Welfare States*, London: Routledge.

Brandth, B and Kvande E (2001) 'Flexible work and flexible fathers' *Work, Employment and Society*, 15(2), London: Sage

Brewer M (2004) 'Will the Government Hit Its Child Poverty Target in 2004-05?' I*FS Briefing Note no. 41*, London: Institute for Fiscal Studies.

Brewer M (2005) 'Maintaining Momentum in Tackling Child Poverty' in Robinson P, Reed J and Delorenzi S (eds) *Maintaining Momentum* London: ippr

Brewer, M and Emmerson, C (2003) *Two Cheers for the Pension Credit?* IFS Briefing Note 39, London: Institute for Fiscal Studies. Available at http://www.ifs.org.uk/bns/bn39.pdf

British Chambers of Commerce (2004), *A New Tax Horizon: How to Simplify Britain's Payroll Tax System* London: British Chambers of Commerce

Brooks, R Robinson, P and Regan, S (2002a) *A New Contract for Retirement*. London: ippr

Brooks, R Robinson, P and Regan, S (2002b) *A New Contract for Retirement: modelling policy options to 2050*. London: ippr

Brooks-Gunn J, Han W and Waldfogel J (2002) 'Maternal Employment and Child Cognitive Outcomes in the First Three Years of Life: The NICHD Study of Early Childcare' *Child Development* 73(4), Oxford: Blackwell

Burchardt T (2003), *Being and Becoming: Social Exclusion and the Onset of Disability*, Centre for the Analysis of Social Exclusion (CASE), London School of Economics, Report no. 21, London: LSE

Carneiro P and Heckman J (2003) 'Human Capital Policy', in Heckman J and Kreuger A (eds), *Inequality in America: What Role for Human Capital Policies?* Cambridge MA: MIT Press

Chatterji P and Markowitz S (2004) 'Does the Length of Maternity Leave Affect Maternal Health?' *NBER Working Papers 10206*, New York: National Bureau of Economic Research

Chote R, Emerson C, Miles R and Oldfield Z (2005) *The IFS Green Budget: January 2005* IFS: London

Crompton R, Brockmann M and Wiggens R (2004) 'A women's place … employment and family life for men and women' in *British Social Attitudes: Continuity and Change over two decades* London: Sage

Currie J (2001) 'Early Childhood Intervention Programs: What Do We Know?' in *Journal of Economic Perspectives* 15, Pittsburgh: American Economic Association

Daly M (2002) 'Care as a Good for Social Policy' *Journal of Social Policy* 31 (2), Cambridge: Cambridge University Press

Daycare Trust (2004) *Universal early education and care in 2020: costs, benefits and funding options* London: Daycare Trust and Social Market Foundation, Policy Paper no. 2.

Daycare Trust (2005) *Parents pay inflation-busting cost of childcare*. Available at http://www.daycaretrust.org.uk/article.php?sld=245

Department for Work and Pensions (DWP) (2005) *Department for Work and Pensions Five Year Strategy: Opportunity and security throughout life* London: HMSO

Dex, S (2003) *Families and Work in the Twenty-First Century.* York: Joseph Rowntree Foundation.

Disney, R and Johnson, P (2001), *Pension Systems and Retirement Incomes Across OECD Countries*,

Esping-Andersen G (2005) 'Social Inheritance and Equal Opportunity Policies' in Robinson P, Reed J and Delorenzi S (eds) *Maintaining Momentum* London: ippr

Fabian Society (2000) *Paying for Progress: A new politics of tax for public spending* London: Fabian Society

Foley J and Ferguson M (2004) *Putting the Brakes on Climate Change: A policy report on road transport and climate change* London: ippr

Fraser N (1997), *Justice Interruptus*. New York: Routledge.

Gershuny, J (2000), *Changing Times*. Oxford: Oxford University Press.

Glennerster, H (1998), 'Welfare with the Lid on', in Glennerster H and Hills J (eds), *The State of Welfare: The Economics of Social Spending*. Oxford: Oxford University Press.

Goos M and Manning A (2004) *Lovely and Lousy Jobs: The rising polarisation of work in Britain* London: Centre for Economic Perfomance (CEP)

Gregg P, Washbrook E, Propper C and Burgess S (forthcoming) 'The Effects of a Mother's Return to Work Decision on Child Development in the UK' *The Economic Journal*, Oxford: Blackwell

Harker L and Kendall L (2003) *An Equal Start: Improving support during pregnancy and the first 12 months* London: ippr

Hedges A and Bromley C (2001) *Public Attitudes towards Taxation* London: Fabian Society.

Hillage J and Mitchell H (2003) *Evaluation of Employer Training Pilots* DfES/HM Treasury/LSC ETP1, London: TSO

Hillage J, Loukas G, Newton B and Tamkin P (2005), *Platform for Progression: Employer Training Pilots Second Year Evaluation Report*, DfES Publications ETP2, London: DfES

400 Social Justice

Hills, J (2004), *Inequality and the State*. Oxford: Oxford University Press.

HM Treasury (2004a) *Choice for Parents, the best start for children: a ten year strategy for childcare* London: TSO

HM Treasury (2004b) *Child poverty review* London: The Stationery Office available online at http://www.hm-treasury.gov.uk./media/985/CC/childpoverty_complete_290704.pdf

HM Treasury (2004c) *Releasing Resources to the Front Line: An Independent Review of Public Sector Efficiency*. London: HMSO. Available at http://www.hm-treasury.gov.uk/media/B2C/11/efficiency_review120704.pdf

HM Treasury (2004d), *2004 Spending Review: Stability, Security and Opportunity for all*, London, HMSO. Available at http://www.hm treasury.gov.uk/spending_review/spend_sr04/report/spend_sr04_repindex.cfm

HM Treasury (2004e), *Tax Ready Reckoner and Tax Reliefs: December 2004*, London, HMSO. Available online at http://www.hm-treasury.gov.uk./media/8F5/9F/pbr04tax_ready_182.pdf

HM Treasury (2005), *Public Finances Databank,* London, HMSO. Available at http://www.hm-treasury.gov.uk/Economic_Data_and_Tools/data_index.cfm

HM Treasury, Department for Work and Pensions, Department for Education and Skills, *Supporting Young People to Achieve: The Government's Response to the Consultation,* March 2005

Holzer H (2004) *Encouraging Job Advancement Among Low-Wage Workers: A New Approach* Washington DC: Brookings Institute. Available at http://www.brookings.edu/es/research/projects/wrb/publications/pb/pb30.htm

Johnson A (2002) *Job Retention and advancement in employment: Review of Research Evidence*, In House Report 98, Department for Work and Pensions, London: HMSO

Kehrer B and Wolin V (1979), 'Impact of income maintenance on low birth weight, evidence from the Gary experiment', *Journal of Human Resources* 1979, 14, Madison: University of Wisconsin Press

Kelly G, Muers S and Mulgan G (2000) *Creating Public Value: an analytical framework for public services reform* London: Cabinet Office. Available at http://www.strategy.gov.uk/files/pdf/public_value2.pdf

Liberal Democrats (2005) *The Real Alternative: Liberal Democrat Manifesto 2005* London: Liberal Democrats

Lister, R (2003), 'Investing in the citizen-workers of the future: transformations in citizenship and the state under New Labour', *Social Policy and Adminstration,* 37(5), 427-443

McQuail S, Mooney A, Cameron C, Candappa M, Moss P and Petrie P (2003) *Early Years and Childcare International Evidence Project: Child Outcomes* London TSO

Maxwell, D (2004) *Fair Dues: towards a more progressive inheritance tax* London: ippr Available online at http://www.ippr.org/research/files/team27/project203/Fairper cent20dues.pdf

Moss P (2001) *The UK at the crossroads: towards an early years European partnership* Facing the Future Policy Paper No.2 London: Daycare Trust

National Association of Pension Funds (NAPF) (2002) *Pensions – Plain and Simple* London: National Association of Pension Funds

National Audit Office (NAO) (2004) *Early Years: progress in developing high quality childcare and early education accessible to all* London: TSO

NICHD Early Childcare Research Network (2002) 'Childcare Structure > Process > Outcome: Direct and Indirect Effects of Child-Care Quality on Young Children's Development' *Psychological Science* 13, Washington: American Psychological Society

NIESR (2005), *National Institute Economic Review*, No. 91, January. London: National Institute for Economic and Social Research

OECD (2001) *Starting Strong: Early Childhood Education and Care* Paris: OECD

OECD (2004) Economic Outlook No. 76 – Statistical Annex Tables Paris: OECD

Office of National Statistics (ONS) (2004) *Youth Cohort Study: The activities and experiences of 18 year olds: England and Wales 2002* London: TSO. Available at http://www.dfes.gov.uk/rsgateway/DB/SFR/s000536/sfr43-2004v5.pdf

Office of National Statistics (ONS) (2005) *Participation in education, training and employment by 16-18 year olds in England: 1985 to 2003 (revised)* London: TSO. Available at http://www.dfes.gov.uk/rsgateway/DB/SFR/s000551/sfr03-2005.pdf

Ofsted (2005), *Registered Childcare Providers and Places in England, 31 March 2005*, London : HMSO. Available at http://www.ofsted.gov.uk/publications/index.cfm?fuseaction=pubs.displayfile&id=3902&type=pdf

Pearce N and Hillman J (1998), *Wasted Youth*, London: ippr

Pension Commission (2004) *Pensions: Challenges and Choices: the first report of the pensions commission* London: TSO

Pensions Policy Institute (PPI) (2004) *Citizen's Pension: lessons from New Zealand* London: PPI available at http://www.pensionspolicyinstitute.org.uk/uploadeddocuments/CPNZ_26_02_04.pdf

Poppe N, Strawn J and Martinson K (2003) 'Whose Job Is It? Creating Opportunities for Advancement Workforce' in Giloth R P (ed) *Intermediaries in the 21st Century* Philadelphia: Temple University Press in 2003. Available at http://www.clasp.org/publications/Adv_chapter.pdf

Robinson, P (2004), *Tough Choices: The 2004 Spending Review*. London : ippr. Available online at http://www.ippr.org/ecomm/files/toughchoices.pdf

Ruhm C (2000) 'Parental Leave and Child Health' in *Journal of Health Economics* 19(6), London: Elsevier

Ruhm C (2004) 'Parental Employment and Child Cognitive Development' in *Journal of Human Resources* 39(1) Madison: University of Wisconsin Press

Saxton J (2004), 'How Competitive is the US Tax System?' Joint Economic Committee, United States Congress, April 2004

Schweinhart L J and Weikart D P (1998) 'Why curriculum matters in early childhood education'in *Educational Leadership*, 55, 6, , Alexandria: Association for Supervision and Curriculum Development

Sefton, J & Van Der Ven, M (2004), 'Does Means Testing Exacerbate Early Retirement?', *NIESR Discussion Paper 244*, London: National Institute of Economic and Social Research.

Sharpe C (2002) *School Starting Age: European Policy and Recent Research* Available at http://www.nfer.ac.uk/research/papers/SSFPAPER.doc

Social Exclusion Unit (SEU) (1999) *Bridging the Gap* London: Social Exclusion Unit

Stafford B (1998) *National Insurance and the Contributory Principle*, DSS

Stanley K and Maxwell D (2004) *Fit For Purpose: the reform of incapacity benefit* London: ippr

Stanley K and Regan S (2003) *The missing million: supporting disabled people into work* London: ippr

Strawn J and Martinson K (2001), *Steady Work and Better Jobs: How to help low-income parents sustain employment and advance in the workplace*, US: Manpower Demonstration Research Corporation

Sylva K, Melmuish E, Sammons P, Siraj-Blatchford I. and Taggart B (2004) *Final Report: Effective Pre-School Education*, Effective Provision of Pre-School Education (EPPE) Project, Technical Paper no. 12, Department for Education and Skills/Institute of Education, University of London, London.

Tanaka S (2005) 'Parental Leave and Child Health Across OECD Countries' *The Economic Journal*, 115 (501): F7-F28 Oxford: Blackwell

Taylor-Gooby P (ed) (2004) *New Risks, New Welfare* Oxford: Oxford University Press

Tomlinson M (2004) 14-19 *Curriculum and Qualifications reform: final report of the working group on 14-19 reform* London: DfES

Woldfogal J (2005) 'Social Mobility, Life Chances and the Early Years' in *Social mobility: building the momentum* Eds. Robinson, Reed and Bush London: ippr

Woodhead M (1989). '"School starts at five...or four years old?": the rationale for changing admission policies in England and Wales', *Journal of Education Policy*, 4, 1, London: Routledge

About the Authors

Tania Burchardt is a Research Fellow at the Centre for Analysis of Social Exclusion (CASE) at the London School of Economics. Her interests span welfare and employment policy, and theoretical frameworks for understanding poverty and social exclusion. Recent publications include 'Capabilities and disability: the capabilities framework and the social model of disability' in *Disability and Society* 19 (7) 2004, *Constraint and opportunity: identifying voluntary non-employment* (with Le Grand J, CASE paper 55, 2002) and 'Social exclusion: concepts and evidence' in Gordon D and Townsend P (eds) (2000) *Breadline Europe: The measurement of poverty*.

Mike Dixon is a Research Assistant at the Institute for Public Policy Research. After graduating from Cambridge in 2002 with a BA in Philosophy, he worked at Ogilvy and Mather for a year before joining ippr.

Julie Foley is a Senior Research Fellow at the ippr. Her previous publications include *Putting the Brakes on Climate Change, Hydrogen: Driving the Future* and *Plane Trading: Policies for Reducing the Climate Change Effects of International Aviation* (2000) with Chris Hewett. She was previously a Policy Analyst for the Energy Saving Trust and is currently Co-Chair of the Socialist Environmental Resources Association (SERA), the Labour Environment Campaign. She is the Secretary of ippr's Commission on Sustainable Development in the South East.

Andrew Gamble is Professor of Politics and Director of the Political Economy Research Centre, University of Sheffield. He is joint editor of the *New Political Economy* and *Political Quarterly*, and his many books include *Britain in Decline, The Free Economy and the String State, Hayek: the Iron Cage of Liberty* and, most recently, *Between Europe and America*.

Steve Gibbons is a Lecturer in Economic Geography in the Department of Geography and Environment at the London School of Economics where he teaches quantitative techniques for spatial analysis and applied urban economics. He is also a Research Associate at the Centre for Economic Performance and the Centre for Economics of Education at the LSE. Current research interests are spatial issues in the economics of education, labour markets, transport and crime, especially the role of local interactions in creating and sustaining social and economic inequalities.

Tony Grayling is Associate Director and Head of the sustainability team at the ippr, which covers a wide range of work on progressive environmental policy, in particular on energy, transport and climate change. He was a special adviser to the UK Minister for Transport, Rt Hon. Dr Gavin Strang MP, 1997–8 during the development of the transport White Paper *A new deal for transport*. From 1994–97 he was environment policy officer for the Labour Party and prior to that was researcher successively to Labour MPs Ron Davies and Anne Campbell.

Anne Green is a Principal Research Fellow at the Institute for Employment Research, University of Warwick. She has a background in geography and works primarily on issues concerned with spatial dimensions of economic, social and demographic change and on aspects of local and regional labour markets. Current work includes 2001 Census based research on the geography of poor skills and access to work.

Paul Gregg is Professor of Economics and Programme Director at the Centre for Market and Public Organisation at the University of Bristol, and a member of the Council of Economic Advisors at HM Treasury. His research interests are mainly on worklessness, welfare to work and poverty. Recent work has looked at intergenerational income mobility, maternity leave and mothers' employment and how mothers' employment patterns and childcare impact on children's development.

Lisa Harker works as a writer, researcher and policy adviser, specialising in issues related to families and social exclusion. She was Deputy Director of the ippr until April 2003 and previously worked for Save the Children, BBC News and the Child Poverty Action Group. Lisa has been Chair of Daycare Trust, the national childcare charity, since 2001. She is a columnist for *Community Care*, *Third Sector* and *Children Now*

magazines and as one of the directors of Aspire Oxfordshire, is involved
in creating employment opportunities for homeless people.

Stephen Machin is Professor of Economics at University College London,
Director of the DfES Centre for the Economics of Education and
Research Director of the Centre for Economic Performance at the
London School of Economics. He is currently one of the editors of the
Economic Journal. Previously he has been visiting professor at Harvard
University and at the Massachusetts Institute of Technology. His research
interests include earnings inequality, educational attainment, intergener-
ational transmissions of earnings and education, and the economics of
crime.

David Mepham is an Associate Director at the ippr and leads its international programme. From 1998 to 2002, he was a special adviser within
the UK's Department for International Development. He made a
substantial contribution to the Government's White Paper *Eliminating
World Poverty, Making Globalisation Work for the Poor* (2000). Prior to
this, David ran the British Foreign Policy Programme for Saferworld
from 1997 to 1998. From 1994 to 1997, he was the international policy
specialist in the Labour Party's policy department and secretary to the
Labour Party's Foreign Policy Commission.

David Miller is Professor of Political Theory at the University of Oxford
and an Official Fellow of Nuffield College. Among his more recent
books are *Market, State and Community* (Oxford: Clarendon Press
1989), *On Nationality* (Oxford: Clarendon Press 1995), *Principles of
Social Justice* (Cambridge, Mass.: Harvard University Press 1999),
Citizenship and National Identity (Cambridge: Polity Press 2000) and
Political Philosophy: A Very Short Introduction (Oxford: Oxford University
Press 2003). He is currently working on national responsibility and
international justice, and on problems of social justice in multicultural
societies. He was elected to a fellowship of the British Academy in 2002.

Geoff Mulgan CBE is Director of the Institute of Community Studies in
London and a visiting professor at the London School of Economics and
University College London. Between 1997 and the autumn of 2004 he
worked in government in a variety of roles, including Head of Policy in
the Prime Minister's office and Director of the Government's Strategy

Unit. Before 1997 he was the founding director of Demos, the London-based research institute. His most recent book is *Connexity* (Harvard Business Press and Jonathan Cape, 1998). Previous books include: *Life After Politics* (Harper Collins, 1997), *Politics in an antipolitical age* (Polity 1994) and *Communication and Control: networks and the new economies of communication* (Blackwells, 1991*)*.

Will Paxton is a Senior Research Fellow at the ippr, where he has published research on savings policy, volunteering and democratic participation, financial exclusion and poverty. Will worked on secondment at the Home Office and Prime Minister's Strategy Unit in 2003. He graduated from the London School of Economics in 2000, where he studied social policy and government.

Nick Pearce has been Director of the ippr since 2004. He was previously a special adviser to David Blunkett MP at the former Department for Education and Employment and the Home Office. He has published books and articles on further and higher education policy; citizenship and social cohesion; asset-based welfare; and socially excluded young people. Between 1997 and 1999, he was Senior Research Fellow in Education at ippr and part-time adviser to the Social Exclusion Unit. Nick was educated at the Universities of Manchester and Oxford.

Raymond Plant is Professor of Jurisprudence and Political Philosophy at King's College London Law School. He has written widely on social, political and legal philosophy including: *Hegel*; *Community and Ideology*; *Politics, Theology and History*; *Modern Political Thought*; *Political Philosophy and Social Welfare* (with H. Lesser and P. Taylor Gooby) and *Philosophy, Politics and Citizenship* (with A. Vincent). He is currently completing a book called *The Neo Liberal State and the Rule of Law*. He is a Labour Member of the House of Lords and was for a time from 1992 an Opposition Spokesman on Home Affairs.

Howard Reed was appointed Research Director of the ippr in 2004. Prior to this he was Director of the Work and Income Research programme at the Institute for Fiscal Studies. He is an economist by training with a range of publications in leading journals such as the *American Economic Review* and the *Economic Journal*. His research interests include the labour market, tax, benefit and tax credit policy, pensions, education and training policy, and disability and ill health. Howard was educated at Keble College, Oxford, and University College London.

Jodie Reed is a Research Fellow at the ippr and works within the Education Team on pre-sixteen policy issues. Her research has focused primarily on educational exclusion and underachievement and she sits on the editorial board of the *International Journal on School Disaffection*. Previously she worked as a Specialist Adviser to Parliament's Joint Committee on Human Rights. Jodie is a first class honours graduate of Manchester University where she was awarded the McKenzie Prize by the Government Department.

Peter Robinson has been Senior Economist at the ippr since October 1997. He leads the ippr teams dealing with economic, employment and industrial policy and public service reform including health and education and the funding of public services. He was a co-author of the final report resulting from the ippr's Commission on Public Private Partnerships. He is also a Research Associate at the Centre for Economic Performance at the London School of Economics and teaches in the Social Policy Department at the LSE.

Dhananjayan Sriskandarajah is a Senior Research Fellow working on migration policy at the ippr. His current research examines the relationship between migration and economic development, and the impact of labour migration. He is the editor of the ippr's Asylum and Migration Working Paper series, and a regular commentator on migration issues. He holds degrees from the Universities of Oxford and Sydney.

Peter Taylor-Gooby runs the ESRC Social Contexts and Responses to Risk research network and the EU Welfare Reform and the Management of Societal Change programme at the University of Kent. He has published widely on current developments in social and public policy. His most recent books are *New Risks, New Welfare* (Oxford University Press, 2004) and *Welfare States under Pressure* (Sage, 2001).